The Tahoe Sierra

By Jeffrey P. Schaffer

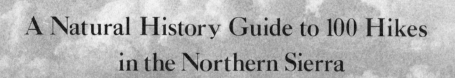

A Natural History Guide to 100 Hikes
in the Northern Sierra

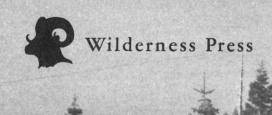

Wilderness Press

iv

Copyright © 1975 by Jeffrey P. Schaffer
All rights reserved
ISBN: 911824-38-3
Library of Congress Card Catalog Number: 74-27686

All maps and photographs by Jeffrey P. Schaffer, except as noted

Front cover: Granite Lake, Emerald Bay and Lake Tahoe
Title page: Emerald Bay and Lake Tahoe

Published by   **Wilderness Press**

2440 Bancroft Way

Berkeley Calif. 94704

Publishers of *The Pacific Crest Trail*, *The Tahoe-Yosemite Trail*, and other trail guides

Acknowledgments

Without the unfailing support of Thomas Winnett, editor-in-chief of Wilderness Press, this book would never have been published. Thanks to his editing, it is now a more readable book. He always strove to translate my scientific jargon into understandable laymen's terms. Where certain esoteric concepts or processes still remain unintelligible, I take the responsibility.

Discussions with Professor Garniss Curtis of the Geology Department of the University of California, Berkeley, gave me a better understanding of this area's geology. Correspondence with Professor Robert Stebbins of the Zoology Department verified my conclusions about certain reptiles. Belated acknowledgments are made to Professor Theodore Oberlander of the Geography Department and to Mitchell Reynolds of the U.S. Geological Survey. The former sharpened by field interpretation of topographic maps, the latter saw to it that I drew in mapped features *exactly* where they should be. Fellow Wilderness Press author J. C. Jenkins showed me how I could still improve the overall quality of my final maps.

Often accompanying me on hikes was Ken Ng, whose fishing expertise contributed greatly to the identification of this guide's fish populations. While hiking alone, I was often comforted by the thought that he would send for Forest Service help should I not return on the appointed day. Accompanying me on shorter excursions were Elaine T. Hussey and Don Masulis, both adding their interpretations of the scenery.

Co-leading the Class 5 climbing I did in this area was my twin, Greg Schaffer, and backing both of us up was one of America's safest belayers, Mike Schaffer.

Finally, credit must be given to the unsung heroes who cared for my home while I was up in the Tahoe Sierra for five months. Foremost of these is Sam Jones, aided on occasion by Vicky Leeds and Ray Ho.

Jeffrey P. Schaffer
Richmond, California
April 2, 1975

vi

Dedication

This book is affectionately dedicated to
Francis and Lorraine Schaffer,
my parents,
who let me as a boy roam the hills
and
encouraged me to study the environment.

Contents

Maps

Introduction

Scope and Purpose of This Book

Certainly no feature in the northern Sierra Nevada so dominates its landscape as does Lake Tahoe. Due to its unique mode of origin, it greatly surpasses all other Sierra lakes in area and depth. During the summer, multitudes of bathers and boaters flock to its shores and waters, while ever-growing numbers of hikers explore its rim of snow-capped mountains. Over 60 of this guide's trips describe hikes within these mountains, while the remaining trips describe hikes in lesser known parts of the northern Sierra.

The trips in this guide are contained in four chapters, each chapter composed of trips whose trailheads can be reached from roads branching off from a major highway. These four highways are—from south to north—U.S. Highway 50, Interstate 80, State Highway 49 and State Highway 70. Each chapter has at least one popular recreation area: for the Highway 50 chapter it is Desolation Wilderness; for 80 it is Granite Chief; for 49 it is Lakes Basin; and for 70 it is Bucks Lake. At the beginning of each chapter is a brief introduction to the trails of its areas.

This book has four purposes. First, it is primarily a **hikers' guide** to virtually all the trails in the northern Sierra that are worth hiking. Many trails not worth hiking are identified in the introduction of each trip chapter, so that the hiker who relies solely on topographic maps won't waste days searching for a good trail. In the northern Sierra, *over half* of the trails shown on topographic maps covering it no longer exist or are unhikeable.

Second, this book is a **climbers' guide** to the northern Sierra. Since the late 1960s, the vertical walls of Yosemite have been overpopulated with climbers. Looking for new, less crowded routes to climb, climbers have often turned to the high country of the central Sierra, but not until the early 1970s did they actively begin exploring possibilities near and around the Tahoe basin. (Lovers Leap and Sugarloaf are exceptions, these being popular even back in the 1960s.) Until now, most of the cliffs and crags in the northern Sierra have remained obscure. For climbers in search of uncrowded climbing areas in the northern Sierra, this guide identifies and briefly describes almost all the faces that can be reached by trail.

Third, this book is a **natural history** of the northern Sierra. The common rocks and vegetation seen from a trail are mentioned in virtually every trip. But this guide goes beyond routine nomenclature; it delves into processes, both geological and biological. Roughly half of the trips elaborate on one or more of the processes seen or related to the environment you'll hike through on the trip. Abundant photographs and several illustrations are included for those who can't hike every trail, yet want to understand these processes. To make space for all these photographs, as well as to lighten the hiker's pack, two or more trips that contain a common trail segment have that segment described in one trip only. The other trips refer the reader back to this trip. In like manner, similar processes elaborated on in one trip may be referred to in other trips—again to save space and weight. Once you begin to understand the processes involved that mold this landscape, you acquire a greater appreciation for what you see as you hike over it.

Finally, this book is a sort of **field textbook**. In Chapter 2 it introduces basic terms and concepts you'll need to understand the processes mentioned in later trips. In these trips, more terms are introduced to further broaden your comprehension of the environment. The author hopes that through this guide you'll not only be better prepared to interpret the natural history of the Tahoe Sierra, but that you'll also learn how to observe and form conclusions about natural processes in other areas outside this region.

Left: Author climbing a glacier-transported granitic boulder *Don Masulis*

Hiking and Backpacking

Most of the trips in this book can be done as day hikes rather than as overnight hikes—although you may want to take more than one day to do many of them. Generally, however, very little planning and preparation for each is required. Novices to backpacking can learn the art by reading a copy of Thomas Winnett's *Backpacking for Fun*—aimed directly at them.

Because *accurate*, up-to-date maps are included in this guide, mileage figures are kept at a minimum. There are, however, numerous instances where vertical distance in feet and horizontal distance in yards are given. The first is given to tell you how much you will have to climb, thereby informing those who like easy hikes what they're in for. The second has a more practical reason: some trail junctions are easily missed, particularly in early season when snow still lingers on.

Duck

Blaze

Therefore, potential hard-to-find junctions are identified by their distance from the nearest identifiable feature—often a creek crossing. Yards are given because they approximately equal long strides—the hiker can pace off the distance when he is in doubt.

Your progress along a trail is often measured with respect to a prominent feature in the landscape, such as a mountain or hill above you. On this guide's topographic maps, many unnamed high points are identified by an **X**, which marks the point, and a number which gives its elevation. This guide refers to these high points as peaks or summits. *Peak* is here used to denote a more impressive high point than *summit*.

Some trails in this guide are poorly maintained and could be hard to follow. Others may have lingering snow patches hiding them. For both, your route can usually be found by watching for blazes, ducks or streamers that mark the trail. A *blaze* is a place on a tree trunk where man has carved away a patch of bark to leave a conspicuous scar. A *duck* is one or several small rocks placed upon a larger rock in such a way that the placement is obviously unnatural. A *streamer* is a plastic ribbon usually tied to a tree branch. Since all these markers can be ephemeral, this guide's route descriptions do not emphasize them.

Climbing

Ascents to mountain tops as well as up steep walls are rated according to a generally accepted classification system. A climb is rated by its difficulty, not by its length. Class 1 is trail and easy cross-country; Class 2 is easy scrambling; Class 3 is scrambling up slopes using your hands as well as your feet. Class 4 requires a rope for safety; Class 5 requires pitons and/or nuts for protection; and Class 6 requires a set of nylon loops to put your feet in and climb up on.

No Class 6 climbs are mentioned in this guide, since this sort of climbing—hanging on to equipment rather than to the rock—is too artificial and therefore, ethically undesirable. Class 5 climbs—the kind preferred by rock climbers—are mentioned more than any other class. A 120-foot rope is adequate for these climbs, since they tend to have many places where the leader can stop. Since you usually have to carry in your equipment a mile or more, you won't feel like bringing along longer, heavier ropes. For leader protection, nuts are recommended over pitons because the latter scar rocks. Furthermore, many climbs in the area are found on volcanic and metamorphic rocks, which can easily fracture if you drive a piton into one of their cracks.

Class 3 climbing

Hazards

Weather. Experienced mountaineers know well the hazards of climbing: loose rock, avalanches, snowstorms, lightning. The hiker need only worry about the last two. Early-season and late-season hikers may encounter snow flurries and rarely, full-fledged storms; and if they plan to camp out overnight, each should carry at least a poncho or protective tarp to shield himself and his sleeping bag from an unexpected storm. Before you drive off to your trailhead, find out what the weather is supposed to be like, but be prepared just in case the weatherman's "clear skies" prediction is wrong.

Even day hikers might carry along a poncho in their day pack, as the author does. One day when he reached the summit of Mt. Tallac at 11:30 a.m., there wasn't a cloud to be seen. When he left it at noon, the sky was half cloudy. A half hour later an intense lightning storm broke loose, first pelting unprepared hikers with half-inch hail, then drenching them in pouring rain. The lesson: a freak storm can suddenly appear out of nowhere—be prepared.

Never climb to a mountain top if clouds are building up above it, particularly if you hear thunder in the cloudy distance. If you see lightning, you can be sure a storm above you isn't very far away. The goal of a summit is not worth the risk of being struck down by lightning.

Growing thunderhead

Injuries. The farther you are from your trailhead, the greater is the problem if you sustain an injury. Rock climbers, who are in a high-risk category, should bear this in mind. Hiking alone is not recommended, since you have no one but yourself to rescue you in an emergency. In popular areas such as Desolation Wilderness and Lakes Basin, however, other hikers are often within shouting distance.

Rattlesnakes, etc. Lying still among a trail's brown grass, dead leaves, twigs and shadows, the well-camouflaged rattlesnake is almost impossible to see. Along the lower trails in the northern Sierra, you stand a chance of encountering this usually shy, poisonous reptile. You are most likely to see them on Trips 1–3, 6, 53–54, 69–75, 93–95, 97 and 100. If you are hiking any of these lower trails in spring or fall, when the temperature is about 50°F or colder, you needn't worry much about the rattlers, for in these temperatures they are very sluggish unless they are warming themselves in the sun. Don't hike at night, since that is the time when they are actively hunting for prey.

Because rattlers are generally shy, the only danger lies in confronting one before it has a chance to escape. Walk cautiously when in rocky, brushy or streamside areas and when stepping over fallen logs. Should you get bitten, *keep calm*, so that the venom enters your system slowly. Many professionals still recommend you make incisions over the fang marks, but the author has met hikers who have been bitten in the past but didn't make incisions. Statistics show that a great majority of healthy adults would survive a bite even without treatment.

A pest found at low elevations, such as at Malakoff Diggins or Feather Falls, is the tick. This quarter-inch relative of spiders has an unpleasant habit of burrowing into unsuspecting hosts and sucking their blood. "How much blood can a tiny tick suck?" you might ask. Not that much, but it can transmit serious diseases, and therein lies the danger.

Less serious but more common is the presence of shiny-leaved poison oak, found along most trails under 3000 feet elevation. Every hiker should learn to recognize its leaves and avoid it, lest they develop a skin rash.

Right: Poison oak

Land-Use Regulations

The trails in the Tahoe Sierra are found mostly on National Forest land, but also on State Park and private land. All these areas have their own regulations, which you ignore only at your risk—risk of physical difficulty as well as possibility of being cited for violations. Listed below are some more-common regulations.

1. A *wilderness permit* is required to enter Desolation Wilderness. It may be obtained at several ranger stations (see Highway 50 road log) or may be obtained by writing to the headquarters of Eldorado National Forest, at 100 Forni Road, Placerville, California 95667. This permit is free.

2. If you are backpacking outside Desolation Wilderness, you will need a *campfire permit* if you intend to build a fire. These can be obtained at ranger stations or at Forest Service headquarters. Campfire permits require each party to carry a shovel. If you don't build any fires but use only gas stoves, then you can leave the shovel behind but you'll still need the permit. A stove is particularly recommended for the high country, where dead and down wood is scarce. Rotting wood should be preserved, since it enriches the soil and hosts organisms which larger animals feed on.

3. A California *fishing license* is required for all persons 16 years old or older who fish. The limit is 10 trout per day, with some exceptions, these given in the state Department of Fish and Game regulations.

4. *Destruction*, injury, defacement, removal or disturbance in any manner of any natural feature or public property is prohibited. This includes:

    a. Molesting any animal, picking flowers or other plants;

    b. Cutting, blazing, marking, driving nails in, or otherwise damaging growing trees or standing snags;

    c. Writing, carving or painting of name or other inscription anywhere;

    d. Destruction, defacement or moving of signs.

5. *Smoking* is not permitted while traveling through vegetated areas. You may stop and smoke in a safe place.

6. Pack and saddle *animals* have the right of way on trials. Hikers should get completely off the trail, on the downhill side if possible, and remain quiet until the stock has passed.

7. It is illegal to cut *switchbacks*. This practice destroys trails.

8. Never camp in meadows or other soft, vegetated spots; an overnight's rest in them will certainly bear your imprint. Don't camp within 100 feet of lakes or streams unless you're certain you won't pollute their water by campfire ashes or accelerated erosion.

9. *Soap* and other *pollutants* should be kept out of lakes and streams. You can use sand rather than detergent to clean your cooking gear.

10. *Toilets* should be in soft soil away from camps and water. Dig a shallow hole and bury all.

11. You are required to *clean up* your camp before you leave. Tin cans, foil, glass, worn-out or useless gear, and other unburnables must be carried out. *Littering* anywhere is an abuse of wilderness.

Selecting Your Trip

The two following tables enable you to, at a glance, get a brief idea of what to expect along each trip. Once you select a trip, you should look it up and see if its features appeal to you and if its hiking season is right for you. The first table lists each trip's classification plus activities you can do while on it. The classification ranges from an easy 1A to a hard 5E. The numbers refer to each trip's mileage, as follows: 1, 0.0–4.9 miles; 2, 5.0–9.9 miles; 3, 10.0–14.9 miles; 4, 15.0–19.9 miles; and 5, 20.0+ miles. The letters refer to the total gain you must climb: A, 0–999 feet; B, 1000–1999 feet; C, 2000–2999 feet; D, 3000–3999 feet; and E, 4000+ feet.

In the first table a plus (+) indicates that a certain activity can be found along a trip; a minus (−) indicates it can't be found. There are, of course, borderline cases. Four straight minuses don't mean a trip is completely unrewarding. Trip 53, for example, falls into this category, yet it stands out because it is the only trip that passes by giant sequoias.

Where there is water, there are usually, but not always, fishing and swimming opportunities. In like manner, the presence of a lake doesn't always mean these two activities are available. No one, for instance, tries to swim in leech-infested Bloodsucker Lake (Trip 9), nor can you swim in some shallow lakes and creeks.

Most trips give you views, some give you good views. Summit views, as used in the table, are those obtained from a distinctive summit—views which alone make the trip worth the effort.

Rock climbing can be done at literally hundreds of places in the northern Sierra, but much of it wouldn't be worth your effort. In this table, rock climbing is limited to trips that contain cliffs worth climbing, and these trips specifically identify these good cliffs.

TABLE OF ACTIVITIES

Trip	Classification	Fishing	Swimming	Summit views	Rock climbing	Trip	Classification	Fishing	Swimming	Summit views	Rock climbing
1	4C	+	+	−	−	51	2B	−	−	−	−
2	3B	+	+	−	−	52	5E	−	−	−	+
3	2B	+	+	−	−	53	1A	−	−	−	−
4	1A	+	+	−	−	54	4C	+	−	−	+
5	1B	+	+	−	−	55	1B	+	−	−	−
6	5E	+	+	−	−	56	3D	+	−	−	+
7	4B	+	+	−	−	57	4D	+	−	−	+
8	3B	+	+	−	+	58	1B	+	+	−	−
9	1A	−	−	−	−	59	4E	+	+	−	+
10	1A	+	+	−	−	60	5E	+	−	+	+
11	2B	+	+	−	−	61	3C	−	−	+	−
12	3B	+	+	−	−	62	4D	+	−	+	−
13	3C	+	+	−	−	63	1A	+	+	−	−
14	2B	+	+	−	−	64	2B	+	+	−	+
15	2B	+	+	−	−	65	2B	+	+	+	+
16	2B	+	+	−	−	66	2B	+	+	−	+
17	2B	+	+	−	+	67	3B	+	+	−	+
18	4D	+	+	−	+	68	3C	−	−	+	−
19	5E	+	+	−	+	69	3B	+	+	−	−
20	5E	+	+	−	+	70	2A	−	+	−	−
21	4D	+	+	−	+	71	1B	+	+	−	−
22	2C	−	−	+	−	72	1A	+	+	−	−
23	3E	+	+	−	−	73	1B	+	+	−	−
24	3D	+	+	−	−	74	2C	+	+	−	−
25	2B	+	+	−	+	75	2B	+	−	−	−
26	3B	+	+	−	+	76	2C	−	−	+	−
27	3C	+	+	−	+	77	1A	−	−	−	−
28	5D	+	+	−	+	78	2B	−	+	−	−
29	5C	+	+	−	−	79	2D	−	−	+	−
30	5E	+	+	−	+	80	2B	+	+	+	+
31	2B	+	+	+	−	81	1B	+	+	−	−
32	2C	+	+	+	−	82	1B	+	+	−	−
33	2A	+	+	−	−	83	1B	+	+	−	−
34	3C	+	+	−	−	84	2B	+	+	+	+
35	3B	+	+	−	−	85	1A	+	+	−	−
36	3D	+	+	+	−	86	1A	+	+	−	+
37	2D	+	−	+	−	87	2B	+	+	−	−
38	1A	+	+	−	−	88	3C	+	+	+	+
39	3C	+	+	−	−	89	1A	−	−	−	−
40	1A	+	+	−	+	90	4E	+	+	+	+
41	3C	+	+	−	+	91	1B	+	+	+	+
42	5E	+	+	−	+	92	1A	+	−	−	−
43	2B	+	−	−	+	93	2C	+	+	−	−
44	1A	−	−	+	+	94	1B	+	+	−	−
45	3C	+	−	−	−	95	2C	+	+	−	+
46	2B	−	−	−	+	96	1A	+	+	−	+
47	1A	−	−	−	−	97	4C	+	+	+	+
48	2B	+	+	−	+	98	2A	+	+	−	−
49	2B	+	+	−	+	99	3B	+	+	−	+
50	3E	−	−	+	+	100	2B	+	+	−	−

TABLE OF SIGHTS

Trip	Lakes	Rocks			Forests			History	Trip	Lakes	Rocks			Forests			History
		Intrusive	Metamorphic	Volcanic	Ponderosa pine	Jeffrey pine	Whitebark pine				Intrusive	Metamorphic	Volcanic	Ponderosa pine	Jeffrey pine	Whitebark pine	
1	−	+	+	−	+	−	−	+	51	−	+	−	+	−	+	−	−
2	−	+	+	−	+	−	−	−	52	−	+	−	+	−	+	−	−
3	+	+	−	−	+	−	−	−	53	−	−	+	−	+	−	−	+
4	+	+	+	−	−	+	−	−	54	−	+	+	+	−	+	−	−
5	+	+	−	−	−	+	−	−	55	−	−	−	+	−	+	−	−
6	+	+	+	−	+	+	−	+	56	−	+	+	+	+	+	−	−
7	+	+	−	−	−	+	−	−	57	−	+	+	+	−	+	−	−
8	+	+	−	−	−	+	−	−	58	+	+	−	+	−	+	−	−
9	+	+	−	−	−	+	−	−	59	+	+	+	+	−	+	−	−
10	+	+	−	−	−	+	−	−	60	+	+	+	+	−	+	+	+
11	+	+	−	−	−	+	−	−	61	−	+	−	+	−	+	+	−
12	+	+	−	−	−	+	−	−	62	−	−	+	+	−	+	+	−
13	+	+	−	−	−	+	−	−	63	+	+	+	−	−	+	−	−
14	+	+	−	−	−	+	−	−	64	+	+	+	−	−	+	−	−
15	+	+	−	−	−	+	−	−	65	+	+	+	+	−	+	−	−
16	+	+	−	−	−	+	−	−	66	+	+	+	−	−	+	−	−
17	+	+	−	−	−	+	−	−	67	+	+	−	+	−	+	−	−
18	+	+	−	−	−	+	+	−	68	−	+	−	+	−	+	+	−
19	+	+	+	−	−	+	+	−	69	−	−	+	−	+	−	−	−
20	+	+	+	−	−	+	+	−	70	−	−	+	−	+	−	−	−
21	+	+	+	−	−	+	+	−	71	−	+	+	−	+	−	−	−
22	−	+	−	−	−	+	+	−	72	+	−	+	+	+	−	−	+
23	+	+	−	−	−	+	−	−	73	−	+	+	−	+	−	−	−
24	+	+	−	−	−	+	−	−	74	−	−	+	+	+	−	−	−
25	+	+	−	−	−	+	−	−	75	−	+	+	+	+	−	−	−
26	+	+	−	−	−	+	−	−	76	−	+	−	+	+	+	−	−
27	+	+	−	−	−	+	−	−	77	−	+	+	−	+	−	−	−
28	+	+	+	−	−	+	+	−	78	+	+	−	+	+	−	−	−
29	+	+	+	−	−	+	−	−	79	−	−	+	−	+	+	−	+
30	+	+	+	−	−	+	+	−	80	+	−	+	−	−	+	−	+
31	+	+	+	−	−	+	−	−	81	+	−	+	−	−	+	−	+
32	+	+	+	−	−	+	+	−	82	+	−	+	−	−	+	−	−
33	+	+	+	−	−	+	−	−	83	+	−	+	−	−	+	−	−
34	+	+	+	−	−	+	−	−	84	+	−	+	−	−	+	−	−
35	+	+	+	−	−	+	−	−	85	+	−	+	−	−	+	−	−
36	+	+	+	−	−	+	+	−	86	+	−	+	−	−	+	−	−
37	+	+	+	−	−	+	+	−	87	+	−	+	−	−	+	−	−
38	+	+	−	−	−	+	−	−	88	+	−	+	−	+	+	−	−
39	+	+	−	−	−	+	−	−	89	+	−	+	−	+	+	−	−
40	+	+	−	−	−	+	−	−	90	+	+	+	+	+	+	−	+
41	+	+	+	−	−	+	−	−	91	+	−	+	−	−	+	−	+
42	+	+	−	−	−	+	−	+	92	−	+	+	−	+	+	−	−
43	−	+	−	−	−	+	−	−	93	−	+	+	−	+	−	−	+
44	−	+	−	−	−	+	−	−	94	−	+	−	−	+	−	−	−
45	−	+	−	−	−	+	−	−	95	−	+	+	+	+	−	−	−
46	−	+	−	−	−	+	−	−	96	+	+	−	−	+	+	−	−
47	−	+	−	−	−	+	−	+	97	+	+	+	+	+	+	−	−
48	+	+	−	+	−	+	−	−	98	+	+	−	−	+	+	−	−
49	+	+	−	+	−	+	−	−	99	+	+	−	−	+	+	−	−
50	−	+	−	−	−	+	+	+	100	−	+	+	+	+	−	−	−

The second table lists sights, which should help photographers and nature lovers plan their trips. "Lake" is taken to mean any large body of water, natural or man-made. A trip with only ponds along it would be classified as minus (−).

Rocks are divided into three groups: intrusive, metamorphic and volcanic. Intrusive rocks are the most common rock type, and about 99% of them are granitic, the remainder being mafic or ultramafic. Volcanic rocks are the least common of the three, but where they occur, they are usually very conspicuous and sometimes are the dominant rock type. Sedimentary rocks, which are rare in the entire Sierra, are not included. The largest exposures of these rocks are found in Trip 72, which explores the Malakoff Diggins.

Vegetation, too, is divided into three groups: ponderosa-pine forest, Jeffrey-pine forest and whitebark-pine forest. The first forest is a low-elevation forest that includes other dominant species such as white fir, sugar pine, incense-cedar, Douglas-fir and black oak. The second is a mid-elevation forest that includes red fir, silver pine and mountain hemlock. The third is a high-elevation sparse forest that includes alpine vegetation. Characteristic bushes and wildflowers are associated with each forest, though some wildflowers and bushes, as well as lodgepole pine, occur in all three forests.

Finally, historical places are mentioned to cater to history buffs. Each trip with a plus (+) is one that contains an elaboration of the history of that trip's nearby area and/or related areas.

Using this Guide

Road log

There are four road logs in this book, each one starting in a principal town along a major trans-Sierra highway. Within most parentheses, two mileages are given. The first mileage is the distance between a point and the preceding point; the second mileage is the total distance from the start of the road log. For example, **Trailhead 1 (0.2, 44.3)**, is 0.2 mile beyond the last road junction and 44.3 miles from Placerville.

Displayed on pages 10–11 is a trailhead map for the Tahoe Sierra. The trailheads, by and large, are numerically arranged in the order you would encounter them as you drove east up each of the four highways. Trailheads 1–36 occur along roads branching from U.S. Highway 50, Trailheads 37–51 along Interstate 80, Trailheads 52–87 along State Highway 49 and Trailheads 88–96 along State Highway 70. In addition to driving directions to trailheads, the road logs list ranger stations, campgrounds and supply centers.

Interpreting each trip's basic data

Certain facts are listed at the beginning of each trip to help you plan and to refer you to the appropriate trailhead and trail map. To reach any trailhead, refer to each highway chapter's road log.

Distance. The total mileage for your hike is given here. It includes the mileages along spur trails when a trip mentions *we* take them, such as the three spur trails to Long Lake (Trip 87). On the maps, these trails are black, solid lines. It excludes the mileages along spur trails when a trip mentions *you* could take them, such as the spur trails to Clyde Lake and Jacks Meadow (Trip 28). On the maps, these trails are gray, dashed lines.

Also included under this heading is the type of hike: round trip, semiloop trip or loop trip. A round trip is one in which you hike to a destination, then return the way you came. A loop trip is one on which you wind across the terrain and return to your trailhead without having to retrace any of your route, except perhaps for a very small part of it. A semiloop trip is a combination of the two; it has at least one segment on which you'll have to retrace your steps plus at least one loop.

Total gain/Net Gain. Total gain is the vertical distance you'll have to climb along your *entire* trip, both going and returning. This is the gain you should consider when planning a trip for it is the amount you'll have to climb. Net gain is the vertical distance between a trip's highest and lowest points. It can be negative, as along the descending South Fork Trail (Trip 2); however, it would be positive if you were to hike that trail in reverse. No plus or minus sign is given.

The ratio between these two figures is a measure of how much up and down you'll have to do. For example, the total gain along the Hell Hole Reservoir Shoreline Traverse (Trip 3) is more than 5 times its net gain (220'). You can visualize it as a rollercoaster path—one with a lot of ups and downs. Since it is a round trip, the gain equals the total loss. You thus gain 1160 feet and lose 1160 feet even though you never get more than 220 feet above Hell Hole Reservoir, the trail's lowest point. In contrast, the No Ear Bar Trail (Trip 94) is very direct; the total and net gains are the same, since this trail plunges down to the Feather River without climbing over any obstacle.

Classification. In this chapter's Table of Activities, trips are rated from 1 to 5 in length and from A to E in total elevation gain. Ratings in which number and letter closely correspond, such as 1A, 2B, 3C, 4D, and 5E, are usually classified as moderate. When a trail has a lower-than-average elevation rating, such as 2A or 4C, it is usually classified as easy. If it has a higher-than-average elevation rating, such as 2C or 4E, it is usually classified as strenuous. There are exceptions, of course. For example, the trails to Smith Lake (Trip 14) and Tyler Lake (Trip 16) are both 2B, but the first is rated strenuous because its gradient is so steep and exhausting.

Season. The season is the period of year you should be able to drive to a trailhead and then hike an essentially snow-free trail. In a few instances, the last bit of road up to the trailhead is in bad condition almost year-round, but these situations are mentioned in road logs found at the beginning of the four Trip chapters. Weather varies considerably from year to year, so that the hiking season may be shorter or longer largely depending on whether the winter-spring precipitation has been above or below normal.

Northern Sierra summer days are usually ideal at higher elevations, warming up to the 70s during the day and cooling down to the 40s by sunrise. Rain is in the form of sporadic thunderstorms, which may occur daily for a whole week, or, more likely, may not occur for weeks at a time. Generally, the morning is cloudless, but clouds build up in the afternoon, only to dissipate around dusk. At lower elevations, such as at Malakoff Diggins and Feather Falls, daytime temperatures soar into the 90s, and these areas are best visited during cooler months unless you specifically intend to go sunbathing and/or swimming.

Those who like to go swimming will generally find lakes warmer than nearby streams. Most lakes warm up to 60° or more—a few even topping 70°F—and almost all are at their maximum in late July through early August. Rivers and streams, continually being fed by cold ground water, rarely climb above the low 60s.

Parking. During the week, there is ample parking space at virtually every trailhead, but some are overflowing on weekends. Consequently, the parking situation for each trip is given to tell you what space, if any, you can expect to find when you get there.

Trailhead/Map. This book's 96 trailheads are generally arranged in the order you would encounter them if you drove northeast from Sacramento, first up Highway 50, then up highways 80, 49 and 70. All the trailheads appear on the Trailhead Map, which shows our area's important roads and towns, and each appears on one or more topographic maps.

This book's 100 trips are shown on 35 topographic maps. Refer to the appropriate map to follow the trail description. Where several maps are required to follow a long trail, they are listed in the order you will need them.

Jumping into Rubicon Lake

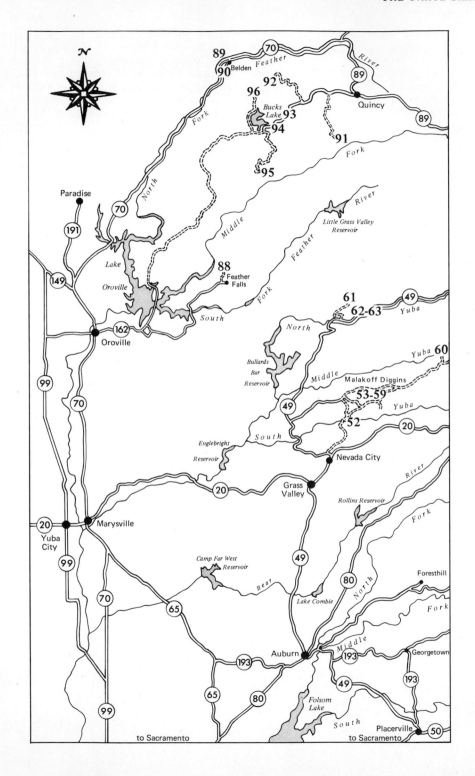

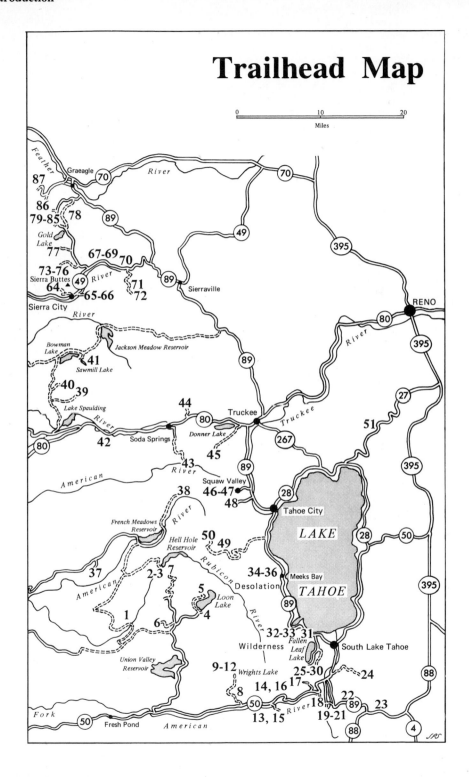

Trailhead Map

0   10   20

Miles

Using the Maps

Every topographic map shows at least one trip, each trip being composed of one or more trail segments. Often, a trail segment is used by two or more trips. In all cases, the number beside a trail segment refers to the trip that best describes it. The larger numbers at the beginning of trails are the trailhead numbers.

All maps except Maps 13 and 23 are oriented so that north is at the top of the page. Unless noted on the map, all have a scale of 1:62,500, or about 1 mile per inch. Maps 7 and 30 have larger-scale map inserts to show the complex road and trail situations at the start of certain hikes. Most maps have contour intervals of 80 feet, but Maps 21 and 34 have 40 feet, Map 31 has 100 feet, and Maps 30, 32, 33 and 35—each being spliced together from several base maps—have two contour intervals. Some maps have shaded portions because they were photographed from topographic maps that were currently available only with green overprint in forested areas.

LEGEND

U.S.G.S. map symbols		Wilderness Press additions	
Heavy-duty road	▬▬	Major road	═══
Medium-duty road	▬ ▬	Secondary road	══════
Improved light-duty road	═══	Jeep road	─ ─ ─
Unimproved dirt road	══════	Described trails	▬▬▬
Trail or jeep road	------	Other added trails	-----

Scale for maps that are 1:62,500

```
0                 1                 2              3 miles
```

An introduction to natural history

Geology

Every mountainous area is diverse in plants and animals and in climates and landscapes. Not all areas, however, are also diverse in minerals and rocks. The Tahoe Sierra is. All three major kinds of rocks—igneous, sedimentary and metamorphic—are found within it, and the ages of these rocks range from Paleozoic to late Tertiary. Minerals, which are the building blocks that make up rocks, are equally diverse in this region.

Most hikers can tell a deciduous tree from an evergreen one, and many can tell a fir from a pine. Happily, an ever increasing number of them carry natural-history guides, and they have learned to identify trees and other flora and fauna. When it comes to identification of rocks, most hikers, through no fault of their own, never progress past a basic classification of rocks: granitic, volcanic, and everything else. The trouble is that geologic guidebooks aren't much help, because, to correctly identify a rock, you often need very expensive laboratory equipment plus knowledge of how to use it. What's a hiker to do? Well, by identifying the major rock types for you, this guide attempts to get you personally acquainted with a variety of rock types and their modes of origin. But it does more than that; it introduces you to geologic processes so that you can appreciate the evolution of the Tahoe Sierra landscape.

Rocks

First, you should get acquainted with the three major rock classes: igneous, sedimentary and metamorphic.

Igneous rocks

Igneous rocks came into being when the liquid (molten) rock material *(magma)* solidified. If the material solidified beneath the earth's surface, the rock is called *intrusive*, or plutonic, and a body of it is a *pluton*. If the material reached the surface and erupted, the rock is called *extrusive*, or volcanic, and a body of it is a usually a lava flow.

Intrusive rocks. The classification of an igneous rock is based on its texture, what minerals compose it, and the relative amounts of each mineral present. Since intrusive rocks cool more slowly than extrusive rocks, their crystals have a longer time to grow. If, in a rock, you can see an abundance of individual crystals, the odds are that it is an intrusive rock. These rocks may be classified by crystal size: fine, medium or coarse-grained, to correspond to average diameters of less than 1 millimeter, 1–5, and greater than 5.

The common minerals in igneous rocks are quartz, feldspar, biotite (black mica), hornblende, pyroxene and olivine. The first two are light-colored minerals; the rest are dark. Not all are likely to be present in a piece of rock; indeed, quartz and olivine are never found together. Intrusive rocks are grouped according to the percentages of minerals in them. The three main igneous groups are *granite, diorite* and *gabbro*. Granite is rich in quartz and potassium feldspar and usually has only small amounts of biotite mica. Diorite is poor in quartz and rich in sodium feldspar, and may have three dark minerals. Gabbro, a *mafic* rock (rich in magnesium and iron), lacks quartz, but is rich in calcium feldspar and pyroxene, and may have hornblende and olivine. You can subdivide the granite-diorite continuum into granite, quartz monzonite, granodiorite, quartz diorite and diorite, and each can be further subdivided into its own related groups. The rocks of this continuum, usually called "granitic rocks" or just plain "granite," are common in the Sierra Nevada. Granodiorite predominates in Desolation Wilderness and the Lake Tahoe environs, whereas in the Bucks Lake area in the north, diorite predominates.

Extrusive rocks. Extrusive, or volcanic, rocks are composed of about the same minerals as intrusive rocks. *Rhyolite, andesite* and *basalt* have approximately the same chemical compositions as granite, diorite and gabbro, respectively. Like the intrusive rocks, these three volcanics can be subdivided into many groups, so it is possible to find ordinary rocks with intimidating names like "quartz latite porphyry"—which is just a volcanic rock with large quartz crystals in a finer matrix, with a composition between that of rhyolite and andesite.

Texture is the key feature distinguishing volcanic from plutonic rocks. Whereas you can see the individual crystals in a plutonic rock, you'll have a hard time finding them in a volcanic one. They may be entirely lacking, or so small, weathered and scarce that they'll just frustrate your attempts to identify them. If you can't recognize the crystals, then how can you identify the type of volcanic rock? Color is a poor indicator at best, for although rhyolites tend to be light gray, andesites dark gray, and basalts black, there is so much variation that each can be found in any shade of red, brown or gray.

One aid to identify recently created volcanic rock types is to look at what landforms are composed of them. In the Tahoe Sierra, however, most of the volcanic landforms were created 5 million or more years ago, and their original surfaces have been almost entirely eroded away. What follows is the description of active or recently active volcanic phenomena in California, so that you can visualize what the Tahoe Sierra's landscape once looked like.

The high silica (SiO_2) content of rhyolite makes it very viscous, and hence the hot gases in rhyolite magma cause violent explosions when the magma nears the surface, forming *explosion pits* and associated rings of erupted material (*ejecta*). For the same reason a rhyolite lava flow (which is simply degassed magma) is thick, short, and steepsided and may not even flow down a moderately steep slope. The Mono and Inyo craters, east of Yosemite National Park, are perhaps the best examples of this volcanic rock in California. At most, you will see only small exposures of it in the Tahoe Sierra.

You'll become very familiar with lava flows composed of andesite, which is the most common volcanic rock in the Tahoe Sierra. The landform characteristically associated with andesite is the *composite cone*, or volcano. Mt. Shasta and some of the peaks in the Lassen Park area, including Lassen Peak, are good examples. These mountains are built up by alternating flows and explosions. In time, *parasitic vents* may develop, such as the cone called Shastina on Mt. Shasta, and the lava being erupted from the volcano may shift to more-silica-rich rock called *dacite*, an intermediate between rhyolite and andesite, which gives rise to tremendous eruptions, like those at Lassen Peak. There are no recent volcanoes like these in our area, but there are remains of past ones, such as Tinker Knob, which can be reached via three different trails.

The least siliceous and also the least explosive of volcanic rocks is basalt. A basaltic eruption typically produces a cinder cone, rarely over 2000 feet high, and a very fluid flow. Cinder Cone and its flows, in Lassen Volcanic National Park, provide a good example, and the cone contrasts sharply with nearby, massive Lassen Peak. Not all basalt flows are thin, however, as can be seen in the area near the Hartman Bar trailhead.

Sedimentary rocks

We tend to think of rocks as being eternal—indeed, they do last a long time. Some of them in the Lakes Basin area are about 250 million years old or older. But even the most resistant polished granite eventually succumbs to the effects of physical and chemical weathering. Next time you're in an old stone granite building, take a look at the steps, even the inside ones. Chances are you'll notice some wear. Constant traffic may account for some of it, but

Lassen Peak

even more may be attributed to their use on rainy days and to repeated cleanings with solutions. In most environments, chemical wear is greater than physical wear. Granite rocks solidified under high pressures and rather high temperatures within the earth. At the surface, pressure and temperature are lower and the rock's chemical environment is different, and in this environment it is unstable. The rocks weather and are gradually transported to a place of deposition. This place may be a lake in the High Sierra, a closed basin with no outlet such as Pyramid Lake basin north of Lake Tahoe, an open structure such as California's great Central Valley, or even the continental shelf of the Pacific Ocean. The rocks formed from the sediment that collects in these basins are called sedimentary rocks.

Most sedimentary rocks are classified by the size of their particles: clay that has been compacted and cemented forms *shale;* silt forms *siltstone,* and sand forms *sandstone.* Sandstone derived from granitic rock superficially resembles its parent rock, but if you look closely, you'll notice that the grains are somewhat rounded and that the spaces between the grains are usually filled with a cement, usually calcite. Pebbles, cobbles and boulders may be cemented in a sand or gravel matrix to form a *conglomerate*. If the larger particles are angular rather than rounded, the resulting rock is called a *breccia.*

Limestone, another type of sedimentary rock, is formed in some marine environments as a chemical precipitate of dissolved calcium carbonate or a physical precipitate of fragments of shells, corals and foraminifers. The individual grains are usually microscopic. If the calcium in limestone is partly replaced by magnesium, the result is *dolomite.*

The Tahoe Sierra, as a whole, is an area that is being eroded rather than a basin receiving sediments, so you'll usually find only very young sediments or very old ones. The young ones may be in the form of alluvium, talus slopes, glacial moraines or lake sediments. The old ones are usually resistant sediments that the intruding granitic plutons bent (*folded*), broke (*faulted*) and changed (*metamorphosed*). Gold-bearing, Eocene-epoch gravels make up a minor but conspicuous third age category.

Climbing on sandstone

Metamorphic rocks

A volcanic or sedimentary rock that undergoes so much alteration (metamorphism) due to heat and pressure that it loses its original characteristics and takes on new ones is a *metavolcanic* or a *metasedimentary* rock. Metavolcanic rocks compose most of the Sierra Buttes-Lakes Basin area, and they are described in certain hikes. Metamorphism may be slight or it may be complete. For example, a shale undergoing progressive metamorphism becomes first a *slate*, then a *phyllite*, and then a *schist*. The slate resembles the shale but is noticeably harder. The schist bears little resemblance to the shale and is well-foliated with flaky minerals such as biotite or other micas clearly visible and aligned in the same plane. The phyllite has intermediate characteristics.

Hornfels is a hard, massive rock not too common in the Tahoe Sierra, formed by con-

tact of an ascending pluton with the overlying sediments. It can take on a variety of
forms. You might find a hornfels that looks
and feels like a slate, but it differs in that it
breaks across the sediment layers rather than
between then.

Gneiss is a coarse-grained metamorphic
rock with the appearance of layered granitic
rock. *Quartzite* is a metamorphosed
sandstone and resembles the parent rock.
The spaces between the grains have become
filled with silica, so that now if the rock is
broken, the fracture passes through the
quartz grains rather than between them as in
sandstone. Metamorphism of limestone
yields *marble*, which is just a crystalline
form of the parent rock. Check out an exposure in the Great Eastern Ravine of Highway 49's Wild Plum area.

Geologic time

You cannot develop a feeling for geology
unless you appreciate the great span of time
that geologic processes have had to operate
within. A few million years' duration is little
more than an instant on the vast geologic
time scale (see Geologic Time Table).
Within this duration a volcano may be born,
die and erode away. Several major "ice ages"
may come and go.

A mountain range takes longer to form.
Granitic plutons of the Sierra Nevada first
made their appearance in the Triassic
period, and intrusion of them continued
through Cretaceous period. Plutons probably formed as late as 30 million years ago,
but these still lie buried under the rocks they
intruded.

GEOLOGIC TIME TABLE

Era	Period	Epoch	Began (years ago)	Duration (years)
Cenozoic	Quaternary	Holocene	12,000	12,000
		Pleistocene	2,000,000	2,000,000
	Tertiary	Pliocene	11,000,000	8,000,000
		Miocene	25,000,000	14,000,000
		Oligocene	40,000,000	15,000,000
		Eocene	60,000,000	20,000,000
		Paleocene	70,000,000	10,000,000
Mesozoic	Cretaceous	*Numerous*	135,000,000	65,000,000
	Jurassic	*epochs*	180,000,000	45,000,000
	Triassic	*recognized*	225,000,000	45,000,000
Paleozoic	Permian	*Numerous*	280,000,000	55,000,000
	Carboniferous		345,000,000	65,000,000
	Devonian	*epochs*	400,000,000	55,000,000
	Silurian		440,000,000	40,000,000
	Ordovician	*recognized*	500,000,000	60,000,000
	Cambrian		570,000,000	70,000,000
Pre-cambrian	No formally accepted chronostratigraphic units; oldest rocks are about 3 billion years old; Earth is about 4½ billion years old.			

Geologic history

As you are reading this book, you are being taken for a ride—literally. Roughly 230 million years ago, North America began to rift apart from Europe and to drift west toward Asia at an average rate of almost one inch per year. If this rate continues, California should collide with Japan in about 400 million years. Californians living west of the San Andreas fault need not worry about that, however, since they are drifting northward at about two inches per year. Los Angeles residents can expect to be juxtaposed alongside San Francisco in about 10 million years and dumped into the Aleutian Trench, off Alaska, about 50 million years later.

The recently discovered fact is that the earth's crust is composed of large, moving plates. Each plate is quite rigid, and as such, it does not readily compress when it is forced against another plate, rather, one plate overrides the other, deformation occurring only at each plate's leading edge. (Plates are in continual contact with one another; one should not infer that they collide.) The overridden plate dives under the top plate at about a 45° angle and continues as a sheet to depths up to 400 miles below the earth's surface before melting.

The key to the geologic interpretation of the Tahoe Sierra starts in the early Mesozoic period, when North America had just broken free from Europe. Paleozoic rocks from the Calaveras formation and other formations in the Tahoe Sierra indicate that long before this time, this area had been part of the North American continent, as it is today. These continental rocks are lighter than ocean-floor rocks; consequently, when the continental plate pushed west against the Pacific Ocean plate, the latter, being denser, was forced to dive under. As the edge of this plate encountered higher pressures and temperatures while it descended, it became hot enough to have low-melting-point, light-weight granitic magma "distilled" off from it, and this magma rose and intruded the continental Paleozoic rocks. If you assume that the edge of the Pacific Ocean plate began to dive east when the Atlantic opened up about 230 million years ago, then you would expect it to reach the longitude of the Sierra Nevada—150 miles east—in about 20 million years. The plate's edge, of course, would be about 150 miles beneath the surface. Interestingly enough, the first plutons in the Sierra formed about this time, 210 million years ago, and this finding tends to lend credence to the argument that they were distilled off from the leading edge of a diving plate.

The formation of plutons continued until about 30 million years ago, when a major

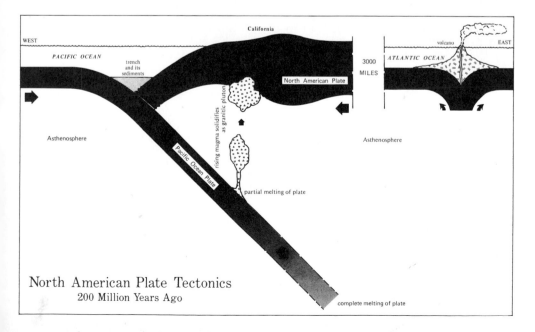

WEST

PACIFIC OCEAN

trench and its sediments

California

North American Plate

3000 MILES

ATLANTIC OCEAN

volcano

EAST

rising magma solidifies as granitic pluton

Asthenosphere

Pacific Ocean Plate

partial melting of plate

Asthenosphere

North American Plate Tectonics
200 Million Years Ago

complete melting of plate

change in forces caused the oceanic plate to glide past, rather than dive under, the continental plate. Since the plate is no longer diving, it shouldn't be producing any more plutons. The lateral movement that has been occurring over the last 30 million years is expressed along the San Andreas fault—the boundary along which the two plates slip. As inferred earlier, the bit of crust attached to the oceanic plate, including Point Reyes, Monterey, Los Angeles and Baja California, is drifting northward.

The intrusion of the granitic plutons did not occur at a uniform rate. Likewise, the primeval Sierra during this period was not always of uniform height or dimensions. We know it did exist, however, since sediments were eroded from it. These Mesozoic sediments—collectively termed the Great Valley sequence—are several miles thick and are seen in the hills that border the west edge of the Central Valley.

The Mesozoic Sierra probably was never very high, for there is no fossil evidence to indicate that the range rose to a great enough height to alter the climate east of it. Certainly by the Eocene epoch, this range in the Tahoe area had been reduced to a low, rolling landscape. Instead of cutting into bedrock and carrying away sediments as Tahoe rivers do today, the rivers back then were depositing their gold-rich sediments.

The low, rolling Tahoe landscape was not significantly changed until the Miocene epoch, when floods of volcanic flows inundated the topography. The volcanic eruptions continued into the Pliocene epoch, and during this time, the Sierran crust began to fracture along faults and was uplifted. By the late Pliocene, the Tahoe Sierra had almost reached its present height, a block of crust had faulted down to form the Lake Tahoe basin, and a lava flow had dammed its drainage, thereby creating Lake Tahoe.

The overall increase in elevation, coupled with a cooler, wetter climate, brought glaciers to the Sierra as early as three million years ago and perhaps earlier. (The Ice Age is usually thought of as being synonymous with the Pleistocene epoch, but in fact, it began earlier.) Glaciers did not exist for a continuous three million years, but rather waxed and waned. The last, major glacial stage ended about 10,000 years ago, and if the past cycles repeat themselves, then we should be plunged into another continental-scale ice age in about 1000 years.

When the Sierran glaciers existed, they effectively cut into the Pliocene mountain range, deepening and widening its stream valleys and removing most of its "newly formed" volcanic rocks. As the hiker tramps through the High Sierra today, he sees abundant evidence of glacial action: lingering moraines and erratics; polished and striated bedrock; cirque lakes and moraine-dammed lakes; and sharp crests above steepened U-shaped valleys. The glaciers did one more thing: they bulldozed away most of the pre-existing soils, leaving the landscape barren when they finally retreated. The soils and vegetation you see in glaciated areas today all developed from 8000 B.C. onward, that is, after the last major glaciers retreated back up to the crest and to their extinction. At least three minor ice ages—collectively called the Little Ice Age—have occurred since that time, but they have had a minimal effect in molding the Tahoe Sierra landscape.

Geologic case histories

In virtually every one of this book's 100 hiking trips, the rocks seen along their trails are mentioned. Many trips also have short case histories that go into detail about specific points of interest you'll see. What follows is a list of these case histories, which are arranged below in an order similar to topics just discussed, which began with igneous rocks. Since most of the Tahoe Sierra landscape was sculptured from late Pliocene through the present, most of the case histories deal with events of this period.

Glacier polish at Twin Lakes

Biology

Even if you don't know much about basic ecology, you can't help noticing that the natural scene in the Tahoe Sierra changes with elevation. The most obvious changes are in the trees, just because trees are the most obvious—the largest—organisms. Furthermore, they don't move around, hide, or migrate in their lifetime, as do animals. When you pay close attention, you notice that not only the trees but the shrubs, flowers and grasses also change with elevation. Then you begin to find altitudinal differences in the animal populations. In other words, there are different *life zones*. These zones, each with numerous habitats, account for the great diversity of flora and fauna.

Flora

If you want to identify plants. A professional botanist, if he had the time and energy, could identify perhaps 1000 plants in the Tahoe Sierra. Other hikers may discover "only" a hundred species, and some will just see trees, bushes and flowers. If you can spare the luxury of an additional 10 ounces in your pack, then carry a copy of *Sierra Nevada Natural History*, which identifies over 270 wildflowers, shrubs and trees and over 480 animals. Not only does it provide illustrations and identifying characteristics of species, it also describes their habitats and gives other interesting facts. If only wildflowers interest you, then carry a copy of *Sierra Wildflowers*, which keys out over 500 species. The two books often disagree on flowers, which leaves the amateur botanist at a loss. For flowers, *Sierra Wildflowers* is certainly more comprehensive and more up to date, but the "common" names used in it are sometimes very uncommon. Our book, therefore, uses many common names found in *Sierra Nevada Natural History*. If you are only interested in recognizing trees, then you can get by with easy-to-use *California Tree Finder*, 1½ ounces light.

Plant geography. Every plant (and every animal) has its own *range, habitat* and *niche*. Some species have a very restricted range; others, a very widespread one. The Sequoia, for example, occurs only in about 70 small groves at mid-elevations in the western Sierra Nevada. It flourishes in a habitat of tall conifers growing on shaded, gentle, well-drained slopes. Its niche—its role in the community—consists in its complex interaction with its environment and every other species in its environment. Dozens of insects utilize the Sequoia's needles and cones, and additional organisms thrive in its surrounding soil. The woolly sunflower, on the other hand, has a tremendous range: from California north to British Columbia and east to the Rocky Mountains. It can be found in brushy habitats from near sea level up to 10,000 feet.

Some species, evidently, can adapt to environments and competitors better than others. Nevertheless, each is restricted by a complex interplay of influences or events.

Climatic influences. Of all influences, temperature and precipitation are probably the most important. Although the mean temperature tends to increase toward the equator, this pattern is camouflaged in California by the dominating effect of the state's highly varied topography. Temperature decreases between 3° and 5.5°F for every 1000-foot gain in elevation, and vegetational changes reflect this cooling trend.

For example, the vegetation along the low-elevation South Yuba Trail is adapted to a hot-summer environment. Annuals by and large have gone to seed when the first day of summer arrives, so they avoid a thirsty struggle. Perennials have leaves that may be reduced, leathery, waxy or succulent—characteristics which reduce water loss. Note, for example, that the relatively large-leaved deer brush, up on higher, wetter slopes, gives way to the small-leaved buckbrush on the sunny, lower slopes. Also note a similar leaf-size change among the trail's oak species. In both the brush and the oak, the heat-tolerant species has stiffer, more-leathery leaves.

Desolation Wilderness, at about three times the elevation of the South Yuba Trail, receives about three times as much annual precipitation, and the moisture-loving conifers—lodgepole and silver pines, red fir and mountain hemlock—predominate. As the temperature steadily decreases with elevation, evaporation of soil water and transpiration of moisture from plant needles and leaves are both reduced. Furthermore, up here the precipitation—about 75 inches—is mostly in the form of snow, which is preserved for months by the shade of the forest until as late as mid-July. When it melts, it is retained by the highly absorbent humus (decayed organic matter) of the forest soil. Consequently, an inch of precipitation on the higher, forested slopes is far more effective than an inch on lower, open-woodland slopes. The plants in Desolation Wilderness at 7500 feet elevation, with a frost-free growth period of only 60 days, have adapted to withstand a long, freezing winter, whereas those at 2500 feet, with a frost-free growth period of about 200 days, take advantage of a long spring and have adapted to withstand the hot summer.

Physiographic influences. As we have just seen, the elevation largely governs the regime of temperature and precipitation. Vegetation is also affected by the location, orientation, steepness and configuration of slopes. It turns out that the temperature decrease associated with a 100-foot gain in elevation is about equivalent to the decrease associated with a 17-mile level traverse north (in the Northern Hemisphere). Since the area covered by the *Tahoe Sierra* is about 85 miles long in a north-south direction, vegetation at, say, 6500 feet elevation at the north end should experience the same temperature and precipitation as vegetation at 7000 feet elevation at the south end of our region. This assumes, of course, that in both instances the topography is similar.

Topography, however, is very diverse. A north-facing slope, because it receives less sunlight than a south-facing slope, is cooler, so evaporation and transpiration on it are less. Consequently, it supports a denser stand of vegetation, which in turn better shades the soil, thereby further reducing evaporation. This denser stand also produces more litter, which results in more humus, so soil water is retained better. In one soil survey conducted by the author, he found that on a north-facing slope about 60% of the soil's weight was due to water, whereas on a nearby south-facing slope, only about 5% was due to water. It is no wonder, then, that one can hike up a brushy, south-facing slope and encounter at its crest a thick, red-fir grove descending the north-facing slope. Steepness of a slope is also important in regulating plant distribution. Red firs grow on steeper, well-drained slopes, but yield to lodgepole pines as the slope gets gentler and more water-saturated.

Edaphic influences. Some plants are particularly adapted to a specific soil. The most notable example of this in the Tahoe Sierra is the relationship between mule ears and andesitic mud flows. The soils developed on talus slopes at the base of these flows are covered with mule ears— to the virtual exclusion of almost every other plant. This aromatic, large-leafed sunflower grows on other soils, but nowhere else except on soils derived from andesitic mud flows does it so monopolize the landscape.

Mule ears in Granite Chief area

A soil can change over time and with it, the vegetation on it. If a forest on a slope is *badly* burned, the organic layer of the forest floor is destroyed, leaving only charred stumps as tombstones. With no protective cover, the rest of the soil is soon attacked by the forces of erosion. This mute landscape may still receive as much precipitation as a neighboring slope, but its effective precipitation is much less; it will take years to make a recovery. Herbs and shrubs will have to pioneer the slope and slowly build up a humus-rich soil again.

Biotic influences. Plants not only adapt to the physical environment—some also develop devices to do in the competition. Certain shrubs secrete toxins that mix with the soil water and prevent nearby seedlings of other species, which tap that water, from developing.

Competition is manifold everywhere. On a descending trek past a string of alpine lakes, you might see several stages of plant succession. The highest lake may be pristine, bordered only by tufts of grass growing between the lichen-crusted rocks. A lower lake may exhibit an invasion of grasses, sedges and pondweeds thriving on the sediments deposited at its inlet. Corn lilies and lemmon willows border its edge. Farther down, a wet meadow may be the remnant of a past lake. White alder and lodgepole pine then make their debut. Finally, you reach the last lake bed, identified by the flatness of the forest floor and a few boulders of a recessional moraine (glacial deposit) that dammed the lake. In this location, a thick stand of white fir has overshadowed and eliminated much of the underlying lodgepole.

When a species becomes too widespread, however, it invites attack, usually by insects. Pure stands of lodgepole pine are subject to attack by the larvae of needleminer moths, which, as their name suggests, tunnel the needles and destroy the forest. Within a well-mixed forest, however, in which lodgepoles are scattered, the moth population doesn't reach epidemic proportion. When an ecosystem—the sum total of organisms and their environment—is oversimplified, it is unstable.

Unquestionably, the greatest biotic agent is man. For example, he has supplanted native species with introduced species. Most of California's native bunchgrass is gone, together with the animals that grazed upon it, replaced by thousands of acres of one-crop fields and by suburban sprawl. Forests near some mining towns have been virtually eliminated. Others have been subjected to ravenous scars inflicted by man-made fires and by clear-cutting logging practices. The Los Angeles basin's smog production has already begun to take its toll of mountain conifers, and Sierra forests may soon experience a similar fate. Wide-scale use of pesticides has not eliminated the pests, but it has greatly reduced the pests' natural predators. Through forestry, agriculture and urban practices, man has attempted to simplify nature, and by upsetting its checks and balances has made it unstable.

The role of fire. Fires were once thought to be detrimental to the overall well-being of the ecosystem, and early foresters attempted to prevent or subdue all fires. This policy led to the accumulation of thick litter, dense brush and overmature trees—all of them prime fuel for a holocaust when a fire inevitably sparked to life. Man-made fires can be prevented, but how does one prevent a lightning fire, so common in the Sierra?

The answer is that fires should not be prevented, but only regulated. Natural fires, if left unchecked, burn stands of mixed conifers about once every 10 years. At this frequency, brush and litter do not accumulate sufficiently to result in a damaging forest fire; only the ground cover is burned over, while the trees remain intact. Hence, through small burns, the forest is protected from flaming catastrophes.

Some pines are adapted to fire. The lodgepole pine, for example, releases its seeds after a fire, as do numbers of shrubs and wildflowers. Seeds of the genus *Ceanothus* are quick to germinate in burned-over ground, and some plants of this genus are among the primary foods of deer. Hence, periodic burns will keep a deer population at its maximum. With too few burns, shrubs become too woody and unproductive for a deer herd. In like manner, gooseberries and other berry plants sprout after fires and help support several different bird populations.

Without fires, a plant community evolves toward a *climax*, or end stage of plant succession. Red fir is the main species in the climax vegetation characteristic of higher forests in the Tahoe Sierra. A pure stand of any species, as mentioned earlier, invites

Deer brush *(Ceanothus)*

Fauna

We have seen how plants adapt to a variety of influences from the environment and from other species. Animals, like plants, are also subject to a variety of influences, but they have the added advantage of mobility. On a hot summer day, a beetle under a scant cover of chaparral can escape the merciless sun by seeking protection under a loose rock or under a mat of dried leaves.

Larger animals, of course, have greater mobility and therefore can better overcome the difficulties of the environment. Reptiles, birds and mammals may frequent the trailside, but they scatter when you—the intruder—approach. At popular campsites, however, the animals come out to meet you, or more exactly, to obtain your food. Of course, almost anywhere along the shady trails you may encounter the ubiquitous mosquito, always looking for a free meal. But in popular campsites you'll meet the robin, the Steller jay, the Clark nutcracker, the mule deer, the Allen, lodgepole and alpine chipmunks, the golden-mantled ground squirrel, and at night, the black bear. You may be tempted to feed them, or they may try to help themselves, but please protect them from your food—they will survive better on the real, "organic" food Mother Nature produces. Furthermore, an artificially large population supported by generous summer hikers may in winter overgraze the vegetation. In the three following examples, we'll take a closer look at population dynamics.

Mule deer. This large mammal can be found throughout the Tahoe Sierra except above the red-fir zone. Mule deer, like other herbivores, do not eat every type of plant they encounter, but tend to be quite specific in their search for food. They typically browse the new vegetation on oaks, ceanothus, cherries and silk tassel; seasonally they may also consume grasses and forbs. Together with other herbivores, parasites and saprophytes (organisms feeding on decaying organic matter), they take care of a small portion of the 100 billion tons of organic matter produced annually on the earth by plants.

Mule deer face a considerable population problem: they have lost some of their predators. With the arrival of "civilized" man in California, the wolves and the grizzly bears were exterminated. In their places, coyotes and black bears have increased in

epidemic attacks and is therefore unstable. Fire promotes stability by giving the nonclimax vegetation a chance to get rooted.

Fire also unlocks nutrients that are stored up in living matter, topsoil and rocks. Vital compounds are released in the form of ash when a fire burns plants and forest litter. Fires also can heat granitic rocks enough to cause them to break up and release their minerals. In one study of a coniferous forest, it was concluded that the weathering of granitic rocks in that area was primarily due to periodic fires.

Natural, periodic fires, then, can be very beneficial for a forest ecosystem, and they should be thought of as an integral process in the plant community. They have, after all, been around as long as terrestrial life has, and for millions of years have been a common process in Sierra forests.

numbers. Coyotes, however, feed principally on rabbits and rodents, and only occasionally attack a fawn or a sick deer. Black bears occasionally kill fawns. The mountain lion, a true specialist in feeding habits, preys mainly on deer. This magnificent animal, unfortunately, has been unjustly persecuted by man, and now many deer that are saved from the big cat are lost to starvation and disease. The California deer population, over one million individuals today, is in poorer health overall than it was a century ago. California's increasing human population compounds the problem. The expansion of settlements causes the big cats to retreat farther, which leaves them farther from the suburban deer. Forests must be logged to feed this expansion of cities, and then the logged-over areas sprout an assemblage of shrubs that are a feast for the deer. The deer population responds to this new food supply by increasing. But then the shrubs mature or the forest grows back, and there is less food for the larger deer population. The larger herd is faced with starvation. The ever-increasing brush fires in California produce the same feast-followed-by-famine effect.

Mule deer

Porcupine. Your chances of seeing this large, lumbering rodent are fairly slim except perhaps during a night visit in its search for salt. Otherwise, it keeps to itself and is rarely seen by the hiker, even though it inhabits Douglas-fir, ponderosa-pine and lodgepole-pine forests. If you happen to notice a conifer with a ring of bark missing, chances are the bark was gnawed off by a porcupine that was dining on the tree's succulent inner bark. By girdling the cambium layer beneath the bark, the porcupine can kill a tree. If the porcupine population gets out of hand—say, due to a decrease in its predators—then it can inflict considerable damage to a forest.

The porcupine has only one *effective* natural enemy, the fisher. This relative of the skunk became valued for its fine pelt earlier in our century, when women's fashions dictated long fur coats. When trapping exterminated the fisher over much of its range, the pine marten and other smaller carnivores partly filled its niche. None, however, was able to control the porcupine population. Hence loggers waged their own war against these "pesky" rodents. Lately, due to a shift in fashions away from fur, the fisher has made the start of a comeback in the forests of California and other states. In the absence of man's interference, the porcupine problem is now slowly getting back under control, and these reclusive rodents can get back to just trimming the forest without tearing it down.

Western rattlesnake. The thought of suddenly encountering one of these reptiles may raise fear in the hiker's mind as he goes cross country over a rocky, brush-covered slope. Indeed, your chances of meeting one greatly increase when you go cross country through rocky or streamside terrain below the red-fir forest belt. Our guide does take you through several miles of cross country and considerably more miles of vegetated, little-used trail. Nevertheless, the danger is not great, because rattlesnakes make an effort to get out of your way. Once while this author was surveying a potential climbing route up a brush-dotted cliff, a rattler made good its escape by slithering between his feet before being seen. The only danger lies in confronting a rattler before it has a chance to escape. Walk cautiously when in rocky, brushy, or streamside areas and when stepping over fallen logs.

The western rattlesnake and other rattle-snakes frequent virtually every type of habitat below the red-fir forest belt. Together they do a significant job in checking the populations of ground squirrels, other rodents and the smaller rabbits. Man, typically, has instigated campaigns to eradicate the rattlesnake and other predators such as hawks and coyotes, thereby causing eruptions in the rodent population (and problems for the ranchers who pushed for such measures). One rattlesnake extermination program carried out in the 1960s eliminated the conspicuous, noisy rattlers, and left the silent ones to breed. A population developed in which the snakes would strike before buzzing. Luckily, most of the rattlers that you might encounter along your route will be glad to get out of your way and will let you know if you get too close for comfort.

In each of the three studies above, each animal has a specific role to perform in its community. A fluctuation in its population will cause a fluctuation in the other species it usually feeds upon or that feed upon it. In each case, man has tried to exterminate a species and in each case an unsuspected adverse result has occurred. As man increasingly asserts his influence over nature, he will have to learn to work within its framework, for he, like any other species, is an integral part of it.

Biological case histories

Every one of this book's 100 hiking trips includes some mention of vegetation—usually of forest cover—to give you an idea of what to expect. As you broaden your hiking experiences, you'll recognize an increasing number of vegetational patterns. For example, in a swampy meadow you'll expect to see corn lilies and shooting stars, and you'll expect it to be fringed with lodgepole pines. Some trips have short case histories that go into detail about specific points of interest generated by what you'll see. The list that follows is an index to these sketches.

Recommended Reading and Source Books

(The books marked* are rather technical and will not be understood by all readers.)

*Bailey, Edgar H., ed., *Geology of Northern California* (California Division of Mines and Geology, Bulletin 190). Sacramento: California Division of Mines and Geology, 1966.

Beck, Eric, *Climber's Guide to Lake Tahoe & Donner Summit*. Tahoe City: Department of Parks and Recreation, 1973.

Burnett, John L., *Geology of the Lake Tahoe Basin* (California Geology, vol. 24: 7). Sacramento: California Division of Mines and Geology, 1971.

Burt, William H., and Richard P. Grossenheider, *A Field Guide to the Mammals,* 2nd ed. Boston: Houghton Mifflin, 1964.

Clark, William B., *Gold Districts of California* (California Division of Mines and Geology, Bulletin 193). Sacramento: California Division of Mines and Geology, 1970.

Crippen, J. R., and B. R. Pavelka, *The Lake Tahoe Basin, California-Nevada* (U.S. Geological Survey, Water-supply Paper 1972). Washington: U.S. Geological Survey, 1970.

*Dodge, F. C., and P. V. Fillo, *Mineral Resources of the Desolation Primitive Area of the Sierra Nevada, California* (U.S. Geological Survey, Bulletin 1261-A). Washington: U.S. Geological Survey, 1967.

*Flint, Richard F., *Glacial and Quaternary Geology.* New York: John Wiley and Sons, Inc., 1971.

*Garner, H. F., *The Origin of Landscapes.* New York: Oxford University Press, 1974.

Heizer, R. F., and M. A. Whipple, *The California Indians.* Berkeley: University of California Press, 1951.

*Hietanen, Anna, *Geology of the Pulga and Bucks Lake Quadrangles, Butte and Plumas Counties, California* (U.S. Geological Survey, Professional Paper 731). Washington: U.S. Geological Survey, 1973.

Hill, Mary, *Geological History of the Sierra Nevada* (California Natural History Guide 37). Berkeley: University of California Press, 1975.

Ingles, Lloyd G., *Mammals of the Pacific States.* Stanford: Stanford University Press, 1965.

*Munz, Philip A., and David D.Keck, *A California Flora.* Berkeley: University of California Press, 1959.

Murie, Olaus J., *A Field Guide to Animal Tracks.* Boston: Houghton Mifflin, 1954.

Niehaus, Theodore F., *Sierra Wildflowers.* Berkeley: University of California Press, 1974.

Odum, Eugene P., *Fundamentals of Ecology,* 3rd ed. Philadelphia: W. B. Saunders, 1971.

*Peterson, Donald W., *et al., Tertiary Gold-bearing Channel Gravel in Northern Nevada County, California* (U.S. Geological Survey, Circular 566). Washington: U.S. Geological Survey, 1968.

Peterson, Roger T.,*A Field Guide to Western Birds,* 2nd ed. Boston: Houghton Mifflin, 1961.

Pough, Frederick H.,*A Field Guide to Rocks and Minerals,* 3rd ed. Boston: Houghton Mifflin, 1960.

Putnam, William C., *Geology,* 2nd ed. New York: Oxford University Press, 1971.

*Scott, Kevin M., and George C. Gravlee, Jr., *Flood Surge on the Rubicon River, California* (U.S. Geological Survey, Professional Paper 422-M). Washington: U.S. Geological Survey, 1968.

Shelton, John S., *Geology Illustrated.* San Francisco: W. H. Freeman, 1966.

Stebbins, Robert C.,*A Field Guide to Western Reptiles and Amphibians.* Boston: Houghton Mifflin, 1966.

Storer, Tracy I., and Robert L. Usinger, *Sierra Nevada Natural History.* Berkeley: University of California Press, 1964.

Sudworth, George B., *Forest Trees of the Pacific Slope.* New York: Dover, 1967.

Watts, Tom, *California Tree Finder.* Berkeley: Nature Study Guild, 1963.

Whitten, D. G. A., with J. R. V. Brooks, *A Dictionary of Geology.* Baltimore: Penquin Books Inc., 1972.

*Wright, H. E., and M. L. Heinselman, eds., *The Ecological Role of Fire in Natural Conifer Forests of Western and Northern America* (Quaternary Research, vol. 3:3). New York: Academic Press, 1973.

Vegetation stabilizing a man-made cliff at Malakoff Diggins

Trails of the Highway 50 Region

Introduction

Over half of the hikes described in this guide are found in the Highway 50 area, and the rest are found in the Highway 80, 49 and 70 areas. The disproportionately large share of hikes in the first area is due to trail-packed Desolation Wilderness (Trips 8–43). This federally designated wilderness exists not so much because of its scenic alpine beauty—though it has lots—but rather because it, unlike most of the Tahoe Sierra, could not be exploited. It had no wealth of minerals, no dense stands of timber, no large, fertile valleys and no highways, and access to it is hampered by a long-lasting snowpack. It was, from an economic standpoint, desolate.

Wilderness it is not. Even if you were dropped into its deepest interior at sunrise, you could easily hike out, perhaps after a swim or a rest, to a trailhead before noon. It is more of a city park, bordered on the east and south by bustling Tahoe settlements and bordered on the west and north by the vacationer-packed Wrights Lake and Crystal Basin recreation areas. Adding to the city-park atmosphere of Desolation Wilderness is its thousands of weekend backpackers.

In order to give every hiker a "true wilderness experience," the Forest Service plans to limit the number and size of hiking parties entering this "wilderness." This policy, it hopes, will make the hiker feel he is truly *alone* in the wilderness. A noble plan, but hopelessly unrealistic.

The Federal government and certain other groups refuse to recognize the *absence* of true wilderness in the conterminous 48 states, for to do so would be tantamount to admitting that we have eradicated all of it. The government, therefore, has converted primitive areas into wilderness areas, pretending they will then become true wildernesses by act of law. They won't. There is no way you can feel you are in the middle of nowhere—hundreds of miles from civilization—in Desolation Wilderness. Yet the Forest Service is charged with executing programs that are supposed to give the hiker a wilderness experience. For the author, a *true wilderness experience* is an excursion into a remote area in which you *know* that if you are injured or get sick, *only* you or members of your party can help you. A true wilderness experience, then, has an element of danger. In contrast, Desolation Wilderness can be traversed from east to west in a day's time.

Back around 1890 America lost its frontiers; the U.S. Cavalry had subdued, enslaved or annihilated all the Indians, thus "civilizing" the continent from sea to shining sea. Geographers and historians lamented the coming of this event, and many people looked upon it as a national tragedy. But according to Manifest Destiny, America *should* expand indefinitely. Since the upsurge of backpacking in the 1960s, wilderness has, in effect, disappeared; virtually no large backcountry area remains untouched each year by hikers' boots. We can lament the passing of wilderness in the continental United States, or we can go on pretending—as the government does—that it still exists. A third choice is to assume a more realistic, mature attitude and admit that our environment is *limited*, and, like the Swiss and the Austrians, learn how to live within it.

Solitude seems to be as American as motherhood and apple pie (neither of which is intrinsically American), but the price we may have to pay for it will be the regulation and

Left: Dicks Peak and Middle Velma Lake

curtailment of many backcountry trips. Will the solitude we find in a High Sierra wilderness be worth it if a ranger dictates how many days we can stay in it and where we can or cannot hike and camp in it? The price we may have to pay for solitude may turn out to be more than we can emotionally afford.

As of 1974, there were no quotas for Desolation Wilderness, and all one needed was a wilderness permit. Camping was prohibited within 100 feet of lakes and streams so that ashes from campfires as well as debris left by careless backpackers would not get carried by heavy, late-spring snowmelt into these waters. This policy is sound logic for lakeside campsites, but not for streamside ones, since streams have an adequate flushing mechanism. Anyway, ecologically minded backpackers carry stoves and leave behind absolutely no litter—not even footprints if they can help it. If the backpacking public was totally educated in the treatment of wilderness, no restrictions would be necessary.

In the Tahoe Sierra outside Desolation Wilderness, there are no foreseeable quotas or restrictions, but the hiker in these areas should treat them with the same conservation-minded respect.

In addition to Desolation Wilderness and its adjacent environs, there are three other hiking areas described in this chapter. The first one encountered as you drive east up Highway 50 is the Crystal Basin Recreation Area (Trips 1–7), which includes trails of the Rubicon River. Below Hell Hole Reservoir, most of the Rubicon's trails have been abandoned, due in part to massive destruction when this reservoir's dam broke (see Trip 1). Bridges were washed out along with trails, and the new ones that replaced them were larger and higher. New roads were built to match these bridges, and these provided incentive for addi-

tional logging roads into areas that previously were too remote for economical logging. Every year sees the extension of a paved forest highway that one day will connect Highway 50 with Interstate 80, via Hell Hole and French Meadows reservoirs. This road may seem an advantage for vacationers, but its main function is to open up access to further logging. The Deer Creek and Parsley Bar trails, both once descending to the Rubicon, were abandoned as much due to logging as to the Rubicon's catastrophic flood.

The multitude of trails in the Crystal Basin proper have fared no better. Their doom, however, was sealed by the Sacramento Municipal Utility District, which built a series of reservoirs—together with generating plants—that flooded most of the basin's trails. Today, water skiers streak along where hikers once trod.

The third hiking area near Highway 50 is located along the upper drainages of the South Fork American and Upper Truckee rivers (Trips 44–49). Through careful planning, one can make a continuous backpack trip along all its trails, starting with either Trip 44 or 49. The trails of this area remain virtually unchanged compared to what they were a generation ago, but trails lower down on each river have suffered attrition.

The final hiking area is the geographically compact Freel Peak area (Trips 50–52). Private ranches plus South Tahoe second-home developments have greatly restricted access to this alpine area, which years ago should have been granted state-park or primitive-area status. A fair number of cross-country routes—more, in fact, than in all the remaining 97 trips—are intentionally described for this area, solely to compensate for the loss of former trails. It deserves the attention of conservationists.

Trailheads reached from Highway 50

The following trailhead mileage logs begin in Placerville, the only major town along Highway 50 between Sacramento and South Lake Tahoe. At the west end of town, just south of the highway, you'll find the Eldorado National Forest headquarters, at 100 Forni Road. Here you can obtain the necessary permits and information you'll need. In town you can get gas, groceries and last-minute supplies.

Trailheads 1–3: Middle Rubicon River access

1   At the Highway 49 junction in Placerville (0.0) turn north and follow this highway to a junction (0.8) where Highway 193 forks right. Take this winding road first down to the South Fork of the American River, then up to Georgetown (15.0, 15.8). Head northeast on this town's main street, the Georgetown-Wentworth Springs Road, 14N01. Take it northeast past the Georgetown Ranger Station (3.8, 19.6) to Stumpy Meadows Lake (formerly Lake Edson) (13.2, 32.8), with its Stumpy Meadows Campground. Now on a poorer road, drive to a junction with the Rubicon River road (6.3, 39.1), branching left, which winds steadily down to the river at the site of former Ellicotts Bridge. Just across a larger, newer bridge (5.0, 44.1), a spur road right descends northeast to the river. About 30 yards before this road curves down to car campsites on a large riverside flat, you reach **Trailhead 1 (0.2, 44.3).**

2,3   From the Rubicon River bridge (44.1), continue your drive, first out of this deep river canyon then into and out of side canyons until you arrive at a signed fork (16.5, 60.6). This fork can also be reached by starting from Auburn. (See the section on Interstate 80 trailheads.) The left fork goes to French Meadows Reservoir. The right fork goes to Hell Hole Reservoir. Take the right fork and follow it to the Big Meadow Campground spur road (5.1, 65.7). This campground, little used compared to others, has better facilities than those found in most Tahoe Sierra campgrounds. Just beyond this spur road we reach the Hell Hole Ranger Station (0.7, 66.4), then start a descent to Hell Hole, soon passing Hell Hole Vista (0.3, 66.7) and Hell Hole Picnic Ground (0.4, 67.1) before arriving at a bend and **Trailhead 2 (1.0, 68.1).** This trailhead is 120 yards west of an open saddle and 20 yards west of a gully. Yellow 1956 California license plates "blaze" our route, a jeep trail. Winding down still farther, we reach a parking lot, **Trailhead 3 (0.5, 68.6),** above the reservoir.

Trailheads 4–7: Crystal Basin Recreation Area

4   From Placerville drive east up Highway 50 to Fresh Pond (17.0), on your right, where there is the USFS Pacific Ranger Station, open weekdays. Also here are a gas station and a cafe. Farther east your highway crosses the South Fork of the American River (5.4, 22.4) and in 50 yards reaches the Crystal Basin Recreation Area turnoff, Ice House Road, on your left. This paved road climbs to a ridge, then descends to Ice House Resort (9.2, 31.4), generally open May through October, which is your last opportunity to purchase fuel, food and supplies. Farther north you reach the Crystal Basin Ranger Station, which is open from Memorial Day weekend to mid-September, when weather conditions permit. If you plan to enter Desolation Wilderness via

Loon Lake, pick up your wilderness permit here if you have not done so already. Before and beyond this station, spur roads to lakes and good, popular campgrounds are passed. Eventually you descend on the paved forest highway to the Robbs Forebay (12.9, 46.0), on the South Fork of the Rubicon River. After a short climb you reach a junction with the Loon Lake Road (0.6, 46.6), climbing right. Follow this paved road to a **Y** (4.6, 51.2) and take the right fork east to a parking lot (0.4, 51.6), on your left, for boaters, bathers and backpackers. Leave your car here and walk 0.2 mile northeast on the road to **Trailhead 4 (0.2, 51.8),** on your right, which is just 20 yards past a campground spur road to sites 1–12, on your left.

5   Back at the **Y** (51.2) branch left and follow the road almost to the end of the second dam (3.3, 54.5), then fork left down a short road that ends in a parking area, **Trailhead 5 (0.2, 54.7),** near the base of this dam.

6   From the Loon Lake Road junction (46.6) drive a short distance to another junction (0.2, 46.8). Turn left (west) and descend the rocky road across a canal (0.7, 47.5) and past the South Fork Campground entrance (0.5, 48.0) to a fork (0.1, 48.1). The left fork leads back up to the paved forest highway and it seems like a better route than the rocky road you just came down. But beware: unless the Forest Service has improved it, it is very likely to be muddy in early season and deeply rutted thereafter. From this fork veer right and curve down to a crossing of the South Fork of the Rubicon River (1.0–49.1). A short drive takes you up to **Trailhead 6 (0.5, 49.6),** on your left, a parking lot signed *South Fork Trail.* You can cut 1.6 miles off the South Fork Trail by continuing 0.8 mile along the road to a fork and then descending the left branch one mile to where it starts to climb (see Trip 2).

7   From the Loon Lake Road junction (46.6) drive north on the forest highway past Gerle Creek and a spur road (2.7, 49.3) that descends southwest to Gerle Creek Campground beside Gerle Creek Reservoir. Continue north almost to Deer Creek, where the Wentworth Springs Road starts up beside it (3.0, 52.3). Soon a branch forks left (0.3, 52.6), crosses the creek, rounds a ridge and climbs to a broad saddle (2.2, 54.8). Now increasingly steep slopes take us up to a junction (2.1, 56.9), where our road switchbacks sharply left. A stiff climb west brings us to another tight switchback (0.5, 57.4), and just beyond it we reach a saddle on which there is a small parking area and **Trailhead 7 (0.1, 57.5).**

Trailheads 8–12: Wrights Lake Recreation Area

8,9   From the Crystal Basin turnoff (22.4), drive up to Kyburz (9.5, 31.9), your last stop for food and gas, and continue to the Wrights Lake Road (5.1, 37.0), branching left. This road climbs 3½ miles to Chimney Flat, curves around it up to a low saddle and makes a short descent to **Trailhead 8 (4.2, 41.2),** on your right. Some backpackers drive 0.4 mile up the spur road to its roadend, with room for only several cars. Just beyond we cross Lyons Creek (0.1, 41.3) then make a winding drive up to a backpackers' parking lot (3.9, 45.2) on our right. As of summer 1974, rangers still allowed people to park at the other Wrights Lake trailheads, but they preferred that hikers park here instead. At the south end of the parking lot, where horses are usually pastured, is **Trailhead 9 (0.1, 45.3).** You could also park at the new Wrights Lake Campground, immediately northeast across the Wrights Lake outlet creek.

10   Just beyond the parking area is the Wrights Lake Ranger Station—where you can obtain your wilderness permits—and a junction (0.2, 45.4) with two roads. The mile-long spur road east goes to the new campground entrance, to the east-shore summer homes and to a trailhead from where a spur trail traverses ½ mile north along or near a meadow's edge to a junction with the Twin Lakes Trail. Since trailhead parking space is very limited, and often is occupied with bathers' cars, parking there is not recommended. The spur road west climbs past the old campground, on the right, up to a low morainal ridge, then descends to **Trailhead 10 (0.8, 46.2),** a small flat by the northeast shore of Dark Lake.

11,12   From the ranger station triple fork, drive north past a picnic ground on the right and the old Wrights Lake campground, on the left, to a fork (0.2, 45.6). The private lakeshore road affords access to the west-shore summer homes. We veer left, climb a rocky road, and then descend it to **Trailhead 11 (0.5, 46.1),** only 50 yards before our reunion with the private lakeshore road. The road ahead quickly becomes bad, particularly in June, when it is still muddy. Nevertheless, hundreds of backpackers drive their cars to **Trailhead 12 (0.5, 46.6),** with parking space for several dozen

cars. It is usually crowded on weekends, when as many as 200 backpackers will hike up toward Rockbound Pass. The Willow Flat Trail starts north up a closed road; about 50 yards southeast of it, the Twin Lakes Trail starts east.

Trailheads 13–18: Upper Highway 50

13   From the Wrights Lake Road turnoff (37.0) continue up Highway 50 to Pyramid Campground (1.8, 38.8) on your right, the only public campground between the Wrights Lake turnoff and South Lake Tahoe. (Two private campgrounds are found at the junction with Upper Truckee Road.) From Pyramid Campground drive east to 42 Mile Picnic Ground (2.0, 40.8), on your right, and take a road from it to a junction immediately past a bridge over the South Fork American River (80 yards). Turn right and follow Strawberry Canyon Road, first south to southeast, then north up to a saddle, after passing several roads branching right. Our road now climbs 0.2 mile south-southeast to a bend, where it curves southeast. Here at the bend you'll see a post which marks **Trailhead 13 (1.0, 41.8),** from which a steep trail climbs to Lovers Leap.

14   Beyond the 42 Mile Picnic Ground turnoff (40.8) we enter the settlement of Strawberry (0.5, 41.3), where gas is available, then continue to Twin Bridges Store and Post Office (1.8, 43.1). Between it and Pyramid Creek, a trail starts north toward Horsetail Falls. This trail is not recommended; see comment at end of Trip 23. Highway 50 now climbs around the mammoth east moraine of Pyramid Creek and reaches Camp Sacramento, on your right, and Sayles Flat Picnic Ground, on your left, which is parking for **Trailhead 14 (1.4, 44.5).**

15   From Sayles Flat the highway climbs east, curves northeast around a bend and quickly reaches a road (0.5, 45.0) which branches right and goes 70 yards southeast across the South Fork to its other bank. Here, obeying a sign, we turn right and head south up Sayles Canyon to road's end at **Trailhead 15 (0.6, 45.6).**

16   Immediately beyond the Sayles Canyon turnoff, Highway 50 meets paved Pinecrest Road (0.1, 45.1), which forks northeast, and we drive to a bend, where we reach **Trailhead 16 (0.2, 45.3),** signed *Ralston Trail.*

17   East of the Pinecrest Road fork (45.1) Highway 50 climbs to another paved road forking left (4.3, 49.4). On this we climb east to a junction with another paved road (0.6, 50.0), on which we climb north, then curve west down to Echo Lake Resort, with gasoline plus a post office. Park your car in the lot just east of and above the resort. **Trailhead 17 (1.2, 51.2)** is at Lower Echo Lake's dam, just a few yards northwest of the resort.

18   Beyond the Echo Lakes road fork (49.4) we immediately encounter Little Norway (0.1, 49.5), which has gas, food and a post office, then drive on to Echo Summit (1.0, 50.5). Just beyond it and a state highway-maintenance station we reach a junction with a dirt road (0.1, 50.6), on which we climb south to its end, to summer homes and to **Trailhead 18 (0.4, 51.0).**

Trailheads 19–20: Upper Truckee Road

19   From Echo Summit (50.5) drive down scenic Meyers Grade toward Lake Tahoe, and immediately beyond a KOA campground entrance reach Upper Truckee Road (3.5, 54.0) on your right. Follow this almost level road south toward the headwaters of the Upper Truckee River. Just before you cross a bridge over this river, take a spur road (3.8, 57.8) to some Bridge Tract summer homes. At the boulder-blocked end of this road is **Trailhead 19 (0.3, 58.1).** Park on a turnout 100 yards before these boulders.

20   From the first spur road above (57.8) drive east across the bridge to a second spur road (0.1, 57.9), and follow it past more Bridge Tract summer homes to **Trailhead 20 (0.2, 58.1).**

Trailheads 21–23: Highway 89 South

21   Not far beyond the Upper Truckee Road junction (54.0) we reach Highway 89 South (0.4, 54.4 miles from Placerville; 5.0 miles south of the Highways 50/89 junction in South Lake Tahoe). Drive south on this steadily climbing highway to a creek crossing, where the highway curves northeast, 3.6 miles before Luther Pass, and reach in 100 yards **Trailhead 21 (5.3, 59.7).** The signed Big Meadow Trail is on the south; roadside parking is on the north.

22   From Trailhead 21 the highway climbs up to a curve at the west end of a large, flat meadow, where we see **Trailhead 22 (1.7, 61.4),** on our left.

23   Highway 89 parallels the north edge of the meadow to Luther Pass (1.8, 63.2) then descends to Hope Valley and a junction with Highway 88 (2.7, 65.9). Turn left and head east past Sorenson's Resort (0.9, 66.8), which has a store, cafe, cabins and gasoline, then to Hope Valley Resort (0.4, 67.2), which has a store, gasoline, and trailer sites. Immediately beyond it you cross the West Fork Carson River and reach Kit Carson Campground (0.2, 67.4), on your left, then arrive at **Trailhead 23 (0.6, 68.0),** on your left and Snowshoe Springs Campground, on your right.

Trailhead 24: Fountain Place

24   From the Highway 89 South junction (54.4) drive north to Pioneer Trail (0.9, 55.3) on your right, and follow this road northeast to Oneidas Street (0.9, 56.2), on which you turn right. At its end (0.2, 56.4) take a dirt road that branches northeast, traverses a ridgetop, passes several junctions with dirt roads, then descends northeast to a fork (0.7, 57.1). Go left here and descend to a flat where a road branches west-northwest to the Burrow Pit just before our road crosses Saxon Creek (0.2, 57.3). Beyond the crossing our road climbs east to a tributary of Trout Creek, 40 yards beyond which we reach a fork (1.8, 59.1). Turn left, cross Trout Creek (0.1, 59.2) then climb up to a barbed-wire cattle fence and closed gate (0.2, 59.4). Close the gate after you pass through it, and make a steep ascent, ignoring spur roads, up to road's end on a forested flat, **Trailhead 24 (2.3, 61.7),** just northwest of a creek and a meadow. No overnight camping is allowed here, so plan to camp along the trail. A word of caution: one mile above the closed gate is a 20-yard stretch of rutted road, which is difficult to negotiate with an ordinary car in mid-August and almost impossible before then. Consider parking below the gate, near Trout Creek.

Trailheads 25–30: Fallen Leaf Lake

25   From the Highway 89 South junction (54.4) drive north on Highway 50/89 to the South Lake Tahoe **Y** (5.0, 59.4, and the end of Highway 50 mileage from Placerville). Since you'll need a Wilderness Permit for most of the hikes from this section's trailheads, turn left (southwest) at this major intersection, drive along Lake Tahoe Boulevard 0.2 mile, then turn left and drive 0.1 mile along Tata Lane to the Tahoe Basin Forest Service Ranger Station. Back at the **Y** (0.0) follow 89 northwest to Fallen Leaf Road (3.2 miles from the **Y**). We soon pass the entrance (0.6, 3.8) to Fallen Leaf Campground, which, like virtually all the others in the Tahoe Basin, is full from July through Labor Day. Farther south we reach Tahoe Mountain Road (1.4, 5.2), onto which we turn and climb southeast. At a fork (0.5, 5.7) we branch right and follow Angora Ridge Road up to Angora Fire Lookout, where, on its north side, is **Trailhead 25 (1.9, 7.6).**

26   Continuing southward from the lookout we descend to a gully with a large parking lot, **Trailhead 26 (1.0, 8.6).** The Fallen Leaf Lake Trail heads northwest over an obvious saddle just above the upper end of the lot. From the southeast end of the lot, this trail continues south up to Lower Angora Lake, from where you follow the closed road south to Upper Angora Lake. A steep, primitive trail climbs from this lake's southeast shore.

27   From the Tahoe Mountain Road junction (5.2), drive south along narrow, heavily used Fallen Leaf Road to bustling Fallen Leaf Lodge, which has a store, coffee shop, post office, campground and cabins. Park near this resort for **Trailhead 27 (2.6, 7.8),** then from the large *Fallen Leaf Lodge* sign hike along the road, climbing southeast and then curving east. At its end, 200 yards from the sign, continue east 80 yards on another road to its end, 20 yards beyond which is the signed *Clark Trail.*

28   West beyond Fallen Leaf Lodge the paved road splits, the branch north across Glen Alpine Creek going to Stanford Sierra Camp. **Trailhead 28 (0.4, 8.2)** starts by a water pipe 30 yards south of this fork.

29,30   Taking the left fork, which passes through Fallen Leaf Lodge's campground before climbing steeply, you soon reach **Trailhead 29 (0.4, 8.6),** then cross Glen Alpine Creek and follow the now gravelly road to a gate, **Trailhead 30 (0.5, 9.1).** Parking for these two trailheads is anywhere you can find space to pull off the road far enough that you don't block traffic.

Trailheads 31–36: Lake Tahoe, Southwest Shore

31   Just north beyond the Fallen Leaf Road junction (3.2) is the Lake Tahoe Visitor Center (0.1, 3.3), which has information, campfire programs, a stream-profile chamber, guided nature tours and 5 self-guided trails. Where Highway 89 curves from west to north, the Spring Creek Summer Homes spur road (1.5, 4.8) departs south. You can follow this road up to **Trailhead 31 (0.8, 5.6),** near the road's end.

32   Beyond the spur road (4.8), Highway 89 climbs and then descends the east lateral moraine of Cascade Lake, then climbs its west lateral moraine and heads to Bay View Picnic Area (3.1, 7.9) on your left, and, 40 yards farther, Inspiration Point Picnic Area, on your right above Emerald Bay. Follow the Bay View Picnic Area loop road to its upper end, **Trailhead 32 (0.1, 8.0).** Just beyond the southernmost table is a branching road. Walk up the right fork, which quickly curves northwest 100 yards up to the Granite Lake Trail.

33   From the Bay View Picnic Area (7.9) drive on an exposed traverse across a rockfall slope then, immediately after crossing Eagle Creek, turn left into the large parking lot of Eagle Falls Picnic Area, which is **Trailhead 33 (1.0, 8.9).**

34   Continuing north on Highway 89 you pass the entrance to D. L. Bliss State Park (2.3, 11.2), with a usually full campground, then wind your way down to Meeks Creek (5.5, 16.7), and just beyond it, Meeks Bay Stables. **Trailhead 34 (0.1, 16.8)** is at the closed road that starts from the north side of the stables. A signed trail begins 1.4 miles up this almost level road. Park where you can find space anywhere along the highway. About 250 yards north of the stables is the entrance to Meeks Bay Resort, which has a campground, fantastic beach and other attractions.

35   Beyond Meeks Bay Stables (16,8) you reach the entrance to Sugar Pine Point State Park day-use area, on your right. You can park your car in it, for a fee, while you're hiking along the General Creek Trail, which starts from a closed road, **Trailhead 35 (1.0, 17.8),** opposite the day-use entrance.

36   North on 89 is another road to the General Creek Trail. Turn left at the General Creek Campground entrance (0.7, 18.5). Since you're entering a fee area, tell the Forest Service attendant your plans and ask him where to park. **Trailhead 36 (0.9, 19.4)** starts at a closed, southwest-heading road opposite campsite 150 on the westernmost camp loop.

You can continue north on Highway 89 through the settlements of Tahoma and Homewood, both having gas and food, then pass by impressive Eagle Rock, just west of the highway, and soon reach Kaspian Picnic Ground (5.2, 24.6). The road leading west from it later branches and climbs up to the Powderhorn trails. To reach these trails see the Interstate 80 trailhead descriptions.

1   Hales Camp Trail, Parsley Bar Trail

Distance: 19.2 miles, round trip

Total gain/Net gain: 2780'/1710'

Classification: Easy

Season: April through November

Parking: More than ample on large riverside flat

Trailhead/Map: 1/1

Features: Due to its low elevation, most of it under 4000 feet, this route has an eight-month-long hiking season. The gently climbing riverside trail provides fishermen with an easy access to dozens of pools inhabited by rainbow and brown trout. During the hot summer months, some of these cold pools make great swimming holes. Students of hydrology or geomorphology will find this hike a very instructive one, for this section of the Rubicon River canyon experienced a catastrophic flood which left in its wake a very altered river environment.

Description: From the signed trailhead the Hales Camp Trail (14E04) climbs up ⅓ mile to a trail intersection on a ridge. Trail 13E13 starts northwest but fades away after 300 yards. An unsigned trail southeast switchbacks steeply down to the brink of the Rubicon gorge, 150 feet above the river. From this exposed vantage point, you could observe the dipping, bedded metamorphic strata on the opposite canyon wall, but more likely you'll be interested in the beautiful pool below, which is reached by hiking upstream from the trailhead parking lot.

Back on the main trail from the ridge intersection we ascend moderately up the ridge, then traverse high above the steep-sided Rubicon gorge before descending gradually to a shady gully opposite the mouth of the South Fork canyon. Fifteen yards beyond this gully's seasonal creek we reach a spur trail that descends 100 yards to boulders and bedrock along the river's edge. Near a rapid that cuts through bedrock is a pleasant, sandy, poolside campsite. Boulder-hopping across this narrow rapid, tricky in early season, gets one to another sandy, sunny campsite at the terminus of the South Fork Trail (see Trip 2). A short, bouldery jaunt down the river's west bank takes you to fast rapids at the start of the scenic upper end of the gorge. Here the river has cut large potholes into the Paleozoic limestone and other sedimentary rocks that line it.

Back on the Hales Camp Trail, we make a short climb up to a curve, from where we can look directly across up the South Fork canyon. One might observe that its north slope is the boundary between the Paleozoic metasediments of the Calaveras Formation, to the south, and Mesozoic diorite, to the north, but a more interesting observation is the jumble of logs piled up on a south-slope bench about 80 feet above the river: they look as if they were left there in the aftermath of a great flood. Is it possible that a surge of water 80 feet high could have left them there in its wake? The answer is an unreassuring "yes."

It was back in December 1964 when all hell broke loose—literally. The Hell Hole Dam, then partly constructed, suddenly gave way. In an hour's time one third of the dam's 2.1-million cubic yards of rockfill was transported downstream in a flood of water that averaged 30-40 feet high. Because the river cuts through a gorge in the South Fork vicinity, the flood here was even higher. If you walked over to the South Fork, you may have seen cables above its 50-foot-high gorge. These are all that remain of the bridge that was washed away by this flood, whose flow averaged better than ¼ million cubic feet per second. On the 61-mile river course from the dam to Folsom Reservoir, where the flood was finally contained, four of the five major bridges were destroyed.

Why did the dam fail in the first place? One reason was that it was only a partly completed, erodable, earthfill dam, composed of an impervious core with rockfill on both sides of it. At the time of the failure, the upstream rockfill and the core had been built only 50 feet high, while the downstream rockfill had been built to a height of 220 feet. No water was being stored behind the dam. Preceding the failure, however, was a torrential, five-day, 22-inch rainfall, which in itself greatly increased the river's flow, and also melted a large portion of the season's fresh snowpack. These two water sources were too great for the temporary dam outlet to handle, and by the third rainy day water had backed up 150 feet high behind the dam—100 feet higher than the top of the protective, impervious core. The dam began eroding away, and at 9:30 a.m. on December 24, the dam broke. Fortunately, the Rubicon River canyon was not inhabited.

Standing on your South Fork canyon observation site, you might consider why your trail climbs so high. As you hike northward, notice how the flood has eroded back the slopes immediately below the trail. Parts of the original trail were washed out when the flood triggered landslides by undercutting the slopes. This is readily noticeable in many places on the opposite canyon wall.

One-third mile northeast of the South Fork canyon we meet the Grey Trail, climbing west. Moving on, we pass many potential riverside campsites before arriving at creekside Hales Camp, now little more than a collapsed cabin and a doorless outhouse. Just 200 yards beyond it, however, we reach a junction from where a spur trail heads 70 yards east to a good, developed riverside campsite with tables and logs. Climbing west from this junction is a trail up toward the canyon's rim.

Continuing our pleasant up-canyon walk through a predominantly Douglas-fir forest that also has incense-cedar, white fir and ponderosa pine, we pass over several moist, shady spots on which dogwoods and broadleaf maples thrive. Farther north we reach a bench with a grassy, wildflowered meadow, in and around which grow a small number of huge, stately ponderosa pines and incense-cedars. Topping 250 feet, the tallest ponderosa ranks as one of the largest of its kind to be found in California—indeed, to be found anywhere. Try to photograph it from top to bottom, and see how far you have to step back to get the full tree into the picture.

The level bench extends northward to a bedrock exposure of diorite, up which we now make a moderate ascent to a view, from above some rapids, of the lower end of long, wide, alder-choked Parsley Bar. In the distance, above unseen Hell Hole Dam, sails Steam-boat Mountain (7347'), its dark slopes being remnants of large volcanic flows erupted during the Pliocene epoch. As you walk along the west edge of Parsley Bar, note the tremendous amount of boulders left behind by the flood waters. This bar is the first large flat downstream from the damsite, and when the floodwaters raged down into it, they spread out and slowed down, thereby losing some of the energy they needed to transport the larger boulders. All the alders among the boulders germinated after the flood, and in the 10 years since that event some have grown to 30 feet—an average growth of three feet per year.

Now on the Parsley Bar Trail (15E01), we have old license plates, nailed high on conifers, marking our route northward. Just as we start to switchback northwest, we reach a 50-yard spur trail to a river campsite, the last one we'll see. Ahead of us is a steep—sometimes very steep—switchbacking ascent. During the summers of 1973 and 1974 some cyclists were sporadically busy rerouting the trail, building longer switchbacks in order to lessen the gradient for their dirt bikes. Both routes cross and recross each other, and the hiker can take his choice. Our exhausting climb takes us up to a huge live oak at the brink of a deep gully. With only 200 vertical feet left to climb, we make a moderate-to-steep ascent 330 yards to the Long John Trail, which starts southwest but goes nowhere. Easier climbing for 270 yards then beings us to a saddle, where our trail becomes a roadway. After a gentle 100-yard north-northeast descent on it, we reach a jeep road at a point where it curves up northwest. Here we turn right and follow it one steep quarter mile northeast down to Trailhead 2 on the Hell Hole road.

Flood erosion at Parsley Bar

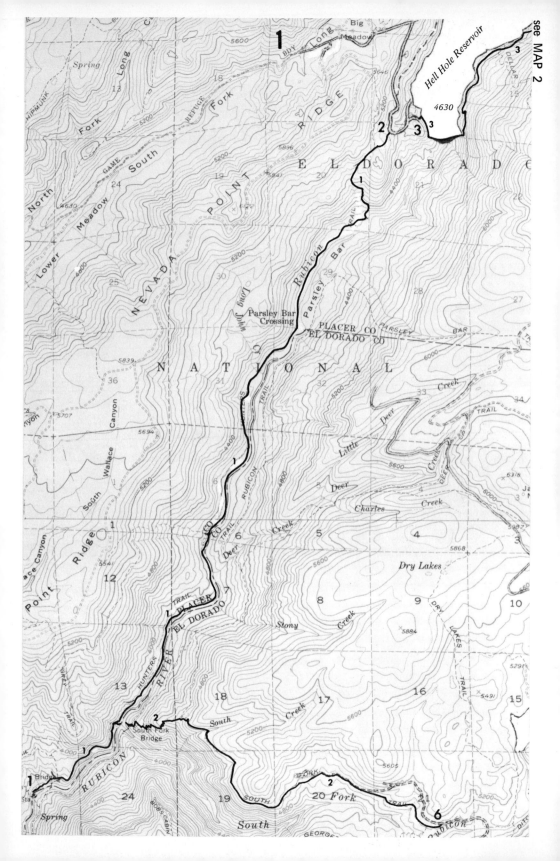

2   South Fork Trail

Distance: 10.2 miles, round trip
Total gain/Net gain: 1920'/1520'
Classification: Moderate
Season: May through October
Parking: Half a dozen cars
Trailhead/Map: 6/1

Features: This trail is a good one for late spring backpacking, for moderate exercise to get you in shape for the summer ahead. Or, if you are vacationing among the reservoirs of Crystal Basin Recreation Area, this trail presents you with a change of pace and a change of scenery. Finally, for those hiking down the Rubicon River (Trip 6), the South Fork Trail provides a rather direct route back up toward their original trailhead.

Description: From the trailhead, our Trail 14E14 makes a sunny traverse west across a brushy, granitic slope into a forest of white fir, sugar pine, incense-cedar and ponderosa pine. Not far beyond the first shady gully, the early-season hiker hears the delightful rhapsody of an azalea-lined cascade joyfully bounding down a small, shady side canyon. So enchanting can it be that some hikers may decide to go no farther. But this show of sound and color is ephemeral, leaving the late-season hiker with only a dry creek bed and little reason to linger. Beyond it the trail traverses the forested slope and is soon overrun and absorbed by a descending logging road. On this you hike ⅓ mile, crossing two gullies. From the second gully the road makes a noticeable climb, and in 100 yards you reach a 20-yard-long clearing, on your left, where the trail commences once again. Late-season hikers may with to park their car at or near this clearing and start their trip from here.

Our forested trail continues its traverse, hanging on to the upper slope of the canyon and providing the hiker with occasional good views up, down and across the deep canyon. Almost four miles from the first trailhead, we make a short, steep descent to South Creek, shaded by more of the conifers we've seen plus dogwood and Douglas-fir. For the up-canyon hiker in particular, this is a necessary, refreshing stop, even a desirable campsite. All too soon beyond this cool retreat, our trail begins a steep ridge descent toward the Rubicon. The river's rapids gradually become audible as granitic rocks give way to metamorphic ones and shady conifers yield to

South Creek

live oak and chaparral. Even lower, a junction with the abandoned Rubicon Trail, starting northward, heralds our approach to the river. Now a few remaining switchbacks take us steeply ¼ mile down to a small, sandy flat on a rocky, potholed riverside terrace. Immediately upstream is a large pool, usually 55-60°F, with shallow and deep sections suitable for fishing, swimming and diving.

If you like spectacular high diving into a cold, deep pool, hike 100 yards up the South Fork and leap off the vertical, 50-foot-high cliffs, if you dare. Lower diving ledges are available to the more cautious. Flirting around the faster running sections of this creek and the river are dippers, or water ouzels, which are chunky, drab-gray birds that seem to be as much at home in the water as the trout are. On a shelf above the creek's south bank is debris left by a catastrophic flood (see Trip 1) and the remains of the South Fork bridge, across which hikers once headed downstream on a now-abandoned trail.

Potholes on metamorphic-rock bench above the Rubicon River

South Fork's deep pool

3   Hell Hole Reservoir Shoreline Traverse

Distance: 9.8 miles, round trip
Total gain/Net gain: 1160'/220'
Classification: Easy
Season: May through October
Parking: More than ample in parking lot above the boat ramp
Trailhead/Map: 3/2

Features: Many small coves—great for fishing, swimming or sunbathing— are easily reached from this little used trail. On a granitic bench overlooking upper Hell Hole Reservoir is a beautiful, woodland campground, which is an ideal site for just pure relaxing.

Description: From the parking lot above the boat ramp, walk down steps to a level road that you follow south toward the west end of the 410-foot-high dam. A large rockfall, about 2000 tons worth, recently fell from the diorite cliff above, but it has since been removed. The area is signed *closed,* but the author was told by one authority that you can enter it *at your own risk* and walk south toward the dam. When you reach the dam, cross its 1570-foot length to the canyon's east side. A project of the Placer County Water Agency, this dam was completed in 1966, but not without incident (see Trip 1). At the dam's southeast corner, an unsigned trail starts out southeast, but goes only six yards before it switchbacks north and climbs 150 feet above the shoreline. Although the trail is unmaintained, it is still in fairly good condition because most of its length traverses erosion-resistant diorite slabs. Seasonal creeks abound in late spring and early summer—so many, in fact, that they might pose a problem, as does a permanent cascading creek you soon must cross on slippery rocks at the base of a splashing cascade. Beyond it, more seasonal creeks are crossed before the trail descends almost to the water's edge and the first good rest spot. Just beyond it, we round a cove, which beckons us to pause, and then continue on to a small flat with a pleasant campsite shaded by ponderosa pines together with incense-cedars, black oaks and live oaks.

By now you might have noticed that the trail climbs and drops in order to follow the large diorite slabs, which are delineated by major joint lines that are almost horizontal. The slab pattern continues as we head toward the northeast end of now-submerged Lower Hell Hole. Just before our trail climbs and leaves the water's edge, Cottonwood Creek, across the reservoir, can be heard but not seen. The trail curves across a bench, from which you can see a pinnacle by Little Steamboat Mountain, to the northeast, before the trail descends east to the water's edge at former Upper Hell Hole. A tempting island lies 150 yards offshore, a good swim at midsummer when the water temperature gets into the 60s, the reservoir is lower, and the distance to swim is less.

As our trail comes almost to the reservoir's high-water level, we see several more islands. From here to a bench ½ mile east, several springs and many seasonal creeks are crossed. Upon making the short ascent up to the bench, we spot a campground with very evident tables, stoves and, less in view, outhouses. The bench is diorite bedrock, but it has numerous, small grassy flats that are ideal for lying on within this rustic environment among scattered ponderosa pines, live oaks, black oaks and Douglas-firs. Take a few days' time to just relax or to explore the environs. Should you wish to continue east along this trail, which shortly deteriorates, see Trip 6, which describes it in detail from east to west.

Little Steamboat Mountain above Hell Hole

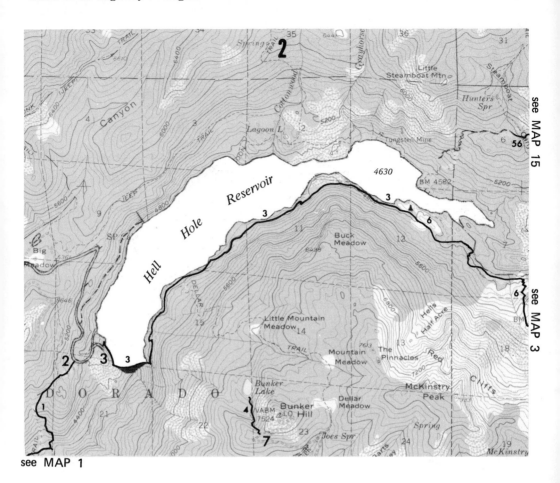

see MAP 1

4   Bunker Lake Trail

Distance: 1.0 mile, round trip
Total gain/Net gain: 600'/600'
Classification: Moderate
Season: Mid-July through mid-October
Parking: Limited, four cars at most
Trailhead/Map: 7/2

Features: Because of the relatively long drive up to it, this trail sees very little use. If you find no cars at the trailhead, you know that you'll get what you drove up for: solitude—there is no other way in to the lake. If a car or two are already at the saddle, you can always change your plans, drive ¾ mile up the road to the Bunker Hill Fire Lookout, and take in the panoramic views of the Crystal Basin to the south and the Crystal Range to the southeast. From the summit a 70-yard-long trail west takes you to an overlook of the Hell Hole Reservoir area.

Description: The unsigned trail starts north from the saddle and steeply descends a gully almost to a hidden spring, whose presence is made known by the lush vegetation as well as by its trickling sound. Leaving the gully, we traverse a brushy slope below gray granitic cliffs, then reach a small, classic lateral moraine, from which we can see that the slope

above us is now orangish brown—metamorphosed marine sediments of the Jurassic period. From the moraine, our beautiful jewel is in sight, and we descend a very steep, short path down a gully to its southeast shore. The best campsite at this moderately deep lake is above its north end, most easily reached by traversing along its west bank on a faint trail just above the brush-choked shore. From the terminal moraine at the lake's north end, you might have expected a great view of Hell Hole, over 2000 feet below, but alas, it is effectively filtered by an abundance of red firs and silver pines.

Much of the brush we passed by, or in a few spots plowed through, is typical of this elevation: chinquapin, huckleberry oak, spiraea and Laborador tea. One species, however, is quite scarce in the Sierra, and its presence here makes the long drive to the trailhead worth the effort. Both on the slope and around the lake you'll see erect stalks with small, white, bell-shaped flowers of the Sierra laurel. The bush is further identified by its evergreen, somewhat leathery leaves. Within the quiet lakeshore environment dozens of other shrubs and wildflowers flourish which should tantalize the amateur botanist.

Bunker Lake

5   Loon Lake to Bugle Lake

Distance: 7.6 miles, round trip

Total gain/Net gain: 1030'/610'

Classification: Moderate

Season: Late June through mid-October

Parking: More than ample at parking area below dam

Trailhead/Map: 5/3

Features: Bugle Lake, off the beaten track, is a pleasant day hike from the Loon Lake area. Those who wish to spend several days in a lakeside environment will find plenty of good campsites here.

Description: Fifty yards beyond the parking area our road crosses the dam's overflow channel and becomes a ducked jeep route over large, barren, glacier-polished slabs that bear glacial striations in a west-southwest orientation—the direction the glacier flowed. The ducks guide us down to the outlet creek and into a swampy lodgepole forest, through which the jeep road remains boggy and mosquito-ridden until mid-July. In addition to finding the usual lodgepole-associated flowers, the midseason hiker will surely spot the Leichtlin's camas, a six-petaled, blue-violet tulip, whose bulbs Indians roasted to give this nourishing food a pleasant vanilla flavor.

At the edge of the forested flat, our jeep road north-northwest meets the Wentworth Jeep Trail at the point where this level "trail" curves northward and starts to climb. About ½ mile west on it is the Wentworth Springs Campground, rather shoddy, and in another ½ mile are the run-down shacks and buildings of Wentworth Springs. Rust-tainted soda springs, with their bubbling water, are seen along the roadside just beyond the east side of this desolate settlement.

From our jeep road junction we immediately start a northward climb, steep at times, up the now almost unusable jeep road. Jeep usage had eroded the road down to the bedrock so that plenty of one- and two-foot-high steps exist, making the route treacherous for jeeps and motorcycles but not for hikers. Just beyond a seasonal creek crossing, the gradient eases and we curve northeast up an obviously glaciated, open slope with a few junipers, across which we can look south to the Loon Lake dam. The route levels off, and we enter a lodgepole forest and soon reach a junction with another jeep road just 40 yards short of refreshing Ellis Creek.

Up this road we tread northwest, almost immediately crossing one of the creek's tributaries. Lodgepoles become subordinate to red firs by the time we reach a fork on a small ridge, 0.9 mile farther. The McKinstry Lake jeep road, branching northwest up to the lake and beyond, is described in Trip 6. We

Bugle Lake

angle left (southwest) and climb this little used road up to a morainal saddle, then make a short descent to Bugle Lake's brushy shore. Continuing along our path, we traverse this island-dotted lake's north shore and reach several good campsites under red firs near its west end. Hikers who enjoy panoramic views can cross the lake's outlet creek, at its west end, and climb an easy slope to a summit immediately south of the lake, from where the Loon Lake Reservoir/Wentworth Springs area unfolds before them.

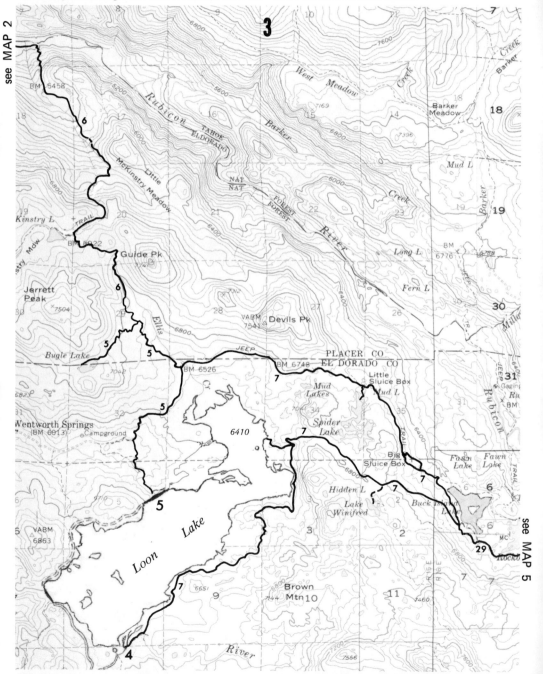

6   Rubicon River Loop

Distance: 39.3 miles, loop trip, or 28.2 miles plus an 11.1-mile shuttle

Total gain/Net gain: 5790'/3510' for the 39.3-mile distance

Classification: Moderate

Season: Early July through mid-October

Parking: More than ample at parking area below dam

Trailhead/Maps: 5/3,2,1

Features: One of the Tahoe Sierra's longer hikes, the Rubicon River loop takes the hiker down through three major environments: red-fir, white-fir and Douglas-fir forests. This trip impresses upon the hiker just how much the vegetation can change with elevation and with aspect, or slope orientation. Flowing or still water parallels most of the route. The unmaintained "Red Cliffs" section of trail offers the backpacker a degree of solitude seldom found anywhere in the entire Sierra Nevada.

Description: Our trail description begins at the Bugle Lake Jeep Road junction, reached by following Trip 5 to it. Beyond this junction on the ridge, we quickly reach a jump-across tributary of Ellis Creek, then climb steeply up a minor ridge, only to descend its other side steeply to an open, sandy flat sandwiched between Ellis Creek and the base of granitic, conical, aptly-named Guide Peak. Several suitable campsites are found along this 100-yard-long flat.

Leaving the flat, we climb an increasingly steep grade north through a forest of red fir, lodgepole and silver pine in upper Ellis Creek canyon, then just below a saddle ahead veer west to a ridge crossing north of and above a second saddle. The jeep road now winds westward down to a boggy flat and crosses several branches of the outlet creek from McKinstry Lake, 200 yards upstream. Forty yards north of the last ford we reach a junction, from where we could walk 300 yards west along a jeep road to adequate campsites along the northeast shore of lodgepole-fringed McKinstry Lake. Rather, we veer right and follow the road northeast, paralleling the creek. The creek curves north, then northwest, greatly increasing its gradient, as does our road. When Hell Hole Reservoir breaks into view, our jeep road narrows to become the McKinstry Trail, which makes a traverse west before curving north and dropping very

steeply to a crossing of the creek we've been paralleling. Along this descent, light gray granitic rocks contrast vividly with reddish-brown metamorphics of McKinstry Peak and the Red Cliffs. The trail down to this crossing isn't too obvious, but about 100 yards before the crossing, our trail passes just five yards west of a huge, five-foot-diameter Jeffrey pine—the largest tree around.

From the crossing our ducked route heads downstream about 50 yards, makes a traversing arc northeast across an open slope, and then descends to a creek. Beyond it we cross a boulder field and reach the main creek, emanating from the Little McKinstry Meadow basin. A diagonal boulder-hop due north across it gets us to a resumption of our ducked trail, on which we descend northwest. Our path parallels the creek at first, then angles away and becomes overgrown with brush. From the other side of a large downed trunk across this unmaintained trail, plow 100 yards straight downslope, and with luck you'll emerge at a small, grassy flat beneath three Jeffrey pines. Now the cross-country is much easier, and the trail becomes obvious—if you've lost it—by the time you reach a rocky flat. If you have the time, spend a day or two of complete solitude camped beside the flat's cheerful creek.

When you must leave this solitude, follow the ducked route to the edge of the flat, then diagonal north steeply down the slope to an obvious gully, just above and beyond which you'll find a free-standing granitic block 50 feet long by 20 feet high. This is a crucial "duck." The trail, which has temporarily disappeared over bedrock, can be found by heading directly downslope from it a few yards until you can locate the ducked trail, which you then follow north steeply down to a small bench above the Rubicon River.

(For those heading up this steep route, bless them, the trail will not be evident. From at least one spot along the Rubicon you can see Guide Peak, a treeless, pointed, light gray summit. The trail is among trees and shrubs to the right of the peak. Starting from the riverside bench, you leave the Rubicon River as your trail makes a short switchback southwest to another bench. Walk a level 45 yards southeast on it, then continue straight ahead 10 more yards to where the trail turns abruptly southwest toward McKinstry Peak. Follow it 15 yards, no farther, for believe it or not, your "trail" now is up the 12-foot-high rock wall on your left. Climb Class 3 up it and then follow ducks 140 yards up the gully ahead of you. Higher, your route curves south-southwest about 50 yards up to a bench, which isn't recognizable as one until you top it. From here many ducks guide you south past junipers up the steep trail to the 50-foot-long granitic block.)

Eighty yards west of the small Rubicon River bench, we reach a large ponderosa pine with an old sign indicating we've just come down the McKinstry Trail. Under heavy forest several creeks are crossed— waded in early season—and then the trail leaves the shady conifers and old blazes behind as it parallels the river, staying about 5 to 30 yards from it, through alders and young conifers that get pretty thick in one spot. As we enter forest again, Guide Peak and the McKinstry Meadow creek cascade disappear from view. The trail starts to climb, and then we make an earnest, 30-yard, steep climb up to a little creek cascading down from Hells Half Acre. Now we make a short traverse, and then a steep switchbacking descent to within 10 yards of the Rubicon at a point where it exits from its gorge.

Just ¼ mile downstream the Rubicon tumbles into a clear, cold, narrow finger of Hell Hole Reservoir, upon whose steep-sided granitic slabs—excellent for diving—are found a few well-secluded campsites nestled among ferns and duff under a forest canopy.

Our trail, rather than descending along this river stretch, veers northwest 60 yards along the base of a northeast-facing cliff, then parallels the south side of a small creek up toward a saddle. One hundred yards below it—east-bound hikers take note—the trail crosses the creek, and then it climbs up to the saddle. Here you are greeted in early-to-mid-season by the music of a seven-foot-high fall splashing into a small pool just south of our trail. This verdant oasis, with sunny nearby slabs, makes an excellent rest spot, lunch stop or bathing pool complete with shower. From the saddle our trail descends moderately for 0.4 mile to a bench above the reservoir, where tables and stoves signal us that we have reached the Hell Hole Campground, which because of its relative isolation above a clear, blue lake is one of the best camping spots in the Tahoe Sierra.

Beyond this campground follow Trip 3 in reverse to its end, Trailhead 3, above Hell Hole Reservoir. Then walk about ½ mile up the road to an open saddle, with views down-river, then 120 yards farther to Trailhead 2 of the Parsley Bar Trail, which is a jeep road "blazed" with yellow 1956 California license plates. From this trailhead, follow Trip 1 in reverse down to a crossing of the Rubicon River at the terminus of the South Fork Trail, Trip 2. Follow 2's trail description in reverse to its start, Trailhead 6. You might have parked a shuttle car here, thereby saving you an 11.1-mile walk on roads, or you might

Rubicon River where McKinstry Trail descends to it

have parked it closer to the Rubicon—as described in the Trailhead 6 approach, thereby saving you an additional 1.6 miles.

If you're walking the complete loop, walk down the road ½ mile to a bridged crossing of the South Fork, and then proceed one mile farther to a road junction. Almost immediately east beyond it you reach the entrance to South Fork Campground, which is a good place to spend the night even though it lacks running water—South Fork is but 100 yards east. Continuing eastward, you cross a canal from Gerle Creek Reservoir, to the north, then climb a rocky road to the paved forest highway, which is slated to extend someday from Highway 50 to Hell Hole Dam and then north to Interstate 80. Head 0.2 mile south on it to the Loon Lake Road junction, then take this road, already familiar to you, 8.1 miles back up to your car.

McKinstry Peak above Rubicon River gorge

7   Buck Island Lake Loop

Distance: 17.1 miles, loop trip, or 13.2 miles
plus a 3.9-mile shuttle

Total gain/Net gain: 1530'/560'for the 17.1-mile
distance

Classification: Moderate

Season: June through October

Parking: More than ample at parking area
below dam.

Trailhead/Map: 4/3

Features: Best in late June and early July when
seasonal creeks are still flowing, this route
takes you past spurs to several good lakes that
are readily accessible while most of the
Desolation Wilderness lakes are still frozen or
just thawing. The walk along the Wentworth
Jeep Trail provides the hiker with an educa-
tion about man's impact upon the landscape.

Description: The first part of our trip is on the
Loon Lake Trail, which gives us many access
points to Loon Lake. After 20 yards on the
trail we reach a closed road and follow it above
Loon Lake Campground for 0.2 mile to the
trail's resumption at a point where the road
climbs east. Our trail starts north, curves

northeast, and generally parallels the lake's
visible shoreline, usually about 100 yards distant. Shaded by white fir, lodgepole and silver
pine, we follow our winding path up low ridges
and across gullies, some with creeks flowing
through mid-July. About 2½ miles from the
trailhead, we climb to a ridge, whose northwest extension almost divides the lake in two.
Before 1967, when the new dam was completed, this ridge separated Pleasant Lake
from Loon Lake. As we make an eastward
descent, we can obtain good views northwest
of Guide Peak's barren summit looming above
the Pleasant Lake lobe, and views east toward
a saddle, between two unnamed peaks, in
which lies Hidden Lake.

After an eastward traverse toward that
saddle, we momentarily turn south into a gully
to cross its creek, then turn north and
gradually descend to a closed road that
terminates at the east arm of Loon Lake. We
make a short climb north up the road to a
glacially polished ridge, from which we can
look southwest down the lake to its dam and
the hills beyond. At the shoreline below us is a
cove along which are some popular campsites.

Pyramidal Guide Peak stands above Loon Lake's north lobe

Spider Lake

More secluded ones may be found by starting from these and following the shoreline north toward Pleasant Campground. In ¼ mile our road reaches a gully and begins a moderate climb west. Here an obscure sign indicates a 0.4-mile-long spur trail to Pleasant Campground. Just before one reaches the actual campground, one has to leave the gully and cross northwest over a low ridge. Boaters have an easier time locating the campground, complete with tables, stoves and an outhouse, for their approach is guided by a prominent sign. Regardless how you arrive at it, you'll probably find your stay a pleasant one.

Back on the closed road again, we climb northwest to a ridge, then follow it up to a broad saddle, exchanging our views of the Loon Lake terrain for those of the gentle Tahoe Sierra crest. Northeast below us we see a ducked route down to a grassy lily-pad pond not far below. By heading east from its shoreline, you'll reach, in about 200 yards, fair-to-good campsites on the westernmost

arm of sprawling Spider Lake. One-quarter mile farther along our road we reach another ducked route, which leads northeast down to the now-visible Spider Lake, arriving at a fair campsite above its shallow south arm. This second route begins just as you reach a long, straight stretch of road. Just before this route junction, you could have followed a ducked route southwest ½ mile up to the Hidden Lake saddle—although the slope up to it is so open that you need not follow any ducked route. We now continue on our road, first gently down, then gently up to a second broad saddle, from which an easy ⅓-mile cross-country jaunt south takes us over a low ridge and down to secluded campsites beside tranquil Lake Winifred.

From the start of the cross-country route leaving the broad saddle, our road east is blocked, in 60 yards, by a large tree purposely felled to discourage motorized traffic. Now our feet protest as we make a long, steady, one-mile descent, crossing a seasonal, cascading creek just before reaching a trail intersection 50 yards from shallow, rocky Buck Island Lake. During most of the summer the lake's level is low and its shoreline desolate. Little water flows out from its dammed outlet; rather, the water flows through a tunnel down to Loon Lake, which, like Rubicon and Rockbound reservoirs upstream and "Lake" Aloha in Desolation Wilderness, are part of Sacramento's water supply system.

Although camping at Buck Island Lake is attractive to marmots, it is unappealing to humans, so you've got several choices: retrace your steps or take the trail southeast or northwest. If you traverse southeast, then in ¼ mile you'll reach a road up from the lake which takes you 20 yards east to the west boundary of Desolation Wilderness. If you intend to follow the road into the wilderness, be sure you have your permit—some rangers do check for it. Consult Trip 29 if you wish to pursue this route from the junction we're at.

Our trip takes the third choice, the trail northwest, which after a 0.6-mile open traverse turns north-northeast and makes an 80-yard descent to the Wentworth Jeep Trail. This obscure junction, by a 3½-foot-high boulder and a 4-foot-diameter ponderosa pine, both on the south side of the jeep road, is 250

Marmot

yards northwest of its crossing of trickling Rubicon River, 70 yards below the Buck Island Lake dam. From this crossing you can follow the jeep road along the lake's north shore, then over a low saddle and down to Rubicon Springs, whose mineral waters were advertised by its resort owners in 1890 as "good for consumptives, asthmatics, persons suffering from chronic bronchitis, catarrh, etc." Beyond the springs, whose abandoned resort hotel collapsed in the winter of 1954, the

Buck Island Lake

Lake Winifred

jeep trail climbs to the McKinney-Rubicon Springs Road, which descends to the Lake Tahoe shore near Tahoma.

We start west-northwest from the obscure junction on the Wentworth Jeep Trail and immediately begin a ¼-mile climb to a fork in the jeep road. The left branch, more direct and exciting, climbs steeply up the Big Sluice Box gully, which has a miniature gorge, a "sluice box," one-third of the way up. Near the top of the gully, leave it at a blaze, bear right, and make a short, steep climb north up to a reunion with the slab route. This route is not recommended for early-season hikers with heavy packs because then there is water tumbling down this chute's large boulders. The right branch, after an initial dip, climbs up open slabs, giving the hiker commanding views of the scenery as he follows tire-skid marks and tape strips up to a reunion with the Big Sluice Box route. Now the road makes a long, rocky, mostly open traverse to the seasonal Spider Lake outlet creek, just 200 yards short of Mud Lake, a knee-deep, grassy, lily-pad pond.

A short climb west of Mud Lake brings us to a saddle just above the Little Sluice Box, a smaller but just as bouldery replica of its southern cousin. Jeep tracks lead 300 yards south from the saddle down to campsites on the north arm of Spider Lake, which has an entirely different look from its shallow southern counterpart. This arm is deep, with good diving rocks, and it makes a warm midsummer swimming hole.

West beyond the Little Sluice Box, the true impact of jeeps and motorcycles upon this route is clearly evident. By spinning their tires in early-season mud, they have dug, in many places, two feet down to the rough bedrock. Two consolations we get from our observations: 1) recreational vehicles have so wrecked this jeep trail that now most of them can't follow it, and 2) the erosion stops at bedrock—it won't go any farther. On a traverse above the Mud Lakes, not to be confused with Mud Lake, we see pyramidal Guide Peak ahead and the high peaks of the Tallant Lakes area behind. After a traverse into a thicker forest, north of Loon Lake's Pleasant Lake arm, we curve down a low ridge and soon reach Ellis Creek, from where we get back to our trailhead by following in reverse the first half of Trip 5 to the parking area below the dam. If you don't have a car waiting here for you, walk up to the lake's edge, where after a refreshing swim a few hundred yards east of the overflow channel, you can start back toward your car, following the dam road around to the southwest lakeshore area.

8   Lyons Creek Trail

Distance: 10.0 miles, round trip

Total gain/Net gain: 1720'/1680'

Classification: Moderate

Season: Late July through mid-October

Parking: Best on the spur road just off Wrights Lake Road or near the bridge across Lyons Creek

Trailhead/Map: 8/4

Features: The numerous meadows found along this trail will reward both botanist and photographer alike. Those who like to frolic in creek pools will find at least three sets of them. Lakes Lyons and Sylvia, each nestled in its own subalpine cirque, add crowning highlights to this trip.

Description: From the trailhead beside Wrights Lake Road, either walk or drive up the 0.4-mile spur road that finally dead-ends at Lyons Creek. A few cars can be squeezed in near this end; no camping is allowed along this stretch. On the southeast side of the roadend the Lyons Creek Trail (16E13) climbs gently eastward. Where the trail almost touches the creek, a short spur goes over to its shallow pools among granitic slabs. Several seasonal tributaries are passed, as well as several meadows, before we reach the site of Lyons at the edge of another meadow. In this meadow, as well as the others, you're lucky to find corn lily, aster, lupine, common monkey flower, ligusticum, senecio, cinquefoil, paintbrush, harvest brodiaea, shooting star, and alpine lily—to name the more prominent species. Just as our trail climbs east to leave this meadow, a trail to Wrights Lake cuts off northwest to Lyons Creek, which is crossed on rocks a few yards downstream (see Trip 9). About midway up our trail, close to the Desolation Wilderness border, you can take a short spur northwest to more slab pools, deeper than those near the trailhead. More climbing up open, granitic slopes takes us to a third set of pools, just before we cross lodgepole-shaded Lyons Creek. Two hundred yards east of the crossing we reach a junction. The branch east traverses a 30-yard-long swath of creeks, which is boggy through early July, then climbs ¼ mile to shallow, placid, trout-inhabited Lake Sylvia. Although this shallow lake lacks impressive views like those found along the Lyons Lake spur trail, it does have a large, good campsite, with running water nearby, under a cover of red fir, mountain hemlock and lodgepole. This site is a good base camp for a climb up Pyramid Peak, towering almost 2000 feet above the lake. You might also investigate the upper cirque lakes northeast of the campsite, and perhaps from these climb over a saddle of the Crystal Range and descend to Lake Aloha.

From the junction east of Lyons Creek, the left fork climbs north steeply up an open granite slope, affording us views of the snowbound lower northwest face of Pyramid Peak. Our steep ascent is quickly over, and we arrive at fair campsites among scattered hemlocks near the Lyons Lake forebay, three feet lower than the dammed lake. Like Lake Sylvia, Lyons Lake is fringed with red heather and Labrador tea. Conifers, however, are much more scarce, creating an entirely different atmosphere than at Sylvia. Its cirque encloses a mountaineer's world, with cliffs crowding in all around the lake, daring the climber to escape. Up the granite walls are found long, easy climbs as well as some short, very difficult ones.

Lyons Lake

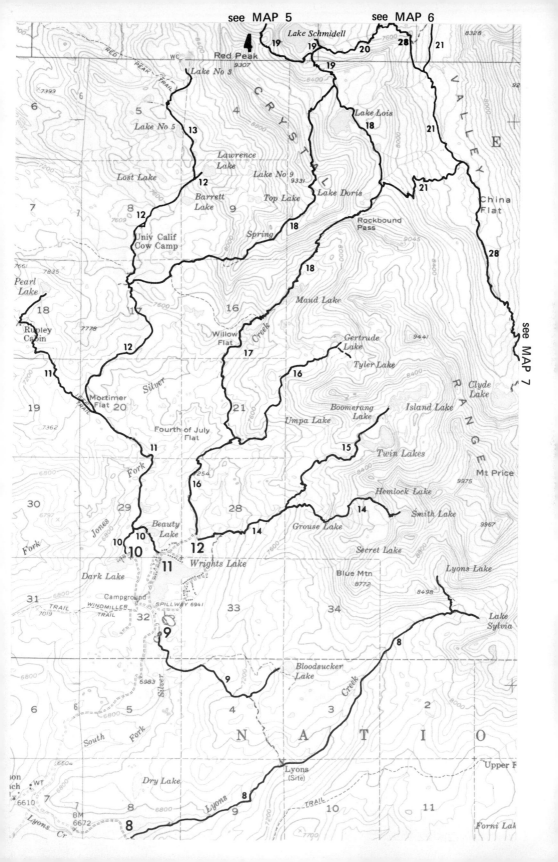

9   Wrights Lake to Bloodsucker Lake

Distance: 3.6 miles, round trip
Total gain/Net gain: 620'/460'
Classification, Moderate
Season: Mid-July through mid-October
Parking: More than ample
Trailhead/Map: 9/4

Features: For those who have seen leeches only in the movies, this trip is an eye-opener. It is also an alternative approach to upper Lyons Creek, Lyons Lake and Lake Sylvia.

Description: From the Wrights Lake Horse Camp at the south end of the parking lot, head south 100 yards on a well-used horse trail to a boulder hop of South Fork Silver Creek, then cross two low ridges of a lateral moraine before reaching a blocked-off road near the top of a third ridge. Up this road we hike east 0.2 mile, to where it curves northeast and starts a moderate climb. Continuing up this road one mile would take you to Bloodsucker Lake, our trip's destination, and this is an alternative return route. At the curve a *Trail* sign tells us to veer southeast, and we cross several alder-lined branches of a Silver Creek tributary, then make a 300-foot gain, climbing southeast through a forest of red fir and lodgepole to a junction with a spur trail, which we take. This trail heads northeast, dropping slightly to a boggy meadow alive with colorful wildflowers that are at their best, unfortunately, when the mosquitoes are at their worst. In addition to seeing the species mentioned in Trip 8, you'll see marsh marigolds. After a short climb from the meadow, we're standing on the previously mentioned road, near Bloodsucker Lake's southwest shore. Sixty yards northwest on the road, and also 60 yards southeast on it, are campsites, although this lake is not conducive to camping, for the knee-deep lake's water is questionable at best.

Blue Mountain, with the Crystal Range as a backdrop, adds to the scenic beauty of the lake, but its main attractions are the bloodsuckers—yes, leeches—up to three inches long. It seems that the only aquatic species that could serve as hosts for these leeches are yellow-legged frogs, of which there are many. In the absence of frogs, however, the leeches could survive on many of the lake's smaller arthropods, for blood is not essential for their subsistence. Just how the leeches got here in the first place is a puzzling question; none of the other shallow lakes of the Tahoe Sierra seem to have them. Perhaps one or more were carried up to that environment in relatively recent times by some unfortunate or unsuspecting host. Students of aquatic entomology will find this lake a well-stocked field laboratory.

Back at the Bloodsucker Lake spur-trail junction, you can continue southeast to Lyons Creek. In 200 yards you pass a shallow, leech-free lake, on your right; then you cross a broad ridge, make a steep descent to Lyons Creek, cross it on rocks a few yards downstream, and climb east through a meadow to a junction with the Lyons Creek Trail. See Trip 8 for its description up to Sylvia and Lyons lakes.

Leech

Bloodsucker Lake and Pyramid Peak

10   Dark Lake to Beauty Lake

Distance: 1.5 miles, loop trip

Total gain/Net gain: 250'/170'

Classification: Easy

Season: Early July through mid-October

Parking: Restricted parking space at either Trailhead 10 or 11. Consider parking at Wrights Lake Picnic Ground

Trailhead/Map: 10/4

Features: This short day hike takes you to Beauty Lake, which, though shallow, lives up to its name.

Description: From the northeast corner of Dark Lake, follow the Red Peak Trail—actually a jeep road—up a gully forested with red fir, lodgepole and silver pine. Atop a moraine and just 15 yards before a reflective pond, you reach the Beauty Lake Trail. Fol-

low this gravelly trail east up a brushy slope, then make a short drop southeast to the lake's forested west shore. Large granitic boulders, left by the last major glacier in this area, add composition and beauty to this quiet lake fringed with bracken fern, spiraea and Laborador tea.

At the southwest shore our trail leaves this sparkling gem, climbs a slight ridge, and then descends south-southeast down a gully, reaching a gate just 25 yards from Trailhead 11 on the Wrights Lake Road. Follow this road up to the low ridge, taking in views of Wrights Lake and the Crystal Range above it as you walk south. Upon reaching the first old campground spur road, follow it southwest past campsites to the Dark Lake Road, then, after a brief ascent on it, descend it to your car.

Beauty Lake

11   Dark Lake to Pearl Lake

Distance: 8.4 miles, round trip

Total gain/Net gain: 1270'/490'

Classification: Easy

Season: Mid-July through mid-October

Parking: 10 cars at most; if full, park at Trailhead 9

Trailhead/Map: 10/4

Features: Isolated from other Silver Creek lakes is little visited Pearl Lake. At the Jones Fork ford of this creek is one of the best creek campsites in the Wrights Lake Recreation Area.

Description: This entire trip is along jeep roads, but if you hike along them before late July, when they are still muddy in a few places, you won't see any recreational vehicles. These aren't allowed on jeep roads until they dry up. The reason for this rule is simple; the rangers don't want these roads to deteriorate into "Wentworth Jeep Trails" (see Trip 7.)

We follow the Red Peak Trail up a gully to a quiet pond that sits atop a moraine 15 yards past a junction with the Beauty Lake Trail (see Trip 10). Then we make a long, partly shady descent north, muddy in places, down to a seasonal creek, then angle northwest a few yards to a fair campsite, shaded by red fir and lodgepole, on the east bank of Jones Fork Silver Creek. Where the road crosses the creek, the ford can be as wide as 15 yards, but by walking upstream far enough you'll be able to cross this large creek on boulders. Farther upstream you'll find some shallow pools that are good for cooling off in. Across the creek near the road ford is a large campsite with plenty of room for one to stretch out, relax and listen to the creek endlessly babble away.

Our road leaves the creekside and the forest cover, climbs northwest, and provides us with a view of Rockbound Pass and the adjacent Crystal Range. Soon we reach a wet meadow, rich with corn lilies, shooting stars, bistort and harvest brodiaea. Here, in Mortimer Flat, the

road splits, and we take the left fork northwest 100 yards to a closed gate, pass through it, and continue our ascent through lodgepole forest up to a morainal ridge rich in granitic boulders. Beyond its crest lies the private property of the Rupley Ranch, so we stay on the road and descend it to a ford of alder-choked Big Silver Creek, which drains the Pearl Lake basin. Beyond the creek we walk about 100 yards west, then follow a spur road northeast ½ mile up a moraine to Pearl Lake. Like almost every lake in the Wrights Lake area, as well as those in adjacent Desolation Wilderness, this lake has a low dam, here built to stabilize summer streamflow and to provide a better year-round habitat for fish.

On the south shore is a fair campsite overlooking the lake's shallow waters, which in the morning peacefully reflect the somber, exfoliating slabs above the northeast shore. To surpass this show of *exfoliation,* one would have to visit Yosemite. These slabs, composed of granodiorite, are exfoliating—peeling off like onion layers—because they are out of equilibrium with the surface environment. When this rock originally cooled to a solid state, about 100 million years ago, it was buried under approximately five miles of rock, at which depth the pressure was about 2200 atmospheres, or roughly 16 tons per square inch. The rock exposed at the earth's surface today is exposed to only *one* atmosphere of pressure, 14.7 pounds per square inch; hence the crystals in it tend to expand and break apart in this new "vacuum" they are exposed to. Because of this tendency to "unload," these rock slabs would gradually peel off even without the aid of any crustal movements to shake them or any weathering processes to etch away at them.

Although Pearl Lake's water is semistagnant, obtaining fresh water is no problem, for just to the south, below the recessional moraine that makes up the lake's natural dam, is a spring-fed creek. You need ask for nothing more.

Exfoliation slabs above Pearl Lake

12   Dark Lake to Lawrence Lake

Distance: 11.6 miles, round trip

Total gain/Net gain: 1810'/930'

Classification: Moderate

Season: Mid-July through mid-October

Parking: 10 cars at most; if full, park at Trailhead 9

Trailhead/Map: 10/4

Features: "The most beautiful lake in the whole area," one old-timer called symmetrical Lawrence Lake. The author tends to agree. Above it is Top Lake, a unique bilobed lake whose water level is two feet higher at its east end than at its west end.

Description: From Mortimer Flat, which we passed en route in Trip 11, we follow the Red Peak Trail—a jeep road—up a little canyon above the flat, curve north up to a low ridge, and then cross a trickling creeklet before reaching an open slab from which we obtain a panorama of the Crystal Range to the east and southeast. From this vantage point the huge Wrights Lake and Lyons Creek moraines are very obvious as moraines, whereas close up, their forest cover and their minor irregularities tend to camouflage their shape. On this open slab our road divides, only to rejoin in a hundred yards, and then it climbs to a marshy, forested flat, curves east across it and turns northward up a ridge. This we eventually cross, and then climb steeply up to a saddle and the intersection of a ridge-crest trail, the Rockbound Stock Driveway. Cattle are still being grazed today in Desolation Wilderness, and one of the routes by which they are led in and out is this trail. Looking gentle and safe where we see it, this driveway becomes, one

Cascade into Lawrence Lake

Terraced Top Lake

mile east, a steep, potentially treacherous route (see Trip 18).

A steep climb 0.2 mile beyond the lake takes us to three junctions, passed in a few heartbeats, from which three short spurs quickly merge into one trail—described in Trip 13—that climbs north to Lake No. 3.

From this ridge we make a descent, steep in places, to a logged-over meadow now being invaded by young lodgepoles. Just past the turn of the century, this plot was sold by the Barrett family to the University of California at Davis, which set up an experimental station here and tried to improve the local herds through selective breeding. From this site we climb, steeply in places, to a broad saddle, on which our jeep road finally diminishes to a trail. After a short, sunny, gravelly descent we reach the swift Barrett Lake outlet creek, a five-yard boulder hop. Now we follow a gully that in places becomes a low chute, and in ¼ mile reach an enormous, flat campsite, under shady red firs, along most of the west shore of Barrett Lake. This site would hold a whole Boy Scout troop with room to spare, and its coves and diving rocks, together with its shallow rock-slab pools below the little dam would keep all the kids active and content.

Easing off, our trail now approaches a fair campsite near the northwest end of the waist-high Lawrence Lake dam. Cross the dam and take a footpath past a small rock island to the outlet creek of Top Lake, which announces itself 150 yards before entering the beautiful, symmetrical lake by cascading 50 feet down a glistening rock slab mantled with a coat of black fungi. To the east is the higher but less spectacular cascade of the outlet creek of Lake No. 9. A half-mile walk up either creek will get you to little-used campsites at its lake.

A side trip to Top Lake is particularly rewarding. Perched at the lip of a cirque, it seems to sit on top of the world, and the backpacker who sets up his camp here sees panoramic sunsets that are hard to match anywhere. On the lake's peninsula, which almost divides it in two, is a picturesque campsite. The most amazing aspect of the lake, however, is its naturally terraced east end, at which the water is ponded up as much as two feet higher than at the west shore. Thick clumps of grass and heather are progressively invading the lake, building dikes and trapping sediments. More vegetation grows upon them and ponds up the water level.

13   Dark Lake to Lakes 3, 4 and 5

Distance: 14.4 miles, round trip
Total gain/Net gain: 2430'/1330'
Classification: Moderate
Season: Late July through mid-October
Parking: 10 cars at most; if full, park at Trailhead 9
Trailhead/Map: 10/4

Features: Unspoiled campsites reward backpackers who hike up to geologically interesting Lake No. 3. From it they can hike cross-country by an easy, novel route into Desolation Wilderness, avoiding much of the usual pedestrian traffic by doing so.

Description: Trip 12 describes the route to Barrett Lake and the lakes above it. From any of three junctions 0.2 mile northeast above Barrett Lake, climb steeply north (the three trails merge) to a forested ridge, then make a short descent to a meadow in which you pass three temporary ponds, all on your right. Flowing from the last of these, as well as from the soggy meadow, is a small creek we must cross before it enters Lake No. 5. This lake is a haunt of spotted sandpipers, who build their nests in the dense grass along the water's edge. If you want to camp at this serene lake, do so on the west bank, a dry, rocky moraine from which you obtain tree-framed views down the glaciated canyon to the west.

Beyond the lake we climb to a saddle, where our trail turns abruptly right. The ducked path straight ahead leads 0.2 mile northwest down to unappealing, semistagnant Lake No. 4. Our faint, ducked trail climbs a fairly open granodiorite slope northeast up to a narrow ridge, one hundred yards beyond which we reach a junction where the Red Peak Trail branches left on its way down to the Van Vleck Ranch. We continue straight ahead through a swampy meadow, head northeast between a rock pile on the left and the main rock slope on the right, and curve northward up to another wet, spongy meadow through which flows the tiny outlet creek from Lake No. 3. Small though it is, this creek nevertheless supports 10-inch trout.

Across the creek we head northwest toward a duck at the base of a moraine and 30 yards west of the creek's cascade. Now it's just a short climb up to Lake No. 3, whose relative isolation from Wrights Lake rewards us with unspoiled lakeside campsites beneath a cover of mountain hemlock and lodgepole and silver

Spotted-sandpiper egg, ½ size

pine. Those wishing to spend a few days here might make an easy cross-country day hike northeast to the saddle between Red Peak and Silver Peak, and then descend to the Leland Lakes. If you take this novel approach into Desolation Wilderness, be sure you have your

wilderness permit. Those wishing to make a
loop trip by continuing over to Lake Lois
should follow, in reverse, part of Trip 19 and
then follow part of Trip 18 if they wish to use
the Rockbound Stock Driveway rather than
the more heavily traveled Rockbound Pass
Trail.

Hikers content to relax at lovely Lake No. 3
might take note of the arc of boulders near its
outlet. These make up a recessional moraine,
which is a moraine formed behind a glacier's
terminal moraine. Most of the lakes we see in
any glaciated country either are dammed by a
recessional moraine or are cirque lakes. Lake
No. 3 stands out because it has such a clear
recessional moraine behind the one that
actually dams the lake. Get to know the
characteristics; then, when you return to
Wrights Lake, go to its picnic area, walk along
the shore of this surprisingly shallow large
lake, and see how many recessional moraines
you can identify.

Recessional moraine in Lake No. 3

14   Wrights Lake to Smith Lake

Distance: 5.8 miles, round trip
Total gain/Net gain: 1810'/1750'
Classification: Strenuous
Season: Late July through mid-October
Parking: Crowded on weekends—then use Trailhead 9
Trailhead/Map: 12/4

Features: Three sparkling subalpine lakes, each with its own special qualities, are the highlights of this trip. From Smith Lake, the highest of the three, you obtain one of the best views of the Wrights Lake and Crystal Basin recreation areas.

Description: Our trail east, the Twin Lakes Trail, immediately log-crosses a clear, cold stream from Umpa Lake and the Twin Lakes basin, then reaches a flat meadow, where a sign indicates that Ed Wright had a cabin and operated a dairy ranch from 1850 to 1900. Before him a group of Washoe Indians used this area as a summer hunting and foraging ground. Wrights Lake, with a maximum depth of only six feet, was longer in their times. After the retreat of the last glacier, about 10,000 years ago, the lake was about a mile long and probably much deeper, but since then half of its length has been filled in with sediments, which have gradually changed to meadow.

Hemlock Lake

Smith Lake

At the meadow's east edge we make a very brief climb up to a low cliff, on our left, which is topped with an erratic boulder left by a glacier, and here meet a spur trail that goes southwest down to some east-shore summer homes. If you're parked at Trailhead 9 or at the south-shore campground, you'll want to start along this alternate trail.

From the junction our trail climbs steadily northeast, often being within hearing distance of the Grouse Lake outlet creek. In one stretch the trail in early summer seems more like a creek than a trail. Where the Twin Lakes Trail turns north to cross the outlet creek (see Trip 15), our trail branches right and follows a ducked route up granitic slabs into an open forest and to a gravelly flat. Turning southeast, our trail then starts to climb gradually, but soon it becomes steep, and then very steep, before easing off atop a moraine that dams Grouse Lake. A few glimpses of Wrights Lake, far below, are obtained near the top of this climb.

Rock-lined Grouse Lake, fringed with red heather and Labrador tea, is a very pleasant lake to linger at, particularly after the strenu-

ous climb. Its shallow, clear water invites a swim. Nearby campsites, on sloping ground above its northeast shore, are only fair.

A steep climb north up a low lateral moraine, then another, longer ascent northeast up a rocky slope brings us to tiny Hemlock Lake, named for the mountain hemlocks that border its south shore. Its small size is compensated for by a dramatic exfoliating cliff above its north shore. A fair camp sits above its southeast shore.

Hiking southeast, we make a final ducked climb and reach nearly treeless Smith Lake, which at 8700 feet elevation is almost at timberline. Its steep, confining slopes, most having snowfields that last well into summer, are also detrimental to growth. Nevertheless, a small stand of lodgepole and silver pines does thrive above the lake's northwest shore. From a rocky, emergency bivouac spot near the lake's outlet we can look out over the Wrights and Crystal Basin recreation areas and identify Wrights Lake and Dark Lake below us and Union Valley Reservoir in the distance. This is the only lake from which you can get such expansive views of these two areas.

15   Wrights Lake to Island Lake

Distance: 6.2 miles, round trip
Total gain/Net gain: 1270'/1190'
Classification: Moderate
Season: Mid-July through mid-October
Parking: Crowded on weekends—then use Trailhead 9
Trailhead/Map: 12/4

Features: One of the more popular trails into Desolation Wilderness, this trail takes you to three fairly large lakes as well as to several small ones.

Description: Follow the route description in Trip 14 to where the Smith Lake Trail leaves our trail at the Grouse Lake outlet creek crossing. From here our trail northward climbs moderately up quite open glacially polished slabs to a ridge, crosses it, and then swings east, passing two small ponds along the Twin Lakes outlet creek. Just beyond the second, we must cross a once-narrow creek lined with a thick, spongy mat of vegetation. Heavy trail use has caused collapse along most of its bank,

thereby widening the crossing to a running jump. A sturdy log placed across the creek would stop, if not reverse, this deteriorating creek environment.

Beyond it, a short climb northeast brings us to Lower Twin Lake, whose outlet creek the trail crosses about 40 yards below its waist-high dam. You'll probably find it more convenient to cross immediately below the dam. Before you cross, however, you might want to stop at the lake's south shore and rest a while or swim and dive from rocks along this fairly deep shore. Anglers will find the lake stocked with brook and rainbow trout. Rainbow were first introduced in 1904 by Joe Minghetti, a local ranch hand, who eventually stocked most of the lakes in the Wrights Lake Recreation Area. Today many of these lakes receive yearly plantings.

Our trail parallels the lake's west shore to a gully at its northwest corner. (An easy cross-country route, rewarding in views, starts west from here, climbs over the low ridge saddle, and descends to Umpa Lake.

Boomerang Lake

From the lake, the route traverses west, staying on the bald slope just below the higher, brushy slope, and then descending a ridge to a saddle where you meet the Tyler Lake Trail.) Our faint, rocky trail climbs northeast from the gully, passes through a 10-foot-deep notch, then reaches Boomerang Lake, named for its shape, from whose west shore on the north arm one can dive from 12-foot ledges into the lake's cold, deep water.

After passing between Boomerang Lake and its tiny northeastern relative, we climb above the western end of a small, linear lake, nourished by a snowfield and two narrow cascades from Island Lake. Just above this silver dagger we reach Island Lake, a fairly large, rock-island, timberline lake. Near its shore, small, fair campsites can be found that are the required 100-foot distance from the lake. Although tall, dark-gray diorite-gabbro cirque walls lend a stark beauty to this subalpine lake, it is not as popular as the Twin Lakes, with their border of sparse trees. At Island Lake you may find more California gulls than backpackers.

From the southeast shore of Island Lake you can go cross-country to Upper Twin Lake—two feet higher than its sibling—by descending southwest to the outlet of the "silver dagger" lake, and then contouring around Upper Twin until you can descend easily to the glacier-polished gentle slabs that separate the twins, on which fair campsites can be found.

Lower Twin Lake

16   Wrights Lake to Tyler Lake

Distance: 7.2 miles, round trip
Total Gain/Net gain: 1670'/1290'
Classification: Moderate
Season: Late July through mid-October
Parking: Crowded on weekends—then use Trailhead 9
Trailhead/Map: 12/4

Features: Two photographic subalpine lakes climax this short hike. Despite their easy accessibility, they remain relatively unvisited because most backpackers prefer lower lakes with less exposed campsites. If you wish to escape the weekend crowd, this hike may be for you.

Description: We start north on the Willow Flat Trail, which for its first 0.2 mile is a spur road to a Forest Service horse pasture and adjacent shed. Beyond them our trail climbs gently northward, then steepens its gradient and loses forest shade before reaching a broad, huckleberry-oak-mantled ridge. This it crosses, and then climbs along the northwest slope before dropping abruptly to a junction in a small, shady flat. From here we follow the Tyler Lake Trail to its end at Gertrude Lake.

Climbing east above the flat, we follow this ducked trail up slabs and a gully to a viewpoint, from where we can trace the outlet streams of Umpa and Twin Lakes flowing—sometimes cascading— over open, glaciated slabs on their way down to Wrights Lake. Our trail makes an unexpected 20-foot-drop, then climbs steeply up a brush-lined gully to a forested, shallow saddle on a ridge. Here you could go cross-country to Twin Lakes by climbing up-ridge about 100 feet elevation and then traversing east past Umpa Lake to a shallow, rocky saddle which lies directly above Lower Twin Lake's west shore.

The Tyler Lake Trail leaves the forested saddle, parallels an ephemeral creeklet, and then climbs steeply north above it, becoming faint before reaching another ridge. Immediately after dropping north to a shallow ridge saddle, it enters a hemlock forest, passes a small, ankle-deep pond, makes a short traverse northeast, and then, at a blazed lodgepole pine, heads north straight downslope 80 yards before curving northeast again. Blazes and ducks guide our traverse across numerous snow-fed creeklets, and then we make a steep, bouldery ascent to a short,

signed spur trail, which descends a willow-choked gully 125 yards to Tyler's grave. Tyler, a local ranch hand, froze to death in a November 1882 snowstorm while trying to round up cattle in this area. Our destination bears his name.

Along a 0.2 mile ascent bisected by Tyler Lake creek, our trail to Gertrude Lake becomes faint. Short on campsites but long on scenery, this shallow lake has an exquisite balance of shoreline slabs and spaced conifers that please the nature photographer.

To reach cirque-bound Tyler Lake, we backtrack to its streaming creek and follow it up open slabs to the lake. Only a few scattered silver pines and mountain hemlocks provide shade at this timberline, slab-surrounded lake. Nevertheless, the naked beauty of its setting will long remain with you. Look for exposed but legal campsites above its rocky east shore.

Tyler Lake

17   Wrights Lake to Maud Lake

Distance: 7.4 miles, round trip

Total gain/Net gain: 1220'/720'

Classification: Moderate

Season: Early July through mid-October

Parking: Crowded on weekends—then use Trailhead 9

Trailhead/Map: 12/4

Features: The most popular backpacker's lake in the Wrights Lake Recreation Area, Maud Lake offers an abundance of campsites near its shores. It serves as a good overnight stop where you can get partially acclimated so that you can better face the steep, long climb up to Rockbound Pass.

Description: Follow the description of Trip 16 to the small, shady flat where the Tyler Lake Trail begins. Staying on the Willow Flat Trail, we immediately cross two snow-fed, ephemeral creeks, and then climb moderately to steeply ½ mile north through a thinning forest to a stagnant pond atop a saddle. An equally long and steep descent from it takes us down brushy slabs to a boulder crossing of Jones Fork Silver Creek one mile below Maud Lake. Beyond the crossing, our route—lined with rocks—ascends a largely barren, low-angle, glacially polished slab upon which rest numerous erratic boulders left behind by the last retreating glacier. Along the massive slab's sparse fractures grow junipers, lodgepoles and other plants that can get a roothold.

We cross a low, minor ridge, parallel it north, and enter the thicket of Willow Flat, which in addition to a dense stand of willows has plenty of bracken ferns, corn lilies and aspens. A short, bouldery, creekside ascent gets us to a shady lodgepole flat, where we jump across the creek just below its slide down a polished ramp. One might camp here, and certainly people do, but all the passing traffic would make this otherwise good site objectionable. Immediately south of it—and north of Willow Flat—is a highly fractured granodiorite knoll that is good exercise for those who enjoy short, roped climbs.

We continue our shady ascent 200 yards to within several yards of the forest's abrupt north edge, where, if you look closely, you'll detect a faint, blazed and ducked lateral trail, which climbs westward to the Rockbound Stock Driveway, an alternative route over the Crystal Range. Out in the sunlight again, our rock-lined trail switchbacks up a barren slope, traverses northeast above the Silver Creek gorge, and then makes a short descent to a pond immediately below Maud Lake.

Campsites abound on the low, rocky benches surrounding Maud Lake. Many of them are illegally within 100 feet of the shoreline, but there are still enough legal ones to accommodate several dozen campers—the typical number of weekend backpackers. Look for fair-to-good campsites west of the trail and also above the northeast and south shores. With heavy use, the lake's water isn't as clear as it used to be. Packers have clouded the situation by making this a rest stop for their dozens of horses. By late August—normally the best time to visit Desolation Wilderness lakes—this lake's inflow is so diminished that its water should be treated before drinking. Evidently one irate backpacker found the semiclear water objectionable, for someone removed the *a* in the *Maud Lake* sign, thus giving it a more appropriate name. Swimmers who venture out in this lake's relatively warm, shallow water can attest to the muddy character of the lake's bottom.

Maud Lake

18 Wrights Lake to Lake Lois, return via Rockbound Stock Driveway

Distance: 15.5 miles, loop trip

Total gain/Net gain: 3080'/2230'

Classification: Strenuous

Season: Early August through mid-October

Parking: Crowded on weekends—then use Trailhead 9

Trailhead/Map: 12/4

Features: Those who are turned on to high-pass routes will appreciate this trip, the views it offers and the lakes it passes.

Description: No one forgets his first climb over Rockbound Pass. Of this steep, 900-foot climb from Maud Lake (see Trip 17), one often hears "It was very grueling" or "I just about died." However, one retired couple, laden down with heavy backpacks, thought the climb wasn't bad at all. The ascent is psychologically defeating only because you almost always see the pass looming up before you, and because its dwarf trees make it look higher and farther away than it is.

The Rockbound Pass Trail was built around 1918, after an early heavy October snow storm of the previous year almost decimated a herd of cattle then grazing in and above Rockbound Valley. Joe Minghetti, a hired hand on the Blakeley Ranch but formerly a Swiss stone mason, was commissioned by the Forest Service to build the trail so that there would be an escape route for the cattle when they had to be quickly evacuated. The trail was not to exceed 15 degrees in grade, but as the backpacker soon finds out, it does.

Our climb from Maud Lake starts out through a sloping, spring-water-saturated meadow—boggy for most of the summer— and then climbs steeply up slopes abundant in huckleberry oak, western serviceberry and wildflowers. The trail's switchbacks—short and steep—are characteristic of old, pre-recreation-trail design standards, when trails were made as steep as the traffic would allow. After the last set of switchbacks we reach a small flat with several large junipers growing on and near it. From this welcome rest spot we can absorb the view of the tarns below, Maud Lake in the middle distance and Wrights Lake beyond.

Rockbound Pass above Lake Doris

Phlox among metamorphic rocks near Lake Doris

Also evident are three granitic plutons, each formed separately—almost certainly at different times—miles below the earth's surface. Each of these light-density molten masses worked its way up through existing rock until it finally cooled to form a solid mass, a pluton. On the opposite canyon wall, from north to south, the three plutons are orange, dark gray and light gray, and their respective compositions are granite, diorite-gabbro and probably granodiorite.

Beyond the junipers it is almost a stroll up to sometimes windy Rockbound Pass, with its weather-beaten, dwarfed mountain hemlocks and lodgepole and whitebark pines. Snowbound through late July, our trail from this pass switchbacks northeast down toward Lake Doris, passing both red and white heather along the way. Among the hemlocks above the north shore is a fair campsite. After briefly touching this shallow lake's east shore—painted yellow with buttercups and marsh marigolds—our trail climbs a few feet, then makes a brief descent to a signed junction, where a lateral trail starts northeast down to Rockbound Valley.

Our trail descends northwest, immediately crosses Lake Doris' outlet, makes a scenic traverse with panoramas to the east, passes just above one pond and then two more on a low, broad saddle, and reaches an east finger of metamorphic-rock-bound Lake Lois. Its rocky cliffs and benches of varying hues are Jurassic marine sediments that were metamorphosed when the neighboring granitic plutons welled up and intruded them. These metasediments, also found in Rockbound Valley, grade upward and eastward into the slightly younger metavolcanics of the Mt. Tallac area.

Popular Lake Lois and its neighbor one mile northwest, Lake Schmidell, both bear the brunt of weekend backpackers. On each you'll find many used sites that are within 100 feet of the shore, and very few sites that are more than 100 feet away. Lake Lois' southeast corner, although only 50°F in mid-August, attracts some backpackers who like to do some brisk high diving—up to 20 or more feet—into its very deep water. Those who just like to swim will find its isolated east finger 10 degrees warmer. Fishing in this stocked lake is fair to excellent, depending largely on your skill.

Paralleling the east finger, our rocky trail winds over to the outlet creek, crosses its low dam, heads briefly west along the north shore, and then climbs to a ridge, where we meet the Rockbound Stock Driveway. Pestered by mosquitoes except in late season, we quickly climb the first half of this damp, open-forest trail, going southwest until we are well above the west shore of Lake Lois. Before early August, parts of this section are still snowbound, and the hiker more or less has to find his way up to a small bench after a second creek crossing. South beyond it, our wide, rocky, open trail soon is climbing moderately to steeply up a talus slope to a shallow saddle immediately east of Summit 9331. One should pause on this ascent, not only to rest, but also to admire the views, which include Phipps Peak (9234') to the northeast, and to admire the very abundant wildflowers along the slope's rills and rivulets.

At the shallow, viewless saddle we have two choices. The first is to go cross-country, following the old Blakeley cattle-drive route down to Lawrence Lake. If you choose this alternative, leave the trail after 200 yards, where it angles briefly southeast, and then pick your way west down the steep, sometimes Class 2 slope to the almost barren slabs between Top Lake and Lake No. 9. From these, the descent to Lawrence Lake is a snap. See Trip 12 for a trail description to a reunion with the Rockbound Stock Driveway.

The second choice, our Rockbound Stock Driveway, starts southwest from the saddle, briefly angles southeast, and then curves south down through a wet, grassy swale, in which you're almost certain to lose the trail. You might find this descent quite isolated and primitive, but then you might also stumble across several dozen cattle. Near the brink of the steep slope above terraced Top Lake, our trail crosses its inlet creek, climbs a low ridge,

and then descends into a shallow bowl with refreshing, ice-cold spring water. Exiting from the barren bowl, our trail curves westward to a ridge on which it descends. Views both east and west highlight this descent through a sparse stand of mountain hemlock and silver pine.

About 200 yards before the ridge plunges south, we reach a five-foot-deep ridge saddle from where our route—believe it or not—makes a plunge of its own—due west straight down a very steep 400-foot slope to a red-fir-shaded flat on a low ridge which we can see west of us. Difficult as this descent may seem, some people still take horses up it!

From the flat our trail descends west one-half mile to a saddle, from where the little-used lateral to Willow Flat departs south. Then it continues another half mile to a junction with the Red Peak Trail. Those who took the cross-country alternative would meet us here. Now we follow in reverse the appropriate trail description of Trip 12 to the Beauty Lake Trail junction, and take that trail, Trip 10, past the lake and down toward the northeast corner of Wrights Lake, a short distance from our car.

Fishing for trout at Lake Lois

19   Wrights Lake to Highland Lake

Distance: 25.2 miles, round trip

Total gain/Net gain: 6250'/1640'

Classification: Strenuous

Season: Early August through mid-October

Parking: Crowded on weekends—then use Trailhead 9

Trailhead/Maps: 12/4,5

Features: Averaging about one lake per mile, this trail gives the backpacker plenty of opportunities to select a campsite. The highlight of the trip is Lake Zitella, with its warm water and its impressive mountain backdrop.

Description: Trips 17 and 18 describe our route to the Rockbound Stock Driveway junction on the ridge above Lake Lois. From this junction we make a fairly steep descent through an open forest, almost touching a small creek before we reach a junction not far from Lake Schmidell. To reach this lake's campsites you could hike northeast 250 yards down a trail to a pond, then 200 yards northwest up to the lake's dammed outlet creek. An easier way to reach its campsites, perched on a mountain-hemlock-and-lodgepole-shaded bench above the lake's southeast shore, is to walk due north 100 yards from our junction.

From the junction above Lake Schmidell we traverse southwest to a cascading creek,

boulder-hop it, and make a scenic though exhausting ascent to a shallow saddle on the granodiorite ridge above the Lake Schmidell talus slopes. The two Leland Lakes quickly come into view as we make an equally steep descent north toward the upper lake. Rather than skirt this lake's grassy east shore, the trail now swings northeast a bit, dips through a boggy meadow, and then descends to the southeast corner of lower Leland Lake. Since all its lakeshore campsites are now off limits, you might look for alternative sites on tiny, grassy flats among the boulders and slabs between the two lakes.

Leaving the lower lake above us, we descend along its cheerful, frolicking outlet creek, cross it in a forested flat, and continue briefly northwest to the forest's edge. Watching for ducks—both the rock kind and in late season the live ones—we follow a faint path that arcs around the west shore of a knee-deep pond called McConnell Lake. Leaving its soggy meadow of grass and heather behind, we reach a low ridge, on which the trail becomes indistinct for a few yards among the brush, then improves as it descends an open slope northwest to the base of an imposing granodiorite wall, which should provide challenging ascents to all types of mountaineers and rock climbers. A prominent low-angle

Vegetation grows along linear master joints above Rockbound Valley

waterfall glides down the middle of this wall, and just after crossing its creek on level ground, we run into route-finding problems. Watch for ducks that mark the route up and down a low slab. Then just beyond it, where the trail climbs over another low slab to a gully with a trickling creek, pay close attention to where the trail actually crosses the creek. Beyond the creek we contour east 100 yards, descend slightly to another short traverse, this one northeast, then top a low, rocky ridge and follow four short, steep switchbacks down to an alluvial flat on which lies shallow, rock-island-speckled Horseshoe Lake. Traversing above the shore to a point just above its northeast corner, we reach a junction from which the Highland Lake Trail climbs northwest up a huckleberry-oak-filled gully. Should you choose to follow the faint trail to 4-Q Lakes, look for ducks standing out against the skyline on the ridge immediately east of you.

We climb steeply up the gully, diagonal left up more open slabs, and take a glance back at photogenic Horseshoe Lake, with the Crystal Range for a dramatic backdrop. Notice how the trees on the granitic slopes beyond the lake are concentrated along *master joints,* which are major fracture lines in this otherwise very resistant rock. Our 200-foot ascent tops out at a saddle, from which our route ahead to seductive Lake Zitella descends ¼ mile to this shallow lake's outlet creek. Just before crossing the outlet, look northeast across Rockbound Valley. If the master joints above Horseshoe Lake weren't obvious to you, then you need a more impressive example. The master joints on the opposite canyon wall are unmistakably clear.

Now that you're at shallow, slightly cloudy Lake Zitella, you might wonder what's so seductive about it. Feel its water temperature; it is the warmest cirque lake—rising into the low 70s—in the entire Desolation Wilderness, and so is an excellent swimming hole, with plenty of shoreline slabs and rock islands to bask upon. Fishing isn't great, though, unless you like yellow-legged frogs, which are abundant. In between swims, climbers might want to explore the easy Class 5 climbing routes on a large, low-angle, exfoliating cliff above the lake's west shore.

Those seeking isolation can now begin an arduous route to Highland Lake. The northwest-bound trail climbing from Lake Zitella's north shore is simple enough, but from the saddle above it, the trail makes an extremely steep descent—almost an uncontrolled slide at times—down a gully. Despite its steepness, it is not very exposed and not very dangerous. This steep route exists because a cliff prevents a traverse west. At the base of the cliff our route turns west and begins to climb. At this point you can take an obvious, open, cross-country route—spread out below you—down to Rubicon Reservoir and from there either follow Trip 29 out to Loon Lake or reverse part of Trips 29 and 20 up the Rubicon River and back to Lake Schmidell.

Watch for ducks that mark our open rock-slab ascent to a crossing of Highland Lake creek at the lip of a cirque, then traverse 150 yards southwest to the northeast shore of an unnamed lakelet. From it our trail makes a winding, ducked ascent in the same direction up to a ridge 70 yards north of a tiny, photogenic lake, whose waters are constantly being aerated by several cascades splashing into it. After a momentary descent, we make a short, steep ascent to a shelf, which we follow south to icy, rockbound, rainbow-trout-stocked Highland Lake, which has some small campsites nearby that are fair at best.

Highland Lake

20 Wrights Lake to Horseshoe Lake, via 4-Q Lakes Trail

Distance: 24.8 miles, semiloop trip

Total gain/Net gain: 5190'/1640'

Classification: Strenuous

Season: Early August through mid-October

Parking: Crowded on weekends—then use Trailhead 9

Trailhead/Maps: 12/4,5,6

Features: An alternative, less used approach to Horseshoe, Zitella and Highland lakes, this route provides you with secluded campsites along the 4-Q Lakes outlet creek.

Description: Our route to Lake Schmidell is described in Trip 17 and in parts of Trips 18 and 19. From the junction at the pond below the Lake Schmidell outlet, stay on the main trail as it makes an eastward, heather-lined descent—muddy and mosquito-ridden through mid-August—to a crossing of the outlet creek. Immediately beyond this we reach a lateral trail for those travelling to upper Rockbound Valley, Mosquito Pass and Lake Aloha (see Trip 28). Beyond this junction we make an equally long, but drier, descent to a second crossing, then in ⅓ mile reach a junction on a bench above the Rubicon River. One hundred yards south of this junction a trail fords the Rubicon and then climbs east to Middle Velma Lake (see Trip 21).

We start north along the Rubicon and in 70 yards reach a short spur trail west to a cold, rusty, seeping mineral spring. After a few minutes' winding walk north, we reach broad, level Camper Flat, where beside a good Rubicon swimming hole is an old campsite. Bearing westward through a lush meadow dense with corn lily, lupine, shooting star, aster, alpine lily and other species, we reach our last crossing of Lake Schmidell's outlet creek. Look for logs upstream on which you can cross it and reach in 70 yards the 4-Q Lakes Trail, branching west. This climbing trail passes several stagnant ponds before we see the first small lake about 40 yards northwest of the trail. One-quarter mile beyond it we reach the signed, second 4-Q Lake, across which we must "walk on water." Two peninsulas almost cut the lake in half, and we cross the shallow, 40-foot strait via rocks and/or logs.

Beyond the lake crossing, our trail curves over to the west shore of this lake, touches upon the north shore of adjacent lake number three, and then makes a brief climb to a stagnant, bush-fringed pond, where you do have to walk on water to follow the trail. Most hikers keep their feet dry by going around and above the pond's west edge, and then relocate the trail, which climbs a few paces west before

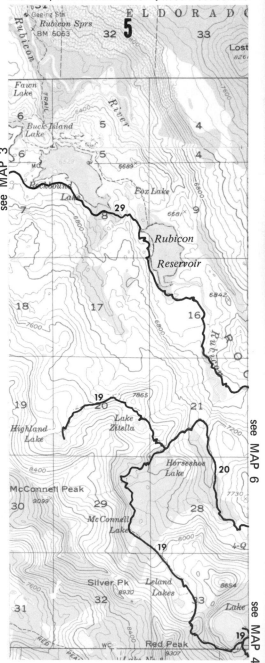

descending southwest to the fourth lake, which is the best of these shallow lakes. When camping near any of these semistagnant lakes, treat your drinking water.

From the north end of the fourth lake, our ducked route makes a moderate descent north down a joint-controlled gully and through red-fir stands, then eases its pleasant, creek-side descent through alternating lodgepole-pine stands and huckleberry-oak-scrub fields. Nearing the end of this 1.4-mile descent, we find ourselves more often than not walking along glaciated granodiorite slabs. Watch carefully for ducks. Our trail crosses the creek just 20 yards above a narrow chute you can jump across. Anywhere in this vicinity you can find rocky campsites whose hardness is more than compensated for by their isolation and by the nearby views north down the Rubi-con canyon.

Now climbing west, it is important to follow the ducks if you want to minimize your effort. The faint trail climbs steeply up a slope, staying about 100-200 yards north of the outlet creek from Horseshoe Lake. Our route reaches a ridge above that lake, and then we follow ducks for about 50 yards west down to a trail junction, from where we can follow Trip 19 either northwest up to Lake Zitella and beyond or southward back to Lake Schmidell.

Sunset over Lake Zitella

Class 5 cliff above Lake Zitella

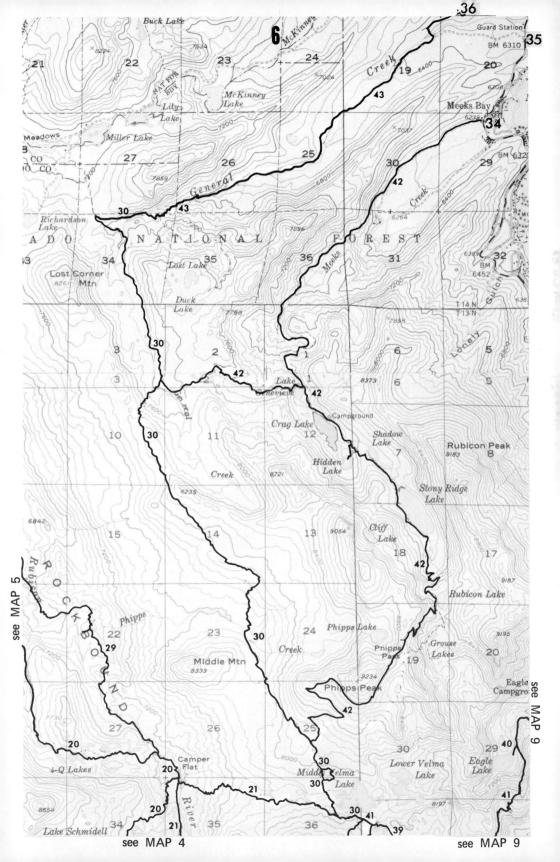

see MAP 5

see MAP 9

see MAP 4

see MAP 9

21   Wrights Lake to Lake Tahoe

Distance: 16.4 miles plus a 40.0-mile shuttle

Total gain/Net gain: 3480'/1680'

Classification: Moderate

Season: Early August through mid-October

Parking: Crowded on weekends—then use Trailhead 9

Trailhead/Maps: 12/4,6,9

Features: Two divides are crossed on this trans-High Sierra hike. Along it the backpacker will encounter cirque-bound and moraine-dammed lakes; one long, glaciated river canyon, several environments, each with its lavish display of wildflowers; and good panoramas of the Desolation Wilderness country and the Tahoe basin.

Description: Follow Trip 17 and part of Trip 18 to the trail junction near Lake Doris' outlet creek. From this junction we make a moderate-to-steep descent that starts in an open mountain-hemlock forest but passes into a moderately dense red-fir and lodgepole-pine forest before we reach a junction with the Rockbound Valley trail a few yards west of the Rubicon River. Trip 28 describes this trail from Echo Lakes north to this junction.

Our route north takes us to a crossing and recrossing of a Rubicon River branch, followed by five creek crossings, the last one being across the churning outlet creek from Lake Lois. Just beyond it we reach a junction, from which Trip 28 follows a one-mile lateral that leads steeply northwest up toward the Lake Schmidell-Camper Flat trail. Along our last stretch, over metamorphosed, rusty Jurassic marine sediments, you're likely to see sagebrush and mule ears interspersed among the lodgepoles, together with lupine, wild parsley, whorled penstemon, phlox, cinquefoil, wild buckwheat and mariposa lily.

From the junction we continue our down-canyon route, first briefly northeast alongside a small creek with a profusion of corn lilies and mosquitoes, then north past a river flat that gives way to a slope as the river tumbles down toward Camper Flat. We descend this slope northward, and soon arrive at a junction on a bench above the Rubicon. The Lake Schmidell-Camper Flat trail junction is just 100 yards north of us, from which Trip 29 carries the description to Loon Lake.

Our route—east—immediately drops to a crossing of the fairly swift Rubicon River, which you may have to wade if you try to cross before late July. On a bench 30 yards beyond the river we see a good campsite, now illegal, and then follow the ducked route up open granodiorite slabs. Route finding can be a problem if you're looking at the scenery rather than looking for ducks; from at least one spot you can look up the glaciated canyon almost to Mosquito Pass, while above the canyon stands the undulating crest of the Crystal Range.

About ½ mile up our trail, we briefly enter a shady oasis in which we step across an alder-bordered creeklet. Then beyond it we make short, open ascent northeast to a southeast jog, at which point a spur trail departs north to a quiet pool at the base of a rock slab. Above, we climb into increasing forest cover, make a short traverse of an open slab, then follow the undulating forest path—generally upward—to a junction with the Pacific Crest/Tahoe-Yosemite Trail about 200 yards south of and above the southwest arm of Middle Velma Lake. Trip 30 describes the PCT northward and Trip 42, followed in reverse, describes the TYT northward. From this junction we make a traverse east, above the south shore of Middle Velma Lake, following Trip 41 in reverse to the Eagle Lake Trail/Granite Lake Trail junction on a saddle. Then we follow Trip 39 in reverse down to Bay View Picnic Area.

Crystal Range, from Camper Flat-Velma Lakes lateral

22   Pinecrest to Ralston Peak

Distance: 7.8 miles, round trip

Total gain/Net gain: 2810'/2690'

Classification: Strenuous

Season: Early July through mid-October

Parking: Crowded on weekends—then park along Pinecrest Road shoulder southwest or east of the signed trailhead

Trailhead/Map: 16/7

Features: Excellent views, both nearby and far-reaching, are obtained from the summit of Ralston Peak. From this summit you can study the different characteristics of the Desolation Wilderness, the river canyons to the west, the Carson Range to the northeast and the Freel Peak area to the east. By inference from the Mt. Tallac erosion surface, you can also mentally visualize what the Desolation Wilderness looked like before the Ice Age.

Description: From the signed trailhead we walk 200 yards due north up to a lateral road, bordered with horse corrals, in the Pinecrest Camp. *Ralston Trail* signs point the way through the west edge of this Seventh Day Adventist camp. We traverse 70 yards west on the lateral road to a minor road north, which we follow for about 150 yards to a second lateral road just south-southwest of the camp's main buildings. On this second lateral we make a very brief climb west to where the road splits into southwest and north-northeast branches. Between them our trail starts a steep ascent north, but after 40 yards curves westward around a little ridge and over to the west side of a gully. Under a white-fir canopy we climb up past chinquapin and the camp's tepees to the top of the gully and a moist, almost level slope. Over the next ¼ mile you'll have a choice of routes, all of them quite steep. The scenic western branch climbs to the bushy crest of Pyramid Creek's 800-foot-high east moraine, from which we can see the near vertical west face of Lovers Leap on the opposite side of the American River.

About 150 yards northeast beyond this viewpoint, this alternate route descends a few feet east to the main trail. Now we have a steep-to-very-steep 1350-foot climb ahead of us up weathered granitic rock largely vegetated with huckleberry oak, manzanita and some chinquapin. A 60-yard-long spur trail west to a disappointing view from a shallow ridge saddle marks the 500-foot point. Continued steep climbing up short switchbacks for 450 more feet brings us to an eastward traverse, along which we pass a trickling spring. A few more short, steep switchbacks are negotiated, and then the gradient eases as we climb to a prominent spur ridge, covered with an open stand of red fir and silver pine. From it a brief initial descent speeds us on our way along a ⅓ mile northwest traverse across a meadowy slope. Some of the more conspicuous flowers you're likely to see here are

Lake Aloha and Lake of the Woods; Jacks and Dicks peaks

Bolander's locoweed, eriogonum, streptanthus, lupine, phlox, pussy paws and
paintbrush.

Just after our traverse turns into a moderate
climb, we encounter two small but profuse
springs, each with its associated cluster of
corn lilies—telltale indicators that water is
nearby. Beyond them a steep, ducked ascent
brings us up to a generally open ridge, but with
clusters of mountain hemlocks, and from it we
can look northwest down at Lake of the
Woods, below us, and beyond at island-dotted
Lake Aloha, which has as a backdrop the
metamorphic masses of Jacks and Dicks
peaks. Pyramid Peak is the prominent granitic
guardian above Aloha's southwest shore.

From this ridge the trail descends a short,
steep north slope to a small, boggy meadow,
and then traverses north to a signed junction
among mountain hemlocks, from which a spur
trail climbs southwest to Ralston Peak. See
Trip 23 for the northward description of the
main trail. Rather than descend the north
slope, which is usually snowbound well into
August, follow the gentle ridge eastward to the
ridge crest, along which you should be able to
locate the faint, ducked trail up it to the
ice-fractured quartz-monzonite summit rocks
of Ralston Peak. At its foot lie three cirque
lakes: Tamarack, Ralston and Cagwin, and to
their east and below them lie moraine-
dammed Upper and Lower Echo lakes.
Above the canyon beyond them are the
granitic summits of the Freel Peak massif,
mostly unglaciated, the closest and tallest
peak being Freel Peak.

Perhaps the most instructive view from our
summit is the view north toward Fallen Leaf
Lake, barely visible, and Lake Tahoe, immediately beyond it. Our view is framed by
the metamorphic mass of Mt. Tallac, on the
left, and the granitic mass of Echo Peak, on
the right. From our vantage point, the lower
southeast slope of Mt. Tallac *appears* to be
almost level, and it forms a conspicuous bench
from which canyon walls drop steeply to
Fallen Leaf Lake. The deep canyon was
carved out during the Pleistocene epoch,
whereas the "bench," or gentle slope, above
it existed before that epoch. Three million
years ago, before the Ice Age, Desolation
Wilderness appeared much more rounded and
subdued, like this bench on Mt. Tallac or the
unglaciated west side of the Carson Range
visible above the east shore of Lake Tahoe
(also see Trip 32).

Summit view: Mt. Tallac bench on left, Fallen Leaf Lake on right, Lake Tahoe behind them, Ralston and Tamarack lakes in foreground

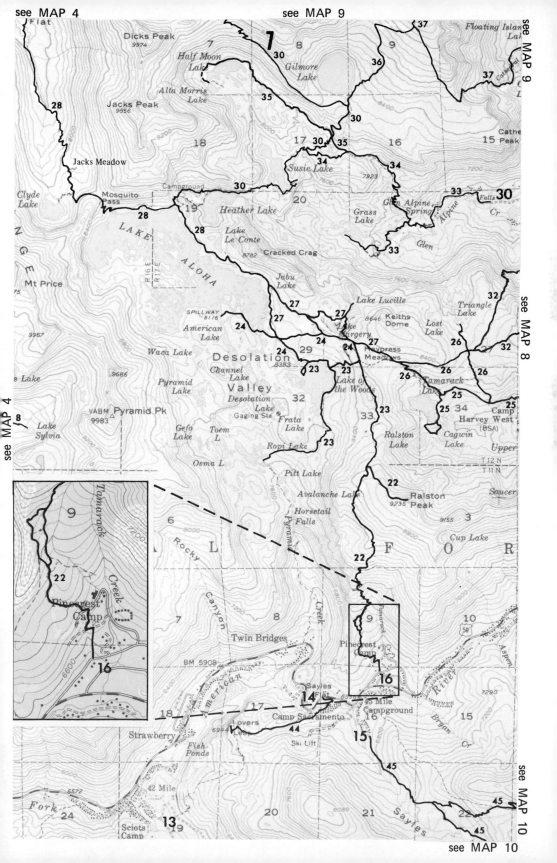

23 Pinecrest to Lake of the Woods and Ropi Lake

Distance: 13.4 miles, round trip

Total gain/Net gain: 4090'/2230'

Classification: Strenuous

Season: Mid-July through mid-October

Parking: Crowded on weekends—then park along Pinecrest Road shoulder southwest or east of the signed trailhead

Trailhead/Map: 16/7

Features: Justifiably popular Lake of the Woods, with its islands, coves, bays and good campsites, is a fine subalpine lake for pure relaxation, and it is stocked with rainbow and brook trout. Ropi Lake, below and beyond it, serves as a base-camp site for forays up and down Pyramid Creek as well as for an ascent of Pyramid Peak—the highest and most dominating peak of the Crystal Range.

Description: From the ridge overlooking Lake of the Woods (mentioned in Trip 22) follow the trail down the short, steep north slope, which is usually buried under snow through early August. The trail may be temporarily lost in a small subalpine meadow, boggy from the snowmelt, but it can be located in a stand of hemlocks and pines occupied by Clark nutcrackers. These large, gray, vociferous cousins of the lower-elevation jays feed primarily on pine-cone seeds, which at this elevation would be those of the thin-barked five-needled whitebark pine. From this conifer stand a signed spur trail climbs ⅔ mile southeast to the summit of Ralston Peak (see Trip 22).

Sunbathing at Lake of the Woods

Clark nutcracker on snow

A northward descent takes us down a gully toward a bench on which there is a pond, with plenty of water-loving wildflowers on the gentle slope above it. We then curve around a flat to a smaller pond, on a saddle, and then start a climb northward up a low knoll. Near its top we obtain a silver-pine filtered view east of the Echo Lakes and of the Sierra beyond. Then we descend to another saddle, where we meet a trail to Haypress Meadows. This lateral descends ⅓ mile east, becoming a multi-laned eyesore through the muddy meadows before reaching a junction with the Tahoe-Yosemite Trail. If we were to continue north from this saddle, we would reach, in ¼ mile, a second junction with the Tahoe-Yosemite Trail (see Trip 24).

Since we're going to Lake of the Woods, we turn left and follow a lateral westward steeply down to the northeast shore, obtaining enticing views of the lake as we descend. In its last few yards before reaching a small peninsula, the trail ramifies into several paths that link up with a shoreline trail. A ¼ mile contour west gets you to a sloping campsite at the northwest corner, from where several ducked trails climb toward Lake Aloha. (The correct route climbs only 80 yards north—the others continue on—then angles west to a gully and switchbacks up it to the west sides of small ponds atop a broad saddle.) Beyond the sloping campsite, the shore trail heads south 300 yards to "land's end" on a rocky, forested peninsula that separates the warm, island-cluttered west arm from the main lake body. Several good-to-excellent campsites are on this large peninsula, and fair-to-good campsites are near the arm and south of it near the west shore.

Our trail to Ropi Lake contours the wetter, more forested east shore and descends to a forested flat where it's easy to get lost by following false ducks too far south. When you reach the flat, you should head west along the south edge of a small, stagnant pond, then immediately cross Lake of the Woods' outlet creek and follow it south. The creek curves westward, as does our faint, ducked trail, and we reach a tiny, swampy flat at the base of a small peak ¼ mile south of Lake of the Woods that serves as a constant landmark.

From the flat we hike west along the peak's south slope down a joint-controlled gully that has red "blazes" painted on rocks. Immediately beyond the gully we arrive at the southeast arm of shallow, snag-infested Ropi Lake. Campsites can be found near its rocky, sinuous shore, and although they and the lake aren't the best, they serve as a base for further exploration of the lakes in this basin. Pyramid Peak can be climbed by many ways, the easiest route being up its southeast spur.

Below Ropi Lake are several ponds and small lakes. Avalanche Lake sits farthest downstream, atop a lip from which plunges upper Horsetail Fall. From this lip a ducked route descends a steep slope to Twin Bridges, on Highway 50. Don't take it. You could slip over a cliff and into the Pyramid Creek gorge. At least nine people have died trying to negotiate this route.

Lake of the Woods and Pyramid Peak

24   Pinecrest to Lake Aloha

Distance: 12.2 miles, semiloop trip

Total gain/Net gain: 3790'/2230'

Classification: Strenuous

Season: Late July through mid-October

Parking: Crowded on weekends—then park along Pinecrest Road shoulder southwest or east of the signed trailhead

Trailhead/Map: 16/7

Features: Most hikes reward you with several lakes; this one rewards you with hundreds of islands—all in one lake. Several other nearby lakes can be visited, but there are no lakes in Desolation Wilderness, and possibly none in the entire Sierra Nevada, that offer such long-range island-hopping possibilities as this one. By late summer, however, this lake is virtually dried up, so you should plan to visit it on or before the Labor Day weekend.

Description, Follow Trip 23 up to the second junction with the Tahoe-Yosemite Trail, which coincides with the Pacific Crest Trail through most of Desolation Wilderness. We turn left on this trail, and after 70 yards reach a junction with a spur trail down to Lake Lucille

(see Trip 27). Continuing west, we traverse a somewhat open slope above placid, forest-bound Lake Margery, passing elderberry, mountain ash and subalpine wildflowers on the way.

No sooner do we start a descent than our trail splits. The Tahoe-Yosemite Trail angles right but our route angles left, and we follow this ducked route down to a wet, sloping meadow 60 yards from the Lake Aloha shore-trail junction. From this fragile meadow a narrow path we'll be taking back climbs southeast toward Lake of the Woods. A minute's walk northwest from this junction and we're at the shore trail. The 0.6-mile segment north along the shore will take you to the TYT, which continues a shore traverse northwest, but since our destination is the Lake Aloha dam, we head west along the lake's southeast shore. The trail crosses a spillway, winds and climbs northwest along this rocky, irregular shoreline, and then curves west and finally southwest down to the dam.

When the lake's water is high—through

Pseudo-panorama: Crystal Range (Pyramid Peak is far left), Channel Lake on left,

mid-August—one can jump or dive off the dam's high point, five feet above the water level, into pleasantly cool water 20 feet deep. By mid- to late-September, however, after most of the users of this lake are back in school, the days are still warm but the lake's temperature is below 60°F, and its water level may be 5-10 feet lower, allowing you to walk out to many of the lake's islands that you earlier would have had to swim to. There are so many islands, ranging from a few yards to a few hundred yards long, that even on a crowded weekend there seem to be at least a dozen islands for each person. You could make a leisurely traverse of this two-mile long, mostly five-foot-deep lake by swimming and/ or wading from island to island. One would expect a lake of this shallowness to be rather stagnant. It isn't. It is crystal clear due partly to a complete flushing of the basin with each year's heavy snowfall and partly to the nature of this desolate basin—virtually devoid of erodable soil and organic matter. This lake, a reservoir for the city of Sacramento, now floods much of the barren, flat granodiorite floor of Desolation Valley, after which the wilderness was named.

Leaving the heart of this wilderness, you can follow the east side of the lake's outlet creek cross-country toward Lake of the Woods. Deep American Lake, with nearby good campsites, is first encountered, then shallow, picturesque Channel Lake. Beyond it you may end up climbing Class 3 down to the north shore of an unnamed lake, then following its east shore southeastward down to the fourth lake in this joint-controlled, linear chain—Desolation Lake. From it you can either head east over a low ridge to the south tip of Lake of the Woods or you can continue downstream to Ropi Lake. In either case, you'll end up backtracking the route described in Trip 23.

Those preferring to stick to the shorter, trail route should take the narrow path that starts from the previously mentioned sloping meadow near Lake Aloha, follow it up to the west sides of ponds atop a broad saddle, then switchback down a gully and over to Lake of the Woods' northwest shore. A ¼-mile shoreline traverse east then takes you to a small peninsula at the lake's northeast corner, from which you follow a trail steeply upslope—the reverse of Trip 23.

Lake Aloha on right

25   Echo Lake to Tamarack, Ralston and Cagwin Lakes

Distance: 8.8 miles, round trip, or 3.6 miles plus water taxi

Total gain/Net gain: 1340'/450'

Classification: Easy

Season: Early July through late October

Parking: Usually crowded; park in or near lot above resort

Trailhead/Map: 17/8

Features: A good day hike is a walk up to the Ralston Peak basin lakes. If you're out of shape, you can take a scenic water-taxi ride from the Echo Lake Resort over to the public pier on Upper Echo Lake's north shore, then later take it back again. The Echo Lakes are stocked with rainbow trout and Kokanee salmon.

Description: Over half the distance to and from the Ralston Peak basin lakes can be eliminated by taking the Echo Lakes water taxi, which in 1974 cost $1.25 per person, with a three-passenger minimum per trip. Since P.G.&E. owns the top 12 feet of the lake (because they've dammed it that high), they have the right to lower the water by that amount, and by mid-September they have to do so. Then the lake reverts to its natural, upper-lower pair of lakes, and the taxi service stops.

Our signed trail is the Tahoe-Yosemite Trail, which starts near Meeks Bay, on Lake Tahoe, and extends south to Tuolumne Meadows in Yosemite National Park. The Pacific Crest Trail, extending from the Canadian to the Mexican border, coincides with the TYT through most of Desolation Wilderness, the two splitting just north of Middle Velma Lake. We cross Lower Echo Lake's dam, make an initial climb south, and then head west on this sparsely treed, rollercoaster trail.

Our trail traverses below some prominent granodiorite cliffs, on which you might see a rock climber struggling up the cracks, and then it passes below a saddle 140 feet above the trail. From it you would get a fair view of the southern part of the Lake Tahoe basin and the Freel Peak massif above it. Beyond this slope our trail switchbacks twice and climbs high above lakeshore summer homes. Scattered Jeffrey pines give way to thick groves of lodgepoles as we descend toward the lake's north shore. Then we traverse to a rusty, granitic knoll, round it to forested slopes above Upper Echo Lake, and continue westward. The tree cover is thick enough to blot out any possible view of the public pier at which the water taxis land, and several short trails down to the lake add to the confusion. If

Dark inclusions cut by a younger feldspar-rich dike; pencil for scale

Lodgepole pines at Cagwin Lake

you've taken the taxi, you'll know which trail to take back. One can follow any of them down to the shore, then follow a shoreline trail to the obvious pier on the lake's north corner.

Beyond the lake we climb a rocky tread up open slopes of slightly metamorphosed quartz monzonite and quickly reach a cryptic junction with a lateral trail to a saddle. To this junction Trip 26 from Triangle Lake descends, following this steep lateral. This junction is just 20 yards past a small bend which has conspicuous junipers growing on it and 70 yards before you enter an obvious, small, shady grove of lodgepoles. The dark inclusions you've been seeing in the rocks over the last stretch are clusters of high-melting-point crystals, which are the first ones to solidify in the molten, cooling mass of a newly forming pluton.

The next junction, with the trail to the Ralston Peak basin lakes, is also not very obvious. Six-tenths mile past the Triangle Lake lateral, our trail rounds a bend and passes through a blasted, five-foot-high trail cut, then in 40 yards reaches a trail junction. From here the TYT continues to climb, an older TYT segment traverses west before it climbs back up to the TYT, and our ducked trail descends south over barren bedrock to Tamarack Lake, largest of the Ralston Peak basin lakes and, like the other two, fringed with mountain hemlock and lodgepole and silver pine. From the south tip of this shallow lake you can head south on a ducked route directly over a low ridge and descend to the north shore of moderately deep, red-heather-and-Labrador-tea-lined Cagwin Lake, or you can follow a trail southwest over the west end of the ridge and down to deep Ralston Lake, which is totally surrounded by steep slopes. The best campsites are near the east shore of Tamarack Lake and beside a trail midway between Ralston and Cagwin lakes.

26   Echo Lake to Triangle Lake

Distance: 10.0 miles, semiloop trip, or 4.8 miles plus water taxi

Total gain/Net gain: 1800'/940'

Classification: Moderate

Season: Early July through late October

Parking: Usually crowded; park in or near lot above resort

Trailhead/Map: 17/8

Features: This route not only takes you past the readily accessible Ralston Peak basin lakes, but it also leads you—on a well-graded trail—up to a fantastic viewpoint before bringing you to a saddle where you can descend to tranquil Triangle Lake or climb moderately to the Echo Peak ridge for an encore of fantastic views.

Description: From the Ralston Peak basin trail junction, mentioned in Trip 25, continue west up the Tahoe-Yosemite Trail to a tiny creek in a gully, which is a good place to rest after your moderate climb. Rather than shortcut up the gully, as too many careless hikers have done, we follow two switchbacks up to a bench, from where we see a lateral trail traversing east across a slope predominantly colored with paintbrush and sagebrush, but also with pennyroyal, cinquefoil, aster, mariposa lily and cushion stenotus, the last species being a low, yellow sunflower that is fairly abundant in this local area.

We take this lateral trail east, passing occasional junipers and viewing with changing perspective the Ralston Peak basin lakes below and the peak above. We then make a brief climb to a ridge and bang! a panorama explodes so suddenly upon us that it almost knocks us over. To the east we get an aerial view of both Echo Lakes and the Sierra beyond; to the west looms Pyramid Peak above Haypress Meadows; to the south we have a detailed inspection of the basin lakes below us; and to the north we even see a bit of Lake Tahoe beyond Angora Peak. Most of the ridge crest of the Crystal Range, from Becker Peak northwest to around Rockbound Pass, is visible in one sweeping glance. Still stunned by the sudden shock of this grandstand panorama, we meander with new thoughts and vivid emotions northeast down to a flat saddle, where we intersect a lateral that leads 0.4 mile down to Triangle Lake.

Descending this lateral northward, first through a meadow and then across ducked quartz-monzonite bedrock above the lake's south shore, we obtain an excellent inspection of Mt. Tallac's gentle southeast slope, a Pliocene erosion surface (see Trips 22 and 32 for elaboration). After 40 yards down the jagged bedrock we drop a few yards east to a creeklet and follow a faint duff trail down to the shallow, grassy south end of Triangle Lake. From good diving rocks above the lake's northwest shore we can look down into the water and see 8- to 10-inch brook trout swimming lazily in this deep arm. Small, fair campsites can be found in nooks among the ice-fractured rocks above the lake. Its water is of questionable purity, so you might consider treating it or drinking from the inlet creek.

To return to the Echo Lakes, we retrace our steps to the flat saddle, and then continue south along a forested path that becomes increasingly more open as we approach the Tahoe-Yosemite Trail. For those who first want to climb Echo Peak, one mile east of the flat saddle, follow a trail 85 yards east-northeast to a pile of rocks, where the main trail turns northeast, but the faint Echo Peak trail continues east-northeast (see Trip 32 for route descriptions along both these trails).

**Echo Lakes
from
Triangle Lake
Trail**

27   Echo Lake to Lake Aloha

Distance: 13.1 miles, semiloop trip, or 7.9 miles plus water taxi

Total gain/Net gain: 2080'/930'

Classification: Moderate

Season: Mid-July through mid-October

Parking: Usually crowded; park in or near lot above resort

Trailhead/Maps: 17/8,7

Features: The most popular lake in Desolation Wilderness is Lake Aloha, and this trip leads you there—with a side excursion to Lakes Lucille and Margery thrown in for added spice. Our route is mostly along a stretch of the famous Pacific Crest Trail, which also, in this area, coincides with the signed Tahoe-Yosemite Trail. You get to walk along two high-status trails while putting forth the effort for only one!

Description: Just 0.1 mile past the lateral east toward Triangle Lake, mentioned in Trip 26, the Tahoe-Yosemite Trail brings us to the east fringe of Haypress Meadows, rich in lupine, aster, paintbrush and corn lilies. Here a lateral trail forks west, unfortunately, across the boggy part of the meadows. In an effort to keep their feet dry, hikers to Lake of the Woods have selected paths of their own, and the result is that up to five ruts now cross the meadows. Rather than worsen this muddy situation, hikers should hike northwest another half mile on the TYT, which is rerouted around the north end of the meadows, then reach a north-facing slope on which another lateral leaves our route and climbs south-southwest to a saddle. From this they can descend west to Lake of the Woods without damaging Haypress Meadows.

From the north-facing-slope junction, we contour only 70 yards before we come to a third lateral, this one veering right and winding down to Lake Lucille. At its northwest shore we find a small, scenic peninsula, almost an island, which is a good meditative, relaxing spot for lunch. Enriched with food and thought, and perhaps with a view from the end of this lake down at Fallen Leaf Lake and Lake Tahoe, we make a short, moderate ascent southwest along the northwest side of Lake Margery's outlet creek. Pausing at this shallow, rocky lake, we can see backpackers traversing the TYT high above us, their numbers making that trail seem more like an expressway than a path. Our route back will

be on that "expressway," which on a Sunday afternoon resembles rush-hour traffic.

Leaving the forest-canopied shoreline of Lake Margery behind, we climb west up to three ankle-deep ponds, and just beyond the westernmost one we rejoin the wide TYT. Now we enter a thick forest and soon descend on a broad trail, supported in places by railroad ties, down to a junction above Lake Aloha, which contains brook trout. To continue north on the TYT, see Trip 28. We head south along the east shore of Lake Aloha, spying several good campsites 100 legal feet or more from the lake's shore.

After a pleasant stay relaxing or exploring, head south to the very tip of Lake Aloha, from where you can go west toward the dam for great swimming. When you're finally ready to leave this swimmer's paradise (see Trip 24), start a southeast ascent from the tip of Lake Aloha. In 60 yards you'll reach a narrow spur trail that goes southeast to Lake of the Woods (see Trip 24), but our route climbs east ½ mile to a point on the TYT above Lake Margery and ¼ mile southeast of the TYT's junction with the spur trail east down to that lake. On the TYT we traverse east across the sometimes rocky slope above Lake Margery, then continue down our usually broad, well-graded trail to the Echo Lakes.

Lake Margery, from the TYT

28   Echo Lake to Wrights Lake

Distance: 23.2 miles plus a 23.8-mile shuttle

Total gain/Net gain: 3570'/1600'

Classification: Moderate

Season: Early August through mid-October

Parking: Usually crowded; park in or near lot above resort

Trailhead/Maps: 17/8,7,4

Features: Subalpine lake basins and a long river valley offer the backpacker two contrasting views of this glaciated landscape. During the last major glaciation, which ended about 12,000 years ago, every inch of this route was under ice—even high Rockbound Pass. While hiking along this fine subalpine route, keep in mind that all the soil and vegetation you see have appeared since the retreat of the glaciers.

Description: See Trips 25-27 for route description along the Tahoe-Yosemite Trail from Echo Lake Resort to the east shore of brook-trout-stocked Lake Aloha. From the junction with the lakeshore trail we follow the lake's unsightly northeast edge, which has hundreds of dead lodgepole snags that once grew in this basin, Desolation Valley, before the city officials of Sacramento decided it had to be flooded to supply water to their growing population.

Soon our trail—the TYT or PCT, depending on your preference—takes us alongside a fairly clear, chest-deep, large pond, on our left, which like Aloha, warms up to the mid-sixties in midsummer. Walking 150 yards beyond it, we reach a gully, up which our trail seems to head. A snowbank, lasting through July, obscures the correct route, which makes a brief climb southwest before traversing northwest again. Had you gone straight ahead, you would have reached chilly, rockbound Lake LeConte, stocked with rainbow trout. This diversion would have provided you with a view of two high summits, Jacks and Dicks Peaks. Jacks Peak, the closer, is equally divided between brown metasedimentary rocks north of the summit and gray granitic rocks south of it.

Lake LeConte, Jacks Peak

Lake Aloha; Cracked Crag on left, Ralston Peak on right

Continuing northwest just above Lake Aloha, we now traverse along a nicer, snag-free section of lake, and then reach its northeast corner, which has a two-foot-high retaining wall to prevent the lake from spilling over into Heather Lake, below us to the east. Climbing just a few yards beyond the wall, we reach a junction, from where the TYT/PCT descends first north and then east to Heather Lake, but we turn west, following Lake Aloha's north shore toward Mosquito Pass. The TYT/PCT description to Heather Lake and beyond is continued in Trip 30.

Now upon a less used trail, we stroll along Lake Aloha's picturesque north shore, and after ½ mile reach a long, grassy flat, which has suitable campsites. Not far beyond it, we climb via five switchbacks through a sparse stand of mountain hemlock to Mosquito Pass, leaving broad, flat, glacier-resistant Desolation Valley behind us. One hundred yards closer to Rockbound Valley, but still on the wide pass, we reach a crude, stone windbreak which serves as an emergency shelter. Beyond it our rock-blasted trail arcs southwest, passing seeps with ferns, columbines and corn lilies and providing us with open views north down Rockbound Valley. It then switchbacks north down to a junction by a seasonal creek, from where a steeply descending spur trail goes down a large-block talus slope to Clyde Lake. Although lower than Lake Aloha, this cirque lake is much colder, usually reflecting a snowfield across its protected waters until well into August. The steep walls above three of its sides perpetuate a sense of chill in this glacier-carved environment. In addition to the steep trail and the bleak environment, a lack of good campsites is

another argument for not visiting the lake. It does, however, have some positive features: it is often good for the seeker of solitude, and it is stocked with rainbow, brook and golden trout.

One-third mile farther down the main trail we hit another spur, this one striking 100 yards east to swampy Jacks Meadow, currently being invaded by willows, heather and mosquitoes. In pursuit of a decent campsite, we descend onward, down a rock trail through an open forest of red fir, mountain hemlock, silver pine and lodgepole pine, to the Rubicon River. Here we find what we've been looking for, our first good campsite since the north shore of Lake Aloha. The river is up to seven yards wide, but by following its east bank about 30 yards downstream, we can cross a narrow stretch of it on large boulders. Now on the west bank, we walk back up to another good campsite, this one by the trail ford, which is on a point of land immediately below where two large tributaries join the Rubicon.

Our gentle descent north now crosses many creeks as it parallels the Rubicon, which is largely unseen due to the thick, lush vegetation. Hidden campsites as well as hidden fishing holes await the inquiring backpacker. One mile from the first Rubicon ford we must ford the river again, and this time we have no large boulders on which to make a dry crossing. However, the wide river is quite shallow, and if you run fast and lightly enough, you'll barely get your boots wet.

From the Rubicon's east, lodgepole-lined bank, we regain our composure, head northeast across a meadow, and then tread north for ¼ mile to large, shady-but-open China Flat Public Camp, an ideal base camp for the complete fisherman. Three hundred yards north of it, we reach a third ford of the Rubicon, this one up to 15 yards wide and six inches deep. Look downstream for a log crossing or be prepared to get your feet wet.

After another 300 yards, along a curving path over a low ridge, we reach a junction with a trail, described in Trip 21, which climbs moderately to steeply west up to Rockbound Pass. Not ready to face civilization yet, we continue our Rubicon odyssey, crossing and recrossing a branch of the Rubicon, then jumping several streams, including several branches of the Lake Lois outlet creek. Just 25 yards beyond the last branch we reach, amid lush creekside vegetation, a trail fork. We veer left, make an exhausting initial ascent northwest up a steep, meadowy slope, then a more reasonable one north to a saddle on a ridge that separates the Lake Schmidell drainage from that of the Rubicon. Fifty yards before this rocky saddle, you'll reach an old, abandoned trail that descends steeply 0.4 mile to the Rubicon River trail at the north end of a long, swampy flat.

Leaving the saddle, we descend west to the south bank of Lake Schmidell's outlet creek.

Since an incredible horde of mosquitoes inhabits the moist creekside environment from here up to the lake, hike this stretch after mid-August or be prepared for the worst. Just before reaching the Lake Schmidell-Camper Flat lateral, our soggy trail fords the wide outlet creek. Rather than look for a way to cross it, continue upstream about 100 yards to where you'll reach the lateral. By making this short cross-country detour, you avoid the need for crossing and then immediately recrossing the lively creek.

Along the lateral trail, lined with mosquito-harboring mountain hemlocks, we walk briskly up to a soggy trail junction near the southwest edge of a large pond bordered by both red and white heather. From it a three-minute walk upstream brings us to a bench above the southeast shore of deep, cold Lake Schmidell, upon which we get gentle breezes that waft away our pesky, pursuing pests. See Trip 19 for a digression on the geomorphic activity at Lake Schmidell as well as for a brief trail description up to a ridge south of this lake, from which you follow in reverse part of Trip 18 and all of Trip 17 to Wrights Lake.

Clyde Lake

29   Echo Lake to Loon Lake

Distance: 28.4 miles plus a 56.2-mile shuttle

Total gain/Net gain: 2790'/2020'

Classification: Easy

Season: Mid-July through mid-October

Parking: Usually crowded; park in or near lot above resort

Trailhead/Maps: 17/8,7,4,6,5,3

Features: A traverse along the east side of the entire Crystal Range is achieved by those who complete this generally easy, mostly downhill trip. Some of the Tahoe Sierra's finest swimming holes are found along a three-mile stretch of the Rubicon River below Camper Flat, and surprisingly enough, this stretch is one of the least visited areas in Desolation Wilderness. Along the Rubicon you may expect to catch rainbow and brook trout.

Description: Trip 28 describes our route to a junction immediately north of the Lake Lois outlet creek not far above its union with the Rubicon River. From this junction our trail descends north-northeast alongside a small creeklet, soon crosses it, and then traverses a

forested slope north, staying just above a moist flat through which flows the Rubicon. As we pass the north end of this flat, we encounter an old, abandoned trail, still followable, which climbs steeply upslope to reach a lateral to the Lake Schmidell-Camper Flat trail only 50 yards before the lateral crosses a shallow ridge saddle.

After a slight ascent our trail north becomes a moderate descent, then almost levels off alongside a very low granodiorite ridge, on our left, which it parallels for 0.2 mile north to a trail junction on a bench above the Rubicon. Here a trail descends 30 yards to the wide river, fords it, and then climbs east to Middle Velma Lake (see Trip 21).

Only 100 level yards north of this junction we arrive at another junction, this one with the Lake Schmidell-Camper Flat trail. Continuing north along the Rubicon, we pass in 70 yards a short spur trail west to a cold, seeping, rust-stained mineral spring, then shortly beyond that arrive at spacious Camper Flat, which has a large, but now illegal, campsite

Rubicon River pool at AAA camp

adjacent to a good Rubicon River swimming hole.

Beyond the campsite we wade through a dense meadow rich in corn lily, lupine, shooting star, aster, alpine lily and other species, then come upon Lake Schmidell's outlet creek. If it is too high and wide to jump across, look upstream for logs on which to cross. Seventy yards beyond it we meet the 4-Q Lakes Trail, branching west and climbing.

After several minutes' hiking, we are beside the Rubicon again, and we traverse a bench where the river cuts through a miniature gorge. The river emerges westward from its gorge by cascading five feet down into a 10-foot-deep, 40-yard-long, slab-bordered, crystal-clear pool, the first of many we'll pass in the next three miles. Not far beyond it is a second, equally large emerald-green pool. Then we soon leave the river's side and traverse west-northwest ¼-mile across a wide bench to the north side of a stagnant pond. The trail beyond it is hard to follow, so watch closely for ducks that mark the 80-yard stretch to our fourth crossing of the Rubicon along this backpack trip.

The best crossing, on a log if you're fortunate, is at a narrow constriction of the river, 25 yards northwest of a bend. When you reach the east bank, look for the trail in the lodgepole thicket at the river's bend. Your trail now descends northward, passes large, shallow pools, and ⅓-mile from the crossing makes a short, steep climb up a somewhat brushy gully to a small, hidden flat atop a saddle on a low ridge. The next ⅔-mile stretch of trail to a spur trail has a lot of minor ups and downs and is anything but straight. Watch carefully for ducks. From the saddle the trail descends north past huckleberry oaks, which

are later joined by lodgepoles, then by Jeffrey pines and junipers. Eventually we make a brief climb west, back on to the ridge, which now is very low, broad and glacially polished, and then we arc northwest to where ducks mark a 200-yard traverse west from the trail to "AAA Camp" just above the Rubicon, where it cascades into a 10-foot-deep pool—brisk, but excellent for diving, cooling off or just frolicking around in.

After a memorable stay at this lodgepole-shaded camp, we retrace our steps back to the main trail and start north again down the glaciated river canyon. The river is in general quite straight, and when it makes a major deviation, it usually does so at right angles to the canyon. Its course is controlled by long fractures in the granodiorite that are called joints. The largest of these, the master joints, trend north-northwest, and along them the ancestral Rubicon River was able to incise a channel. Ensuing Pleistocene glaciers followed that channel and deepened it to form the Rockbound Valley we see today. Look on the canyon's east wall for lines of trees, tell-tale indicators of the location of master joints.

Our trail winds 0.2 mile along the broad, open ridge, then makes a sudden, brief plunge east to the south end of a shallow, wide pool on Phipps Creek. Once across its inlet, we follow our blazed, ducked, paint-marked trail through a lodgepole flat that is saturated with a bed of bracken ferns, then head west and make a winding descent briefly touching the Rubicon, and finally wind northwest down to a riverside bench beside a long, shallow pool. Three hundred yards beyond it, at some low-angle exfoliation slabs, the north-northwest-flowing river turns abruptly north-northeast. Here our ducked route crosses the

Rubicon Reservoir

wide, ankle-deep river on bedrock. If you want to keep your boots dry, you might try boulder-crossing it 60 yards downriver.

Once across, we descend north at a distance from the river, angle northwest gently up to two stagnant ponds on a large, high bench, and then make a westward descent toward the inlet of shallow Rubicon Reservoir. Our trail soon parallels the west shore of this reservoir, which turns into an unattractive mud-and-boulder flat late in the summer. Nevertheless, it is home to some furry marmots and some feathery spotted sandpipers. We then arrive at a road above its northwest lobe, where water empties into a quarter-mile-long tunnel northwest toward Rockbound Lake; the Rubicon River channel is left dry.

Hiking northwest up the road almost to a saddle, we spy Fox Lake, a short 300-yard cross-country jaunt north of us. On a small island—a peninsula in late summer—grow several lodgepoles beside two large, dark erratic boulders, which were left behind by the same glacier that scoured out this basin. Glacial striations, bearing north-northwest, mark the direction of its flow.

From the saddle overlooking Fox Lake we follow the closed road west moderately down to the "new Rubicon River," up to 15 yards wide, gushing from the tunnel outlet 150 yards upstream. Rather than wade this fast, knee-deep river, you can cross 50 yards upstream via a cable-slung, water-gauge trolley, perhaps the most unique "ford" you'll make in the entire Tahoe Sierra.

A 300-yard shady traverse west brings us to a lodgepole-sheltered, poolside campsite 20 yards north of where we cross a wide creek on logs. Beyond it we lose our forest cover and follow a sunny road up above the curving south shore of appealing, fairly deep Rockbound Lake, which has been further deepened by the addition of a low dam. Look for small campsites under the sparse tree cover near the shoreline.

Beyond the lake's southwest finger, our road traverses briefly northwest, and then we spy Buck Island Lake, rocky and muddy like Rubicon Reservoir. We descend toward that lake, leave Desolation Wilderness at the signed west boundary, and in 20 yards leave the road on a trail branching left. After another 20 yards we ford two step-across creeks, then make a somewhat shady, wildflowered traverse to a road junction 50 yards southwest of the lake. Now we follow in reverse the route description of the first half of Trip 7, which guides us to the Loon Lake Campground. A longer alternative is to follow the second half of Trip 7 to the junction immediately past Ellis Creek, then most of Trip 6, which takes you down the Rubicon all the way to its South Fork, from which a trail leads up to roads that take you back to Loon Lake.

Erratic boulder on Fox Lake's island

30   Echo Lake to Lake Tahoe

Distance: 31.0 miles plus a 31.2-mile shuttle

Total gain/Net gain: 4620'/3060'

Classification: Moderate

Season: Late July through mid-October

Parking: Usually crowded; park in or near lot above resort

Trailhead/Maps: 17/8,7,9,6

Features: This enjoyable backpack trip takes you along a segment of the justly famous Pacific Crest Trail. Along your route you cross the highest pass in Desolation Wilderness and encounter lakes of all sizes and shapes. Although this trip traverses relatively rugged country, it is only moderately difficult to hike.

Description: The Pacific Crest Trail from Echo Lake Resort to the northeast corner of Lake Aloha is described in Trips 25 through 28. A retaining wall at this corner prevents the large, shallow lake from spilling over into the Heather Lake basin. At the east end of this wall a trail, often partly snowbound, descends to a shallow tarn and then parallels a creek as both descend to Heather Lake. The PCT leaves the west end of the wall and descends east, giving us views of the Freel Peak massif to the east. A switchback takes us to a delicate 20-foot-high waterfall just above deep Heather Lake's northwest shore. Here we

meet a shoreline trail, which contours southeast and eventually climbs up to the shallow tarn. Near a large red fir and the fall's creek—which supports a colorful ribbon of wildflowers—is an adequate campsite. Fishermen will find this subalpine cirque lake stocked with rainbow, brook and brown trout.

Not much heather is found around this Heather Lake; instead you'll see alder, dogwood, willow and aspen, all dwarfed by the long, cold winters. That part of each bush which remains buried and protected within the winter snow survives; any part protruding above it is likely to be killed by the icy winds of winter.

Most of the lakes we've seen in Desolation Wilderness have islands in them, but none has an island as high as the chunky, massive one in Heather Lake, which stoutly resisted glacial attempts to wear it down.

As we traverse east above the lake's north shore, we can glance back over the lake and see ragged Pyramid Peak, crowning the southern end of the snow-mantled Crystal Range. Our trail then leaves the lake at its low dam, climbs a low, barren ridge, and descends to a cove on the southwest shore of red- and white-heather-bound Susie Lake. In the late 1800s, routes to this and other lakes were blazed by Nathan Gilmore, discoverer of Glen Alpine Springs, and this lake was named after his oldest daughter.

Heather Lake; Pyramid Peak on left

On a weekend several dozen backpackers may be seen camped at poor, tiny campsites along this easily accessible dark-shored lake below the towering, rusty, metamorphic shoulder of Jacks Peak. The best campsites are on a small bench, shaded by mountain hemlock and lodgepole pine, 70 yards down the lake's outlet creek. We cross the outlet creek, follow the rocky trail over a low ridge, pass two stagnant ponds, and descend to a flowery, swampy meadow, where the trail forks. A well-used trail to the Fallen Leaf Lake area branches southwest across the meadow (see Trip 34).

The PCT is now all uphill to Dicks Pass, and it first switchbacks northeast up to a junction with a second trail southeast down to the Fallen Leaf Lake area. This trail also continues northwest to Half Moon and Alta Morris lakes (see Trip 35). Beyond this trail intersection the PCT switchbacks up to a junction with a lateral trail that takes you ¼ mile to good campsites above the south and east shores of orbicular Gilmore Lake, then 1¾ miles farther to the top of Mt. Tallac (see Trip 36).

As we start west up toward Dicks Pass, we get a peek through the lodgepole forest at Gilmore Lake, and then we ascend steadily northwest, climbing high above the pale brown metavolcanic rock basin that holds Half Moon and Alta Morris lakes. Below them to the southeast is open Susie Lake, cradled in a bed of metamorphic rock, and beyond the ridge above it we barely see Lake Aloha, nestled at the foot of Pyramid Peak and the Crystal Range. Partway up our ascent we parallel a rocky lateral moraine on our left, composed of rocks that fell onto the side of a cirque glacier which once filled the bowl beneath us to this height.

This climb is enhanced by a large variety of flowers: senecio, aster, yarrow, eriogonum, knotweed, paintbrush, pussy paws, Douglas phlox and streptanthus clothe the slope in color together with lupine, sagebrush and juniper, which add pleasant aromas to the rarified air. In a rainstorm, the strong, delicious odor of wild parsley makes this small, often overlooked flower very noticeable. Lodgepoles, mountain hemlocks and silver pines—occupied by chirping Oregon juncoes and singing mountain chickadees—are soon joined by whitebark pine, the harbinger of timberline, as we approach a saddle east of Dicks Peak. From it, a faint but popular unofficial trail leads hikers up a ridge to the rusty peak's summit.

Rather than descend from the saddle, our trail climbs east up alongside the ridge crest in order to bypass the steep slopes and long-lasting snowfields that lie north of it. At 9380 feet elevation our trail reaches Dicks Pass, an almost level area on the ridge, with clusters of dwarfed, wind-trimmed conifers that serve as windbreaks or shelters for those who want to camp overnight here to experience the glorious sunrise upon the richly hued metamorphic massif to the west. Lingering snowpatches usually provide a water source. Here, on the highest pass in Desolation Wilderness—and also the highest pass on the Pacific Crest Trail between Ebbetts Pass on California Highway 4 and the Canadian border, we get far-ranging views both north and south. Dicks Lake, immediately northwest below us, and Fontanillis Lake, just beyond it, are our next goals.

Ducks guide us across Dicks Pass, the boundary between metamorphic rocks to the south and granitic rocks to the north, and then we descend on hemlock-lined switchbacks, rich in thick gravel from the deeply weathered granodiorite bedrock. Descending northwest to a rocky saddle with sparse lodgepoles that sometimes harbor mountain bluebirds, we reach a junction. From here the Pacific Crest Trail descends 0.1 mile southwest to a union with a second trail from the saddle (see Trip 39). It then descends another 0.1 mile south to a spur trail, which in turn descends 100 yards to a shoreline trail that leads you to campsites along the north shore and east peninsula of Dicks Lake.

We follow the PCT down to the Dicks Lake spur trail, stop at the lake's northeast, rockbound corner to fish or to admire the scenery, then get back on the PCT and follow it down to a large tarn with a good campsite by a low ridge that blocks our view of Fontanillis Lake, immediately beyond it. Another tarn is passed before we descend a gully to a small cove on the lake's east shore and parallel this shore northwest to the outlet creek. Campsites are fair to poor around this lake, but fishermen hike up to it from the Velma Lakes to fish for brook trout.

From the north end of Fontanillis Lake, southbound PCT trekkers can identify Dicks Pass as the seemingly unvegetated skyline flat ¼ mile east of the lowest saddle. To leave this rockbound lake, rimmed with spiraea and two kinds of heather, we cross the outlet creek, make a brief climb north to a young lateral moraine shaded by red fir, silver pine and mountain hemlock, and then descend part way along its crest before curving left, jumping an intermorainal creek and descending a not-much-older lateral moraine to a trail junction above the south shore of Middle Velma Lake. Eastward, a trail climbs and then descends to Bay View Picnic Area and to Eagle Falls Picnic Area, both above Lake Tahoe's Emerald Bay (see Trips 39 and 41).

Seventy yards west on this trail we reach a sign *Middle Velma Lake*, from which you'll probably want to descend to campsites on the lake's shore, which are the best you'll find between General Creek, to the north, and Lake Aloha, to the south. On weekends this lakeshore is crowded, since it is readily accessible from Emerald Bay and it has inviting water, tempting hikers to swim out to and dive or sunbathe on one or more of the lake's rock-slab islands. Other hikers may be found fishing for rainbow trout in this amorphous-shaped lake. Situated on a bedrock flat between Upper and Lower Velma lakes, it drains west into the Rubicon River, whose waters eventually reach the Pacific Ocean. The other two lakes drain into Lake Tahoe, whose waters eventually reach the desert east of the Sierra. Another glacial episode could alter the drainage pattern, so that Middle Velma drained east into Tahoe or Upper Velma drained northwest into the Rubicon. Only Lower Velma is set in her ways.

After climbing from the south shore back up to the PCT, we follow it west, reaching—35 yards beyond a sluggish creek—a trail that descends 2¼ miles to Camper Flat, on the east bank of the Rubicon River (see Trip 21). Then we descend north to a southwest arm of Middle Velma Lake, negotiate a muddy traverse across its swampy outlet, and head north to an abrupt change in gradient. Unless you're looking closely for the new trail, you'll climb north straight ahead up the steep, old one. That's okay. The longer, new segment climbs east and then curves northwest to a junction with the old one, from which we climb 0.3 mile north to an important junction.

Susie Lake and Pyramid Peak, from near Gilmore Lake junction

Here, the Tahoe-Yosemite Trail, which has coincided with the Pacific Crest Trail, forks northeast and makes long switchbacks up to Phipps Pass. For a route description along this beautiful paternoster-lake-lined TYT segment, follow Trip 42 in reverse.

Our blazed PCT forks northwest, briefly ascends a shallow gully to an almost imperceptible spur ridge, and then makes a long, gentle-to-moderate descent to seasonal Phipps Creek. By early August this creek and others between Middle Velma Lake and *lower* General Creek will be either stagnant or dry.

On glacier-polished granodiorite slabs just north of the sluggish creek you can find campsites that are relatively mosquito-free. Beyond it we climb moderately to better water, which flows down a rock into a small pool. Then we cross its outlet, make a gentle climb to a forested spur-ridge saddle, and descend a shallow gully along the edge of a narrow meadow that runs down it. Our blazed trail passes northeast of a 50-yard-long pond, crosses a boggy meadow beyond it, and then commences a 200-foot climb almost to the top of Peak 8235.

At our trail's high point we can take a 40-yard spur trail southwest to some rocks, from which we can see Rubicon, Rockbound and Buck Island reservoirs in the deep canyon west of us. A tunnel diverts water from Rubicon Reservoir to Rockbound Lake, Rockbound drains into Buck Island Lake, and a tunnel from it transports the water west, through the north end of the Crystal Range to Loon Lake. This engineering project of the Sacramento Utility District leaves the river channel below Rubicon Reservoir quite depleted, thereby depriving Hell Hole Reservoir, a downriver project of the Placer County Water Agency, of some water. It, however, receives water from a tunnel that starts at French Meadows Reservoir, on the other side of the ridge north of it. Hell Hole Reservoir, stingy like Rubicon Reservoir, *usually* doesn't let much water slip out down the Rubicon to Parsley Bar (see Trip 1), but rather tunnels it through a divide to another reservoir. And so it flows—very unnaturally.

From our spur-trail viewpoint the PCT descends steeply to a level, northwest-trending ridge, which has erratic boulders perched on it, left behind by a former glacier. We follow this ridge through an open forest with blazed trees, then curve north to a gully and descend it via short, steep switchbacks to

a crossing of torpid General Creek. About 150 yards northeast of this crossing we reach a junction from which a faint but well-blazed lateral trail climbs east to the TYT and Lake Genevieve, lowest of the Tallant Lakes. Our trail north parallels General Creek, usually unseen below us to the west, and then after 1¾ miles crosses it at a steep section that almost always has good, aerated water.

We make a brief, curving climb around a low ridge to the creek's west tributary, cross it, and climb an aromatic, mule-eared slope to a road on a saddle. The Pacific Crest Trail continues north toward Canada (see *The Pacific Crest Trail*) but we follow this wide dirt road east down to a ford of General Creek. To keep your feet dry, boulder-hop the creek immediately upstream and then walk to the road and hike up it 300 yards to a low ridge opposite a huge cliff. Here the road turns south and begins a steep climb up to the logged-over Lost Lake/Duck Lake basin. On the low ridge look for ducks that mark the General Creek Trail, and follow this fine creekside route northeast to the General Creek Campground. This trail is described, east to west, in Trip 43.

Dicks Pass from near outlet of Dicks Lake

31   Fallen Leaf Lake to Angora Fire Lookout and Angora Lakes

Distance: 5.4 miles, loop trip

Total gain/Net Gain: 1140'/1030'

Classification: Moderate

Season: Late June through late October

Parking: Always crowded; park where you can, but don't obstruct access

Trailhead/Map: 27/8

Features: This hike offers you a lot of possibilities for its short distance. If you only want breathtaking views, hike up the Clark Trail and return down it, two miles round trip. If you want to do some swimming, diving, boating or fishing, continue to Upper Angora Lake. This lake, at the end of a closed road, is so attractive you might find yourself eventually spending many weekends at it.

Description: Just beyond and above the easternmost cabin of Fallen Leaf Resort, we begin a stiff climb up the Clark Trail. Half way

up it our gradient becomes more moderate, the forest cover of white fir and red fir thins, and Jeffrey pine together with huckleberry oak, chinquapin and manzanita become more predominant. The more open ascent lets us gaze across Fallen Leaf Lake toward Tahoe as we climb above the noise and congestion below. High on the slope, the seductive aroma of tobacco brush above lures us on to the crest, where our trail ends, the trailhead lying between the Angora Fire Lookout and the fire-watcher's residence just north of it.

From the lookout we obtain a commanding view of the southern Tahoe basin. High above it in the east we see deeply weathered granitic peaks. Freel Peak, at 10,881 feet, is the highest peak in the Tahoe Sierra, just barely nudging above its more glaciated close relative, Jobs Sister, immediately northeast of it. To the southeast we can look up the Upper Truckee canyon, in which the last receding glacier left 10 recessional moraines as it retreated up-canyon. Each moraine consists of a collection of rocks and debris left by the leading edge of a glacier while it was

Upper Angora Lake

temporarily stationary because the front of the glacier was melting at the same rate as more ice was arriving via glacial flow. To the south, more icy evidence is seen in the form of two cirques that have been gouged deep into the northeast face of Echo Peak. Unseen beyond its southeast ridge lie the popular Echo Lakes. Directly west and above us is Cathedral Peak, which is not a true peak but rather the steep, lower southwest flank of Mt. Tallac.

At the foot of Mt. Tallac and beyond, northwest of us, stand some imposing lateral moraines. Impressive though they are, they are a mile shorter and 400 feet lower than the mammoth moraine we're standing on. Ours forks into two ridges just north of us. If you were to walk about half a mile north and compare the two ridges, you'd find that the western one has more rocks and less soil compared to the eastern one, which is older and whose rocks have been longer exposed to weathering. About 15,000 years ago a glacier was spilling down Glen Alpine canyon into the valley filled today by Fallen Leaf Lake. This moving ice sheet was so thick that it stood higher than—and built up—the ridge we've just climbed up.

After soaking up all the views you can, follow the dusty Angora Ridge Road south to a parking lot just before a gate across the road. Here in a broad gully, our route back to Fallen Leaf Lake climbs northwest over a low saddle. If you've brought your bathing suit along, you might want to make a one-mile hike to the south shore of Upper Angora Lake. The Angora Lakes, and Angora Peak west of them, were named for the herds of Angora goats that were pastured by Nathan Gilmore, an early cattleman who discovered Glen Alpine Springs. From the southeast end of the lot take either the road or the trail up to Lower Angora Lake, then continue on the road to the upper lake. Here you can rent boats from Angora Lakes Resort and buy snacks at its small store. Hikers who've brought along their fishing rods will find both lakes stocked with native cutthroat trout. Swimmers may traverse the talus of the east shore to reach some good diving rocks above the south shore of this deep cirque lake. For super-high dives, up to 50+ feet, try the west cliffs.

Returning to the parking lot, we climb to a saddle, and then descend a forested trail—with several verdant oases of lush vegetation—steeply down to Trailhead 28, at the road fork by Fallen Leak Lake's southwest shore. If you were wondering about the change in rock textures and colors, it occurred because the grantic rocks above gave way to metamorphic rocks below. From Trailhead 28 walk 0.4 mile east along the paved road to Trailhead 27, Fallen Leaf Resort.

Fallen Leaf Lake and Lake Tahoe beyond

32   Tamarack Trail to Echo Peak

Distance: 7.0 miles, loop trip

Total gain/Net gain: 2650'/2450'

Classification: Strenuous

Season: Mid-July through mid-October

Parking: Always crowded; park where you can but don't obstruct access

Trailhead/Map: 29/8

Features: Almost every ascent to a mountain's summit provides the climber with far-ranging, panoramic views. This trip to the Echo Peak ridge and summit area certainly is no exception, but in addition it routes your return trip past Upper Angora Lake, an ideal relaxing site after your arduous climb. The wildflowers along the ascent are so abundant that the amateur botanist may feel fulfilled even if he never makes it to the top.

Description: Starting on metamorphic bedrock with granitic boulders transported here by a glacier, our trail enters an open forest of white fir and lodgepole and Jeffrey pine, with a rich substory of aspen, alder, willow, vine maple, tobacco brush, currant and spiraea. Beyond a low knoll we get a view of Mt. Tallac's dark back side, then enter a shady forest where we see white thimbleberry (with pink berries in late season), red columbine, purple monkshood and the green fronds of bracken fern. Less common is pine drops, and rare is snow plant, both being red saprophytes that live off decaying organic matter. Two large white firs mark the start of a steep ascent, but thirst on this climb can be slaked at a number of creeklets, each with its refreshing water plus its own population of water-loving plants.

Our grade eases and the forest opens as we approach a second knoll, from which we can look west-northwest at the two brownish-red metamorphic summits of Jacks and Dicks peaks. Perched nearby us is a huge, 20-foot-high orange-and-gray boulder of metamorphic rock in contact with the granitic rock that

Echo Peak

Indian Rock, Fallen Leaf Lake and Lake Tahoe

intruded the metamorphic rock just over 100 million years ago. Beyond it we are soon climbing up steep switchbacks through an overwhelming amount of vegetation. Finally emerging from this jungle, we make a short traverse west to a relatively barren flat on which a few hardy junipers survive. From here we see most of Fallen Leaf Lake and part of Tahoe beyond it. Now also visible are the summit rocks of rusty Mt. Tallac. Just above this flat is an exposed campsite, relatively close to a long-lasting snowfield; its rock may be hard, but its views down the glacier-carved canyon are heard to beat.

A short, climbing traverse west brings us to a dangerous creek we must jump across; should you slip, you're likely to go over the brink of a very steep cascade—a one-way trip. Short, steep switchbacks up a path gloriously lined with wildflowers take us to a safe recrossing of the creek and to some good rocks to stop at and rest, from which we can photograph the magnificent canyon and lateral moraines north of us.

Refreshed, we climb steeply up the wildflowered east bank of the creek, cross it after a 250-foot climb, and then continue up an increasingly easy grade that eventually levels off. Here we see a panorama from Tahoe, in the north, past Tallac, Dicks and Jacks summits to barely showing Pyramid Peak, in the west-southwest. The forest is now an open one of juniper, silver pine and mountain hemlock, and on the grassy slopes grow sagebrush, lupine, streptanthus, eriogonum, senecio, aster, cushion stenotus and phlox. If you are quiet you might observe a chicken-sized, chunky blue grouse nibbling away on berries or pine needles. An easy stroll now takes us down to a flat saddle with a trail intersection. To the north, the trail descends to Triangle Lake; south, it descends to the Echo Lakes (see Trip 26 for more details).

To climb Echo Peak, we retrace our steps 85 yards east to a rockpile, from where a faint, unmaintained trail continues east while the main trail we came up curves left. Fallen trees make the trail hard to follow in a few places, but the slope's topography and vegetation are so amenable to cross-country travel that you need not stick to the trail. From the junction, the trail soon turns northeast and then climbs steadily through an open forest that now includes whitebark pine; then, as it approaches the rocky northeast ridge of Echo Peak, it fades into nothingness.

Here it behooves you to walk 130 yards north to the brink of the ridge, from where you not only see everything you might have seen from the Angora Fire Lookout (Trip 31), but also have a better perspective of it all. Very conspicuous is Mt. Tallac's preglacial, almost flat erosion surface, which has remained little changed over the past few million years except that glaciers have cut a deep canyon into it. Before these ice-rivers came, the gentle southeast slope of Mt. Tallac descended almost to the spur one mile northwest of Echo Peak. Glaciers cut back into both of these rounded peaks, sculpting out steep, ragged faces, and successive glaciers cut back up the Glen Alpine Creek canyon, deepening it by 1300 feet and steepening its sides considerably.

An easy, ducked path southeast takes us to granitic, potholed Echo Peak, which provides us with an additional panorama, this one of the Crystal Range to the south and west. On the southeast horizon near Carson Pass stand Stevens and Red Lake peaks, both 10,061 feet in elevation. Like every other Tahoe peak, ours has its resident golden-mantled ground squirrel to inspect you or your pack, if you leave it for a minute.

To descend to Upper Angora Lake, follow a ducked trail northeast down through gruss, which is largely a surface accumulation of feldspar and quartz crystals that have broken off weathered granitic rock after the dark minerals disintegrated and freed them. The trail descends a very steep, minor northeast ridge of Echo Peak, and then continues down a gully so rich in gruss that you can almost ski down it. Large backpacks are definitely not recommended on this very steep descent. Several short-switchback routes descend northeast down this gully and merge on a flat 300 feet above the lake. Midway down the very steep gully you'll pass a facetious sign, *Caution—Maximum Speed 25 Mi.*

From the flat we descend northwest very steeply down another gully to Upper Angora Lake's southeast corner. Here you can traverse west to a rock slab above the south shore, from which you can high-dive into water that is incredibly deep for a lake this size. Lower diving points are available for the more cautious, but so too are very high rocks for any "Acapulco" diver. There is also plenty of room on the slab for those who just like to stretch out in the sun.

The trail from the southeast shore consists of a traverse across a large-block talus slope to the lake's outlet, then a walk northwest to Angora Lakes Resort. From here follow the Trip 31 description down to Trailhead 28 and hike southwest from it 0.4 mile back to your car near Trailhead 29.

Potholes and arch on Echo Peak; Freel Peak in background

33   Glen Alpine to Grass Lake

Distance: 5.0 miles, round trip

Total gain/Net gain: 740'/660'

Classification: Easy

Season: Early July through late October

Parking: Always crowded; park where you can, but don't obstruct access

Trailhead/Map: 30/8

Features: An easy day hike, this route leads you up to a rockbound lake with a dramatic cascade on the cliffs beyond it. Its fairly warm water is just right for a midsummer afternoon swim.

Description: From the gate follow the closed road past private residences as it more or less parallels Glen Alpine Creek westward to where the trail begins at the Desolation Wilderness border, just beyond Glen Alpine Springs. Nathan Gilmore discovered these iron-rich mineral springs while looking for his stray cattle in 1863. They were then gushing at about 200 gallons an hour. In the late 1870's Gilmore began bottling the carbonated water, which soon achieved a reputation, and he developed Glen Alpine Springs into a very popular resort.

We start up the Glen Alpine Trail, which climbs southeast about 200 yards before climbing west up a rocky, joint-controlled gully. An earlier trail, still visible, climbed up a gully above 100 yards from the trailhead. We make a switchback south out of our gully, curve around a low ridge, and walk west again to a small, waist-deep pool with a tiny fall splashing into it. Just beyond this cool bathtub, on a flat immediately before the trail bends northeast as it starts a switchbacking climb, we reach an easily missed junction with the Grass Lake Trail. From here, head a few

yards west past a frequently used campsite, jump across the creek from Gilmore Lake, and then follow the trail southwest up a brushy slope, inhabited by mountain quail, to reach a grassy pond that is an overflow of Glen Alpine Creek. The best spot to cross this creek is at some rapids below the pond, where water flows east down a small, granitic, 20-foot-high V gorge.

Beyond this crossing our trail winds almost up to the audible outlet creek of Lake Lucille. The older trail still climbs southwest to it before curving northwest to Grass Lake, but our trail curves north, passes northwest through a V trough, and then curves southwest and descends through another one. Joint control certainly expresses itself in this granodiorite bedrock. Just beyond the second trough our newer trail meets the older trail, and 100 yards farther we are at the southeast corner of shallow Grass Lake. The trail continues for 0.2 mile to a shallow bay, passing several campsites located too close to the shoreline to be legal. We then reach a campsite just east of the bay on a bench covered with fir and pine.

East of this are some open metavolcanic rocks, below which is the lake's deepest water. Here, an eight-foot-high rock bench makes an ideal platform for diving into the lake's fairly clear water, which warms up into the mid-60s. These brown rocks contrast strongly with the gray, joint-controlled granitic rocks that dam the lake's east end.

Fishing is poor because the lake is relatively small and is heavily fished. However, what may be lost in the way of a fish dinner is made up for by the lovely lakeside surroundings, including a silvery cascade from Susie Lake that plunges down the cliff northwest of us.

Grass Lake

34 Glen Alpine to Lake Aloha

Distance: 11.4 miles, round trip

Total gain/Net gain: 2050'1550'

Classification: Moderate

Season: Mid-July through mid-October

Parking: Always crowded; park where you can but don't obstruct access

Trailhead/Map: 30/7

Features: This trip takes you up to large, shallow Lake Aloha, which is probably the most popular lake in Desolation Wilderness. By arriving at its scenic northeast shore, however, you avoid most backpackers, who generally camp at its south shore. Rockbound Susie Lake, two-thirds of the way up to Aloha, is a favorite lake of many backpackers, and for late-season excursions it is a well chosen goal, because much of Aloha dries up after Labor Day.

Description: As in Trip 33 we start at the closed gate, walk 0.8 mile up the road to the Desolation Wilderness boundary, and then hike up the new Glen Alpine Trail to a small flat just above a splashing trailside pool. Above this flat we take a newer trail segment that switchbacks north up a brushy, open-forested granitic slope, where frisky golden-mantled ground squirrels scamper about. Immediately before reaching an alder-lined, step-across creeklet, we meet a junction with

the older trail, which climbed straight up to here from the flat.

After a refreshing sip from the creeklet, we start up our trail and quickly reach a third segment of newer trail, which we climb northwest to a reunion with the older and steeper but shady creekside segment. An ascent west up creekside metamorphic bedrock gets us to Gilmore Lake's outlet creek—which we must wade in early summer—and then in 30 yards we reach a signed trail fork. The right fork climbs to a junction with trails to Dicks Pass, Gilmore Lake and Mt. Tallac. We take the left fork, which makes an initial climb west, traverses through a lodgepole forest past four lily-pad ponds, and then descends westward to join the Tahoe-Yosemite/Pacific Crest Trail. Here, at the upper end of a boggy meadow, you can identify an abundant variety of wildflowers—after mid-August, when the mosquitoes aren't pestering you to death. Identified by their aromas are swamp onion, lupine and pennyroyal. Also look for alpine lilies, corn lilies, buttercup, ligusticum, paintbrush, arnica, yarrow, aster and columbine.

From the junction our route follows the TYT/PCT west past Susie and Heather lakes up to Lake Aloha. See the first part of Trip 30 for a more complete description, in reverse.

Golden-mantled ground squirrel

35   Glen Alpine to Half Moon and Alta Morris Lakes

Distance: 10.4 miles, round trip

Total gain/Net gain: 1910'/1600'

Classification: Moderate

Season: Late July through mid-October

Parking: Always crowded; park where you can but don't obstruct access

Trailhead/Map: 30/7

Features: Situated on the corrugated bedrock floor of an immense cirque, these two lakes see relatively little use despite their accessibility; they are bypassed for lakes in more demure settings along the highly popular Tahoe-Yosemite/Pacific Crest Trail. Within this cirque basin you're almost guaranteed to find a suitable, isolated campsite.

Description: From the Gilmore Lake outlet creek junction where Trip 34 forks left, our route forks right. We make a ¼-mile ascent up a rocky path, climbing steadily above a shallow tarn below us to a juniper-flat junction

with the Tahoe-Yosemite/Pacific Crest Trail, and go straight ahead.

Our trail starts a contour northwest as a narrow footpath, then becomes more distinct as it arcs west across a small, forested bowl. Leaving the bowl, we climb to a low ridge and see Susie Lake, nestled in her metamorphic bed. On the skyline, granitic Pyramid Peak stands at the south end of a long, snowy stretch of the Crystal Range. Leaving this viewpoint, we descend slightly into a shallow gully, go up it, cross a low ridge bordering it, and then traverse a lodgepole flat and a mucky-banked creeklet flowing through it. With mud falling from our boots, we climb up the southwest slope of yet another gully and soon approach a chest-deep pond, on the left, which has drinkable water and at times an aquatic garter snake or two. After passing two smaller ponds on our right, which support pond lilies and other aquatic vegetation, we come to a grass-lined pond with a campsite on

Half Moon Lake

its northeast shore. Since this site is within 100 feet of the shoreline, it is off limits to camping, so if you want to camp in this vicinity, try above the south or west shores.

From a low ridge immediately beyond the last pond, we see clear, blue, appropriately named Half Moon Lake, which occupies almost the entire width of the huge cirque carved out between Jacks Peak and Dicks Pass. Not only is this the largest cirque in Desolation Wilderness, but it is also the deepest, and the lake is hemmed in on three sides by a dark wall of steep rock that averages ¼ mile high.

The trail makes an undulating traverse across the meadowy talus slope of metamorphic rock that borders the lake's north and west shores. In some places the trail is boggy; in others it is indistinct and somewhat overgrown with willows. Eventually you'll reach a fairly large campsite, nestled under silver pines and mountain hemlocks, on a bench above the northwest shore of Alta

Morris Lake. This lake, perhaps the most scenic cirque lake in Desolation Wilderness, rests above the southwest corner of Half Moon Lake, and it can be approached by a more direct, drier, cross-country route.

Starting this route when you first see Half Moon Lake, head west and stay on the rocky bench above its south shore. On the map this route looks almost level, but in reality you ascend and descend across a number of small, glacier-cut gullies. Midway across your washboard traverse you'll cross Half Moon's outlet creek, which cascades into a clear, linear, grassy-bottomed lake—nice for swimming in or camping nearby. Continuing west toward the dark rusty-brown metasediments that buttress Jacks Peak, we walk across buff-colored metavolcanic bedrock that contrast strongly with them. Soon we reach one or more small, semistagnant ponds and, just beyond them, the northeast bench above Alta Morris Lake. This lake, like Half Moon Lake, is stocked with both brown and golden trout.

36   Glen Alpine to Gilmore Lake and Mt. Tallac

Distance: 11.6 miles, round trip

Total gain/Net gain: 3230'/3170'

Classification: Moderate

Season: Early July through mid-October

Parking: Always crowded; park where you can, but don't obstruct access

Trailhead/Maps: 30/8,9

Features: Of all the significant peaks you can climb by trail, Mt. Tallac is the closest one to the shore of Lake Tahoe. Consequently, your view of the lake is truly exceptional, and it is highlighted by the dramatic topography of the prodigous lateral moraines that border Emerald Bay, Cascade Lake and Fallen Leaf Lake. Gilmore Lake, along your ascent route, is an ideal spot to rest or camp before making the final push for the summit.

Description: Follow Trip 34 and up to the Gilmore Lake outlet creek junction, fork right, and climb to the juniper-flat Tahoe-Yosemite/Pacific Crest Trail junction. From here Trip 35 continues straight ahead to Half Moon and Alta Morris lakes, but this trip switchbacks north up a ½-mile segment of the TYT/PCT. Along this open ascent past large, rusty-barked junipers, we can look south to shallow Grass Lake and southwest to sparsely tree-lined Susie Lake. Just before our trail comes alongside Gilmore Lake's cascading outlet creek, we catch a glimpse of granite-lined Lake Aloha in the southwest. Veering slightly away from the creek, we reach an almost level junction in an open lodgepole forest.

The TYT/PCT turns west and continues its climb to Dicks Pass (see Trip 30), but we head north, cross the creek and arrive at good, lodgepole-shaded campsites above the south-

east shore of Gilmore Lake. In the entire Sierra there is hardly a lake more circular than this one, and it is amazing that it doesn't bear the name *Round Lake,* especially when you consider how many noncircular lakes in the Sierra do bear this name. Instead, it was named in honor of Nathan Gilmore, a local settler from 1863 onward, who in 1887 stocked this lake with 20 black bass. Now it has a population of rainbow, brook and brown trout.

Beyond this lake our trail climbs steeply, first northeast and then north, heading up through a rapidly thinning forest of lodgepole and whitebark pines and crossing three flower-lined creeklets. We hike to within 200 yards of a 9000-foot saddle, then switchback east up the grass- and sagebrush-lined trail. Mixed with these shrubs are subalpine wildflowers such as cushion stenotus, aster, senecio, ligusticum, pennyroyal, phlox, eriogonum and mariposa lily. *Mariposa* in Spanish means "butterfly", and indeed, the creamy-white petals of this flower surely do resemble butterfly wings.

Four hundred feet below the summit we reach a junction with the faint Floating Island Trail, which descends Tallac's southeast slope and then curves north down toward Highway 89. Trip 37 describes the route from this junction to the summit, the views seen and the significant geomorphic features. You can make a loop trip by following Trip 37 down to a junction with the Stanford Sierra Camp-Mt. Tallac Trail, then following that trail down to the camp and from there hiking back up the road to your car.

Crystal Range and Gilmore Lake

37   Mt. Tallac via Floating Island Trail

Distance: 9.2 miles, round trip
Total gain/Net gain: 3320'/3260'
Classification: Strenuous
Season: Mid-July through mid-October
Parking: Adequate parking along roadside
Trailhead/Map: 31/9

Features: Like Trip 36, this one takes you to Tallac's summit, but it does so in fewer miles. Two small lakes—one of them unique—are passed along your way up this route, which has more views but fewer campsites than Trip 36.

Description: From a signed trailhead where the road bends southwest away from Tallac Creek, we start out southeast, cross the creek after 60 yards, and parallel its northbound tributary from Floating Island Lake. Our initial trail through a dense white-fir forest, with occasional aspens, becomes increasingly steeper, wider and more open, with spacious Jeffrey pines, scrubby huckleberry oaks, thorny snow bush, red-barked manzanita and aromatic tobacco brush. About one mile up the trail, where red firs become conspicuous, we cross the quiet creek and climb steeply to a

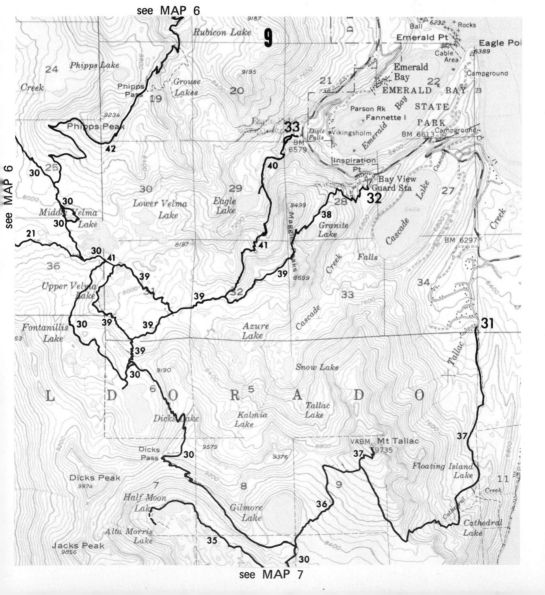

see MAP 6

see MAP 7

Fallen Leaf Lake, Tahoe Keys and Freel Peak

recrossing of it. We get a short breather in a traverse of a block-filled depression, but then are forced to make another stiff climb, which takes us up to a crossing of the creek just below the outlet of shallow Floating Island Lake. In 1890 this lake was noted as having a 20-foot-diameter floating mat of grass and shrubs, whence the name. In 1974 there was still a grassy mat. Along the trail above the lake's northeast shore is a fair, well-used campsite. Mosquitoes, however, will prevent you from enjoying it until they diminish in numbers around mid-August.

We now climb southwest above the lake, and then, near the inlet creek and just past a small pond, reach a junction with an unmaintained trail that descends southeast and to join the ducked route. That trail then crosses Cathedral Creek and immediately joins the Stanford Sierra Camp-Cathedral Lake Trail. We continue southwest steeply up our trail, lined with wildflowers, currant, western serviceberry, sagebrush and the other shrubs we've seen, and soon we come to a saddle immediately west of a little rocky knoll. From its juniper-covered summit, free of mosquitoes, we can relax and take in a panorama that includes most of Lake Tahoe, some of Fallen Leaf Lake and beyond it the granitic summits of the Freel Peak massif.

Mt. Tallac's summit area is now visible, and it beckons us onward, so we make a brief descent to Cathedral Creek, cross it, pass the Stanford Sierra Camp-Cathedral Lake Trail junction, and then, in a few minutes, reach Cathedral Lake. Named for its proximity to Cathedral Peak—which is not a peak but rather a cliff on Tallac's southeast ridge—this shallow, barren lake is a disappointment. However, its water is more drinkable than that of Floating Island Lake.

After climbing very steeply west 200 feet above this lake, we reach a trail segment with fresh, cold water running along it. Bordered with common monkey flower, forget-me-not, tall larkspur, fireweed, thimbleberry and other hydrophytic wildflowers, this short stretch is an excellent place to take a lunch break, since it may be your last dependable source of water. Beyond it our trail climbs steadily and steeply up the sloping floor of a cirque toward its headwall, which usually has snow fields well into August. Several trails, formed on talus through continual use, try to avoid most of the snow. The correct route has a switchback leg that climbs south up to the ridge and tops it at a point immediately west of where the trail curves from southeast to east. Standing atop it, we get great views east, south and west—a taste of what's to come.

We leave the edge of the ridge as we hike northwest up an increasingly steep trail bordered by currant, gooseberry, snow bush, spiraea and sagebrush. Scattered clumps of silver, lodgepole and whitebark pines speckle the slope. Near the 9000-foot level, the brush diminishes and wildflowers become more predominant. Finally we reach a junction with the larger, more evident trail from Gilmore Lake (see Trip 36). Enjoying a breather while taking in a view of many lakes below, we can identify circular Gilmore Lake in its cirque southwest of us, Susie Lake on a bench beyond it, and Lake Aloha along the east base of the granitic Crystal Range.

There being now only 400 vertical feet to climb to the summit, we start with more determination than ever, climbing north steeply up an increasingly faint though ducked trail, or up one of its parallel branches. Midway to the summit this trail cuts east up to a weatherbeaten clump of conifers, which makes a good wind-protected emergency shelter, but it is no place to sit out a lightning storm. You shouldn't attempt to climb to this summit—or any summit—if a storm is impending.

We now follow a rocky route, first northeast to the brink of a dangerously steep avalanche chute, then diagonally northwest for the last few steps to the pointed summit. Most panoramas from any high summit are spectacular, and those from dark, metamorphic Mt. Tallac certainly are. Because it stands so close to Lake Tahoe, it provides us with a view of almost the entire lake. Standing above Tahoe's northeast end is andesite-capped Mt. Rose, which at 10,776 feet is the basin's third highest peak. Along the east shore rise the granitic western slopes of the Carson Range, which remain unglaciated because they lie within a rain shadow cast by the Sierra crest above Tahoe's western shore. Today the western crest receives 70–90 inches of precipitation annually, whereas the eastern crest receives only about 30–40 inches.

Along the lake's south shore are the readily visible Tahoe Keys, which together with the high rises stand out in this basin as a monument to man's economic exploitation of a unique, fault-dropped, high-mountain lake basin. Southeast of this shore rise Freel Peak (10,881') and Jobs Sister (10,823'), ranking first and second among the basin's peaks. In the distance to the southeast is the 10,000-foot-high ridge near Carson Pass. To the south rises granitic Echo Peak, and beyond it Ralston Peak, the unseen Echo Lakes lying between them. West of Ralston Peak is Pyramid Peak, the high point and south end of the Crystal Range.

Of much interest are the huge, linear, lateral moraines that border Emerald Bay, Cascade Lake and Fallen Leaf Lake. Towering up to 900 feet above their basins, the heights of these moraines indicate the minimum thickness of the glacier that filled the basins. Since each of these glaciers also scoured its basin and made it deeper, it is likely, in the case of the Fallen Leaf glacier, that the glacier was ¼ mile thick. The Tahoe basin must have been an extremely impressive sight 15,000 years ago. At times, equally large glaciers from Squaw Valley, and from Pole Creek north of it, dammed Tahoe's northwest outlet and raised the lake's level by as much as 600 feet. Then these glacial-ice dams broke, creating catastrophic floods much larger than the recent one along the Rubicon River (see Trip 1). Take your time at the summit, crowded on weekends, and try to visualize the evolving landscape of this majestic basin.

Up here with all the hikers you might find a fat marmot freeloading off their luncheon leftovers. Other fauna include a variety of insects wafted up here by updrafts.

Cascade Lake, Emerald Bay and Lake Tahoe

38   Bay View to Granite Lake

Distance: 2.4 miles, round trip

Total gain/Net gain: 810'/810'

Classification: Moderate

Season: Early July through late October

Parking: Bay View Picnic Area; if crowded, use Inspiration Point Picnic Area

Trailhead/Map: 32/9

Features: A pleasant day hike, the Granite Lake Trail leads you up to the fragrant shores of lovely Granite Lake, a good lake for swimming since it is one of the Tahoe basin's warmest lakes.

Description: From the top end of the loop in Bay View Picnic Area we walk 40 yards upslope to a road that immediately forks. We take the right fork, which curves northwest, and in 100 yards reach the start of the Granite Lake Trail. Climbing moderately on it through a dense white-fir forest with a chinquapin understory, we switchback up to a sharp bend in a jeep road. We could have hiked southwest up this very steep road to reach this bend, but the effort wouldn't have been worth it. Now we follow it northwest up to the top of a ridge of weathered granodiorite bedrock, and there leave it for a trail that climbs southeast alongside Granite Lake's trickling, alder-lined outlet creek. Also along it we find water-loving wildflowers, including Bolander's yampah, or olaski, as the Miwok Indians called it, who ate the roots of this wild carrot. Don't pick this plant because first, it is illegal to do so, and second, there are some poisonous wild carrots that closely resemble it.

The sensuous aroma of tobacco brush heralds our approach to clear, moderately large Granite Lake. If you're descending to this lake, as in Trip 21, you'll appreciate the relatively warm water—up to 70°F—of this moraine-dammed lake. There are no large campsites, but small ones lie along its east and north shores.

Brook trout

39 Bay View to Dicks Lake and the Velma Lakes

Distance: 10.9 miles, semiloop trip
Total gain/Net gain: 2890'/1630'
Classification: Strenuous
Season: Mid-July through mid-October
Parking: Bay View Picnic Area; if crowded, use Inspiration Point Picnic Area
Trailhead/Map: 32/9

Features: A good weekend backpack trip, this route exposes you to a variety of popular lakes. The numerous trails in the Velma Lakes area allows you to put together a custom tour through it.

Description: Trip 38 describes our route up to Granite Lake. From just above the west shore we climb three sandy switchback legs up through manzanita and chinquapin under the canopy of an open stand of red fir, silver pine and lodgepole pine. Nearing the base of an exposed, weathered granodiorite ridge, we climb steeply south along it up to a set of tight, steep switchbacks. Breathing heavily from this unrelenting ascent, we stop, catch our breath and take in the stunning view below (front-cover photograph). At our feet rests deep-blue Granite Lake. Beyond it and encompassed by large lateral moraines lie Cascade Lake and Emerald Bay. If Lake Tahoe, which we see beyond them, were to have its level raised by 250 feet or more, as has happened in the past, then Cascade Lake would be transformed into an Emerald Bay and then, like Emerald Bay, it might qualify for state-park status. It is, like so much of the Tahoe basin, still in private hands.

After completing the switchbacks, we cross over the ridge that joins the two Maggie Peaks, and, a few steps northwest of the trail, look dizzily down at Eagle Lake. Our hike is now an easy one, as we traverse the conifer-clad northwest slope of South Maggies Peak, and then descend to a shallow saddle from which we switchback down to the crest of the peak's slabby southwest ridge. Following a meandering path that gradually arcs west-ward, we reach, after ⅓ mile, a junction with the Eagle Lake Trail (Trip 41), which descends steeply northeast.

We continue west, reach a small granitic flat that can be wet until early August, and then engage a short, rocky climb up a brushy slope almost to a saddle. Here we reach an ankle-deep, 10-yard-long tarn on our left. The main trail to the Velma Lakes turns northwest

here and in 100 yards tops the saddle, on which you'll find another tarn, twice as long. We make an easy climb southwest, soon losing our brief sight of the dark-gray, metamorphic-capped summit of Mt. Tallac in the southeast, and then we pass two small tarns before passing a third one that is ringed with lodgepoles. Beyond it we quickly reach a shallow, serene lakelet that drains northwest into Upper Velma Lake. If you've wondered what exactly is meant by *joint control,* then take a close look at the glaciated granodiorite slope above this lakelet. The straight, usually snowfilled gash descending across it is a good example. The forces that brought about the

Joint-controlled gully

uplift of this mountain range caused the rock to fracture. The fractures, termed *joints* by geologists, are straight lines in which plants can get a roothold, along which glaciers can quarry, and down which water can run. Consequently, these straight cracks get progressively more eroded, first to troughs, then to gullies, and finally to canyons. Since the development of a drainage system is not random but rather is concentrated along the more erodable joints, the landscape is said to be "joint-controlled."

After perhaps taking a lunch break or a brief swim in this snow-fed lakelet, we leave it and its abundant frog population, cross its outlet creek, and then climb gently southwest 200 yards to a junction with a trail that we'll follow northwest down to Upper Velma Lake. But first we'll climb up to Dicks Lake, since it is too scenic to miss now that we've come so close to it.

One-third mile of short switchbacks brings us to a saddle from where two trail forks lead south and east, both short spurs going to the Tahoe-Yosemite Trail. Follow the south spur a brief 250 yards downslope, then take another short spur to campsites along the north shore of dramatically rimmed Dicks Lake. The metamorphic, dark, rusty-brown west cliffs below Dicks Peak contrast strongly with the gray granitic rocks we've been treading on. After your stay at this lake, however long or short, you can hike north or south along the Tahoe-Yosemite Trail—which here coincides with the Pacific Crest Trail—by consulting Trip 30.

For this trip, 39, we return to the trail leading northwest down to Upper Velma Lake. Starting down it, we quickly reach a

knee-deep pond on our left, then continue along a ducked, winding, slab route down to the south end of heather-fringed Upper Velma Lake. Soon we boulder-hop a creek coming down from Fontanillis Lake, pass by a linear pond on our right, and then curve north to a peninsula on the west side of Upper Velma Lake. This lake's "claim to fame" is its "lake within a lake." You can step across on rocks to its large, tree-covered island and see for yourself. The lake on it isn't too impressive though—just a grassy, semistagnant pond. Because this lake abounds with shoreline mountain hemlock, Labrador tea and red heather—all being havens for mosquitoes—expect to be bitten until after mid-August. Or you could continue north ½ mile to a trail junction where there are better campsites. Fresh running water is obtained east of them at the fairly deep outlet creek of a shallow, unnamed lake immediately below Upper Velma Lake.

At the trail junction one could proceed west 180 yards to a reunion with the TYT/PCT above the popular south shore of Middle Velma Lake, but our route heads east and crosses a five-yard-wide creek. To keep your feet dry, try crossing about 30 yards upstream. We promptly pass two small tarns, one on each side, and then reach the unnamed lake, fringed with grass and lodgepoles growing on bedrock, a popular camping area on weekends. On our trail beyond it, we negotiate a winding, sometimes stiff ascent through an open forest up to a saddle with a tarn, 100 yards beyond which we intercept the faint trail we took to Dicks Lake. From here we retrace our steps back to Granite Lake and Bay View Picnic Area.

Upper Velma Lake

40   Emerald Bay to Eagle Lake

Distance: 2.0 miles, round trip

Total gain/Net gain: 530'/420'

Classification: Moderate

Season: Early July through late October

Parking: About three dozen cars; overflowing on weekends—then park alongside highway

Trailhead/Map: 33/9

Features: Best as a dayhike, this trip introduces you to a popular fishermen's lake. For climbers, this lake serves as a base camp from which they can try extended, difficult climbing on the steep walls of Eagle Lake canyon.

Description: Fifty yards west of the parking lot, a road forks south 25 yards to a choice of two trails. You can either climb moderately up a trail lined with thick, tall brush—no hiking shorts or wide packs, please—or you can contour southwest to Eagle Lake's outlet creek and then climb—literally, with hands as well as feet—up to the top of a rock cliff, on which you meet the other branch. From here the route descends to a bridge, crosses it and heads south toward an obvious *Trail* sign nailed to a lodgepole pine.

Our trail traverses the foot of a blocky talus slope, climbs up to a bench, and then swings west to a second bench, on which lie erratic boulders transported down-canyon by a glacier. From this bench we can look northeast down at Emerald Bay and out to the Carson Range above Tahoe. Beyond the bench we cross a small lodgepole flat where people have camped, round a low headwall, and parallel Eagle Lake's outlet creek. Shortly we reach another flat, shaded by white fir and Jeffrey pine, on which there is a fair campsite between the trail and the creek. We now make a brief ascent, see the creek's rapids, and catch a glimpse of Eagle Lake as we reach a well-used spur trail that goes 200 yards over the bedrock to the lake.

Hemmed in by granitic cliffs, this picturesque lake is a good area for climbers, who can establish a base camp above the north shore. A climbers guide, published by and available from the Tahoe City Department of Parks and Recreation, adequately describes some of the climbs in this canyon. The guide, however, is unbelievably vague in describing approaches to these climbs, and finding them is half the challenge for the climber. Nonclimbers will find a photogenic lake to relax at, to photograph or to fish in. The lake is stocked with rainbow, brook and brown trout.

Eagle Lake

41   Emerald Bay to Middle Velma, Fontanillis and Dicks Lakes

Distance: 10.9 miles, semiloop trip

Total gain/Net gain: 2750'/1920'

Classification: Strenuous

Season: Mid-July through mid-October

Parking: About three dozen cars; overflowing on weekends—then park alongside highway

Trailhead/Map: 33/9

Features: Despite its difficulty, the trail up Eagle Lake canyon is one of the most popular in the Lake Tahoe region, for it takes you, in a few hours time, to the Dicks Lake-Velma Lakes area. By making a loop through this area, we pass five lakes and one lakelet, all good for swimming in or camping by.

Description: Trip 40 describes the moderate ascent up to Eagle Lake. Beyond this lake, the Eagle Lake Trail climbs steeply up to a saddle and a junction with the Granite Lake Trail. On this strenuous climb, aromatic tobacco brush, drab huckleberry oak, and needle-tipped snow bush dominate the vegetation. This section is a bad one for wearing shorts along or carrying a large pack up.

After we pass under the towering cliff of North Maggies Peak—a challenge to rock climbers—we arrive at a gully, shaded by pine and fir, that has a small creek trickling down it.

Short, steep switchbacks take us up the gully's west side, and as the gradient eases, an old branch of the trail climbs west out of the forest cover, but our route switchbacks southeast one more time before curving west and rejoining the old route. From the reunion, follow ducks up a barren slab to a small lodgepole flat, whose west side the trail traverses for 50 yards before it climbs south-southwest up to and through a clump of alders, arriving at the base of an outcrop. After an initial 30-yard climb west along this base, our trail—indistinct over the last ¼ mile—becomes obvious, and we climb south steeply up a slope and then traverse to a rocky bench on the west ridge of South Maggies Peak. These two similar, pointed peaks, popular conversation pieces for 19th century Lake Tahoe boaters, were not named for Maggie, but rather for part of her anatomy. Back in those days, however, the two peaks' names were more explicit.

A short, steep switchback leg takes us down from the bench, and then we make a traverse high above a large pond overgrown with grass and lily pads. Along the trail we find, in an alder thicket, a trickling spring, which is our last dependable fresh water until we reach Velma Lakes creek, about two miles farther.

Middle Velma Lake

Beyond the spring we switchback up to an ephemeral creek, cross it, and climb a gradually easing slope up to the saddle on which we meet the Granite Lake Trail. Now we follow part of Trip 39, heading west 0.6 mile to a junction beside a 30-yard-long shallow tarn. We go right, immediately top a broad saddle, and then descend northwest to a shallow, unnamed Velma lake and cross its wide outlet creek 30 yards upstream from where the trail actually crosses it. By hiking downstream 0.4 mile cross-country, you can reach less crowded Lower Velma Lake. In 100 yards we reach campsites at a junction with a trail to Upper Velma and Dicks lakes (see Trip 39).

Continuing west for 180 more yards, we meet the Pacific Crest Trail, which descends north from hemlock-bordered Fontanillis Lake. We walk west on the PCT a short distance, until we see rainbow-trout-stocked Middle Velma Lake, a fairly large, island-dotted lake that is better for swimming than for fishing. When you are ready to leave this popular lake, rather than retrace your steps back to the trailhead, climb south up the PCT to Fontanillis and Dicks lakes, following part of Trip 30 in reverse. Then from Dicks Lake head north to the low saddle above it, following part of Trip 39 in reverse. You'll descend past a lakelet below a steep joint-controlled slope before you'll reach the trail junction next to the 30-yard-long tarn, near a saddle, that you earlier hiked by. From it, retrace your steps back to Emerald Bay.

42   Meeks Bay to Middle Velma Lake

Distance: 25.9 miles, semiloop trip
Total gain/Net gain: 4130'/2220'
Classification: Moderate
Season: Late July through mid-October
Parking: Roadside parking, very crowded on weekends
Trailhead/Map: 34/6

Features: This route takes the backpacker along the northernmost part of the Tahoe-Yosemite Trail, which also happens to be one of its best parts, since along it we pass one lake right after another. Our return is partly along the famous Pacific Crest Trail, which offers us a forested, lakeless environment before we take a lateral back to the TYT again.

Description: Our route starts west along a closed road at the north edge of Meeks Bay Stables. The road is supposedly closed to all vehicles, but there seems to be some use along it and the side roads branching from it. A horse trail from the stables parallels the road, crossing and recrossing it. After passing two forks going left, our 1⅓-mile-long road—lined with white fir, incense-cedar and lodgepole, ponderosa and sugar pines—enters Forest Service land.

Near the upper end of a grassy swamp, on the left, we reach the signed trailhead for the Tahoe-Yosemite Trail, on our right. The road continues ⅓ mile to Meeks Camp. On trail, we climb moderately for ⅓ mile up the huge lateral moraine the road was following, and meet a spur trail that descends southeast to Meeks Camp. One hundred yards later we pass a dripping trailside spring, and then continue up a now gentler trail to flower-lined Meeks Creek. Here we find swamp whiteheads, asters, Indian pinks, thimbleberries and bracken ferns as well as the inevitable alders and willows that try to monopolize its waters.

Our ascent now becomes almost negligible as we progress southwest, paralleling the usually unseen creek along a large, mostly forested flat. We hike along the south edges of three dry meadows that sprout variable amounts of lupine and mule ears, and offer potential campsites along their border. Beyond the last one we parallel the creek up a moderate ascent that has two older trail segments along it, both branching left but quickly rejoining the TYT. Where we reach a second forested flat, we also reach a third trail segment, this branching right and dying out upstream.

In this higher, forested valley, the more alpine red fir, Jeffrey pine and silver pine have replaced their less alpine look-alikes: white fir, ponderosa pine and sugar pine. Incense-cedar was the first to go, but a somewhat similar tree, the juniper, will be seen on exposed rocky benches above. Lodgepole pine—an inhabitant of several vegetational, climatic and edaphic zones—remains with us.

Crag Peak, from Hidden Lake

We angle south gently down to a quickly reached large campsite beside Meeks Creek, find suitable rocks on which to cross the creek, and climb a moderately ascending path as it arcs east into a shady, moist, red-fir-forested cove rich in vine maple, currant, thimbleberry and fireweed. Then, winding southwest up the cove's south slope, we soon arrive at a much drier, more open ridge, a good resting spot from which we can just barely see Lake Tahoe. Climbing again, we have a short, pleasant stretch beside cascading Meeks Creek as we hike up to warm, shallow Lake Genevieve, lowest of the Tallant Lakes. In 1895, California's Fish Commission authorized the stocking of these lakes with Great Lakes Mackinaw fingerlings. When fully grown, these trout top 30 pounds. They migrated down Meeks Creek into Lake Tahoe, grew, and were eventually blamed by Tahoe fishermen with destroying Tahoe's native cutthroat trout. Since all large trout are known to cannibalize smaller trout, the Mackinaws weren't the only culprits. Besides, commercial fishing had been going on unrestricted for decades, first to feed the mining populations in western Nevada's silver mines, then later to supply more distant markets, and very little effort had been put into restocking the lake. (In like manner, the forests were mowed down to provide timber for mines, fuel and mining buildings, and then the denuded slopes were abandoned.) Today you'll have to go to the Angora Lakes (Trip 31) to catch cutthroats; Tahoe has Mackinaw, rainbow and brown trout and Kokanee salmon, but no cutthroat trout. The Tallant Lakes have Mackinaw, rainbow, brown and brook trout.

Along Lake Genevieve's northeast shore you'll see old blazes that mark a narrow trail striking northwest toward the lake's outlet. We'll be returning on this trail later in our trip. There are campsites around this lake, some even with a good view of domineering Crag Peak (Peak 9054 on the map), but since most of them are within 100 feet of the lake, we move onward upstream and quickly reach larger, more appealing Crag Lake, from which Crag Peak rises in all its granitic glory. Like Lake Genevieve downstream and Stony Ridge Lake upstream, Crag Lake has a low dam, so you can expect its water to fluctuate slightly. Good trailside campsites are found along much of its northeast shore, and those willing to make the extra effort will find more secluded campsites on a granitic bench midway along the lake's southwest shore.

Shadow Lake

After a pleasant stay, continue your TYT trek southeast, climbing up to a boulder-hop ford of Meeks Creek, and then encounter an unsigned trail junction on a ridge just beyond it. This side trail descends to shallow Hidden Lake, nestled at the foot of Crag Peak. Climbers wishing to attempt one or more of the very difficult Class 5 routes up the 400-foot northeast cliff of Crag Peak can reach it by following the glacial trough that curves up to it from the south end of this lake.

From the Hidden Lake Trail junction, we climb up the ridge, a lateral moraine, and then curve east to another ridge, this one being a recessional moraine that has dammed diminishing Shadow Lake, below us. The eventual fate of all lakes is extinction, and Shadow Lake is well on its way. Sediments have filled it to such an extent that pond lilies have invaded the upper half of the lake. Close behind them in the marshy water are hydrophytic grasses and wildflowers. Pursuing them on mucky soil are currants and alders. In time the lower half will become a meadow, while the upper half will be sprouting lodgepole pines and mountain hemlocks. Eventually almost all traces of the lake will disappear under the floor of a red fir and silver pine forest. About that time—perhaps 1000 years hence—a glacier may well be advancing down the Tallant Lakes canyon, obliterating all the vegetation in its path.

Leaving this swampy lake behind, we hike along a moderately graded trail that momen-tarily becomes steeper as it climbs alongside Meeks Creek, whose water is tumbling in cascades and rapids down a granitic gorge. Above the gorge we reach Stony Ridge Lake, largest of the Tallant Lakes. Here, the best campsite of many available may be the one above its north end, just across the low dam. Our trail contours the long, southwest shoreline, briefly crosses some mafic rock, and fords several creeks, which are bordered by yampah, larkspur, columbine, common monkey flower and other wildflowers. The dark, mafic bedrock is similar to granitic bedrock in that it was intruded from below up into overlying rocks that have since been eroded. It differs in that it is much richer in iron and magnesium—hence the darker color.

At the lake's southwest corner we cross and immediately recross the lake's inlet creek, proceed south along the west edge of a boggy meadow, and then, near an impressive, low-angle cliff of granodiorite, start up a series of well-graded switchbacks, bounded by two tributaries. After almost reaching a steep, churning cascade, we turn onto the last switchback, climb southwest, and get hemlock-framed views below of Stony Ridge Lake and its damp meadow. We soon curve south into a little, willow-lined creek cove, bordered by steep, vertical-jointed cliffs. Now a short climb southeast past a tiny tarn takes us to Rubicon Lake's west shore. Dammed by a ridge of resistant bedrock, beautiful Rubicon Lake is the highest of the Tallant Lakes, which, because they form a line of "beads" along the creek that connects them, are called *paternoster lakes,* after their resemblance to beads on a rosary. Fairly close to the water is a good campsite under mountain hemlocks and lodgepole pines. A large decaying log near the camp serves as home and food for large, black carpenter ants and other invertebrates as well as home for golden-mantled ground squirrels, who may find your pack their most enjoyable source of food. Don't spoil them on processed food.

The lake's water is a bit nippy, reaching only into the low 60s, but a tempting rock just off the west shore beckons one to jump into the cold, clear water. After you climb out to bask atop this rock, you can peer over its edge and see 10-inch trout swimming lazily below you.

Above the lake's south end we reach an unsigned trail that descends to the Grouse Lakes, which are a bit stagnant, and then 15 yards beyond the junction we top a saddle. Our trail then switchbacks up to a granodiorite outlier, just beyond which we can look back at it and see how joints—elaborated upon in Trip 39—really control its angular shape. We pass a small gully, snowbound as late as early August, then reach a switchback. Before climbing any farther, you might stop, rest under a juniper or a silver pine, and enjoy the view in the southeast. Looking beyond the north end of Fallen Leaf Lake, we see Tahoe Mountain immediately above it, and from its slopes a long, level ridge—debris left by glaciers—extends southward. Although this ridge, a glacial moraine, towers 900 feet above the lake, that doesn't mean the morainal deposits are 900 feet deep; if we were to tunnel into it, we would surely find granitic bedrock underlying these *surficial* sediments.

A switchback leg north takes us higher up the joint-controlled rocks, and then our trail climbs moderately southward and crosses a gully. You can climb a very steep unmaintained trail up this gully to the crest, about 120 feet above, and descend 320 feet down an equally steep slope to cold, circular Phipps Lake. The TYT, reinforced with railroad ties, now climbs above Phipps Pass, which is the saddle about 50 feet below us.

The route ahead, except for a few trivial gains, is all downhill. After almost cresting the ridge, our trail traverses granitic slabs and boulders along the southeast slope of Phipps Peak, named after General William Phipps,

who settled along his ("the General's") creek near Sugar Pine Point. We encounter a spring, then swing around to the peak's open south slope, from which we can see the Velma Lakes in the gray, granitic basin below us, and the rusty, metamorphic summit of Dicks Peak towering above it. The contact between the two rock types is clearly evident.

On the TYT we curve northwest, re-enter an open forest of mountain hemlocks and lodgepole, silver and whitebark pines, pass some scolding Clark nutcrackers flying from tree to tree, and then come within 40 yards of a ridge. Here we get poor, hemlock-blocked views northward. Our route now descends southwest, almost reaching the ridge again, then traces three long, well-graded switchback legs down to a junction with the Pacific Crest Trail. Along this descent we thrice cross a trickling creek and we pass many large red firs. Some of the older firs, now in the process of decay, have had their rotting trunks excavated by busy pine martens—larger cousins of the weasel—who chase down ground squirrels, which might also nest in these rotting trunks.

At the junction, we're only about a mile from and 200 feet above Middle Velma Lake, so we head down to this swimmer's paradise, since it will be, from midsummer onward, the last dependable fresh water we'll see until we rejoin Meeks Creek at Lake Genevieve. After a refreshing stay at Middle Velma, we return to the junction and hike northwest along the Pacific Crest Trail, following part of Trip 30, from this junction to another trail junction 170 yards beyond our crossing of sluggish General Creek.

There, we leave our PCT segment, signed the *Miller Lake Trail,* walk southeast upstream, and then climb east up a gully, approaching a lodgepole-fringed lily-pad pond on the flat above it. After crossing between the pond's south end and a meadow's north end, we follow a winding trail that essentially takes us east across a relatively gentle, mostly bedrock surface. With all the winding that you do along it, you are liable to get misoriented, so watch for blazes and ducks. Near its end this 2-mile lateral climbs the lower part of a prominent ridge, from which we descend in a few minutes' time to the northeast shore of Lake Genevieve. Our route now is back down the Tahoe-Yosemite Trail, on the lake's east shore, which we follow to our car at Meeks Bay.

43 General Creek Trail

Distance: 9.0 miles, round trip

Total gain/Net gain: 1100'/820'

Classification: Easy

Season: July through October

Parking: In or near General Creek Campground

Trailhead/Map: 36/6

Features: Although stocked with rainbow, brook and brown trout, General Creek sees very few fishermen, for there are no signs pointing the way to it. Those who enjoy spacious, relatively isolated creekside camping will appreciate the many sites found along the flatter, lower stretch in moraine-bound General Creek valley.

Description: From Campsite 150 on the westernmost loop of General Creek Campground, we start southwest on a road signed *Vehicles Prohibited,* and reach a junction with a similar closed road from Campsite 153. Merged together as one road, this route goes past two short trails leading down to shady General Creek, then past one climbing north. One-third mile from the trailhead we turn left on a road that descends southeast to General Creek, crosses it, climbs above its bank and terminates at another road. Walking east on this one, we would reach, in ⅔ mile, the entrance to Sugar Pine Point State Park's day-use area.

We parallel the creek upstream, hiking up a sandy road bordered by mule ears, aster and lupine, and passing granitic boulders abandoned by a retreating glacier. Leaving the unseen murmuring creek, we soon enter a long flat, covered with an open forest of Jeffrey and lodgepole pines, along which we can find numerous campsites between our road and the creek.

Our views of the two huge lateral moraines that border this creek valley disappear as we enter a thick, shady forest and soon cross willow- and alder-lined General Creek. Beyond it our road becomes overgrown and reduces to a footpath, which cuts across sometimes soggy soils before it climbs south to higher, drier ground in the form of a recessional moraine. Rounding this landform westward, we traverse a wide, open, creekside bench, pass by a nice campsite near mule-ears-cloaked slopes, and then enter shadier terrain. Our route now ascends for about ¾ mile alongside the creek, climbing over another recessional moraine and passing through stands of conical white firs and shrubby huckleberry oaks before reaching a trail fork. Straight ahead, the trail reaches a small creekside campsite in 30 yards, then fades into oblivion upstream.

Our well-maintained route goes left and crosses General Creek just a few yards below several trout-inhabited small pools. Most fishermen and hikers won't venture beyond this verdant spot, but backpackers climbing west toward the Pacific Crest Trail can follow the switchbacking trail up to a road by a flat spot on a granitic ridge that is just opposite a 400-foot cliff that should challenge qualified climbers. See Trip 30's trail description if you intend to hike south on the PCT. If you intend to hike north along it, consult *The Pacific Crest Trail.*

Small trailside pool along General Creek

44   Lovers Leap

Distance: 2.8 miles, round trip, or 3.0 miles
plus a 4.7-mile shuttle
Total gain/Net gain: 630'/530'
Classification: Moderate
Season: Mid-June through late October
Parking: More than ample
Trailhead/Map: 14/7

Features: This short ascent takes you up the
easiest route to the summit called Lovers
Leap. There are dozens of extremely difficult
Class 5 climbing routes up its near-vertical
west face. From the top you can see Pyramid
Peak, the lateral moraines of Pyramid Creek,
and much of the deep South Fork American
River canyon.

Description: From the Sayles Flat Picnic
Ground, walk across Highway 50, follow a
road east to a bridge over the South Fork
American River, cross it and arrive in Camp
Sacramento, which is operated by that city for
the benefit of its citizens. The road takes you
between two main buildings, from which you
fork right and traverse southwest to a trailhead
just behind Cabin 53.

Our trail immediately enters a ski-lift
clearing, then re-enters forest cover and
crosses several seasonal creeks. Along each
you may see mountain bluebells, thumbleber-
ry, alpine lilies, corn lilies, tall larkspur, red
columbine, lupine, common monkey flower
and sunflowers such as arnica and aster. Since
each species has its own time for blooming,
you may not see all of these in blossom, but
you may see others. Associated with the
wildflowers in this moist environment are
bracken fern, creek dogwood, alder and
aspen. Soon we spy the silvery plumes of
Horsetail Falls in Pyramid Creek's canyon,
north of us, and then encounter drier slopes on
which thrive chinquapin, manzanita, snow
bush and huckleberry oak together with their
wildflower assemblage.

Our trail takes us just above a saddle that
separates a low summit, on our right, from the
main slope. Beyond it our climb steepens and
switchbacks up to the weathered, gravelly
ridge of Lovers Leap, clothed with a few
Jeffrey pines that stand watch over the
scrubby huckleberry oaks and manzanita. A
short walk north takes us to the brink of the
leap. Be very careful if you want to get a look
down the near-vertical face; the gruss, or
granitic gravel, is slippery! Also be careful not

Lovers Leap

to jar loose rocks that might hit climbers
below.

The long, steep face of Lovers Leap,
glaciated and structurally resembling that of
Half Dome in Yosemite, is considered by
many—including the author—to be the best
climbing area in the Tahoe Sierra. Near-
vertical joints, along which glaciers plucked
off large slabs, account for the steepness of the
face. The low knoll north of and below you has
lower-angle joints, so its slopes aren't as
steep.

What sets Lovers Leap climbing apart from
other Sierra climbing is the great numbers of
horizontal dikes that have infused this rock.

Long before any of its granodiorite was every exposed to the earth's surface, this rock was intensely fractured, mostly along horizontal planes, and fingers of a molten mass, rising from below, were squeezed into these fractures, later to solidify as veins that geologists call *dikes*. Because they are rich in quartz and feldspar and are virtually devoid of any dark minerals—which are the first ones to weather—these dikes are more resistant than their relatively dark-mineral-rich host body is.

Consequently, the dikes stand out from the faster-weathering granodiorite face, thereby providing climbers with convenient ledges to reach for and to stand up on, making otherwise nearly impossible routes considerably easier.

When you have had your share of views, and on weekends seen your share of climbers, return the way you came, or descend along a steeper, longer undesirable trail, which crosses a gully with spring-fed water in it to Trailhead 13.

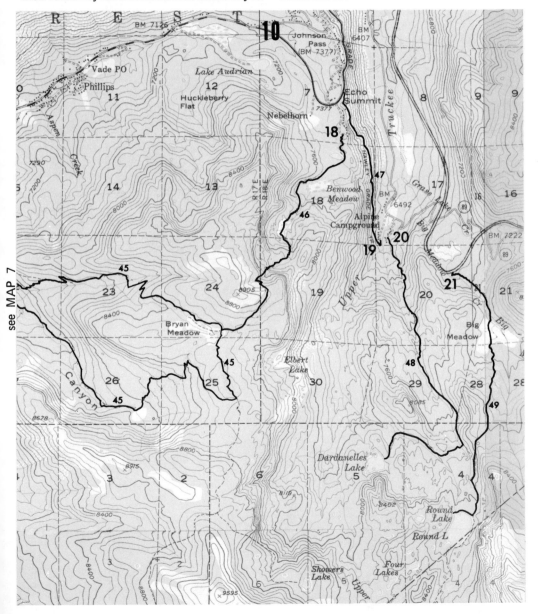

45   Sayles Canyon and Bryan Meadow Trails

Distance: 11.3 miles, semiloop trip

Total gain/Net gain: 2100'/2030'

Classification: Moderate

Season: Late July through mid-October

Parking: Four cars at most; crowded on weekends. If no room, use Trailhead 14, walk over to Camp Sacramento and then east up a road to Sayles Creek. Cross the creek and follow a creekside road up to Trailhead 15. This approach adds 0.9 mile, each way, to your hike.

Trailhead/Maps: 15/7,10

Features: One of the best trips to go botanizing along, this creekside trip exposes you to about 300 species of flora. Those hiking the Pacific Crest Trail south starting from Highway 50 will find the Sayles Canyon Trail up to it a better route than the first three miles of the PCT south from Echo Summit.

Description: Starting among red firs and lodgepole, silver and Jeffrey pines, we hike under a cool, protective forest cover whose floor is adorned with a variety of colorful wildflowers. Almost always conspicious are the strongly scented, pale-purple clusters of flowers belonging to pennyroyal. Having a more subtle odor are the pale-purple, pea-family flowers of lupine. Pastel blue colors are represented by the nodding mountain bluebell and the fragile Sierra forget-me-not. Tall larkspur, growing to a height of six feet, has spurred flowers that are a dark bluish-purple. Red is represented by two *saprophytes*–

Pine drops

Snow plant

plants living on decaying organic matter—the delicate pine drops and the chunky snow plant. Tinged with yellow are the gracefully bowing flowers of the red columbine, while the common monkey flower stands open-mouthed, a bright sunshine yellow beneath. Also having some yellow are cinquefoil and at least three common types of sunflowers: arnica, aster and senecio. As if vying for our attention, scarlet paintbrush and orange alpine lily produce a brilliant display. Adding greenish-white to this spectrum of colors are the small, pale terminal flowers of the corn lily, the delicate petals of Richardson's geranium, the creamy "cotton balls" of knotweed, the umbrella arrangements of several parsleys and the gold-tinged petals of triteleia. If you're not in any hurry, you can identify dozens more. The peak of flowering season, unfortunately, coincides with the peak of mosquitoes.

Leaving the ribbon of creekside flowers temporarily behind, we ascend a bouldery, rocky trail southeast to scrub-vegetated granodiorite slopes, and, before curving east around a low moraine, we can glance back and see Pyramid Peak towering above barely visible Horsetail Falls. Curving east between the moraine and a creeklet alongside it, we quickly reach a junction with the signed Bryan Meadow Trail, down which we'll be returning. After crossing the creeklet, we soon reach an alder-lined Sayles Canyon creek tributary from Bryan Meadow. Rather than ford the shallow creek where the trail does, veer east 20 yards upstream to a boulder-hop crossing near some cold pools up to three feet deep. Here, under lodgepoles, you'll find a nice, flat campsite near the creek's north bank.

Beyond the ford our well-maintained, verdant pathway climbs southeast up the stepped canyon floor, at times almost touching Sayles Canyon creek. We pass some large boulders—up to 20 feet high—then traverse through a meadow largely overgrown with willows, alders and corn lilies before we ford lushly vegetated Sayles Canyon creek. Then we tread a progressively easier trail east up to the northwest corner of grassy Round Meadow, which a few thousand years ago would have been called Round Lake; now only its flat surface and a trace of a moraine indicate a once-present lake. By digging below the meadow's deep soils, however, we would find lake evidence in the form of *varves*. Usually well under an inch thick, each varve is composed of a relatively thick layer of coarser sediments, which are deposited on a lake's bottom during the late-spring/early-summer heavy runoff, and of a relatively thin layer of finer sediments, which are deposited later in the year when incoming water is scanty. Pollen grains trapped in these varves tell us what kind of vegetation once grew around this area, and by noting shifts in this prehistoric vegetation, such as a shift to more alpine species, we can infer—in this example—that the climate then was probably cooler.

Of more immediate concern to you is "Where does the trail go from here?" Near the meadow's north edge, the trail starts out along the south side of a clump of willows, heads east-southeast to a quick crossing of trout-inhabited upper Sayles Canyon creek, and then diagonals east-northeast toward some corn lilies and some girdled, dead lodgepoles. Beyond them it reaches slopes at

the forest's edge, from which the trail upward is well blazed and also ducked. Mosquitoes, abundant through mid-August, make this damp meadow an undesirable camping area in early and mid season.

On a trail that is bouldery at first, we ascend moderately up through the red-fir-and-lodgepole forest, parallel eastward a linear corn-lily meadow, climb steeply north, and make a long, relatively gentle uphill traverse

Red columbine

southeast before curving east up to a saddle. Here we encounter the Pacific Crest Trail, which also coincides for some distance with the Tahoe-Yosemite Trail. To follow this trail southward, consult *The Pacific Crest Trail* or *The Tahoe-Yosemite Trail*.

Tracing the Pacific Crest Trail northward, we climb to a low summit, with weathered boulders but no views, gradually descend through an open forest of mountain hemlock and lodgepole pine, cross a mucky slough that annually sprouts a magenta field of blazing shooting stars, and reach a trail junction at Bryan Meadow's upper east end. Here the Pacific Crest Trail turns east, ascends 200 yards to a low saddle, and winds along a knee-pounding route down to Benwood Meadows before ascending to Echo Summit (see Trip 46 for an elaboration of this route).

An old trail once cut straight down Bryan Meadow, and we can follow it 50 yards west down to a small, poor campsite in a cluster of lodgepoles. A newer trail heads north a short distance, curves west to a gully, and then parallels the north edge of Bryan Meadow. In a number of spots we walk along the meadow's thick soils, rich in humus and clay.

Both hold a lot of water. The clay is derived from micas that have been weathered and eroded from the adjacent granodiorite slopes. Beyond the meadow our trail traverses a slope while paralleling Bryan Meadow's creek, below us. The trail here is drier, for the slope has a typical cover of *gruss*—the chunky, residual quartz and feldspar crystals that are left behind after most of the micas and other dark minerals decompose and are carried away. At this elevation, ice wedging (see Trip 50) hastens the formation of gruss. We descend a ridge crest, switchback down its more forested north slope, ford several branches of a creek and then curve westward as we descend to a fairly large, forested flat. At the west end, the creek tumbles down a steeper slope while our trail switchbacks down to a sloping meadow. Just west of it, we encounter a wretched motorcycle trail up which cyclists drive, sometimes to Bryan Meadow and beyond, even though they are prohibited from doing so. At the junction our trail forks left and descends via short and long switchback legs through more open forest back down to the Sayles Canyon Trail, on which we retrace our steps to the trailhead.

Pyramid Peak

46   Echo Summit to Bryan Meadow

Distance: 6.6 miles, round trip

Total gain/Net gain: 1730'/1280'

Classification: Strenuous

Season: Mid-July through late October

Parking: Space for about four cars at trailhead; crowded on weekends—then park farther north along the road

Trailhead/Map: 18/10

Features: This not-too-rewarding hike is very popular because it is along a readily accessible segment of the Pacific Crest/Tahoe-Yosemite Trail. Its principal drawback is that it goes straight up several natural chutes, thereby making the ascent very taxing. On the plus side, you'll encounter a unique pond, pass perhaps hundreds of wildflower species and—if you're a climber—find some rocks midway up the trail that are worth your time and effort to climb.

Description: From a small flat just north of a cluster of summer homes, we wind southward along a boulder-lined path atop a mammoth moraine that towers up to 1100 feet above the Upper Truckee River's bouldery canyon floor. Soon our trail descends past a lily-pad pond, west of us, and crosses its southeast-flowing outlet creek. The pond resembles so many others we've seen in the glaciated High Sierra, but it is distinct in its mode of origin. Rather than being dammed behind a recessional moraine, as most are, this pond was dammed *between* two *lateral* moraines. The huge Upper Truckee canyon lateral moraine blocked the creek's drainage eastward and another lateral moraine extending east from the north edge of Benwood Meadow blocked its drainage southward, thereby ponding up the creek.

On the low, Benwood Meadow moraine we traverse to the northwest edge of that swampy meadow. To avoid this beautifully wildflowered but mosquito-ridden bog, our trail circles the lower slopes west of it. Beyond a small creekside campsite, it begins a steep climb that takes us alongside a cascading creek. Near a huge, five-foot-diameter juniper, our trail climbs past a second creekside campsite, on a small flat. Approaching a rocky, forested saddle, we reach a slightly larger campsite, this one between the trail and a small creek on our left. From the saddle you quickly reach another meadow, not too swampy, through which you traverse toward a prominent 60-foot-high, near-vertical face on a 100-foot-high rock. This rock and its larger, more visible neighbor west of it offer some short, extremely difficult climbs that should please more avid Class 5 rock climbers.

From its base we parallel the meadow's southern edge eastward, then commence an even steeper ascent than the last one as we labor up beside a creek—a refreshing comfort—to a willowy flat on which there is a minimal campsite. You might as well pause here, for the next climb, believe it or not, is even more strenuous, averaging about 30-plus degrees in steepness. Breathing heavily, we struggle up this last steep ascent—dangerous when snow covered—through a forest of red firs and mountain hemlocks, and finally emerge at a lovely cove beneath a conspicuous dark cliff of remnant volcanic rocks that date back to the Pliocene epoch. The contact between them and the underlying granodiorite marks where the earth's surface was when they solidified on it several million years ago. As you can tell by the deep Upper Truckee canyon east of you, a lot of erosion, much of it due to glaciers, has taken place since then.

We cross a sparkling creeklet that drains from the melting snowfield clinging to the upper slopes, then begin a reasonable ascent southeast to the gentle volcanic summit's forested east shoulder. Then we descend southwest on volcanic soils which, due to the porosity of their rocky particles, are much drier. Flowers of mule ears and lupines, both with unmistakable scents, thrive in these soils. We get a brief view of peaks to the southeast but then submerge under the forest's cover once again as we descend, sometimes steeply, on granitic soils to a ravine with a tiny creeklet.

A short, easy climb west now takes us to a thickly cloaked saddle above Bryan Meadow, which has fair-to-poor campsites along its fringe. Descending about 200 yards to the meadow's east edge, we reach a trail junction from which the Bryan Meadow Trail curves north and the Pacific Crest Trail turns south. See Trip 45 for descriptions along these two trails. Southbound trekkers should consult *The Tahoe-Yosemite Trail* for a trail description south of the Sayles Canyon Trail junction.

One can put together a fairly long, vigorous Sierra canyon route by continuing down the Bryan Meadow Trail to the Sayles Canyon

Crest above Upper Truckee River canyon

Trail, as in Trip 45, then going down to its trailhead and beyond, almost to the banks of the American River. Here you cross Sayles Canyon creek, take a road west into Camp Sacramento and, following Trip 44, climb beyond it to Lovers Leap. From it you descend southwest to Trailhead 13, one mile from Highway 50's 42 Mile Picnic Ground.

47   Hawley Grade Trail

Distance: 3.8 miles, round trip

Total gain/Net gain: 800'/800'

Classification: Easy

Season: Late June through early November

Parking: Half a dozen cars at most; if crowded, park alongside road, but don't obstruct access

Trailhead/Map: 19/10

Features: Along the Hawley Grade you relive a bit of California's history by hiking up the first wagon road to be built across the central Sierra.

Description: The Hawley's Grade was a short-lived but key link in a trans-Sierra route to Hangtown and Sacramento. By 1850 Hangtown—today's Placerville—had become the unofficial capital of northern California's gold-mining region, and two years later a route of sorts was built from it to Johnson Pass—¾ mile north of today's Echo Summit—whence dropped into Lake Valley. Drop it did, so steeply in fact that block and tackle had to be used to haul westbound wagons up it. An alternative grade had to be found.

A route over Luther Pass, to the east, was surveyed in the winter of 1854 for the purpose of providing a wagon road to Sacramento and Hangtown that would be better than Johnson Pass and also shorter and easier than the primitive Carson Pass route. That spring, Asa Hawley established a trading post in upper Lake Valley near a part of the Upper Truckee canyon's wall that quickly became known as Hawley's Hill. Construction soon began on a grade that would be gentle enough to safely accommodate wagons. Financed by private interests, this route—Hawley's Grade—was completed in 1857, making it the first conventional wagon road to cross the central Sierra. Combined with the recently constructed Luther Pass segment, this grade fast became *the* route to take. In 1858 El Dorado and Sacramento counties improved western segments of this largely-one-lane toll road, making it far superior to the higher, longer-snowbound Carson Pass route to the south.

Palisades above Round Lake, from Hawley Grade

Lake Tahoe and the distant Carson Range

Timing couldn't have been better, for in 1859 silver was discovered in the Comstock Lode at Virginia Town, today's Virginia City. Traffic was reversed on this road as a flood of miners from California's gold fields scrambled east over this toll road to try their luck at or near Virginia Town. Alas, even as Hawley's Grade was constructed to channel westbound miners and pioneers into California's Mother Lode country faster than was possible along the Carson Grade, so too were plans made to convey miners and others east to the Comstock by a faster route. By the summer of 1860, a wagon-and-stage toll road—abandoned today—had been constructed down Meyer's Grade, then east to climb over Daggett Pass, situated above Tahoe's southeast shore. Hawley's Grade, briefly a shortcut that siphoned traffic from the Carson Pass route, now became the longer, unprofitable toll road.

From the boulders that today block the road, we start our hike up this historic grade by walking south about 100 yards, to where the road bends sharply and commences its climb to Echo Summit. From this bend, if you choose, you can first follow a good trail 50 yards south to the tumbling waters of the Upper Truckee River. The road quickly reduces to a trail and we soon encounter a tangle of alders, bushes and wildflowers that take advantage of the preponderance of springs and creeklets in this area. Beyond them we're on a narrow road again with more spacious vegetation. Scattered Jeffrey pines and other conifers break the monotony of the slope's mantle of huckleberry oak, and in shady spots bracken fern, thimbleberry and Indian hemp add variety. In October the leaves of this diminutive hemp turn a bright yellow, making the plant one of the more conspicuous species. After the first fall frost, Indians would collect its stems in order to make string which would be used for basket weaving and for bowstrings.

Midway along the ascent we reach our first good view north, then enter a gully down which a creek from Benwood Meadow and a pond north of it falls and cascades toward us, splashing on the large boulders we must cross. Although our path across this gully is partly washed out, we have little difficulty crossing, and from its north side we can look back and see the tall volcanic cliffs that loom above Round Lake (Trip 49). Soon we get a glimpse of Lake Tahoe and spy trucks climbing up Highway 50's present Meyer's Grade. We can also see how growth along Tahoe's south shore is spreading southward, gradually transforming the forested valley below us into a suburb of South Lake Tahoe. This valley could house thousands of new residents, but crystal-clear, deep-blue Lake Tahoe could not withstand the added sewage they would contribute. Tahoe-basin residents plan to export their treated sewage to other drainage systems rather than see their lake undergo eutrophication and lose its purity and its brilliant color.

Our views of Tahoe improve as we climb steadily north, but soon we veer west into a forest of white fir and Jeffrey pine and lose the views. Replacing them are the undesirable noise from traffic on Highway 50, which we're rapidly approaching, and the highly desirable aroma of a spread of tobacco brush. You can follow Hawley's Grade all the way to Highway 50's embankment, but this shoulderless highway is dangerous to walk along. When you see this embankment you can instead climb west up a shady gully and reach Highway 50 at its junction with a narrow road leading south to Trailhead 18, at the start of the Benwood Trail—Trip 46. Most hikers, however, will want to retrace their gentle route back to its trailhead.

48 Dardanelles Lake Trail

Distance: 8.0 miles, round trip

Total gain/Net gain: 1810'/1310'

Classification: Moderate

Season: Mid-July through mid-October

Parking: Three cars at most; if crowded, park alongside road, but don't obstruct access

Trailhead/Map: 20/10

Features: Hundreds of wildflowers, a warm, trout-stocked lake, and imposing cliffs provide the botanist, swimmer, fisherman and climber with rewarding goals.

Description: Like the Sayles Canyon Trail (Trip 45), our trail starts in a shady forest whose floor and slopes are adorned with a variety of colorful wildflowers. In addition to the wildflowers mentioned in that trip are the trumpet-shaped flowers of scarlet gilia and the unpleasantly scented, pale-pink flowers of nettle-leaved horse mint.

Our trail starts to climb immediately, and quickly reaches the large boulders of a talus slope, which it traverses. Then it climbs steeply through the forest up to a more open, minor ridge. Here we contour toward a trickling creek, and then make a steep ascent alongside it to a crossing of it just before topping a not-too-evident second minor ridge. Catching our breath once again, we prepare to assault the third rise, but it turns out to be shorter and less steep than the first two. A steeper, older trail segment on our right parallels our route over the final minor ridge.

Yellow buttercups and spiny thistles make an appearance as our trail eases off and approaches a gurgling tributary of the Upper Truckee River. We make a relaxing stroll upstream beside this alder- and willow-lined creek, but then we must climb moderately again as we reach a section of rapids. Eventually our steady ascent comes to a junction in a predominantly red-fir stand of conifers that also includes Jeffrey, silver and lodgepole pines. The main trail continues

Volcanic-mudflow boulder

south-southeast 0.2 mile gently up to a union with the more popular Big Meadow Trail (Trip 49), from where they climb south as one trail to Round Lake.

Since Dardanelles Lake is our goal, we veer southwest and descend 30 steep yards toward the creek we've been paralleling—but first we are likely to gape at the strange, 10-foot-high boulder beside us, which differs markedly from any granitic boulder we've seen downstream. This boulder broke off from the impressive palisade of Tertiary volcanic rocks that towers above Round Lake. The cluster of smaller volcanic rocks that make up the large boulder we see are just a biopsy of one of the large volcanic mudflows we would see on Trip 49, which elaborates about the preponderance of these flows.

After a pleasant lunch stop, we jump across the spring-fed creek, which receives its water from subterranean channels that flow through the volcanic rocks downstream from Round Lake, ⅔ mile south of us. Our trail traverses a broad, low slope, covered with glacier-transported volcanic sediments with a lily-pad pond among them, and then descends to Round Lake's second outlet creek, one that

leaves a dam at the lake's northwest corner and tumbles down a narrow, curving canyon. At one point these two outlet creeks are almost a mile apart, before they finally merge 200 yards upstream from our trailhead.

Our creekside journey downstream soon takes up past an aged patriarch—a seven-foot-diameter juniper—then past many creek-side willow thickets to a ford of this creek. We tread across some low, glacially polished granodiorite slabs, and then climb south-southwest on a ducked trail up a straight, easy, joint-controlled gully leading to rock slabs above the east shore of Dardanelles Lake. From its south shore rise the steep granodiorite cliffs of Summit 8402, which, for climbers, are the reward of this long ascent. Non-climbers will have to admit that the cliffs do add to the beauty of this shallow lake, which in midsummer warms up to 70 degrees or more, making it ideal for swimming; fishermen can try to catch a tasty brook-trout dinner. Late in the summer the lake's water becomes slightly cloudy, and then it should be purified before drinking. Fair-to-good campsites can be found among scattered junipers and lodgepoles on slabs bordering the east and northwest shores.

Dardanelles Lake and Summit 8402

49   Big Meadow Trail to Round Lake

Distance: 6.4 miles, round trip

Total gain/Net gain: 1370'/990'

Classification: Moderate

Season: Early July through mid-October

Parking: About one dozen cars fit into the highway turnout; on weekends use additional nearby turnouts

Trailhead/Map: 21/10

Features: Because it has volcanic and granitic soils in various stages of development, the Upper Truckee River's uppermost basin supports approximately 300 species of wildflowers, shrubs and trees, and it supports a similarly diverse invertebrate fauna. The Big Meadow Trail is your easiest trail into this lake-dotted, volcanic-rimmed basin, which offers climbers some interesting routes.

Description: From the signed trailhead we make an initial ascent south toward Big Meadow Creek, jog east, and then pant southeast up an increasingly steep slope of weathered, glacier-deposited granodiorite boulders. Near the top of our climb we encounter a closed gate, and 200 yards later we leave lodgepoles and aspens behind as we arrive at the north end of grassy, enormous Big Meadow. Just within it, beyond a clump of willows, our trail curves slightly right (southwest) and fords trout-inhabited, jump-across Big Meadow Creek.

Beyond the creek crossing, our path turns south again and we pass two conspicuous wooden posts along this very level traverse before we enter forest cover again, in a cluster of mature lodgepoles that trespass into the southeast corner of the meadow. Now our path winds south up the lodgepole-covered slope, which also is cloaked with clusters of red firs in some places and with open patches of mule ears and sagebrush in others. Near the top of our climb the grade eases off and the trail swings southwest, passes through a barbed-wire stock fence, and then begins a moderate descent from a broad, forested saddle.

On the fairly steep slope of volcanic rubble that we descend, the trees aren't as densely packed as were those along our ascent, so we can survey the basin we are about to enter. At the base of a prominent granodiorite cliff one mile west lies shallow, unseen Dardanelles Lake; above and beyond both stands a volcanic ridge, usually laced with snow and

composed of many flows that are discernible by the naked eye. At the base of the massive volcanic cliffs ahead of us lies our unseen destination, Round Lake.

After passing some fine specimens of Jeffrey pine, whose deeply furrowed bark emits a butterscotch odor that permeates the warm air, we meet the Round Lake Trail, which has climbed up a tributary of the Upper Truckee River. A gentle 0.2 mile descent along its aspen-covered banks will take you to a junction where the 1¼-mile-long Dardanelles Lake Trail branches west (see Trip 48). We continue south, climbing up, down and around on hummocky terrain of volcanic mudflow deposits and blocks. Our trail, now over fine-grained volcanic soils, is considerably dustier than the coarser-grained granitic soils we started on. Several minutes before we reach a flat above Round Lake's northeast shore, we pass one large mudflow block that has a five-foot-long granitic boulder cemented into it, indicating that the mudflow must have packed a lot of power to have lifted this two-ton boulder.

Arriving at Round Lake, we see it is different from all the other lakes of the other Highway 50 trips. Bordered by volcanic deposits along its north, east and south shores, the lake is brownish-green in color due to super-fine volcanic particles held in suspension. Since you'll probably not want to drink this water, hike 170 yards along the lodgepole- and cottonwood-lined east shore and obtain water from a trickling creek. Fair campsites are scattered about the northern half of the lake, the southern half being too vegetated and swampy. Perhaps the best site is at the lake's outlet. From the northeast corner follow a narrow path west past Jeffrey pines, junipers, sagebrush, mule ears and frosty eriogonum to a small campsite on a grandiorite bench just west of the head-high dam. Beneath red firs and lodgepoles you can take in superb sunsets that set the towering volcanic palisade east of you ablaze with color. Just east of this campsite is a small cove in which you can enjoy a refreshing swim or can fish for some of the lake's cutthroat trout.

Just beyond a trickling creek flowing down to the lake's northeast shore, the trail encounters an enormous block that, like so many around us here, has broken off from the vertical-to-overhanging cliffs above us. Climbers who like to go "bouldering" will find

Volcanic palisades above Round Lake

this an ideal block to climb on. Since some routes are overhanging and others are as long as 40 feet, and since the flat-sided handholds aren't always secure, a top rope is desirable. More daring climbers may want to try the potentially dangerous deep fissures on the vertical cliffs above.

These mudflow cliffs are part of the Mehrten formation, which is an assortment of andesitic flows and structures that are several thousand feet thick in some places. From the middle Miocene epoch through the late Pliocene, thick andesitic lava flows poured from summits that probably resembled today's Oregon Cascades, and they covered an area of the slowly rising Sierra Nevada that extended from Sonora Pass north to Lassen Park and from east of the present Sierra crest to west beneath the Central Valley. As the thick lava flows cooled while flowing along their downward paths, they became less and less able to move, particularly along their rapidly cooling edges, and eventually these edges solidified. But then the edges were fractured by the pressure of the still-flowing internal molten material.

The *autobrecciation* of flows—the self-fracturing of a flow's rocks by its own movements—was responsible for the overwhelming quantity of *lahars,* or volcanic mudflows, which characterize the Mehrten formation. A lahar flows when an accumulation of fragmental debris becomes saturated with water. The extensive autobrecciation of these andesite flows produced a very abundant supply of fragments—"food" enough to feed hundreds of lahars like the ones that compose the thousand-foot-thick wall above us. Pleistocene glaciers, in conjunction with some faulting (see Trip 52), have removed most of the lahar deposits that once filled Round Lake's basin.

From Round Lake you can continue south along the Meiss Meadow Trail, explore more of the basin's rocks and lakes, and see more than 100 species of subalpine and alpine flowers that have adapted to this rocky, often snow-covered environment.

50   Freel Peak

Distance: 13.8 miles, round trip

Total gain/Net gain: 4160′/3040′

Classification: Strenuous

Season: Mid-July through early October

Parking: Adequate for those who can drive all the way to trailhead, which is virtually impossible to reach before mid-August

Trailhead/Maps: 24/11,12

Features: Three of the four Tahoe basin peaks higher than 10,000 feet lie along or close to this route; from Horse Meadow all three can easily be climbed in a day. The Fountain Face provides good-to-excellent Class 5 rock climbing, and the north face of Jobs Sister provides fair-to-good climbing and excellent mountaineering opportunities. Of the three routes to the Horse Meadow area, this one is the shortest and easiest.

Description: In 1859 silver was discovered in Virginia Town's Comstock Lode (see Trip 47). In that year, Garret Fountain started

grazing beef cattle and milk cows along the headwaters of Trout Creek, and he thought that Armstrong Pass might provide a faster route for the miners who were leaving California's Mother Lode in droves and scrambling east, via Luther Pass, to the Comstock Lode. In 1860 he built a way station at what today is known as the Fountain Place, hoping to profit from the passing traffic. Armstrong Pass, however, never did become a popular route, for the Comstock Lode mine operators financed the construction of a road over Daggett Pass, north of Freel Peak. No buildings remain standing at the Fountain Place today, but the cattle remain.

From the parking area at the end of the road, we immediately leave the forest's cover, jump across a creek, and contour south-southeast across a meadow that is being invaded by willows and cows. Cow paths obscure the real

The Fountain Face

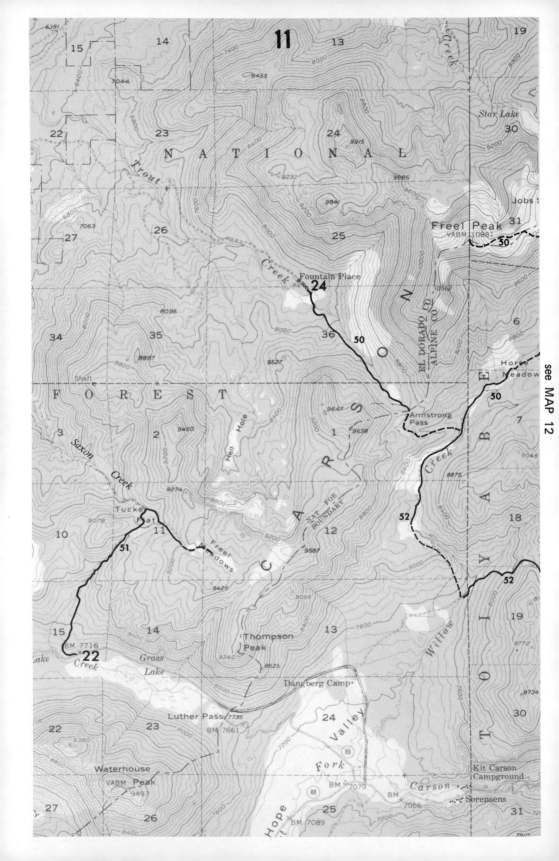

see MAP 12

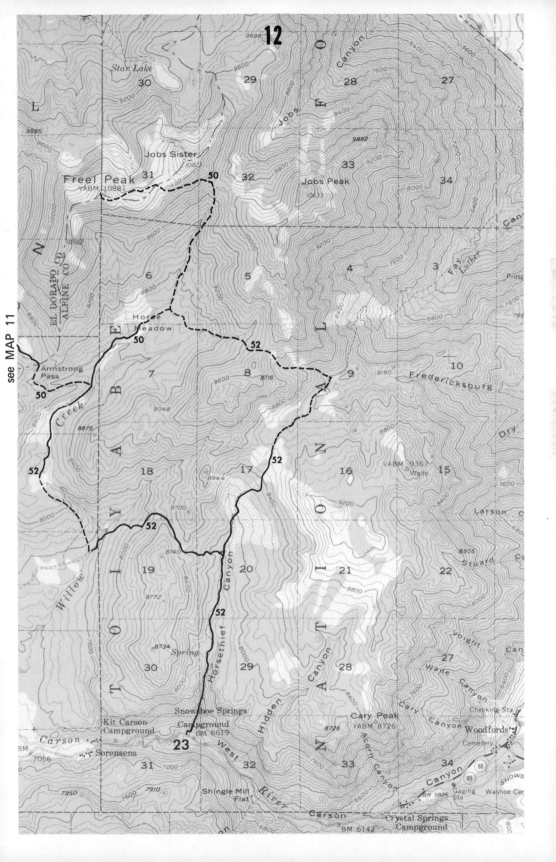

see MAP 11

trail as we enter a forest of lodgepoles and aspens; then, in less than 50 yards, we jump across Trout Creek. The next 200 yards of trail up to a trickling tributary of Trout Creek are obscure and hard to follow. After it, however, the trail becomes quite obvious, and we parallel the usually unseen creek as we climb moderately toward Armstrong Pass.

Midway up our ascent through a red-fir and silver-pine forest, we can gaze across the canyon and see the Fountain Face, a 300-foot-high granitic cliff that is riven with vertical cracks which provide climbers with over one dozen routes ranging from easy to extremely difficult Class 5. The climbing routes are quite clean, even though the cliff was never scoured by glaciers. What keeps it clean is *ice wedging:* when the temperature drops, water that has seeped behind crystals and into tiny cracks freezes, and in doing so expands by about 10 per cent in volume. This expansion gradually splits off loose crystals—whose presence is undesirable for climbers. Under ideal conditions, when water turns to ice it can exert a force of 1000 pounds per square inch as it tries to expand. This force is equal to that which you would experience if you could skin-dive to a depth of 2300 feet, or if you were buried under 800 feet of rock—a very impressive force. The more opportunity water has to repeatedly freeze and thaw, the more it will weather a rock by ice wedging. The rugged crags we see north of and above the Fountain Face are more broken up because of more intense ice wedging, and the high peaks we'll climb are even more so. When too much ice wedging occurs, the rock then becomes unsafe for climbing.

Whitebark pines now line our path as we continue upward, and soon its gradient eases as we approach and traverse the southwest edge of a meadow. Above it, we climb briefly on a ducked, faint trail up to a stock fence, and then in 100 yards top viewless, forested Armstrong Pass. No real trail exists from this pass down to Willow Creek, but the short cross-country route ahead is easy to follow. Descend steeply south toward the open, gentle slope below you and cross it in its lower part—that is, through the corn lilies rather than through the tangle of willows above them. Down its south side flows a permanent creeklet, up which you can climb southwest to the Tahoe basin's rim and then traverse southwest on the rim to the Freel Meadows area (see Trip 51). Beyond the creeklet, our cross-country route contours southeast toward an open-forested ridge that has a fairly deep layer of *gruss*. This soft layer, combined with pine needles, makes our descent east to the Willow Creek Trail very easy on the feet. You need not follow the ridge crest down to that trail; you can traverse the ridge's easy north slope to it.

Turning left on the trail, we quickly step across the creeklet we first crossed just below Armstrong Pass, then proceed upstream on one of several cow paths. In general, the higher the path, the drier it will be; the creekside path tends to be quite boggy, and it has many willow patches that impede progress. When you reach Horse Meadow, almost one mile upstream on the Willow Creek Trail, cross the creek and hike northeast cross-country up the crest of a low ridge. Three-tenths mile from our creek crossing, the low ridge suddenly steepens, which signals those who intend to make a one-day ascent of Freel Peak to leave their heavy backpacks here and carry only a day pack up the steep route ahead. From this broad, dry, open-forested ridge—a better place to camp at than damp Horse Meadow—Trip 52 commences a cross-country contour east.

Our cross-country route is a steep climb that parallels Willow Creek's east bank. Red fir drops out of the forest cover as we tread up the gruss-covered slopes, and soon whitebark predominates over lodgepole pine. The creek has incised a steep-walled gully in its deeply weathered canyon, and it could be dangerous if you were to slip down into it; stay at least a few feet back from its lip. The last 400-foot climb to our first saddle is up an open slope clothed with sagebrush, whose fragrant aroma tempts us to linger awhile and enjoy it. After yielding to temptation—mostly to catch our breath in this rarified high-altitude air—we continue up to the deeply weathered saddle, whose wind-trimmed, chest-high whitebark pines show in what direction the dominating winds blow. Before mid-August, violent thunderstorms develop almost daily in the Freel Peak area. Don't try to climb any summit if the weather looks in the least bit threatening. A full storm *can* develop out of a clear, blue sky in less than two hours.

Scanning northeast down Jobs Canyon and beyond, we can see the irrigated fields of the Carson Valley below. Peak baggers who like to "collect" summits may first want to make a moderate climb east over to the saddle south of Jobs Peak, from which the rest of the easy climb to that peak is "in the bag." If you were to descend from it to Point 9892, on its northeast ridge, you could then look due north along the fault that conspicuously separates the Carson Range from the Carson Valley. The Carson Range is a *horst,* a fault-block mountain, which now stands up to a mile or more above its matching granitic bedrock, which lies buried under the Carson Valley's deep alluvium. The Lake Tahoe basin, like Carson Valley, is a *graben,* a basin formed when a block slipped down between two faults. This dramatic topography developed mostly during the Miocene and Pliocene epochs. Since then, glaciers and other eroding forces have chiseled at the protruding highlands, sculpturing them into the complex landscape we see today.

Having mastered the first saddle without too much difficulty, we now diagonal almost due west to a second saddle, about 600 feet higher. The slope up to it has been extensively weathered by ice wedging, and consequently our route goes through a deep mantle of gruss. The climb, however, isn't all that bad, because grasses, shrubs and whitebark pines help hold the loose material in place. Had we climbed to Freel Peak directly from Horse Meadow, we would have had to struggle all the way up a steep scree slope.

Upon attaining the second saddle, we can see that it is a more inhospitable environment for plants. No grasses, shrubs or trees grow on this broad, barren saddle; whitebark pines on both sides of it, however, form a dense, waist-high thicket. From this saddle we have a choice of routes. Jobs Sister, a 15-minute climb to the northeast, offers better views than any other peak in this southern end of the Carson Range. Its views to the east equal those of Jobs Peak; its views to the north, west and south equal those of Freel Peak; and its deeply glaciated north face is far higher and steeper than that of any nearby peak.

Backpackers who have carried their packs this far may want to follow the northwest ridge of Jobs Sister down to fairly large, isolated Star Lake. Mountaineers and climbers may want to establish base camps here to try ascents up the ragged cirque wall that is the north face of Jobs Sister. Routes there range from relaxing to terrifying. Ice wedging has made the rock rough and easy to grasp—great for handholds and footholds—but it has also broken faces into large, semistable slabs,

which could prove dangerous. Proceed with caution.

Most hikers will want to climb Freel Peak, which is the highest peak on the Tahoe basin rim—indeed, the highest peak in the Tahoe Sierra. Leaving the saddle, we follow a narrow footpath that makes an initial drop and then traverses steadily up around the north slope of an intermediate summit. We reach a third saddle, and then make a short, steep, 15-minute climb up the narrow trail as it ascends the southeast slope to the summit.

Pinnacle on Jobs Sister

Our conquest, greeted by the hum of a microwave-relay tower, is a bit disappointing. Like many high peaks outside the Desolation Wilderness and Granite Chief areas, this one now serves 20th century man. The views, however, are not blocked. In the south is a ribbon of Highway 88; in the west-southwest beyond Echo Summit is the incised South Fork American River canyon. Unmistakable Pyramid Peak looms above the Echo Lakes to our west. In the northwest, the slopes of dark, metamorphic-capped Mt. Tallac descend to Tahoe's shoreline. Above the lake's northeast corner stands volcanic-capped Mt. Rose, whose summit, at 10,776 feet, is third highest in the Tahoe basin, ranking below only Freel Peak and Jobs Sister. Viewing Jobs Sister, we can identify two parallel, massive, quartz-vein dikes that paint its west slope white with rocky "snow." Lake Tahoe, of course, is the main feature that captures the eye. This deep, blue gem seems to be too large to be in so high a basin—we almost expect it to overflow into the lower, dry desert to the east.

Atop the summit grow small clumps of whitebark pines, here only knee-high, and above them mountain bluebirds dart swiftly after insects wafted here by updrafts. When you are ready to leave, you could retrace your steps, but there is a better way. Return to the second saddle and then descend, in leaps and bounds, the southeast-facing scree slope. You should be able to make the 1900-foot descent to Horse Meadow in about half an hour.

Freel Peak

51   Freel Meadows

Distance: 6.2 miles, round trip
Total gain/Net gain: 1870'/1530'
Classification: Strenuous
Season: Early July through mid-October
Parking: Ample parking along highway
Trailhead/Map: 22/11

Features: Solitude is almost guaranteed along this trip. From Freel Meadows you can go cross-country to Horse Meadow, normally approached from Armstrong Pass (Trip 50), but the road to that trail isn't negotiable until early August. If you're attempting to climb the Freel peaks before that time, you should consider this trip as an alternative, drier way to them.

Description: For most of our route we will be hiking along the signed Tucker Flat Trail. In an open Jeffrey-pine forest that includes specimens of juniper, red fir and sagebrush, we begin an easy climb west, paralleling the highway, and then arc north to a gully, where we cross an alder-lined, trickling creek. Watching for ducks and old blazes, we progress on our trail up this sometimes-damp, wildflowered gully to drier granitic soils on the slope above. As the slope levels off, we cross a seep lined with gooseberries, then wander among corn lilies, mule ears, lupine and various sunflowers before we make a slight descent northwest to a bubbling creek.

We cross this permanent creek, quickly recross it, and commence a long, steep pull up beside it through a red-fir forest. Our shady route winds among large granitic boulders, usually staying near the creek, and soon we approach a side canyon that descends from the northwest. On the lower slope of this canyon, just away from our creek, is an adequate campsite under red firs.

When we continue to climb, we lose sight of our creek where it audibly churns its way downslope beneath a layer of large boulders—some more than 10 feet high—beneath a cover of red fir, lodgepole pine and silver pine. Where our steep gradient abruptly becomes a more moderate one, we cross over the creek's now-dry channel and walk up to a broad, bouldery saddle. From here, the best route to Freel Meadows is to head east toward them up the fairly easy slopes. However, the Tucker Flat Trail descends northeast from the saddle, and then skirts the southwest edge of Tucker "Flat," a wet, gentle slope rich in grasses and water-loving wildflowers. Staying alert for blazes and ducks, we reach the meadow's west edge, then descend northeast and quickly arrive at a trail junction several yards west of the Tucker Flat creeklet. A trail that starts northwest down alongside Saxon Creek, below us, is no longer maintained; if you try to follow it down to a residential development south of the Pioneer Trail road, you'll find yourself fighting your way through dozens of alder thickets. The first ¾ mile of trail, however, is in acceptable condition, and this stretch will take you steeply down to a large, almost flat, forest-and-meadow bowl, where you'll be rewarded with a true feeling of wilderness, for within it the hand of man is virtually impossible to detect.

From the trail junction near Tucker Flat, our route follows a faint trail east, which takes us, after a two-minute walk, to Saxon Creek, above whose north bank one can camp under conifers growing on a dry, gentle slope at the east end of a meadow. Our trail to West Freel Meadow now fades almost into oblivion, so climb the steep but easy slope any way you wish, staying relatively close to Saxon Creek. Mountain hemlocks, along with other conifers, now line our gravelly, cross-country route. When you spy grassy West Freel Meadow—a collection of sediments "dammed" behind resistant granitic bedrock at its west end—traverse over to it and follow a small, sluggish creeklet east up to a flat, dry saddle, which has convenient lodgepole-shaded campsites. From these dry sites we obtain a view southeast of Hawkins Peak (9961'), which barely pokes its summit nipple above the conifers at the far end of large East Freel Meadow.

If you've hiked in the Desolation Wilderness area, west of here, you might have noticed how different its landscapes are compared with those of the Freel peaks area. The difference is due mainly to the *rain shadow* cast by the high ridges of Desolation Wilderness. Most storms approach the Sierra from the west, and they unleash most of their precipitation—usually snow—as they rise up the western slope, because air cools as it rises, and the colder the air is, the less water vapor it can hold. By the time a storm has worked its way from the Sacramento Valley, near sea level, 9000 feet up to the Sierra crest, its air mass has cooled about 30° Fahrenheit and its water-vapor capacity has been halved—the other half having been converted to precipitation. When the storm then passes over the Freel peaks area, it is pretty much "milked dry," and as a result, this high country receives only about half the precipitation received by Desolation Wilderness, about 10 miles west.

How does this precipitation difference affect landscape development? During the Pleistocene epoch, snowfields covered the Desolation ridges and were the source of huge glaciers that scoured out canyons east and west of the ridges. With considerably less precipitation than its counterpart, the Freel peaks area spawned very few glaciers, the only significant one growing from the north wall of Jobs Sister (see Trip 50). Consequently, the terrain we tramp through in Trips 50–52 has V-shaped canyons rather than U-shaped ones.

More important, since almost none of the canyons were scoured by glaciers, the soils were not removed. Whereas most of Desolation's soils have formed since the retreat of the

last major glaciers, about 12,000 years ago, those of this area have not been interrupted for probably more than a million years. Erosion, of course, has stripped away the soils that existed then, but the soil cover has continually been replenished by newly weathered fragments of bedrock—the normal situation.

The immediate advantage is that these deep soils hold more water than the new discontinuous soils of Desolation. Therefore, while most creeks are rapidly drying up in Desolation after the snow melts, the creeks in this area still flow, since abundant water is stored in the deep soil. Furthermore, this soil, being older and better developed, supports more vegetation, and together with the humus that accumulates from dead plant life, the vegetation further retards water runoff, thereby permitting the storage of even more water.

At Freel Meadows you can enjoy the solitude of a seldom visited place, or you can make a cross-country wilderness trek to Willow Creek, east of us. To do this, traverse east up toward Peak 9587 on the crest, then

East Freel Meadow and Hawkins Peak

traverse for about one mile northeast, staying on or near the crest. When you reach a broad, forested saddle south of ragged Peak 9638, descend a gully for ¾ mile until you are immediately south of recognizable Armstrong Pass. Here you can join Trip 50's short cross-country segment east down to the Willow Creek trail.

When you're ready to leave Freel Meadows, you might consider a scenic alternative route back to Tucker Flat. From the northwest corner of West Freel Meadow, arc northward across a gentle slope, staying just above the large granitic boulders to the west. State geologic maps show no volcanic rocks existing in the Freel Peak massif west of Willow Creek, but you can't miss the dark ones on your right, upslope from the lighter colored granitic rocks we've seen. Dating as far back as the late Miocene, these volcanic rocks were then part of extensive flows that buried shallow canyons. Today, perched along a ridge crest, they serve as a clue to the geologic past.

About ⅓ mile north of the meadow we arrive at a shallow, broad saddle, and from it we make a short, easy ascent northwest to large, granitic blocks at the summit of Peak 9274. From this whitebark-pine-clad summit we can survey the country beyond. North and well above boggy, mosquito-ridden Hell Hole below us stands Freel Peak, the highest summit in the Carson Range.

Leaving this serene summit, descend southwest, straight downslope, staying southeast of the creeklet in a prominent gully. There is some bushwacking along this route, but since you're descending, not much effort is required in the few spots where you might have to plow through bushes. At the end of your cross-country descent, you'll arrive at the camping area above the north bank of Saxon Creek and find the faint trail. Walk west on it to the quickly reached trail junction, and return on the Tucker Flat Trail.

Hell Hole and Freel Peak

52   Horsethief Canyon Trail to Horse Meadow

Distance: 25.0 miles, semiloop trip

Total gain/Net gain: 4320'/2810'

Classification: Strenuous

Season: Mid-July through mid-October

Parking: Plenty of parking near water fountain; don't monopolize the few campsites in the small campground below you

Trailhead/Map: 23/12

Features: The third and longest route to the Freel peaks, this semiloop trip takes you past miles of delightfully scented brush interspersed with abundant stands of timber. Campsites along this route are limited only by your imagination.

Description: From the wayside drinking fountain 40 yards west of the Snowshoe Springs Campground entrance, cross the highway and find the signed trailhead beside a large Jeffrey pine. Our trail swings east through an open cover of mountain mahogany, manzanita, tobacco brush and mullein, and then we execute 10 short, incredibly steep switchbacks that guide us up to a point almost beside a roaring, unseen creek that lies just around a low ridge.

Topping the low ridge, we find both the creek and a starkly grotesque cliff of pinnacles and goblins—the eroded product of andesite flows dating back as far as the late Miocene epoch. Here, the daring climber will find hundreds of semisolid or semiloose—depending on your state of mind—handholds and footholds by which he can scale the vertical formations. Safety-minded climbers will want a top rope. Knobs are abundant on this cliff because it is an andesitic mudflow derived from an autobrecciated lava flow, such as the ones explained in Trip 49.

Surrounded by the pervasive aroma of tobacco brush, we labor steeply up the trail, which is occasionally bordered by junipers, and reach a taller bank of andesite cliffs, these being clearly recognizable as old lava flows. Stop a minute—you'll want to anyway,

Mudflow cliffs

because of the grueling climb—and notice how the flows *dip*—that is, are inclined—slightly westward down toward us, and how they stop abruptly at the creek. Only highly weathered granitic rocks lie west of the creek. "Why don't these flows continue westward?" one might logically ask. The answer lies—literally—along Horsethief Canyon creek, which is eroding down along a *fault*—a fracture in the earth's crust. We don't see any volcanic rocks west of the creek because the block of granitic rock we're standing on has been lifted in relation to the block on the east side. Consequently, along the fault granitic rocks on the west are juxtaposed against volcanic rocks on the east, and we expect to find, and do find, some volcanics on our ascending trail higher on the west slope. (See the diagram in Trip 68, which depicts the same situation as here, except that the block west of the fault here moved up.)

Our ascent becomes more moderate and takes us up to a gate in a cattle fence. Beyond it we hike up an increasingly easy trail that passes through an open forest interspersed with slightly fragrant sagebrush and very fragrant mule ears. Past a spring-fed creeklet, partly bordered by aspens, we make a pleasant one-mile stroll, passing a dilapidated shelter and potential campsites to our right. Then 10 minutes beyond the shelter, we enter the south end of a meadow and spy a shack at its northeast edge. This is a crucial meadow for staying on route. Ignore cow paths and follow the trail past creekside willows and into a lodgepole forest. At the first dry wash you encounter, less than two feet deep, leave the trail and head west-northwest up alongside it. The wash quickly turns into a gully, and along its south side you'll recognize a cattlemen's trail, which is blazed. Up this we climb west—very steeply at times—to a viewless saddle whose forest floor is overgrown with a mat of dwarf manzanita.

From the saddle our blazed trail descends northwest along the southwest slope of a shady, forested gully, then curves west and begins a steep-to-very steep descent across drier slopes dotted with aspen and cloaked with tobacco brush, chinquapin, juniper and some conifers. Upon reaching Willow Creek just above where it debouches onto an open slope at the mouth of a canyon, we hop on large boulders to its west bank.

A trail once climbed to the middle reaches of Willow Creek, but it no longer exists. You have a choice of climbing straight up the canyon's slope, which is quite brushy in the lower section, or following the cattlemen's trail west ⅓ mile and then commencing a climb north from it. This is the preferred route, for it is less brushy and initially less steep.

Above a canal, the slope gradually transforms into a well-defined ridge, and we progress steadily up its increasingly barren granitic surface until we finally reach its Jeffrey-pine- and juniper-covered top. This minor, flat, granitic summit has been weathered for so long (see Trip 51) that very little bedrock protrudes. To the south we can look down Hope Valley and see Highway 88 climbing toward Carson Pass. A cattle fence runs west along most of our now-level ridge. Cross it and descend northwest to a huge, grassy meadow, in which you'll easily locate a jeep road paralleling Willow Creek upstream. For the next 2½ miles between this meadow and Horse Meadow, there are numerous potential campsites, some occasionally used by cattlemen.

Beyond the huge meadow our road crosses a willow-choked gully and soon diminishes to a trail. The trail, sometimes a choice of several cow paths, makes a gentle northward ascent over open slopes abundant with creeklets, springs and mud. The higher cow paths above Willow Creek are the drier ones. We angle northeast, make an almost imperceptible climb, and arc north to curve around a low, broad ridge. Should you wish to exit to the Lake Tahoe area, you can climb this low ridge and then swerve north to Armstrong Pass (see Trip 50).

Beyond the low ridge, we step across a creeklet from the pass area, then follow well-named Willow Creek for about a mile to Horse Meadow. Our trail deteriorates as we approach it, but no matter, for all routes beyond it are cross-country. At the meadow's ill-defined lower end, we cross the creek and follow a gentle ridge 0.3 mile northeast to where it suddenly becomes steeper. From good, dry campsites on this ridge, Trip 50 guides you up to the alpine landscapes of the Freel peaks. If you've hiked this far, you'll probably want to make this extra side trip. This trip, Trip 52, however, sends you packing on an eastward traverse across gruss-covered slopes and gullies toward a conspicuous broad-arc saddle that you must climb to.

Hope Valley and juniper

At the end of the traverse, we reach a refreshing creek that is sometimes watched over by some gregarious Steller jays. This is your last chance for good late-summer water until you once again reach Horsethief Canyon. Confronting the 900-foot ascent east to the saddle, you can console yourself that if you were walking in the opposite direction, you'd have to climb up a *scree* slope that is both steeper and longer. Your route direction is also less confining, allowing you to make your own switchbacks up the very steep slopes of granitic bedrock.

At the saddle we get a framed view eastward down Fredricksburg Canyon of Nevada's 9000-foot Pine Mountains. Just as the high ridge crests of Desolation Wilderness cast a rain shadow on us (see Trip 51), so this ridge crest casts one on these drier, open-forested Nevada mountains.

From the saddle, the first 300 vertical feet of very steep descent can be dangerous, for only a thin layer of gruss coats the weathered granitic bedrock, and this thin layer can act like a sheet of ball bearings to speed you on your way downslope. If you're cautious, however, you should be able to negotiate it even with the largest pack. Where the gradient eases off, we now have an enjoyable ski downslope on the loose scree. Parallel the dry wash down the canyon until it drops off steeply, then climb down—sometimes Class 2—along the wash, which is lined with aromatic tobacco brush as well as with chinquapin and sagebrush.

The wash leads us down to a "flat" shaded by red fir and lodgepole and silver pine, and just east of it is a low knoll that has a thin coating of volcanic rocks scattered across its weathered granitic boulders. Isolated from any water supply, this knoll is an outlier for more drought-resistant species such as mountain mahogany.

Our route essentially follows the Horsethief

Canyon fault, which generally divides exposed granitic rocks to the west from volcanic-covered ones to the east. We commence hiking south, round a low-angle slope of volcanic rock, and soon enter a meadow with sagebrush, mule ears, grasses and willows. Our cross-country route is now an obvious one: hike southwest along the upper Fredricksburg Canyon creek drainage and eventually parallel the east side of this creek up to a long east-west saddle. A trail of sorts heads up this creek, but it is not important that you stay on it until you reach the saddle.

From the saddle's lowest point—which isn't all that obvious—we embark on a sometimes winding trail descent southwest, first dominated by "scent-uous" sagebrush and mule ears, then overseen by junipers, mountain mahogany and, finally, aspen. Rock ducks plus blazes on aspens distinguish this moderate-to-steep descending trail from numerous cow paths. Back in the meadows of upper Horsethief Canyon, follow the creek's west bank. Soon you'll recognize the terrain up which you hiked, and you can lope south down the familiar Horsethief Canyon Trail.

Trails of the Interstate 80 Region

Introduction

Just as over half of the trips in the Highway 50 region are in and around Desolation Wilderness, so too over half of the trips in the Interstate 80 region are in and around smaller Granite Chief Motor Vehicle Closure Area (Trips 54-62). Although its elevations and its amount of glaciation are similar to those of Desolation Wilderness, Granite Chief presents the hiker with a strikingly different landscape—one with few lakes but with towering volcanic cliffs whose talus slopes are often covered with large fields of aromatic mule ears.

Like the lower elevations of the Highway 50, 49 and 70 regions, however, the lower elevations of this region are unsuitable for hiking. An example of this is Green Valley, which is two miles southeast of Interstate 80's settlement of Alta, in the bottom of a deep, spectacular canyon cut by the North Fork American River. The *Colfax* 15-minute topographic map (1950) shows Green Valley and its immediate environs ramified with trails. What really exists: The trail from near Interstate 80 to Green Valley does exist, but like virtually all of the old, utilitarian trails that are so typical of the western Sierra canyon country, it is uncomfortably steep. Furthermore, this trail, like so many others, is unmaintained, and it dies out before reaching the river. If you did plow down to the river through the brush—thereby running the risk of encountering rattlesnakes, ticks or perhaps poison oak—you would be disappointed with the debris earlier travelers have left behind. Two trails that once traversed east across Green Valley to other trails no longer exist. Another mapped trail, heading down-river from Green Valley, quickly reaches private property.

Trespassing at lower elevations is definitely *not* recommended. As one sign points out, "Survivors will be prosecuted," and the gun-toting owners mean it. Hundreds of small mining claims dot the lower Tahoe Sierra, and the prospectors that work them are often trigger-happy. As one old prospector told the author, he would kill anyone he *thought* might want to steal his gold (he had less than an ounce worth).

Armed natives, then, are the greatest danger to hikers who want to explore anywhere in the lower Tahoe Sierra. If you still decide to explore these elevations, then be prepared to find only a small fraction of their trails in existence. New roads plus logging operations have taken their toll of trails.

In addition to Granite Chief, five other hiking areas exist in the Interstate 80 region. Lowest and most isolated of these is Placer County Big Tree Grove (Trip 53), which is the only grove of giant sequoias in the Tahoe Sierra. If you decide to drive the long, winding road to it, you might as well take in some equally remote, nearby hikes (Trips 1, 3, 54). Here too, logging operations have obliterated most of the trails that once existed in this area.

Whereas most areas have had many trails widened into roads, the Grouse Ridge Recreation Area (Trips 63–65) is largely composed of jeep roads that have been converted into hiking trails. As in the Granite Chief area, volcanic, granitic and metamorphic terrains are found in this smaller, lake-dotted area. Private property is still held around beautiful Culbertson Lake and nearby vista-packed Bowman Mountain, with its marvelous views, both unfortunately off-limits to the public.

Driving east up Interstate 80 to the Big Bend offramp, you'll come to an even smaller lakes basin, the Loch Leven Lakes area (Trip 66). The short trail up into it is one of the best-constructed and maintained trails in the Tahoe Sierra, which can't be said of the deteriorating or logged-over trails just outside the Loch Leven area. The Loch Leven Lakes, being shallow and not fed by long-lasting snowfields, are among the first natural lakes in the Tahoe Sierra to warm up to reasonable swimming temperatures. By late season, however, all but High Loch Leven Lake become slightly stagnant.

Cyclists and jeepsters have made virtually all hiking north of Interstate 80 in the Donner Pass area undesirable. Although frequently visited by these noisy, often boisterous-and-littering motorists, Paradise Lake (Trip 67) is nevertheless included in this guide because it can be paradise when you have it to yourself, which you some-

Left, climbing on Sanford Lake slab

times can during the week. Larger White Rock Lake, north of it, is accessible in pickup trucks as well as motorcycles and jeeps. The Mt. Lola Trail, north of this lake, starts from Perazzo Meadows and traverses across well-posted private property. Other private holdings plus an expanding ski-development hamper west-bound access to lakes east of Paradise Lake. Southwest of this lake lie the Lola Montez Lakes, but like others, they are accessible to cyclists and jeepsters. West Lakes have been obliterated by Interstate 80, but Azalea, Flora and Angela lakes, south of it, are somewhat accessible from the freeway's rest area or from Donner Pass along old Highway 40.

Despite the abundance of trails depicted on maps of the Mt. Rose area, only one still remains open to the public—the short trail up to the peak itself. From the mid-1800s

onward, the forests of the Mt. Rose environs provided timber for mines and mining towns that sprang up around Virginia City's Comstock Lode. Private interests ruthlessly exploited the forest reserves of the Carson Range, and today the Toiyabe National Forest is still only a sparse patchwork of plots throughout the range. Trails that haven't been converted to jeep roads are either long-abandoned, like the Martis Peak-Mt. Rose trail, or they are inaccessible. Rutted roads, private property and private logging tracts prevent trail access to the Mt. Rose high country via any route other than by the Mt. Rose Trail (Trip 68). Detracting from the wilderness feeling in this area are encroaching ski areas and a radio transmitting tower. The hike to the mountain's summit, nevertheless, is well-graded, vista-packed, and is certainly worth the effort.

Trailheads reached from Interstate 80

The following trailhead descriptions begin from Auburn, which is about 34 miles northeast from Sacramento via Interstate 80. Our mileage begins at the Highway 49 junction in Auburn. Trailhead 1 can be reached by driving south 3.2 miles on Highway 49 to its junction with Highway 193, and then taking this highway 12.7 miles east to Georgetown. From there you follow the Highway 50 log to Trailhead 1 (44.4 miles from Auburn).

Trailheads 1–3, 37–38: Middle Fork American River

37 From the Highway 49 crossing (0.0), drive northeast up Interstate 80 and take the Auburn Ravine Road offramp (2.0). Lining this busy intersection are plenty of gas stations and coffee shops. We follow *Foresthill* signs as we take the Auburn-Foresthill Road northeast, passing the Foresthill Ranger Station (15.5, 17.5) before reaching that settlement (2.0, 19.5). In it we fork right on Mosquito Ridge Road, signed *French Meadows*, and follow this scenic, winding, gorge-traversing road until we come to a junction with a spur road (25.1, 44.6) This road curves southward to a parking lot and **Trailhead 37 (0.7, 45.3)**, in Placer County Big Tree Grove.

1,2,3 From the spur road junction (44.6), we continue on the main road, pass the Greek

Store Fire Station entrance (1.0, 45.6), and eventually reach the north end (9.5, 55.1) of French Meadows Reservoir dam. At the dam's south end (0.5, 55.6) there is a choice. By turning right you can follow Road 17N12 to a junction (6.6, 62.2) by the North Fork of Long Canyon Creek. From this junction— mile 60.6 of the detailed Highway 50 trailhead log—drive southwest to reach **Trailhead 1 (16.7, 78.9)** or drive northeast to reach **Trailhead 2 (7.5, 69.7)** and **Trailhead 3 (0.5, 70.2)**.

38 If you turn left at the dam's south end (55.6), you'll parallel the reservoir's southeast shore and pass several recreational facilities before you cross a bridge (5.0, 60.6) over the Middle Fork American River, just above the reservoir's north end. The pavement ends after we pass a fork (0.3, 60.9) to west-shore recreation sites, and we soon reach Ahart Campground (0.7, 61.6), on our right. We continue upstream to a junction (2.1, 63.7), from where a recently improved road starts a climb left up toward Soda Springs. Someday a paved road may run from Highway 50 to our canyon, then up it to Interstate 80, which will undoubtedly intensify logging operations near its route. Farther up-canyon, we branch right (1.0, 64.7) on a narrow road and negotiate this rutted route to **Trailhead 38 (1.0, 65.7)** at Talbot Campground. During midsummer 1974 a logging road was being built into the campground, and future backpackers may find this road a better way into the campground. If you can successfully drive across Talbot Creek, then you can drive an additional 0.8 mile to the start of the Picayune Valley Trail.

Trailheads 39–41: Grouse Ridge Recreation Area

39   From the Highway 49 crossing (0.0) in Auburn, drive north on Interstate 80, passing cafes and gas stations before reaching the Highway 20 offramp, on which you exit right, curve clockwise under Interstate 80 (45.0), and drive southwest to a junction with Road 18N18 (4.1, 49.1). Descend this road north to a bridge over the South Yuba River (1.4, 50.5), then wind up to Fuller Lake's south end (2.3, 52.8) and Fuller Lake Campground, which extends northward along the lake's west shore. Continuing on 18N18, we pass a road (1.2, 54.0) to Rucker and Blue lakes, then meet the Grouse Ridge Road (1.6, 55.6) as Road 18N18 starts to curve clockwise around a ridge. We turn right and climb up the Grouse Ridge Road, ignoring well-graded logging roads. Nearing Grouse Ridge, we see the start of the Grouse Ridge Trail, on our right, which descends to a jeep road. Seventy yards later we cross a cattle guard and a spur ridge (5.4, 61.0). Beyond it, our now-rutted road quickly forks (0.1, 61.1), the left branch climbing 0.8 mile to the Grouse Ridge Fire Lookout. We take the right branch, traverse a meadow, and reach outhouses and a pipe spring of sloping Grouse Ridge Campground, which serves as **Trailhead 39 (0.1, 61.2)**.

40   From the Grouse Ridge Road junction (55.6), drive north on Road 18N18, crossing Fall and Clear creeks, and arrive at a junction with Road 18N16 (2.2, 57.8), branching right. Drive north up this fair-to-good road, then east to Carr Lake Campground (2.9, 60.7), which begins at the west end of Carr Lake. Camping niches are found among the dense shore vegetation as you head eastward and climb up to Feeley Lake's dam, reaching in 20 yards **Trailhead 40 (0.3, 61.0)**. It is better to park in one of the sites around Carr Lake than at the cramped turnaround by Feeley Lake.

North of the 18N16 junction (57.8), Road 18N18 soon meets Road 18N15A (2.6, 60.4), which climbs east to a YMCA camp, the Lindsey Lakes, bad roads and private property. Don't expect to reach the Rock Lakes via this road. Continuing north on 18N18 we wind our way past spur roads and signed Canyon

Creek Trail (3.7, 64.1), to the left, which is an unmaintained trail that dies out after descending almost to that creek. Our road now deteriorates to fair—poor in places—crosses Canyon Creek and climbs steeply to a junction (2.7, 66.8) above Bowman Lake's west end. You can drive west 6.4 miles on Road 19N14 to Merk's, at the west end of Graniteville, where from the start of the fishing season to the end of the hunting season—roughly late May through late October—you can obtain gas and a minimal supply of food. Road mileages on 19N14 west of Graniteville are given in the Highway 49 trailhead log.

41   Leaving the junction with Road 19N14 (66.8), we follow a rough road along Bowman Lake's precipitous north shore, passing campsites at the lake's east end and campsites just before a junction with Road 18N13 (3.6, 70.4). Drive south up this road to where a spur road forks right (1.2, 71.6) and follow it west to road's end, **Trailhead 41 (0.3, 71.9)**.

Trailheads 42–45: Donner Summit Area

42   From Interstate 80's crossing of Highway 20 (45.0), drive east past Cisco Grove (gas, food) to the Big Bend offramp, which you take to a junction with old Highway 40 (5.5, 50.5). Head east on it across the South Yuba River and reach in 70 yards, **Trailhead 42 (0.2, 50.7)**, which is signed *private road, public trail*. Northeast 140 yards is Big Bend Ranger Station and the entrance to Big Bend Campground.

43   From Interstate 80's crossing of Highway 20 (45.0), drive east and take the offramp to Soda Springs (13.1, 58.1), which has gas, food and lodging, Follow old Highway 40 through this town to the Soda Springs Road (0.7, 58.8), on which you drive south. At the south end of the Ice Lakes ski-cabin development the pavement ends (2.3, 61.1), and our road winds down to Onion Creek (4.4, 65.5), near which you can camp, then continues beyond it past Cedar Creek (1.9, 67.4) and summer homes to a road fork. Stay left, not crossing the American River, and reach in 100 yards a closed gate, **Trailhead 43 (0.4, 67.8)**.

44   From Interstate 80's crossing of Highway 20 (45.0), drive east and take the Boreal Springs offramp, near which is a highly visible Shell Station. The offramp terminates at Boreal Ridge Road (15.8, 60.8), which you follow north under the divided freeway, then drive east and curve gently up into Castle Valley, on whose west slope the road climbs northwest to a parking area, **Trailhead 44 (1.8, 62.6),** from which a trail parallels the right side of a jeep road up to a nearby saddle. Before early August, the last half-mile of road to the trailhead may be too muddy to drive.

45   Drive east on Interstate 80, crossing the Sierra just east of the Boreal Ridge Road crossing (60.8), then descend past large, deep-blue Donner Lake and veer right on the Donner Memorial State Park offramp, which curves down to an intersection with the Donner Lake-Truckee road (old Highway 40) (8.4, 69.2). Here, you'll find a gas station, a cafe and a motel. You may camp in Donner Memorial State Park, whose entrance is 0.3 mile west on old Highway 40. We drive southward, paralleling the Teichert Aggregates property to where the pavement ends (0.5, 69.7), then curve left and cross that company's private haul road (0.1, 69.8) and curve right. Our dirt road, posted with *Emigrant Trail* signs, parallels the company's operations, on our right, and Cold Creek, on our left, then comes to a crossing of Southern Pacific's railroad tracks (3.1, 72.9). Only 140 yards beyond this crossing, we pass a road climbing north toward the site of Eder, then 140 yards later reach a fork. Keep left for 110 yards to another fork, at which you veer right and drive ¼ mile to **Trailhead 45 (0.5, 73.4),** a deceptively easy-looking jeep road that branches left across a Cold Creek meadow.

Trailheads 46–50: East Approaches to Granite Chief

46,47   From the Donner Lake area, follow Interstate 80 past the Donner Park offramp (69.2) and take the next offramp, which leads you to a junction with Highway 89 (2.2, 71.4). Heading south up this Truckee River highway, we pass Granite Flat (1.0, 72.4), Grouse Meadow (3.1, 75.5) and Silver Creek (2.5, 78.0) campgrounds before reaching a junction with Squaw Valley Road (1.3, 79.3). Drive up it past a small shopping center with a post office (1.9, 81.2) to a junction by the Squaw Valley Fire Station, **Trailhead 46 (0.4, 81.6).** Turn left (south) and drive to a large parking lot beyond the Cable Car aerial tramway and just east of the Village Store. Park here for Trailhead 46 and for **Trailhead 47 (0.3, 81.9),** which is located at the start of a dirt road at the base of lift KT-22.

48   Beyond the Squaw Valley Road junction (79.3), Highway 89 crosses to the east bank of the Truckee River and reaches the Alpine Meadows Road junction (1.4, 80.7). Drive west up paved Alpine Meadows Road to a junction with Deer Park Drive, where you'll encounter **Trailhead 48 (2.2, 82.9).**

From the Alpine Meadows Road junction (80.7), drive up Highway 89 to the Tahoe City Y (3.9, 84.6), then follow the highway south through Tahoe Park (store plus gas station) (2.3, 86.9) to the Kaspian Picnic Ground (2.1, 89.0). You can continue south 5.2 miles on Highway 89 through the settlements of Homewood and Tahoma, both with gas and food, to the General Creek Campground entrance, from which mileages south are given in the Highway 50 trailhead log.

49,50   We turn west at Kaspian Picnic Ground, drive west up a road paralleling unseen Blackwood Creek, then at a junction (2.3, 91.3) drive south, crossing the creek (0.1, 91.4) and climbing to the Sierra crest (4.7, 96.1) ½ mile south of the original Barker Pass Trail. Our road descends northward to this jeep trail, then curves west and makes a winding traverse to a junction (1.8, 97.9) at a spur ridge, down which a southbound road descends 2.6 miles to Barker Creek and Barker Meadow, a convenient camping area. Beyond the spur ridge our road quickly reaches a gully and **Trailhead 49 (0.3, 98.2),** then winds west gradually down to a fork (1.7, 99.9). We climb up the right branch almost to a saddle, then follow a narrow logging road 250 yards northwest up to it, on which is located **Trailhead 50 (0.9, 100.8).** Don't obstruct passage along this narrow road, which may be quite muddy and undrivable before early August.

Trailhead 51: Mt. Rose

51   East beyond Interstate 80's Donner Park offramp (69.2), take the Highway 267 offramp down into central Truckee. There, turn south on 267 (2.4, 71.6) and follow it all the way to its junction with Highway 28 (12.3, 83.9), on Lake Tahoe's north shore 9.5 miles northeast of the Y at Tahoe City. On Highway 28, drive east into Nevada and reach Highway 27 (4.6, 88.5) up which you drive to **Trailhead 51 (8.1, 96.6).** Highway 27 continues 0.3 mile up to the Mt. Rose Campground entrance, immediately crosses the crest at 8924 feet, then descends 17.0 miles to Highway 395.

53   Placer County Big Trees

Distance: 1.8 miles of trail in the park
Total gain/Net gain: Negligible
Classification: Easy
Season: May through October
Parking: More than ample
Trailhead/Map: 37/13

Features: If you have time to spare after completing Trips 1, 3, or 54, then you might stop at this grove of sequoias and marvel at the height and bulk of these big trees, the only ones found in the Tahoe Sierra.

Description: At the trailhead beside the parking lot is a map of this park's Forest View Trail and Big Trees Trail. The Forest View Trail, starting near the drinking fountain, is

Sequoia cone, ½ actual size

225-foot-high Pershing tree

exactly what it claims to be: a view of trees and the interesting plant life beneath them, not a view of scenic panoramas. The Big Trees Trail, starting at the map, has signs that identify trees, shrubs and features, and give the dimensions of the larger sequoias. Since both trails are so obvious, no trail description is necessary. Take the Big Trees Trail first, so that you will recognize some of the species you'll see along the Forest View Trail.

Two trail signs deserve elaboration. The first one is the *fallen tree* sign, which states that this sequoia trunk, 154 feet long by 10 feet in diameter, fell in 1861. Had the trunk belonged to any other species of tree that grows in this grove, it would have long since decayed into oblivion. The bark and wood of the sequoia, however, are very resistant to insect infestation and fungal attack. That this trunk—and the larger Roosevelt Tree trunk near it—has survived over a century is amazing when you consider that chemical and biochemical processes in this area are quite strong.

Only one other tree, the bristlecone pine, can withstand decay better. Preferring timberline slopes in drier ranges east of the Sierra, this pine has an extremely short growing season—a month or so—and consequently it grows very slowly, producing extremely close-spaced annual rings that are very resistant to all kinds of attack. Until the 1950s it had been thought that the sequoia was the world's longest-living tree, but not now. The bristlecone pine not only lives longer—5000 years versus 3000 years—but its dead trunks also survive longer. By counting and matching tree rings in both living and dead pines, scientists discovered that some trunks have survived thousands of years; a few pines whose seeds germinated 9000 years ago have their dead trunks lying around today. Since

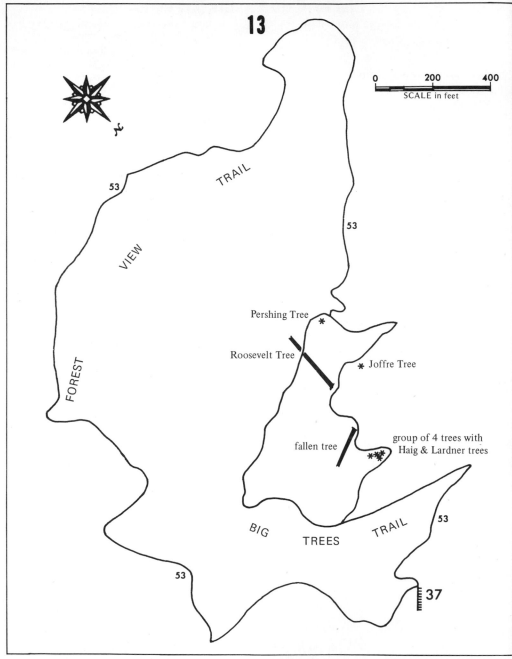

this tree's annual rings reflect precipitation—rings spaced farther apart when there is more of it—scientists have been able to piece together a 9000-year-long climatic history for the Basin and Range province, which includes most of Nevada and adjacent parts of neighboring states.

The second trail sign worth noting is *streams underground,* next to which we can look down into some small holes, one or two feet deep, and see water flowing in an underground channel. It is channels like these from which the shallow, far-ranging sequoia roots get the water they need; no surface water is necessary. If you hike both trails in this park, you'll notice that the sequoias are found only on the lower slopes, which are laced with ephemeral creeklets—sure signs of abundant groundwater below. Note that the vegetation in the sequoia grove is composed of water-loving species such as dogwood, alder and azalea, while the slopes above have manzanita. Throughout this small park you'll see trees found in virtually every one of California's 70 sequoia groves: sugar pine, ponderosa pine, white fir and Douglas fir. Also seen in this locality are scrub tanbark oak and black oak.

The present boundaries of California's sequoia groves appear to be quite stable; they are neither expanding nor contracting. Because few seeds are sprouting, however, most of these groves are underoing a gradual decrease in numbers of sequoias. This gradual decrease in numbers has been going on for at least 500 years, so Western man isn't really at fault—although early entrepreneurs tried to lumber the groves. The sheer bulk of these giants caused them to shatter into useless splinters when they hit the ground, so most of the sequoia trees—unlike its close cousin, the coast redwood—were spared from the ax. This Placer County grove was discovered in 1855 by miners who were searching for gold among the quartz veins which infuse the Paleozoic marine sediments that underlie its fairly deep mineral soil.

It is this moist mineral soil that the sequoia seedling needs to survive, not the mat of drier litter atop it. A survey of three controlled burns in Kings Canyon National Park showed that a year after the fires burned off the litter, there were about 1500 sequoia seedlings sprouting in the mineral soil for every mature

sequoia in the burns. In an adjacent, unburned grove, no seedlings sprouted. Burned sequoia litter holds up to three times more water than does unburned litter. Fires also aid seedlings by killing fungi, eliminating some plant competition and driving off small rodents that feed on the seedlings. Still, mortality is high: only about 30 seedlings per parent survive by the end of the third year.

Once the sequoia grows large enough to develop a good, protective bark, which will eventually get to be over a foot thick, it becomes immune to virtually everything, fire and lightning included. What, then, kills these giants? The author concludes, after having visited at least half a dozen sequoia groves, that these giants die due to loosening of their roots by erosion of the soil that supports them. The soils are typically about five feet deep, and in this shallow layer the roots radiate out 100 feet or more from the trunk. Over a 2000-year period, easily half of this soil can be eroded away, exposing many roots and leaving the tree defenseless against a large windstorm, such as the one in 1861 that toppled two giants in this Placer County grove. Unlike short-lived giants such as sugar and ponderosa pines, sequoias do not reach old age and die to leave a snag that eventually falls over. Rather, these giants are *undercut* while in their prime—they don't reach old age. People can accelerate erosion by trampling around the ground; this was probably a factor in the felling of Yosemite's popular Tunnel Tree. Bristlecone pines, such as those in California's White Mountains, grow on slower-eroding slopes, and this may increase their longevity. Nevertheless, they too, because of their long lives, are faced with the same problem.

Cones of the ponderosa pine (top), Douglas-fir (right) and sugar pine (bottom), 1/3 actual size

54   Picayune Valley Trail

Distance: 15.2 miles, round trip

Total gain/Net gain: 2580'/2030'

Classification: Moderate

Season: Mid-July through early October

Parking: More than ample at Talbot Campground, but the spur road into it may be undriveable until late August—before then, park along the main road and hike one mile to the campground

Trailhead/Map: 38/14

Features: The Picayune Valley Trail is the only reasonable trail into the Granite Chief area from the west. Ascending a deep, glaciated canyon, the trail parallels the Middle Fork American River, whose middle reaches sport fair-to-good, isolated campsites. Rock climbers specializing on volcanic cliffs will appreciate those along the crest above the head of the canyon.

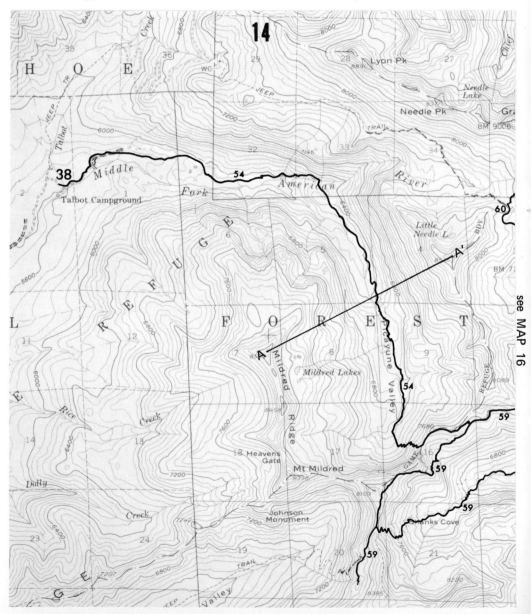

Description: Starting from hard-to-reach Talbot Campground, we immediately cross Talbot Creek, then follow an almost level road one-half mile northeast to a fork. Here, a trail between the two forks climbs straight ahead from us. Our road branches left, climbs to a quick reunion with this trail, and then gradually levels off over the next ¼ mile as it approaches a road block. The road curves left around this, but we jump over it and find ourselves at the start of the Picayune Valley Trail.

In 1974 one began an easy walk through a forest of incense-cedar, white fir and Jeffrey pine, but future hikers may find this flat terrain logged over. As we climb toward a notch between a low knoll and the north slopes above us, we enter the signed Granite Chief Motor Vehicle Closure Area. A minor descent southeast from the notch takes us down to the start of a gently undulating eastward ascent that parallels the unseen Middle Fork American River for one mile. By walking south 100–200 yards along the forest's open floor, you can reach this unused section of river and find a place to establish a good campsite for yourself.

Where our trail crosses the river's first permanent tributary since Talbot Creek, the route begins a moderate-to-steep climb. A second tributary surprises us with its delightful, short fall into a churning, refreshing pool that supplies us with the best water available on this trip. Our trail now veers south and climbs up to a second low notch, from which we can look north and see a skyline cliff of gray granitic rock, which is a spur ridge that was severely abraded by glaciers. To the southwest, dark-brown metamorphic cliffs rise above Picayune canyon. These two rock types—granitic and metamorphic—have an irregular boundary between them that our southbound canyon-floor path crosses and recrosses.

After a brief descent from the notch, we reach a fair campsite—under an open lodgepole cover—that lies between the trail and some nearby small pools on Picayune Creek. Our southbound adventure now proceeds across several short stretches of wet trail that remain soggy even in late September. In mid-July, bring your rain boots. We pass meadow after boggy cow-meadow, divided by aspens, cottonwoods, alders and willows, and finally dry our boots as we climb a short, rocky trail section that transports us up to the north edge of flat Picayune Valley.

Standing at the rocky brink of the valley's north end, we can gaze northward downcanyon and identify three major rock types. The multihued rocks we're standing on, together with those of the canyon's west slopes, are Jurassic sediments, most of which were deposited as silt and sand in a shallow ocean basin, then later compacted to siltstone and sandstone. When they were subjected to deep burial and folding, these sediments were metamorphosed to slate and quartzite.

Granitic plutons, rising from below, intruded these *metasediments* and further metamorphosed their lower zones to varieties of schist, a rock that shows the highest degree of metamorphism. Plutonic rocks, chiefly granodiorite, comprise most of the steep, chaparral-mantled, east slopes of the canyon, including the prominent, vertical-fractured cliff—a source of joy to rock climbers.

On the forested, gentler slopes above the granitic band lie the dark-brown andesite rocks that flowed during the early Pliocene.

Topographic inversion. Volcanic rocks flowed down two prevolcanic canyons (1 & 2), deeply burying them. Today, the rocks that buried these canyons form high slopes and ridges, whereas the ancient prevolcanic ridge has been eroded down to a deep canyon. This cross section is marked on Map 14 as A-A'.

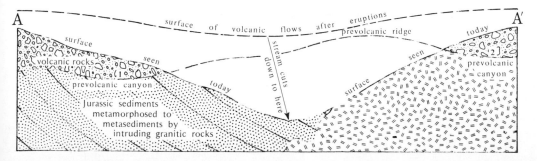

These rocks show a classic example of *topographic inversion:* they once flowed down a shallow canyon—a topographic low—but today they form the upper slopes and ridge crest—a topographic high. After these flows flooded the ancestral canyon, streams began to cut down along the canyon's slopes between the bedrock and the flows' edges, and eventually the streams cut noticeable canyons that were later transformed into spectacular ones after glaciers repeatedly sculptured them. Because these andesite flows erupted about 10 million years ago, and because the maximum erosion since then is *at least* 3000 feet—the height from the volcanic ridge crest down to the canyon floor—the erosion of this landscape has been occurring at a minimum average rate of 3.6 inches per 1000 years. The continental U.S., as a whole, is being denuded at the rate of about 2.4 inches per 1000 years, or one third less than that of the Middle Fork American River drainage. (Repeated uplifts prevent the continent from ever being reduced to sea level.)

Of more immediate interest to the hiker are two pools connected by a low waterfall. In the lower pool is a circular, waist-deep pothole, which makes an invigorating bathtub. Scattered about the generally barren, rumpled bench west of these pools are potential campsites; but upstream, the water is sluggish, poorly aerated and frequented by many cows, so camping is undesirable.

Our trail once climbed up an extremely steep volcanic slope above Picayune Valley's south end, but now it switchbacks up to a saddle just north of an impressive band of deeply grooved andesite cliffs of autobrecciated lava flows (see Trip 49). Climbers will find an abundance of handholds up the two dozen or so deep grooves of these nearly vertical, 200-foot-high cliffs, which require expansion bolts to protect the leader.

Leaving the saddle, we follow an ascending crest route that takes us past much lower volcanic cliffs, which for the climber are alone worth the relatively long hike up to them. Nonclimbers will appreciate the interesting composition of these stark landforms as well as the ridge-crest views obtained. On the horizon in the south-southeast, the high peaks of the granitic Crystal Range poke up above the notch that marks the head of Big Powderhorn canyon.

Our crest route levels off, we enter a red-fir

View north from Picayune Valley: Volcanic crest, granitic cliffs and metamorphic foreground

forest, and then we make a short descent to a trail junction amid a tremendous field of mule ears that covers the slopes. No single plant in the Granite Chief area so dominates its volcanic slopes as does this aromatic, large-leaved sunflower. Trip 54 ends at this junction, but you, of course, can continue northeast toward Whisky Creek Camp or southwest toward Shanks Cove, both directions of this trail being covered in Trip 59. If you're heading southwest, you'll want to descend cross-country straight down to the trail from where our trail crosses the crest at the saddle, thereby saving a mile of needless ascending and descending.

55 Little Powderhorn Trail to Powderhorn Creek

Distance: 5.6 miles, round trip

Total gain/Net gain: 1710'/1680'

Classification: Moderate

Season: Late July through early October

Parking: Several cars at most; don't park in the way of logging equipment

Trailhead/Map: 50/15

Features: Although the drive to the trailhead is a little longer and somewhat more difficult than others, the Little Powderhorn Trail is the hiker's shortest and fastest route into the southern portion of the Granite Chief Motor Vehicle Closure Area.

Description: Our trail begins atop a forested saddle in a township section of Forest Service land that is being selectively logged. Fire rings indicate that people camp here, but by mid-July most of the snow one can use for water has melted. Mornings from the saddle are heralded by the warm glow of the skyline crest that includes Needle Peak, Granite Chief and Squaw Peak, north of us.

Descending into a forest of mountain hemlock and lodgepole pine, we cautiously hike down a steep, switchbacking trail, watching our footing on the loose volcanic rocks. We relax our braking as the grade eases off in the head of an unnamed, meadowy cove that marks the southern border of section 3, owned by the Southern Pacific Land Company, which has a checkerboard pattern of land holdings in much of the Granite Chief area. Our trail hugs the meadow's west side at first, then disappears in the meadow. Near its brushy north edge, we cross the headwaters of Little Powderhorn Creek and pass a fair campsite beneath lodgepoles. Beyond the meadow, we hike down the stream's east bank, keeping an alert eye open for the blazes and ducks that mark the trail.

After a fairly steep descent, we see towering above us steep cliffs of andesite lava that have the vertical columns—generally hexagonal in cross section—so characteristic of thick flows (see Trip 56). We quickly reach the creek and cross the steep-sided gully it has cut into a volcanic mudflow (see Trip 49). After a 300-foot descent along the alder-lined creek, we cross back to its east bank and then gradually veer away from the creek as we descend through a sometimes-open forest of Jeffrey pine and white fir.

We soon reach a junction with Trail 15E12, on which we can traverse 120 yards southeast to turbulent Little Powderhorn Creek. Just 130 yards past it, this traversing trail intersects

From trailhead: Needle Peak (left), Granite Chief (middle) and Squaw Peak (right)

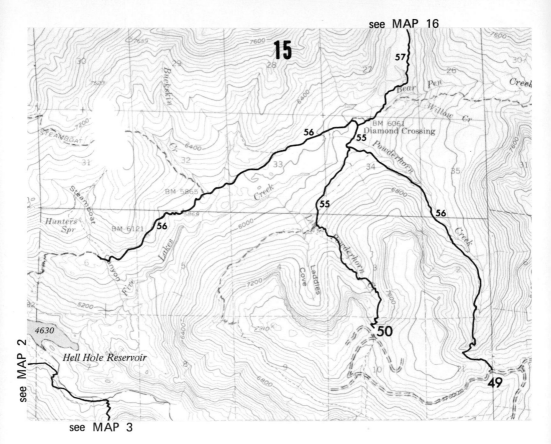

an equal-sized creek draining Laddies Cove.
A 350-foot ascent up alongside this creek
would reward you with forest's-edge
campsites in secluded Laddies Cove, from
whose upper end you can gaze north at the
crests of the Granite Chief area, Beyond the
Laddies Cove creek, Trail 15E12 gradually
curves southward, climbs steeply to a ridge,
and then becomes severely overgrown as it
starts a long traverse across a southwest-
facing slope.

Back at the trail junction, our route, Trail
15E12, descends one mile north to a level,
grassy meadow, in which we meet the Big
Powderhorn Trail. Just north of this meadow,
atop a bench above Powderhorn Creek's
south bank, we reach a large, good campsite, a
fine place to set up a base camp for further
exploration of the trails that thread Granite
Chief's canyons.

56
Big Powderhorn Trail to
Diamond Crossing and Trails West

Distance: 14.6 miles, round trip

Total gain/Net gain: 3410'/1990'

Classification: Moderate

Season: Mid-July through early October

Parking: About half a dozen cars can park at trailhead; latecomers use other nearby turnouts along road

Trailhead/Map: 49/15

Features: This popular trail down to Diamond Crossing takes you to some good creek campsites—ideal spots for just relaxing. The route continues beyond them to some more-isolated parts of the Tahoe Sierra, in which the inquisitive backpacker can do some exploring on his own.

Description: Near a gully excavated from loose volcanic rocks, our signed trail starts a steep ascent up a mule-ears-covered slope to a broad saddle clothed in red fir—the tree that nearby loggers are after. In addition to red fir, we encounter silver pine and mountain hemlock as our trail descends west, then steeply descends via switchbacks to the headwaters of Powderhorn Creek. At the bottom of the loose, volcanic boulders and sediments of its sometimes dry channel, one will always find water flowing through this porous rock. We cross to the creek's west bank, which we'll parallel—though at a distance—all the way

down to a junction on a flat meadow with Trail 15E12.

Our gradient is now mostly a moderate one as our trail leads us north down through more open areas that are abundant in sagebrush, mule ears and pennyroyal. In one of these clearings we pass a huge, trailside boulder, on our right, that broke loose from the slopes above us. This boulder is a characteristic portion of a mudflow, which in turn was derived from an autobrecciated lava flow (see Trip 49), for it is composed of a wide assortment of smaller, angular boulders that range up to two feet in diameter. Some volcanic mudflows also contain nonvolcanic rocks, because surface rocks get intermixed with them as they flow downslope. Notice how the texture of this huge boulder differs from that of smaller boulders that were derived from lava flows composing the cliffs way above us.

Beyond the boulder our trail soon curves northwest and takes us to better views of the columnar, andesitic lava flows that form cliffs on the upper slopes of both canyon walls. Because these flows were so thick—up to 200 feet or more—they took a long time to cool—10 to 20 years. Like most liquid masses, these flows tended to contract as they solidified, and as the bottom of the flow—in

Autobrecciated mudflow boulder

contact with "cold" rock beneath—solidified rather uniformly, contraction of the bottom layer occurred about many almost equally spaced centers. This contraction created tension between the centers, resulting in a network of short, straight cracks that grew vertically upward as the lava cooled and solidified upward. A similar process was taking place at the cooling top surface of the flow, and other vertical cracks grew downward. When the entire flow finally solidified, the cracks from top and bottom grew together, creating vertical columns, typically several feet in diameter, which usually have a hexagonal cross section. Five-, four-, and sometimes three-sided cross sections are also found. Climbers will appreciate these vertical columns, for the cracks between them provide routes and nut protection up the cliff. Readily accessible Devils Postpile National Monument, a few miles southeast of Yosemite National Park, is California's best-known example of columnar jointing in lava flows—although its columns are no match for the giant ones we see well above us.

After crossing several ephemeral creeks and touching the lower edge of the talus slope derived from these flows, our trail enters a moderately dense forest of white fir and Jeffrey pine, which gradually becomes increasingly infiltrated with incense-cedar as red fir and silver pine drop from the ranks. After descending gentle slopes, we enter a level, grassy meadow, hike west through it, and reach a junction with Trail 15E12. Trip 55 tells you what to expect if you hike south up this trail. We start north through the meadow, swing northeast past a large campsite, and boulder-hop Powderhorn Creek.

About 250 yards beyond the creek, as we near a large meadow known as Diamond Crossing, we peel left on a shortcut trail, arc westward and soon pass cottonwoods, lodgepoles, alders, Jeffrey pines and white firs that line boulder-bottomed Five Lakes Creek. On the creek's west bank we discover a good campsite, but more secluded ones that are just as good or better can be found by hikers who are willing to spend a few minutes looking upstream or downstream. Most backpackers will be content to stay at the campsites they find around here, but Trip 56 continues for three more miles.

Our trail makes an initial ascent southwest, undulates through a sometimes shady forest as it passes four low knolls on the left, and then makes a moderate descent to signed Little Buckskin Creek. We no sooner climb out of its shallow gully than we find ourselves making a brief descent to Buckskin Creek. Just 30 yards beyond it we reach a fair campsite on a small flat, and 60 yards beyond that arrive at a junction with the Steamboat Trail.

Trail 15E13, the Steamboat Trail, makes an interesting, well-graded climb up to a red-fir saddle east of Steamboat Mountain, from which it descends to milky Grayhorse Creek. Along this entire descent there are trees marked for logging, and it may not be too long before the loggers actually cut them. As of 1974, logging operations in Grayhorse Valley had already made it hard to find Miranda Cabin, which lies west of a meadow beyond the creek. Due to the maze of logging roads that lace this valley, the hiker descending a trail at its east end will face the impossible task of locating the cabin. Once that hiker is considerably upslope toward the red-fir saddle, however, he should be able to find Trail 15E13. Heading northeast up one of the valley's logging roads, we would have an equally difficult time locating the lower section of the trail that descends from its east end. Consequently, a hike into or through Grayhorse Valley is not recommended.

Our route continues southwest, passes trailside Bench Mark 5869, and rollercoasters up to Fletcher Ravine, which divides mudflow deposits to the east from granitic bedrock to the west. A stiff climb out of it takes us up to Bench Mark 6121, emplaced on a ridge of exposed metamorphic bedrock. Standing here, we can look south across the Rubicon River's deep canyon and see the bald top of granitic Guide Peak perched above the reddish-brown metamorphic slopes beneath it. Down these slopes winds the McKinstry Trail, a crucial part of Trip 6.

Beyond this outcrop, we tread once again on granitic soils, re-enter forest—now composed largely of ponderosa pine, black oak and incense-cedar—and descend rather steeply to Steamboat Canyon creek, where nearby flat campsites mark the end of Trip 56. The trail continues west, steeply descending a gully, then begins a winding, sometimes brushy, sometimes live-oak-shaded, very steep descent toward Hell Hole Reservoir. About 400 feet above the reservoir, this faint, ducked path becomes very brushy and in effect ceases to exist. The presence of rattlesnakes will deter the more cautious from descending any farther.

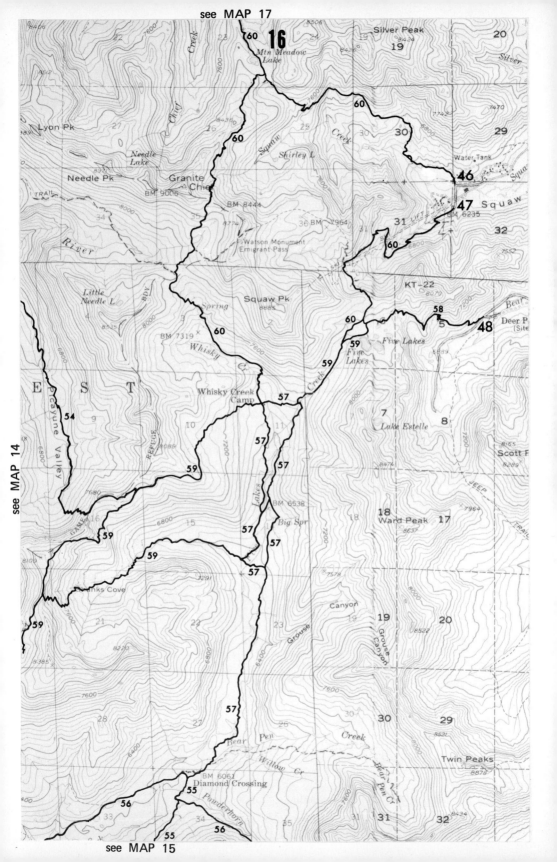

see MAP 17

16

Silver Peak
19

20

60

Mtn Meadow Lake

Silver

Chief

Creek

60

60

30

30

29

8406

7600

8506

8424

Lyon Pk

Needle Lake

Needle Pk

Granite Chief

BM 9006

Squaw

Shirley L

Water Tank

46

TRAIL

River

BM 8444

Watson Monument
Emigrant Pass

47

Squaw

47

BM 6235

LIFT

32

60

Little Needle L

Spring

Squaw Pk

60

KT-22

Whisky

BM 7319

60

59

Five Lakes

58

48

Deer P
(Site)

59

Five Lakes

59

57

Creek

E   S   T

54

Whisky Creek Camp

57

7

Lake Estelle

8

Scott

REFUGE

57

Picayune Valley

59

57

57

BM 6538

Big Spr

18

Ward Peak

17

59

59

Shanks Cove

57

57

Canyon

19

20

Grouse Canyon

59

Grouse

Canyon

57

30

29

Bear   Pen   Creek

Twin Peaks

Willow Cr

Bear Pen Cr

BM 6061
Diamond Crossing

55

56

Powderhorn

31

32

55

56

see MAP 15

see MAP 14

57   Big Powderhorn Trail to Upper Five Lakes Creek

Distance: 18.0 miles, semiloop trip

Total gain/Net gain: 3360'/1780'

Classification: Moderate

Season: Mid-July through early October

Parking: About half a dozen cars can park at trailhead; latecomers use other nearby turnouts along road

Trailhead/Maps: 49/15,16

Features: Most of the trails that compose this trip parallel Five Lakes Creek or one of its tributaries, thereby providing the hiker with many opportunities to set up a creekside campsite. Even more numerous are the opportunities to fish along this trout-inhabited creek.

Description: Follow the route description in Trip 56 to the edge of a large, dry meadow—Diamond Crossing—250 yards beyond Powderhorn Creek. Hiking along the Pacific Crest Trail, we make a gentle uphill traverse northeast across this meadow, passing midway through it a trail that descends west to Five Lakes Creek. Leaving this meadow, bordered by tall Jeffrey pines, we enter a forest of mixed conifers and quickly reach a signed junction from where the Bear Pen Trail climbs 2.9 miles up to the Bear Pen—a small, meadowy cove at the upper end of the boxed-in canyon. Under mountain hemlock, red fir, lodgepole pine and silver pine which borders the meadow's north edge, you'll find a campsite just east of trickling, alder-lined Bear Pen Creek.

Immediately beyond the Bear Pen Trail junction, we descend the south bank of Bear Pen Creek, cross it on boulders just east of a miniature gorge, and commence a winding, forested walk northward. Numerous low outcrops of metamorphic rocks are passed, and one short, boggy flat is crossed before our 2½-mile trail segment gently ascends to a meadowy junction with the Shanks Cove Trail, on which we'll be returning. Anywhere along this stretch you can find secluded campsites by walking west 100 yards or so to the east bank of Five Lakes Creek.

Continuing north, we leave the meadow and hike up to a seasonal wash. Immediately north of it and west of the trail we see water gushing forth from Big Spring—a point where the ground water in the alluvium makes a dramatic surface appearance. Our trail now contours northwest, crossing a meadow fringed with Jeffrey pine and sagebrush, then 15 yards beyond the meadow's north end merges with a faint trail climbing north-northeast from Five Lakes Creek. The gradient soon increases as we progress northward, and we get occasional glimpses of the creek, mostly hidden by alders, aspens, cottonwoods and lodgepoles. Climbing past white firs and Jeffrey pines, we acknowledge the usual trailside decorations of corn lily, knotweed, Indian hemp, thistle and aster. At the end of a moderate climb, we cross Five Lakes Creek and reach a junction from which the Five Lakes Basin Trail climbs about 1¼ miles northeast to the shallow lakes of that granitic basin.

Going left at the junction, our mostly forested route traverses west, descends past gooseberries—ripe in September—crosses a low ridge and arrives at Whisky Creek. After climbing up the creek's bank we spy a shack, shed and fireplace that make up most of Whisky Creek Camp, and just beyond these is a trail intersection where the Pacific Crest Trail starts a northwest traverse (see Trip 60). Fifty yards beyond this junction, under shady conifers, is a large, good campsite that has several tables together with plenty of logs to sit on (the trail west is described in Trip 59). We head south on the faint Pacific Crest Trail, which becomes more evident as we top a low recessional moraine left by a glacier when its icy front stagnated a few yards south of the flat Whisky Creek Camp area.

Our winding "crest" trail parallels the largely unseen creek southward, and in a few spots we can look east and identify a trail above the creek's east bank. The descent eases from moderate to gentle, then levels off and passes through a small meadow. Beyond, it joins a more prominent trail that descends northeast a few yards to a wide creek crossing before climbing to a forest's-edge junction with the east-bank trail on which we hiked north.

We continue south along the Pacific Crest Trail, shaded by Jeffrey and lodgepole pines and by red and white firs. Then, after a short, moderate descent, we diagonal southwest to a junction with the Shanks Cove Trail, in a dense stand of lodgepoles. The descent along this trail to this junction is described in Trip 59. The Pacific Crest Trail—our route—makes a quick traverse to bouldery Five

Five Lakes Creek

Lakes Creek, on whose east bank a good, though small, trailside campsite is encountered. If you wish to avoid other backpackers while camping around here, use one of the adequate campsites on the fairly level terrain just downstream or upstream from the creek crossing.

Leaving this delightful streamside environment, we wind eastward to a meadowy junction, then follow the Pacific Crest Trail southward down to the Big Powderhorn Trail, up which we hike to the trailhead.

58   Deer Park Trail to Five Lakes Basin

Distance: 4.4 miles, round trip

Total gain/Net gain: 1080'/1000'

Classification: Moderate

Season: Early July through late October

Parking: Ample space along shoulder of paved Alpine Meadows Road

Trailhead/Map: 48/16

Features: Ascending this wide, well-graded, popular trail, the weekend backpacker can reach the Five Lakes basin in only an hour's time, leaving many hours to fish, swim, explore and camp around these lakes.

Description: We start west along volcanic talus, derived from the andesite cliffs above us, and hike past dense stands of huckleberry oak beneath a scattered cover of Jeffrey pines and white firs. Rounding a broad ridge, we can look south toward the upper canyon, whose slopes support the hardly visible ski lifts of forested Alpine Meadows—quite a contrast to the many highly visible lifts in open Squaw Valley, north of us.

Our dusty trail becomes a gravelly one as volcanic rocks give way to granitic ones, some of them stained reddish by iron oxide in the rock. A few switchbacks through dense brush transport us higher up the slope, and then we arc southwest to a switchback on a weathered granitic ridge. From it we can look east, back the way we came, and see the clear contact between the medium-gray Pliocene volcanic rocks and the lighter Mesozoic granitic bedrock west of them.

After passing stunted Jeffrey pines that struggle in the shallow soils of this dry granitic ridge, we soon find ourselves contouring northwest to a set of concrete-and-rock stairs—perhaps unnecessary—that take us across exposed bedrock. Soon we reach a gully, up which we make a short, steep, winding ascent past some dark-red granite. As the gradient eases beyond the gully, we enter a lodgepole forest at the border of the Granite Chief Motor Vehicle Closure Area. Our path quickly levels off, and where it curves from southwest to northwest, a spur trail descends to the northernmost of the Five Lakes—a shallow, grassy body of water dotted with granitic boulders. In late summer and early fall, after most hikers have departed, ducks rest here while on their southward migratory flight.

A few minutes' walk beyond this spur, the Deer Park Trail meets a trail that curves north to a low saddle before descending into Squaw Valley. We veer south, round a low ridge and soon spy the westernmost and largest of the Five Lakes. A spur trail departs south toward its east-shore campsites, and a fork from this spur trail traverses east to a second lake, which is actually an almost separate lobe of the westernmost lake. Draining into the north and southeast corners of this "lobe" are creeklets from two of the basin's other lakes, which can be reached by heading up the creeklets. Within this glaciated granodiorite basin, plenty of campsites can be found around the warm, shallow lakes. Late-season hikers will find the best drinking water along Five Lakes Creek, which emanates near campsites above the north end of the westernmost lake.

Squaw Peak and westernmost of the Five Lakes

59   An East-West Traverse of the Granite Chief

Distance: 17.1 miles, semiloop trip
Total gain/Net gain: 4270'/1720'
Classification: Strenuous
Season: Mid-July through early October
Parking: Ample space along shoulder of paved
   Alpine Meadows Road
Trailhead/Map: 48/16

Features: Scenic diversity is the key feature of
this hike. Stream environments contrast with
the Five Lakes basin, exposed ridge traverses
contrast with shady valley floors, and open
meadows contrast with dense forest. Rock
types and vegetational assemblages constantly vary as we trek along this undulating
route.

Description: Trip 58 describes the route to the
westernmost lake of Five Lakes basin. Leaving campsites under lodgepoles, silver pines
and red firs along its north shore, we hike west
down to a trickling creek, immediately beyond
which we meet a trail leading north toward
Squaw Valley. This route segment is described in Trip 60.

From the junction we trek through a sloping
meadow that is being invaded by willows and
aspens, and then make a creekside descent
through an open forest down to a second
junction, this one beside the frolicking creek.
After taking a refreshing sip from its clear
waters, we traverse west, as in Trip 57, and
descend to Whisky Creek Camp and an
intersection of the faint Pacific Crest Trail 90
yards beyond a boulder hop of Whisky Creek.

A level traverse west leads us past a large,
obvious campsite before we hit a small, steep
slope. Short switchbacks take us to a gentler
slope above, colored and scented by mule
ears. Beyond it, our trail climbs steeply once
again, entering a forest of red firs and silver
pines. Midway up our haul to a ridge, we
encounter an alder-lined trickling creek,
which gives us an excuse to rest. Since this is
the last dependable water before our
campsite, almost four miles farther, we fill up.

Once on the fairly open ridge, we have
another excuse to pause, for we can admire a
panorama that extends from Granite Chief,
north of us, southward along the ridge-crest
andesite flows that cap Squaw, Ward and
Twin peaks. A low ridge-crest notch to the
south is the saddle over which the Big
Powderhorn Trail climbs. Looking through

Mule ears

the Five Lakes basin notch, we can see the
distant, broad, saddle-shaped summit of Mt.
Rose (10,776'), third highest of the Tahoe-
basin peaks.

We climb up the ridge briefly, then make a
descending, westward traverse through one of
the Sierra's largest field of mule ears (a larger
one is crossed in Trip 60). This 40+ acre
spread of large-leaved sunflowers saturates
our visual and olfactory senses. Characteristic
of, but not limited to, slopes of volcanic soils,
mule ears tend to grow in almost-pure fields,
leading one to suspect that their aromatic
leaves produce substances that reach the top
soil and prevent the germination or sub-
sequent growth of competing wildflowers.
This phenomenon has been observed in other
plants—particularly in aromatic ones—and it
is interesting to note that where there are
plants associated with mule ears, they are
usually sagebrush, pennyroyal or some other
aromatic species.

After rounding a forested slope, we traverse
through a second large field of mule ears and

come to a junction, near a shallow gully, with a signed trail that makes a short ascent before descending along the ridge crest and down into Picayune Valley (see Trip 54). Beyond the junction, we descend through a red-fir forest to an open, sometimes wet cove below an impressive array of deep, vertical grooves that striate a huge cliff of volcanic mudflow deposits (see Trip 49), above us. Rock climbers may wish to try to scale this cliff via one of its deep grooves. Leaving the cove, we follow our blazed path past red firs, then scramble up as it climbs very steeply toward a ridge. The firs on this shaded ascent allow snow patches to remain as late as early August. Because the trail is composed of volcanic rubble, it can be slippery and potentially dangerous, so watch your footing up to the ridge and beyond.

Struggling up the ridge of blocky volcanic rock, we pass some grotesque formations before the trail eases its ascent and reaches an east-west saddle from which we can gaze down Picayune Valley. Bordered by brown metamorphic rocks on its west slope and light-gray granitic rocks on its east slope, Picayune Valley sits deep beneath the dark-gray andesite flows that cap the two ridges above its slopes (see Trip 54 for a geologic interpretation). From this viewpoint we climb southwest through a forest of hemlock and pine to a long north-south saddle. From it we can see—due west of us—Johnson Monument, which is a large, isolated, severely

Johnson Monument

overhanging volcanic block atop a narrow pedestal. In the northeast, Mt. Rose again projects its broad summit above the Five Lakes basin gap.

At the long, open saddle's south end, the trail forks, each branch descending into a canyon. In search of a nearby campsite, we veer right, traverse the upper east slopes of Grayhorse Valley, and then descend slightly to a shallow gully, down which the main trail starts to switchback toward the valley floor. Rock climbers will find additional challenge in the 200-foot-high cliff readily visible just northwest of us. The trail that once descended to now-dilapidated Miranda Cabin, in Grayhorse Valley, is today obscured by a plethora of logging roads. Still in search of a campsite, we traverse a cattlemen's trail ¼ mile to a spring-fed gully, 60 yards beyond which we find our goal under mountain hemlocks in an isolated, miniature hanging valley.

After a pleasant stay, we leave our camp, make the short climb back up to the saddle's south end, and begin a switchbacking descent east toward Shanks Cove. When we reach this almost level cove, which stands apart from most others in that it is completely forested, we cross a trickling creek, then parallel it over a winding path down metamorphic bedrock. As the gradient decreases, we recross the creek—now more substantial—and parallel its trout-inhabited waters east through a lodgepole forest down to a flat where we meet the Pacific Crest Trail. Fair-to-good campsites can be found along Five Lakes Creek, which is 180 yards southeast on the trail.

Our route, however, winds northeast up the Pacific Crest Trail for 0.6 mile, to where we fork right and cross the creek, while the PCT continues up the creek's west slopes. Immediately upstream and downstream from this broad crossing are additional potential campsites for the backpacker who is unwilling to return to civilization. Beyond it we skirt the west border of a fairly large meadow; then just within the forest's edge at its north end we join a larger trail. Staying temptingly close to Five Lakes Creek, this trail beckons us to linger awhile before leaving the Granite Chief area. We finally recross this creek, instantly come to a junction with the Five Lakes Basin Trail—on which we originally descended—and retrace our steps up this trail to the Deer Park trailhead.

60   Squaw Valley to Tinker Nob

Distance: 20.4 miles, semiloop trip
Total gain/Net gain: 5500'/2710'
Classification: Strenuous
Season: Late July through early October
Parking: More than ample in large parking lot
Trailhead/Maps: 46/16,17
Features: A route with plenty of rock-climbing opportunities, this semiloop trip is bound to please Class 5 climbers. Nonclimbers will appreciate the panoramas obtained from the summits and high saddles attained along this trip through the heart of the Granite Chief area.

Description: Starting at a brown post at a road junction, our trail bears north along the east edge of the Squaw Valley Fire Station's lawn, curves west above and behind some housing developments, and climbs toward Squaw Creek. Just before reaching this creek, the trail branches, but the branches rejoin within 100 yards. If you take the left fork, which is more obvious to downhill hikers, you'll follow ducks across granitic bedrock that lead you almost to the lip of a 20-foot-deep gorge, down which Squaw Creek once flowed. Now it is cutting a channel immediately west of this minor gorge.

We parallel the creek a short distance, then cross a seasonal tributary and begin a moderate-to-steep ascent beside it. Soon, we cross it in a grove of cottonwoods, and higher up recross it in a thicket of alders. Our path now climbs west through an open forest dominated by white firs and Jeffrey pines, and it closely parallels the contact between the volcanic rocks above and the granitic bedrock below. Forest cover gives way to brush, particularly snow bush, whose thorny branch tips crowd the trail.

Beyond a small slope painted green and yellow with mule ears, we come across a small, spring-fed creek, from which our trail follows a ducked route up sloping, joint-controlled (see Trip 39) granodiorite slabs. Rock climbers will appreciate the short leads, usually under 50 feet, up near-vertical cracks on walls that our route passes. We cross two small, level benches and, immediately beyond the second, enter a gully, then switchback northeast through brush to a small flat. Our trail now heads west to a seasonal creeklet and follows it northwest, exchanging snow bush, huckleberry oak and juniper for red fir,

mountain hemlock and silver pine, and granodiorite for metamorphic rock. Coming to shady cove's headwall, we make a short, strenuous haul up it to a saddle, immediately north of which we join the Pacific Crest Trail where it bends from east to north. From here we'll make an excursion to Tinker Knob and back, a hike that takes only several hours round trip. You may wish to leave your backpack near this junction and carry only a light day pack.

From the junction a gentle descent through a sloping meadow, sometimes visited by coyotes, brings us to Mountain Meadow Lake's forested east shore, which would make a fairly good campsite were it not on private property. Although most maps show a creek draining north from this shallow lake, there isn't one. Rather, the lake drains through the sediments that dam it; then this water surfaces as a spring in the narrow gully north of the lake. Down this lushly flowered gully we proceed, observing the maze of light-colored *dikes,* rich in feldspar, which infuse the dark, sparkling, fine-grained metasedimentary rocks of Jurassic age. The source of these dikes is the nearby granitic mass, which during the Cretaceous age intruded the metamorphic rocks of this canyon.

Our gully soon curves northeast, but we continue straight ahead, following a second, shorter gully that is being eroded along the same fracture line as the first. As our trail's gradient eases where the trail curves northwest, a sign alerts us to turn onto a trail to Tinker Knob, which makes a short descent northeast to the canyon's granitic bedrock floor.

Climbing north out of the canyon is at first a struggle, for the trail, marked by painted blazes and stone ducks, winds steeply up brushy slopes from slab to granitic slab. As we curve into a minor cove, however, the nature of our trail changes dramatically. Here, above a spring-fed creeklet, is a good campsite within a grove of red firs, lodgepoles and silver pines, from which we have a grand view of the impressive volcanic palisade above us. Now on volcanic soils, we make a steep initial climb northwest from the creeklet, then follow a well-graded trail, largely through a huge, continuous field of mule ears, 1.5 miles up to a saddle on the ridge crest. Six-tenths mile along this segment, we leave our last permanent

From Tinker Knob: view south; Lake Tahoe is far left

source of water as we pass several alder-lined springs.

Once on the narrow, windswept crest, we stop a minute to absorb the new views to the east, then at the saddle's north end meet the Tinker Knob Trail, which has climbed south from a road in the Donner Lake area. From this junction several paths bear northwest toward Tinker Knob. The correct path is one that goes 100 yards to a very conspicuous cluster of conifers, then continues northwest from it past mule ears, sagebrush and silver-leaved lupine—all aromatic—to the north slope of Tinker Knob. From here, the obvious trail continues north along the broad ridge crest to a Sierra Club hut, but our route, a second-class climb, leads us south up a faint trail to the highly fractured summit of Tinker Knob.

Like Squaw Peak (8885'), south of us, and Castle Peak (9013'), north-northwest of us above Interstate 80, Tinker Knob is the remains of a Pliocene volcano. The resistant rock that solidified in the volcano's ancient throat today stands as a pinnacle on a volcanic ridge. When you consider that this volcano might once have towered 1000 feet above today's summit, you realize that a lot of erosion, perhaps 4000 feet worth, has taken place since it existed. Before its eruption, and the eruption of other Pliocene volcanoes, the Tahoe Sierra looked considerably different.

The range was lower, unglaciated, more rounded and, except for some late-Miocene eruptions, largely devoid of volcanic rock.

Inspecting the terrain seen from today's summit, we view a volcanic landscape that has undergone severe erosion, largely due to glaciers, which have exposed the underlying granitic and metamorphic bedrock. Among the more prominent landmarks is Mt. Rose (10,776'), also of Pliocene andesite, which stands as guardian above Lake Tahoe's glistening northeast corner. To the south stands aptly named Granite Chief, devoid of volcanic rock, and in the distant south shines the snowy, granitic Crystal Range, which forms the backbone of Desolation Wilderness. Catching our eye in the west is Royal Gorge, a 4000-foot-deep cut by the North Fork American River through early Mesozoic volcanic rocks that were subsequently metamorphosed. The rugged terrain visible from Tinker Knob merits a long stay atop it—though not in threatening weather. After you've had your share of views, return to the Pacific Crest Trail junction between Mountain Meadow Lake and the saddle just south of it, and turn right onto the PCT.

After a short jog west, the Pacific Crest Trail climbs south, traverses an open slope with outcroppings of vein quartz, and passes clumps of willows, in which you may spot a chicken-sized dusky grouse. Just beyond them, we get our first views of Squaw Valley and Lake Tahoe since Tinker Knob, which continue as we climb south through a forest of red fir, lodgepole pine and mountain hemlock. Along this ascending traverse one sees plenty of short cracks on the cliffs above, which will tempt the rock climber. A small flat, covered with gruss, provides an adequate campsite, and 200 yards southeast of it, our briefly descending trail crosses the headwaters of Squaw Creek at the eastern edge of a fragile, subalpine meadow. We follow this edge, then negotiate a series of short, steep switchbacks that take us up to a minor ridge-crest saddle. (Northbound, early-season hikers please note that this saddle is about 300 yards west of the large, obvious one.)

Granite Chief's subalpine meadow

Leaving the ridge and its conifer-filtered views of Mt. Rose and Lake Tahoe, we follow blazes and ducks along a faint, coarse-sand path that leads down a fairly open boulder field as we head south toward the distant Crystal Range. Easing off, the trail comes to the step-across headwaters creeklet of the Middle Fork American River. An adequate, though small, campsite lies just south of this creek, upslope from the trail.

In 100 yards we meet a junction with the Tevis Cup Trail, up which you could hike— steeply at times—0.6 mile east to the Watson Monument at Emigrant Pass. The monument's plaque, missing in 1974, told of this historic trail, first negotiated in the gold-rush days of 1849. First known as "Scott's Route," it became the "Placer County Emigrant Route" in 1852 after that county invested $20,000 to clear and grade it. This Squaw Valley route was short-lived, for by the late 1850s virtually all traffic from Carson City to Sacramento had been siphoned off along the easier Donner Pass, Hawley Grade and Carson Pass routes. From the monument much of the Tahoe landscape is visible, including—clockwise—Mt. Rose, the Freel peaks, Dicks Peak, the Crystal Range, Needle Peak, Granite Chief and Tinker Knob. Seen everywhere on Squaw Valley's slopes are lifts and roads. From Emigrant Pass you can descend an obvious road down to Squaw Valley, should you wish to cut short this trip.

Dark, volcanic flows of Peak 8774 rest upon a light, granitic base

The Tevis Cup Trail is part of the old Scott's Route, and on it—which is also the Pacific Crest Trail at this point—we descend a short distance to a junction just below and west of a saddle, from where the Pacific Crest Trail climbs southeast to the saddle. Climbers may wish to follow the Tevis Cup Trail 2¼ miles west to the crest of a very prominent, 400-foot-high granitic cliff. The trail to it, being an old one, takes the route of least resistance, climbing and descending wildly before it reaches a red-fir flat—an isolated campsite—immediately north of the challenging Class 5 cliff. Some springs just before the flat provide unfailing water for those who wish to climb or relax here.

From the junction near the saddle, our route—still the Pacific Crest Trail—swings across the saddle and goes briefly up over a low ridge, then winds and switchbacks down to a seasonal creek. A short traverse east takes us across a small flat to a volcanic slope down which our trail plows through a 50-acre field of mule ears. We approach Whisky Creek and some small campsites hidden under the dense cover of trees beside it, then parallel this largely unseen creek east to where the valley floor drops off sharply. Before we start a series of short, steep, brushy switchbacks down granitic terrain, a down-canyon view opens before us, and we can identify the obvious, closely spaced Twin Peaks and Bear Pen canyon, a large side canyon south of and below them.

Below the switchbacks we jump across trout-inhabited Whisky Creek, then traverse south across a flat to a trail intersection in Whisky Creek Camp, which has a large, popular campsite at its west end. We hike east, cross Whisky Creek in 90 yards, and make a short climb to a trail junction beside Five

Class 5 granitic cliff, seen from Trip 54

View down Five Lakes Creek canyon

Lakes Creek. Retracing some steps of Trip 59, we climb northeast moderately up a creekside trail, cross a sloping meadow being invaded by willows, and arrive at a trail fork just before a trickling creek. The main trail veers right to close-by Five Lakes and beyond—a worthwhile alternate route—but our trail veers left, crosses the trickling creek, and on a low ridge joins a trail from the Five Lakes basin. A short haul brings us to the west edge of a saddle, from which we see the lifts and roads of Squaw Valley.

Intermittently during the Pleistocene epoch, large glaciers filled this canyon below us and Pole Creek canyon—immediately north of Squaw—and they repeatedly dammed the Truckee River when they reached and obstructed that river's canyon. At times, these ice dams temporarily raised Tahoe's level by as much as 600 feet—the approximate thickness of these two glaciers—and then they broke, sending catas-

trophic floods of rampaging water down the Truckee, transporting house-sized boulders for miles.

Leaving the saddle, we descend gently north at first, then, from a viewpoint, brake down one of several steep trail branches. Each branch ends at a road on the gently sloping basin floor, and since these roads all merge as one hikes northwest, we go in that direction, contouring the slopes. A ski-lift maintenance road, climbing to Emigrant Pass, is encountered just before we cross a year-round creek, from which our road makes a winding northeast descent, recrossing this creek about midway down to Squaw Valley. After this ford several trail segments leave and rejoin our road, these making the descent a little shorter, but also a little steeper. Our dirt road, which has *W S TRAIL* signs posted along it, ends at the bottom of lift KT-22, about two minutes' walk from the large parking lot in which we left our car.

61   Tinker Knob via Tinker Knob Trail

Distance: 10.2 miles, round trip

Total gain/Net gain: 2720'/2680'

Classification: Strenuous

Season: Mid-July through mid-October

Parking: Ample parking along roadside or by meadow's edge

Trailhead/Map: 45/17

Features: The shortest and steepest of three routes to the summit of Tinker Knob, this route—a jeep trail for most of its length—is a good one for day-hiking peak baggers.

Description: From the trailhead, the Tinker Knob Trail traverses east across a meadow, through which Cold Creek runs. Beyond the meadow, it climbs south steeply up a low morainal ridge, then contours southward above the entrenched South Fork of Cold Creek, which has cut a gash through loose volcanic-mudflow sediments. Below us we soon see a tributary joining the South Fork; then we pass a roadside stand of aspens and arrive at a junction. One could go left, cross the creek and find a suitable nearby campsite, but the blazed Tinker Knob Trail parallels the creek and climbs an increasingly steep slope southward.

White firs found among this canyon's lodgepole-pine forest begin to give way to red firs as we approach a spring-fed creek, which has a fair campsite near its east bank. A minute's walk beyond it, our jeep road reduces to a trail, which immediately crosses the South Fork—our last permanent-water source. This trail climbs steeply northeast toward a ridge, switchbacks south up to it, and then climbs very steeply up its crest. Scattered

Jeffrey and silver pines provide occasional shade, and aromatic tobacco brush pleasantly distracts us from our labors.

Tinker Knob, towering way above us, is seen soon after we start up the ridge crest. Below us to the west are granitic cliffs—of interest to rock climbers—not far upslope from the fair campsite we passed. As the crest's gradient eases, we enter a shady forest of fir, hemlock and pine. Our blazed trail becomes more open in about 200 yards, and gradually widens to become an old road. This road soon takes us past old stumps in a red-fir forest which was selectively logged, rather than clear-cut. Most of the conifers are still standing, so our route is pleasant enough.

After almost touching the headwaters of the South Fork, this old logging road switchbacks east almost up to a saddle, then jogs southward around a small knoll and crests at a second saddle. Beyond the eroded pinnacles and cliffs of the volcanic slope northeast of us, we see a distant, saddle-shaped summit, Mt. Rose, in the east-northeast.

A few paces up this crest road, it forks. We stay right, and go up a steep ridge road, which quickly diminishes to a trail. This path winds up the open ridge of mule ears and sagebrush before climbing south through a grove of conifers. In this grove, as in other subalpine groves, Clark nutcrackers, which are large, gray members of the jay family, may be seen searching for pine nuts. Just beyond a pair of switchbacks, our trail eases off and climbs gently south to a junction with a trail from the North Fork American River. See Trip 60 for a route description to the summit of Tinker Knob and for the views obtained from it.

Distant Lake Tahoe and Carson Range, from Tinker Knob

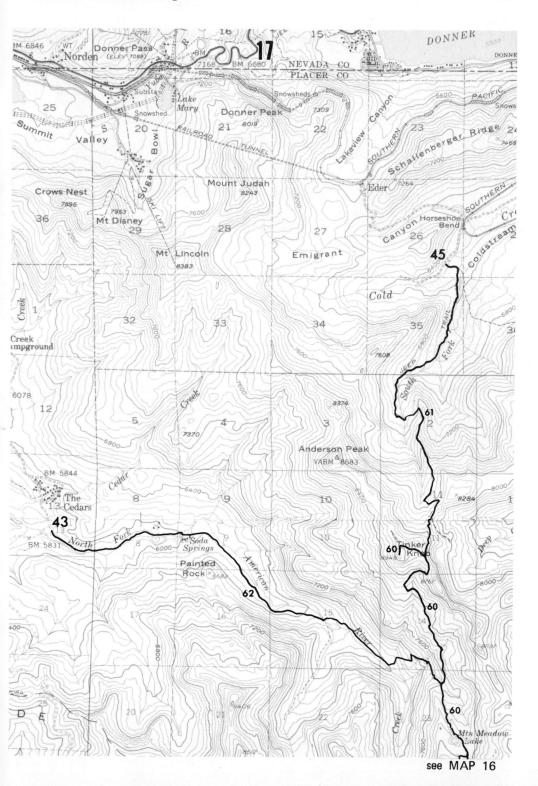

see MAP 16

62   Tinker Knob via Painted Rock Trail

Distance: 15.6 miles, round trip

Total gain/Net gain: 3450'/3130'

Classification: Strenuous

Season: Early July through mid-October

Parking: Ample parking along roadside near gate

Trailhead/Map: 43/17

Features: This third approach to the summit of Tinker Knob is the most enjoyable one, for along most of its length it parallels the North Fork American River.

Description: From the closed gate across Pinehurst Road, walk 1.6 miles east along this little-used road to its bridge across the North Fork American River. About 15 yards beyond it we reach the trailhead for the Painted Rock Trail. Starting up it, we pass half a dozen private summer homes, then beyond them encounter several soda springs which emanate from cracks and crevices, coating the granitic bedrock orange and red with their iron-rich waters.

Rounding the north toe of Painted Rock, we can see how this colorful outcrop of metamorphosed Jurassic sediments received its name. Now hiking southeast within the Granite Chief Motor Vehicle Closure Area, we are still traversing across private property and will continue to do so until we reach Section 14 (see Map 17). Our trail presents us

with a variety of environments, some shady, some open, and although the river is seldom seen, it is usually heard. Just before we cross it—a wade in early season—an unsigned trail departs southward and climbs into Forest Service land where it enters Section 22, about ½ mile up.

Once on the river's northeast bank, the Painted Rock Trail parallels it, passing several seasonal creeklets before veering northeast and switchbacking up the slopes. At the start of this ascent—on Forest Service land—you can camp in or near the river's grassy flat.

Our steep climb up through snow bush, manzanita and huckleberry oak leads past occasional junipers and Jeffrey pines and provides us with a steadily improving view down-canyon. Beyond a seasonal creek, we negotiate a few short, steep switchbacks that take us up to a recrossing of the North Fork American River. This jump-across ford is made on the lip of a hanging valley, from which the infant river plunges down into the deep, glaciated canyon below. A short, easy jaunt to a signed junction with a trail to Tinker Knob takes us across granitic bedrock that has been polished and striated by abrasive materials transported along the bottom of the river of ice that flowed slowly down this canyon as recently as 12,000 years ago. Trip 60 describes the route from the junction up to Tinker Knob.

Trail up to saddle immediately east of Tinker Knob

63   Feeley Lake and Round Lake Trails

Distance: 4.4 miles, round trip
Total gain/Net gain: 570'/390'
Classification: Easy
Season: Late June through late October
Parking: Crowded, especially on weekends; then park within Carr Lake Campground
Trailhead/Map: 40/18

Features: One lake right after another is encountered along this short, enjoyable route.

Description: Our trip starts beside Feeley Lake, which is a fairly large, moderately deep, clear lake that in the still of the morning vibrantly reflects the red-brown colors of dominating Fall Creek Mountain. In the early morning, fishermen may be seen in their small boats hoping to catch a good trout breakfast. Along this lake, whose water level has been raised by a low dam, we leave the signed Feeley Lake trailhead as we hike east on a closed road that parallels the shoreline. A short, moderate climb up a gully shaded with red firs gets us to a crossing of a subordinate ridge, from which we drop slightly as we cross a minor gully. Then we reach a tranquil lily-pad pond, which originated when the low lateral moraine immediately north of it blocked the drainage down the slopes to the south. This origin contrasts with that of most ponds, which usually form between two lateral moraines after a glacier recedes.

After crossing the outlet creek of this acre-size pond, we tread a narrow route between it and the moraine, then parallel a wet meadow east of the pond. Sediments plus accumulation of dead organic matter have formed this meadow and have decreased the pond's size to about one third of what it originally was when the glacier that filled this area finally disappeared.

At the meadow's end we crest the low moraine, which has hidden the view to the north, and we are greeted by a delightful, small lake with a photogenic, lodgepole-covered island. On the low, narrow, rocky bench that separates it from Island Lake, east of it, we find shady campsites. Trip 64, heading south, crosses this bench and joins our trail—now called the Round Lake Trail—here. We quickly encounter Island Lake, which has some fair campsites along its south shore. From granitic benches of varying height that border the southeast edge of the lake, one can dive into the cool, deep, refreshing water. Also from these benches one can gaze down toward the lake's bottom, 15 feet or more beneath the surface, and see trout swimming lazily.

Island Lake floods most of a narrow, north-south mass of Mesozoic volcanic rock, which was intruded and metamorphosed by the somewhat younger granitic rock that makes up the lake's east shore. In contact with the metamorphosed rock along the lake's west shore are Paleozoic marine metasediments, whose iron-rich content accounts for the red-brown color of Fall Creek Mountain and the adjoining landscape. Because these two units of metamorphic rock are so different in age—millions of years apart—their contact is a surface of *unconformity*—one which represents a gap in the geologic record. After a long period of deposition of Paleozoic sediments in a shallow marine basin, regional earth movements slowly uplifted these sediments, eventually exposing them to forces of erosion, which stripped away the younger sediments at the surface. Then, during the Triassic and/or Jurassic periods, volcanic sediments were deposited atop the remaining sedimentary layers. Because these old marine sediments had been tilted somewhat when they had been uplifted, the plane of their beds was at an angle to the new, overlying volcanic beds. Hence this kind of unconformity is called an *angular unconformity*.

From a trail view of Island Lake's south shore, we climb east to a north-trending, sunny, bedrock ridge, from which we can see the island-speckled lake below us, and can also see, on the north horizon, the unmistakable sawtooth crest of towering Sierra Buttes (Trip 79). Leaving the ridge, we descend northeast to the inlet creek of Long Lake, which we cross, and then we climb a low bench and catch a glimpse of that lake as we continue northeast. Where our trail curves east along bedrock, a faint trail descends 60 yards to a small gully, immediately north of us, and descends down the gully to the east shore of Long Lake. As we continue east toward Round Lake's outlet creek, we meet a second Long Lake spur trail, this one striking west to the gully and joining the first spur trail. Scenic Long Lake appears to be purposely designed for the best visual effect, for it has just the proper balance and arrangement between

An unnamed "island lake"

conifers and granitic benches. The lake's rocky shore, however, is not conducive to enjoyable camping, for it supports mountain hemlock, heather and Labrador tea, all of which harbor mosquitoes—even after Labor Day, when many Sierra lakes are virtually mosquito-free. Slightly cloudy water also makes this lake an undesirable camping area.

Twenty yards beyond the second Long Lake spur trail, we reach a junction, from which a short spur trail branches south and parallels a creek up to noncircular Round Lake. This trail traverses to a good campsite on the lake's south shore, then splits into quickly fading branches. Mountain ash, a usually inconspicuous bush, makes its presence known here in late season when it produces bright red-orange berries that easily outshine the red ones on nearby elderberries. Warm Round Lake provides excellent midsummer swimming, and one can dive into it from gray granitic rocks along its northeast shore.

From the Round Lake spur junction, we go down the outlet creek a short way, cross it, and climb steeply up a closed jeep road to where it forks just below a ridge crest. Both branches, of approximately equal length, climb to the main ridge and the route of Trip 64. Rather than branching left and climbing along the north slope of a spur ridge, we branch right, climb, and then descend briefly to shallow, greenish Milk Lake, on whose northwest bank is a fair campsite under forest cover. The trail to the main ridge is a narrow footpath along the base of the morainal spur ridge, whose lower slope is densely vegetated with bracken ferns, wildflowers and shrubs. The trail is barely above the waterline in places, and the thick vegetation at times almost forces one into the lake. Below a flat above the lake's northeast corner you'll find another fair campsite, often used by those who descend from Grouse Ridge Campground. On the flat is a reunion with the other spur-ridge route, and from this junction one can head 100 yards either southeast or northeast up narrow roads to the main ridge route, a closed jeep road.

64   Grouse Ridge Lakes Loop

Distance: 9.7 miles, semiloop trip.
Total gain/Net gain: 1580'/960'
Classification: Moderate
Season: Mid-July through early October
Parking: Ample parking in campground
Trailhead/Map: 39/18

Features: Except for in the Lakes Basin area, more lakes are encountered along this trip than perhaps any other 10-mile hike in the Tahoe Sierra. Although not all of them are sparkling gems, enough are, and the remainder serve to remind us that every lake has a history of changing states.

Description: The Grouse Ridge area has such an abundance of lakes within its complex, though not difficult, topography that you may first want to make an easy hike up to the fire lookout in order to study the terrain. From it you'll see a much larger landscape, one that extends from Lassen Peak (10,457'), in the north, to the Crystal Range of Desolation Wilderness, in the south.

Our route—a closed jeep road like many routes in this area—is not obvious at first, since several roads head north from the ill-defined Grouse Lakes Campground. All take you to our ridge route, but the best one is the lowest, and from it a short trail descends

northeast across a curving slope to the ridge and the jeep road on it. From this junction we pass an old, abandoned pickup truck and in 150 yards reach a second junction, from where a jeep road descends southeast to a ridge above Sanford Lake's north shore. A cryptic path continues down to a campsite on that shore, then winds around the lake's north arm to a crossing of the outlet creek and quickly terminates at the east arm, which also has an outlet—a very rare occurrence. Standing on the east brink of this hanging cirque lake, we can look southeast and inspect the terrain over which two ribbons of concrete—Interstate 80—meander.

Of interest to climbers is the 500-foot-high, low-angle cliff immediately south of Sanford Lake. Almost countless climbing routes exist up it, for hundreds of shallow, vertical cracks striate this wall of fine-grained granitic rock. Because the cracks are shallow, however, protection along many routes is virtually impossible with climbing nuts, and adequate only with pitons. Climbers can best approach the base of this cliff by descending directly from the campground.

From the Sanford Lake spur-road junction, our crest route swings north, descends past two closely spaced roads that meet on a flat above Milk Lake (see Trip 63), and then snakes northeast through the forest down to a

Feeley Lake (left), Island Lake (center) and Fall Creek Mountain

broad, level saddle. Along this descent, hikers and fishermen sometimes depart eastward down one or more easy cross-country routes that lead to the northwest shore of attractive Downey Lake. From rock benches above its north edge, you can high-dive into refreshing, deep water.

On the level saddle is a meadow from which we get a tree-framed view of the ragged Black Buttes in the east. The main route continues northeast, soon to climb Sand Ridge, but we peel off to the left 80 yards before the meadow and follow a path, faint at first, which becomes

more evident as we descend its winding course northwest. Then we head north across a gully to a low ridge, veer west, parallel the gully and its seasonal creek, and curve north through a narrow meadow. At its north end the trail is indistinct, and unaware hikers generally curve northwest over a very low bedrock ridge and follow an erroneous, ducked route down its slopes toward Middle Lake. The correct, blazed route veers northeast at the meadow's north end, in 50 yards crosses a creeklet, and then gently descends northwest through a pleasant forest on an approach to Middle

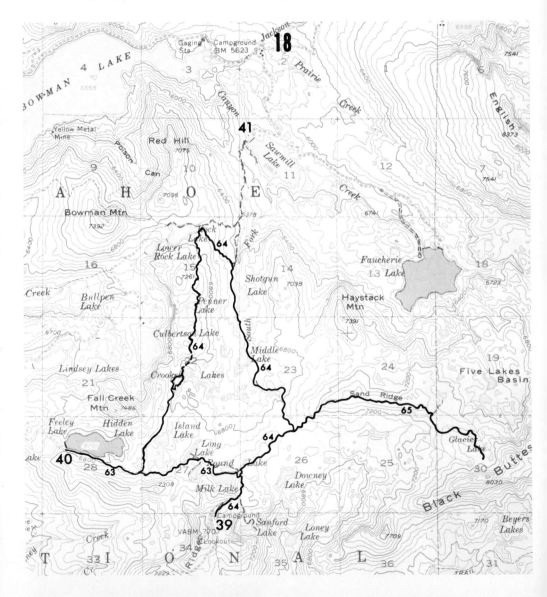

Lake. The trail never touches this shallow lake's shore—probably for the better, since it has snags and it suffers from cow pollution. People still camp by it, though.

Shotgun Lake, one-half mile downstream from Middle Lake, won't stir your heart either. After a 100-yard slog through a muddy flat, you cross its inlet creek, then diagonal northwest from it, looking desperately for blazes on the trees that border the lake's grassy west shore. Lake indeed! A late-October hiker could almost walk entirely across it and not find it, for this lake is in a late stage of ecological succession: in early summer it is a grassy pond at best; in late summer it is a wet meadow. Lodgepole pines will soon invade this meadow and lower the level of its ground water, thereby making it susceptible to further invasion by red firs and silver pines.

The South Fork of Canyon Creek, which drains Shotgun Lake, descends down a small, though impressive, gorge through bedrock just north of the lake. Not the product of recent stream erosion, this gorge was almost entirely cut by the late-Pleistocene glacier that flowed down South Fork canyon.

After going a short distance along the rim of the gorge, we reach an ephemeral creeklet, from whose bank a narrow trail starts westward. This is the trail we'll follow to Rock Lake. Beyond this junction the main trail quickly leaves the rim and descends ½ mile to a junction with a second trail to Rock Lake, this one climbing west. Beyond the junction, the main trail descends to a gully near Sawmill Lake's dam. (Hikers who want to reach this trail by starting from the Sawmill Lake trailhead—Trailhead 41—should cross Canyon Creek near or on the dam, and from the spillway's west end ascend 60 yards west, then descend 85 yards southeast to the gully. Here, 15 yards from the shoreline, look for the trail south up the gully; don't follow the shore trail unless you want a campsite.)

On the first Rock Lake lateral trail, we follow blazes and ducks up largely open slopes to a jeep road atop a shady ridge. Sixty yards north on it we reach the second Rock Lake lateral trail, which contours west along Rock Lake's north shore, then widens to a jeep road beyond it. Along the east shore of this good swimming lake, you can find an adequate campsite.

To get farther removed from the beaten track, however, leave Rock Lake and hike south up the shaded jeep road that winds to an open-forested ridge, from which the rugged Black Buttes are plainly visible in the southeast. This road then descends through brush and reaches a good campsite under white-fir cover just 20 yards down Penner Lake's outlet creek. An even better campsite is found along this picturesque lake's northeast shore. From this campsite the road climbs southeast to a small Jeffrey pine on a low knoll, then snakes south past the lake's shallow southeast end, near which you may also wish to camp. Beyond it our faint road across bedrock climbs south to a high point on a ridge, descends briefly to a small gap, and curves from east to southeast around a 25-yard-long pond just below and east of the ridgetop. Leaving the pond's southeast corner, we descend south-southeast to road's end on a rocky ridge point, from where you can see the chain of Crooked Lakes below you. South beyond them in the distance is fairly large Island Lake. The Crooked Lake you want to descend cross-country to lies along the same bearing (185°) as does that lake.

Descend along the path of least resistance, heading south-southwest down fairly open bedrock until you are just above the northwest shore of a Crooked Lake. A brief descent through brush takes you to a faint shoreline trail that contours the lake's west shore, staying within forest cover. Near this semi-stagnant, cow-visited lake's meadowy southwest corner, the trail splits, the better branch climbing southwest up to a low ridge above the highest Crooked Lake. The other branch, more brushy, starts southeast before swinging southwest up the highest lake's outlet creek, from which you can fill up on fresh water. At the lake's north shore, it contours west over to the better branch. This quaint little lake may not be good for swimming or fishing, but migrating ducks seem to like it. Granitic boulders, transported here by a past glacier, form miniature islands that add to the lake's charm and give contrast to its red-brown setting in metamorphic bedrock.

Leaving the lake, we parallel the west slope of its inlet creek up to Island Lake, which once had a dam at its north end. Along the northwest shore of this lake are some relatively little-used campsites, but southward beyond a peninsula that almost divides the lake in two, we encounter more-used ones. When we reach the lake's southwest corner, we follow most of Trip 63 east up to Milk Lake, then south back to our trailhead.

65   Glacier Lake and Environs

Distance: 9.4 miles, round trip
Total gain/Net gain: 1480'/620'
Classification: Moderate
Season: Mid-July through early October
Parking: Ample parking in campground
Trailhead/Map: 39/18

Features: Worth the hike alone is subalpine Glacier Lake, but from it you can make excursions into the Five Lakes and Beyers Lakes basins as well as up the rewarding summits of the Black Buttes. By making these side trips you're certain to lose any weekend traffic that might be present along this Sand Ridge route.

Description: From the meadow on the level saddle, our closed jeep road soon winds steeply up the west end of Sand Ridge. This ridge, all that remains of some Pliocene lava flows, is clothed with mule ears, a sunflower that is almost inevitably associated with all of the Tahoe Sierra's volcanic rocks. After a short but tiring climb to the broad, level ridge crest, a pleasant stroll through open clusters of red fir, mountain hemlock, lodgepole pine and silver pine awaits us. Between the conifers grow mule ears plus other aromatic plants, such as pennyroyal, tobacco brush and wild parsley. Unless you stoop close to the parsley, you won't smell it except when you're caught in a rainstorm. Its scent then saturates the air and masks all other scents.

The largely open vegetation allows us to constantly watch the changing perspectives

Lodgepole pine on andesite boulder

around us. The serrated Sierra Buttes (8587'), north of us, contrast with more subdued, closer English Mountain (8373'), in the northeast. The former is constructed of much older rocks than is the latter—Paleozoic metavolcanic rocks versus Mesozoic ones. To the southeast rise the rugged Black Buttes, composed of *mafic* intrusive rocks, which are similar to granite in origin and texture, but are rich in dark minerals, such as pyroxene and olivine. The felspars present in mafic intrusive rocks are calcium-rich rather than sodium-rich, while potassium feldspars and quartz are virtually absent. In addition to these summits, we can see Sanford and Downey lakes plus Interstate 80, and we can trace most of our route from the Grouse Ridge Campground.

As we start to descend the east end of Sand Ridge, we see on the left a small lodgepole tree growing out of a massive, seven-foot-high andesite boulder. Virtually deprived of soil and water, this most adaptable species of Sierra trees seems to be as much at home in this dry environment as it is in waterlogged flats. In addition to occupying a great variety of habitats, this pine also thrives over a great altitudinal range, being found in the lower, drier ponderosa-pine forests as well as in the higher, harsher subalpine forests.

Our short descent takes us to a road fork, from where the left branch descends to a good, shady campsite under conifers 60 yards from the south shore of a shallow, unnamed, trout-stocked lake. This lake sits west of and above more than a dozen lakes of the Five Lakes Basin vicinity, whose larger lakes can be seen from a point a short distance east of the unnamed lake across low, granitic ridges. Once you see these tempting jewels, you'll also see that the open slab descent east-northeast to them is quite easy. You may want to spend a few days exploring around and relaxing at the other lakes in this basin. But don't attempt to descend to Faucherie Reservoir unless you are an experienced cross-country traveller; there are precipitous cliffs to bypass. When its dam was completed in

Beyers Lakes, from Black Buttes

1965, the reservoir flooded a large meadow across which hikers once traversed to a roadend. Now water extends all the way to granitic cliffs, and reaching the reservoir's north-side picnic area is difficult via any route.

From the road fork at the east base of Sand Ridge, the right branch—our main route—traverses a long, rocky saddle through a usually wet flat just below a crest. Don't feel obliged to adhere to the road, an easy cross-country ascent southeast up the ridge will take you to our trip's destination, cirque-bound Glacier Lake. Ducks and blazes along the old road mark its tortuous, winding path—with snow patches through midsummer—almost up to the base of Black Buttes. Once you spot Glacier Lake, just east of the ridge road, you'll also find a good campsite on a red-fir-sheltered flat above the lake's west shore.

Deep Glacier Lake, at the base of Black Buttes, is a scenic site for a base camp. From it you can make day hikes down to the previously mentioned Five Lakes Basin, or you can climb the buttes or explore the Beyers Lakes vicinity. The highest of these dark buttes, which are composed of gabbro and diorite, is reached by hiking southeast up the steep, matted slope to a conspicuous saddle. From it, a short climb west—no more difficult than Class 3—gets you atop Summit 8030, and provides you with a commanding panoramic sweep across the terrain of this part of the Tahoe Sierra.

The shallow, warm Beyers Lakes, immediately apparent from the saddle, can be reached by a fairly easy cross-country route. Rather than descend steep slopes directly to them, diagonal east about ⅔ mile down to a rocky bench and parallel a usually dry creek from it south another ⅔ mile down to the easternmost lake. Our approach to these lakes via Sand Ridge is actually shorter and easier than the Beyers Lake Trail, whose trailhead is reached only by jeep or foot travel along a winding, rough road.

66   Loch Leven Lakes Trail

Distance: 6.4 miles, round trip

Total gain/Net gain: 1460'/1170'

Classification: Moderate

Season: Late June through late October

Parking: Ample parking alongside Old Highway 40

Trailhead/Map: 42/19

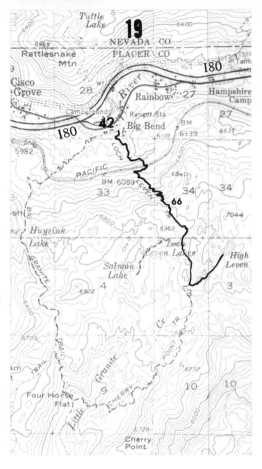

Features: The popular Loch Leven Lakes Trail is probably the best-constructed trail in the Tahoe Sierra. Granitic rocks line and buttress the trail all the way from the railroad tracks to the Loch Leven Lakes basin. The ascending route up to the lakes is never more than moderately steep, and for hikers who like to measure their progress up to these warm lakes, mileage posts are placed every tenth of a mile.

Description: From the sign along old Highway 40, hike south 0.2 mile on the private road, to where it bends west. Here at this bend, the signed Loch Leven Lakes Trail takes off through a forest of lodgepole and Jeffrey pines, then climbs more open granitic slabs adorned with snow bush, huckleberry oak, wild cherry and scattered conifers. Twenty yards past a conspicuous ridge we meet the Devils Peak Trail, which climbs east to a road coming up from old Highway 40 that winds up to that peak's volcanic shoulder. Looking west from the ridge we can see a change in the color of the bedrock, for the granitic rock beneath us gives way to an older assemblage of rocks that are mostly metamorphic in character. Solitary granitic boulders near us bear witness to the past presence of glaciers.

Beyond the trail junction we drop slightly to an alder-lined creeklet that has scattered junipers and incense-cedars growing on slopes above it. An easy climb from the creek takes us past bracken ferns, sagebrush and lodgepoles to the Southern Pacific railroad tracks. On these we walk 50 yards east, almost to the large overhead lights, near which we discover the continuation of our trail, curving west. Well-graded switchbacks take us up through a forest of incense-cedar, white fir, lodgepole pine, Jeffrey pine and silver pine. Interspersed beneath the shady conifers—particularly near seasonal creeklets—are tall vine maples and creeping thimbleberries.

Above a small hill in the north, we can see through the opening forest a metamorphic landscape in which desolate Red Mountain looms above scrubby, reddish-brown Rattlesnake Mountain, which itself rises above Interstate 80. About 50 yards beyond this view is a spring that provides water for late-season hikers. We leave the forest's pleasant, peaceful cover and soon reach Loch Leven Summit, a ridge point above Upper Loch Leven Lake. Down a shrubby slope we descend a short, steep trail segment to this shallow lake's shore, along which we can find small, fair campsites. North-south striations on its shoreline bedrock indicate the direction of movement of a past glacier. Late in the season, this trout-stocked lake becomes somewhat cloudy.

Near the pond lilies at the lake's south end, we encounter a junction with the Salmon Lake Trail. This faint trail—a good side trip—starts west-southwest, but quickly veers northwest up a low ridge, crosses it and descends slightly to an open swale before winding south-southwest down to the base of a low, rocky notch. After crossing this notch the trail continues briefly south down a gully that disgorges on the fairly flat east bench of Salmon Lake. Climbers will find short cliffs northwest of the lake, which require a half-length rope (75 feet) for safety. Fishermen can compete with the belted kingfishers that dart across the lake in search of its small trout.

From the junction with the Salmon Lake Trail, our Loch Leven Lakes Trail quickly crosses the upper lake's ephemeral outlet creek and climbs through a small notch to island-dotted Lower Loch Leven Lake. Immediately north of where our trail meets this lake, there is a fair-to-good campsite, and from it our trail traverses south along the shallow lake's rocky shore to a trail junction at its southwest corner. From it, the Cherry Point Trail descends—steeply at times—2¼ miles to a grassy meadow along a seasonal tributary of Little Granite Creek. Because the total drop to it is substantial, about 800 feet, it is not worth your effort except perhaps in mid-October, when the abundant aspens just north of it turn the canyon gold with color. A trail starting northwest from the meadow eventually leads down to Big Bend, but this uninteresting route is not recommended.

After rounding Lower Loch Leven Lake's southern tip, our trail curves northeast, traverses through a narrow, shady canyon, crosses its creek, and climbs moderately-to-steeply up to trail's end at High Loch Leven

Lake. This lake, purest of all the Loch Leven Lakes, is also best for swimming, and it has a beautiful little island on which one can sunbathe or dive. The combination of cliffs and conifers that border this heather-lined lake make it perhaps the most scenic. You can camp along its southeast shore, or you might backtrack ⅓ mile to a nearby shallow pond and camp on the low saddle between it and Lower Loch Leven Lake, immediately west of it.

High Loch Leven Lake

Salmon Lake

67   Paradise Lake

Distance: 10.0 miles, round trip

Total gain/Net gain: 1900'/810'

Classification: Moderate

Season: Mid-July through mid-October

Parking: Trailhead parking crowded on weekends—then use turnouts farther down road

Trailhead/Map: 44/20

Features: A good weekday trip, this route follows the undulating Pacific Crest Trail for more than three miles before veering east to well-named Paradise Lake. Weekend hikers, however, may find the paradise lost to carousing dirt-bikers.

Description: From the parking area of a small flat beneath red firs and silver pines, a trail and a jeep road intertwine as each proceeds on a course to Paradise Valley. Initially, the trail starts up alongside the road's right edge as both climb steeply but briefly to the open forest of Castle Pass, a saddle that has a thin veneer of andesite rocks atop granitic bedrock. Both paths head north along the crest, then quickly leave it, after which the trail crosses to the road's left side. The two diverge near a secondary ridge crest, the road veering northeast down to Round Valley while the trail veers northwest down to it. As we descend on the trail, we spy the Sierra Club's Peter Grubb Hut, built on the southwest corner of the valley's flat floor. Emerging from a young stand of lodgepole pines that are invading the valley, we pass the hut and reach the trickling headwaters of Castle Creek just beyond. John Muir, who founded the Club in order to preserve the Sierra Nevada, said sheep were "hoofed locusts" that were destroying the Sierra's fragile subalpine meadows. Ironically, in Round Valley you can still find sheep grazing during the summer; treat the waters of Castle Creek with suspicion.

Only 120 yards north of Castle Creek, our faint trail reaches a junction with the signed Sand Ridge trail, which descends west toward jeep roads and small lakes. About 60 yards north beyond this junction, we rejoin the jeep road from Castle Pass, which has cut west across meadowy Round Valley and now turns north. Up it we hike but a short ½ mile, leaving behind the meadow of willows, corn lilies and grasses as we approach a point where the road's gradient becomes noticeably steeper. Here at a large silver pine, marked at

this writing with a metal PCT trail shield, the trail begins again, climbing northwest. We top a low, open ridge and can look west toward Black Buttes and other summits of the Grouse Ridge area (Trips 63–65). In the south we see a prominent ridge split by 4000-foot-deep Royal Gorge, which has been cut by the American River's North Fork.

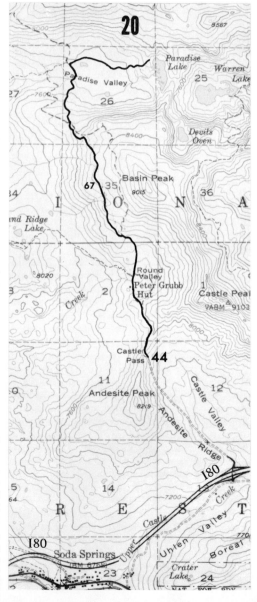

Glacier-carved Paradise Lake canyon, from the Pacific Crest Trail

As we traverse northward across Basin Peak's slopes of volcanic rock, we encounter several springs that muddy our trail but provide us with fresh water. The route then curves northwest, steeply descends a gully, and crosses it before intersecting the jeep road, which is descending a conspicuous ridge. We follow this road 65 yards down to where it curves west through a cluster of large red firs. At the start of this curve we strike northwest 70 yards to a large isolated red fir, from where a faint trail marked with ducks and blazes winds northward down a long, narrow meadow. Beyond the meadow we descend to North Creek, in Paradise Valley—which is not paradise while the mosquitoes here are still actively pursuing victims as late as early August.

In early season North Creek may be up to 10 yards wide, but you can still cross it and keep your feet dry by doing so on large boulders 20 yards upstream. Once on the north bank, we start east, then bend northeast, following a cryptic path that bears north-northwest only 70 yards from the creek's bank. In a forest of lodgepole, mountain hemlock and red fir, we pass granitic boulders up to 30 feet high that were carried here by a powerful glacier. In 160 yards we reach the Magonigal Camp jeep road, just past a small

sign labeled *Castle Valley 4,* in a small, level area (which we should look for when we return). This junction is ¼ mile east of the Magonigal road's junction with the jeep road that has been paralleling and crossing our trail.

The Pacific Crest Trail, on which we've hiked to the Magonigal Camp jeep road, begins again—though faintly at first—only a few yards northwest of this junction. Our route, however, climbs east one mile up the jeep road to the northwest shore of well-named Paradise Lake. The shore of this lake provides excellent campsites when dirt-bikers—who usually ride to it on weekends—are absent. At this picturesque, island-dotted lake you can fish, swim and dive, as well as practice your climbing skills on the good cracks of the surrounding granitic cliffs. An impressive view of glaciated terrain, framed by a well diversified flora, may be had from just over the low east saddle. A glacier once filled this saddle to a depth of several hundred feet and spilled both west down Paradise Valley and east down Carpenter Valley. Today, expanding ski-related developments threaten the serenity of Carpenter Valley and Euer Valley to its south. For the present, you can still descend 500 feet of cross-country rock to cirque-bound, little-used Warren Lake, immediately east of the saddle.

68   Mt. Rose Trail

Distance: 11.8 miles, round trip

Total gain/Net gain: 2620'/1940'

Classification: Moderate

Season: Mid-July through early October

Parking: Very limited; use highway turnouts where permissible or park at Mt. Rose Campground, just up the highway

Trailhead/Map: 51/21

Features: The only hike in this book within Nevada, this trail takes you up to the Tahoe basin's third highest peak, Mt. Rose. The Mt. Rose Trail is short enough and starts high enough that the peak can be easily climbed and descended in one day. Those who want to stay awhile will find that the headwaters of Bronco Creek offer isolated camping.

Description: The first 2½ miles of route are an easy climb up a closed road to a saddle. We start up toward it through an open forest of lodgepole pines, which tap water in the fairly deep soil of weathered granodiorite our road is built upon. Soon, Lake Tahoe and pointed Pyramid Peak rise over the ridges southwest of us, while peaks of the Virginia Range— parent of the Comstock Lode—rise above the framed view through Ophir Creek canyon to the southeast. Along our easy walk, the

pleasing aromas from sagebrush, together with those from mule ears and pennyroyal, complement our visual experience.

Where our road makes a noticeable curve right, its road cut reveals an anatomical vignette of the volcanic rocks we now tread upon. These layered rocks are not horizontal; rather, they slope down to the east. (Geologists say they *dip* eastward.) A short walk west therefore takes us across increasingly older rocks, probably of early Pliocene age. From east to west we pass through a purplish volcanic mudflow (see Trip 49), then through a buff-colored *tuff* layer, which is the consolidated product of ash that was explosively ejected from a volcano. Next we pass a brown-gray andesite flow, which rests on weathered granodiorite of Cretaceous age. Immediately beyond this small granodiorite exposure we encounter volcanic rocks again. But these aren't older than the granodiorite; they are here because we've just crossed a fault. The rocks west of the fault have dropped in relation to those on the east, so the rock units do not match up—western volcanics are juxtaposed against eastern granodiorite.

Our trail soon curves northwest, leaving behind views of Lake Tahoe and the Incline Lake development, below us. A red-shafted

Cross section through fault. With respect to the rocks that are east (right) of the fault, those west of it have dropped from A to A'; consequently, granitic rocks to the east are juxtaposed against younger volcanic rocks to the west.

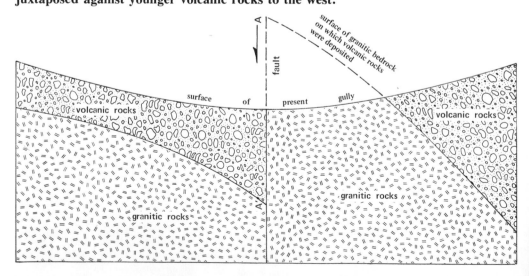

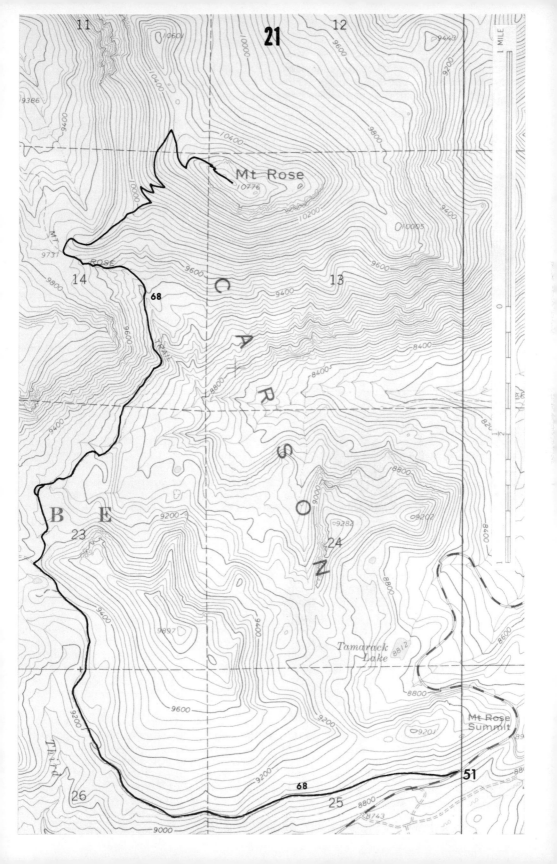

flicker or a Clark nutcracker might be seen flitting from tree to tree, the woodpecker in search of bark insects, the jay in search of pine nuts. Heading north, we parallel a meadow from whose south end a trail descends along the east bank of Third Creek but dissolves among the vegetation just above the Incline Lake development. Bending northwest, our road now takes us past a small dirt road, forking west to nowhere, and past a shallow, semistagnant pond. Immediately beyond it, our road almost crests a saddle.

We leave this service road and fork right (north), immediately cross over the saddle, and descend to a meadow. The road diagonals through it to some trees at its northwest end, and a trail cuts north right through it, to rejoin the road after having saved us a few steps. Near the reunion, a clump of corn lilies signals the presence of a roadside spring emanating from the porous, block-covered, andesitic soil. To the southeast we can look head-on at the fantastically eroded, deeply grooved cliff of easily eroded volcanic mudflows.

Our road descends northeast from the spring, first paralleling overhead powerlines, then bending more northward and crossing a flat with a small, curving moraine perched on the brink of an east-facing slope. You can camp under the lodgepoles on this flat, which has a convenient creek just north of it. Our road winds steeply down to it in about 200 yards and then terminates.

Continuing from the creek, which is our last source of permanent water, we go north on a trail that traverses a bouldery slope and crosses several seasonal creeklets. Wildflowers abound, particularly lupine, tall larkspur, paintbrush, yampah, pennyroyal, mule ears and thistle. Shrubs are represented by sagebrush, currant, elderberry and willow. To the east we can look out well past the ski lifts and see the distant desert ranges.

Our trail climbs moderately northeast, and then at a ridge bends northwest and climbs steeply up the slope of a deeply incised gully. After gradually leveling off, the trail fords the gully's creek, usually flowing through late August, passes a small campsite, and climbs along the northeast bank all the way up to a saddle on which stand some weather-beaten whitebark pines. Descending northwest from it is a faint trail that quickly becomes more prominent as it heads past impressive volcanic cliffs on its way down toward the headwaters of Bronco Creek, along which you can find good, isolated campsites. Before this trail fades into oblivion, it gives rise to two other trails that end at roads which are now closed to the public.

The more popular Mt. Rose Trail turns northeast, then cuts along the crest of a narrow ridge over toward the dark, volcanic hulk of Mt. Rose. We get a superb view northwest down the glaciated canyon of Bronco Creek and see large Stampede Reservoir flooding the valleys among some low hills north of Interstate 80. Our views continue to improve as we switchback up the west slope of Mt. Rose. We now see three reservoirs down-canyon from us which, left to right, are Prosser Creek, Boca and Stampede. On September 12, 1966, an earthquake—magnitude 5.4—cracked Prosser Creek Reservoir's dam; the Tahoe area still has active faults. Lake Tahoe, the Carson Range and Desolation Wilderness come into view to the south. North and just barely below us is an impressive group of granitic "pinnacles," which stand out boldly from the darker andesitic flows above. Along closely spaced vertical joints, or fractures, erosion has worked back, creating deep grooves between narrow arêtes, which have the appearance of pinnacles. Although not too steep, this granitic complex should offer some interesting Class 3 to 5 climbing routes.

By the time we approach the ridge crest, we've left virtually all vegetation behind, and we now see Donner Lake in the west and the unmistakable ribbon of highway called Interstate 80. When we finally do reach the crest, an exciting new panorama opens up before us in the northeast: Reno and the desert ranges beyond it. Now it's only a few minutes' walk to the summit register atop Mt. Rose.

From the summit we can look due south down the granitic backbone of the Carson Range, which separates the Tahoe basin from the Nevada desert. Structural geologists would classify the Tahoe basin as part of the westernmost border of the Basin-and-Range province, which extends across Nevada, for like the basins in that geologic province, the Tahoe basin is faulted down between two mountain blocks. Geochemists and geomorphologists, on the other hand, would classify the basin as part of the Sierra Nevada, for it is largely granitic rock, and its glaciated, adjacent crests are continuous with similar glaciated crests of the Sierra Nevada.

Biologists would classify the basin as

Summit of Mt. Rose

Sierran, but the basin's east ranges have a good share of juniper, sagebrush, mountain mahogany and other high-desert species. As for Mt. Rose, its inhospitable summit supports only the most hardy species, such as dwarf currant, alpine pynocoma (an aster), and ground-hugging species of stonecrop, phlox, eriogonum and grass.

Verifying our views again, we identify, from left to right, Jobs Peak, Jobs Sister and Freel Peak, all on the skyline at the south end of the Carson Range and ranking fourth, second and first among the Tahoe basin's highest peaks. On their summits, as on Mt. Rose, the thickness of the air you breathe is a full one-third less than that at sea level. West of them stand several dark summits of the Carson Pass area. Continuing our clockwise scan, we can spot pointed Pyramid Peak. Contrasting with it is the broad, metamorphic summit of Mt. Tallac.

When you descend from Mt. Rose, please don't cut switchbacks, as others have done. You might have noticed that the trail's gradient was just about perfect for the ascent, and it would be unfortunate if you were to ruin it for others.

Trails of the Highway 49 Region

Introduction

Crowning the northern Sierra in the Highway 49 region is a south-north swath of lake-dotted, subalpine scenery. From the Sierra Buttes northward, this area includes the Sardine Lakes, Salmon Lakes and Gold Lake canyons, Lakes Basin Recreation Area and Plumas-Eureka State Park (Trips 79—92). Perhaps no other area in the entire Sierra Nevada has such easy access to as many lakes as this one does, which accounts for its popularity. If it were reached by Interstate 80 instead of winding Highway 49, it would be far more popular. The central attraction, Lakes Basin Recreation Area, rivals Desolation Wilderness in beauty, though not in size. Wisely, the Forest Service has made Lakes Basin itself a day-use-only area, thereby eliminating the need for restrictions that exist in Desolation Wilderness. Since every lake in this basin can be reached within an hour's walk from a trailhead, no one suffers and everyone benefits—lake shores are not deteriorating despite heavy use.

The first area you come to as you drive north up Highway 49 from Nevada City is the Malakoff Diggins area, which includes a state park, its nearby environs and the South Yuba Trail (Trips 69–72). This trail at present is about six miles long. It may soon be extended to Missouri Bar, and we hope that in its final form it will extend from Highway 49 east 25 miles up the South Yuba River to the sleepy settlement of Washington. This low-elevation area provides almost year-round hiking opportunities.

Isolated midway between the Malakoff Diggins area and Interstate 80's Grouse Ridge Recreation Area is the Bedbug Smith Trail (Trip 73), which is one of the few remaining maintained canyon trails and is the only one in this guidebook that descends to the Middle Yuba River.

The North Yuba River is much more accessible, because Highway 49 runs beside it for many miles. Trails along this river and highway can be divided into three groups: the Ramshorn area, the Wild Plum area and the upper North Yuba area. All are characterized by steep-canyon topography with a few pools and almost no lakes. The Ramshorn area, being lowest, has the longest hiking season—about eight months—while the North Yuba area's season is only half that. Throughout most of the Highway 49 region—home of the Mother Lode and other gold pockets—mining claims by the hundreds dot the landscape. As mentioned in the Interstate 80 introduction, all claims should be avoided to avoid being shot at. Few mining claims exist in the higher, forested areas, but virtually all the trails in them, which were utilitarian rather than recreational in nature, have been obliterated by logging operations.

Trailheads reached from Highway 49

The following trailhead descriptions begin from Nevada City, which is about 29 miles north from Auburn via Highway 49. Our mileage begins at the junction where Highway 49 branches west from northeast-curving Highway 20. If you are driving to Trailheads 52 through 60, then Nevada City will be the last town where you can purchase gas, food and supplies.

Trailheads 52–59: South Yuba River

52 From the junction where Highway 49 branches west (0.0), we drive in that direction and immediately pass on our right the headquarters of the Tahoe National Forest. Highway 49 descends to a bridge across the South Fork Yuba River (7.2), then climbs to paved Foote Crossing Road (4.3, 11.5), on which we turn right and drive northeast to the very rural settlement of North Columbia (8.3, 19.8). Here we turn right and drive southward along the Grizzly Hill Road to a junction with the North Bloomfield Back Bone Road (3.2, 23.0). (Since South Yuba Campground doesn't yet have a permanent water system, you may want to stock up on some water by driving

Left, Sierra Buttes Fire Lookout

southward down toward Edwards Crossing. Nine-tenths mile down this road you'll encounter Rattling Jack Spring, on your right, beneath a shady broad-leaf maple.) If you have water, turn left (northeast) and curve eastward on the Back Bone Road to the South Yuba Campground entrance road (0.2, 23.2) and down it reach **Trailhead 52 (0.1, 23.3),** located at the end of a large, day-use parking lot on your left. You can also drive two-tenths mile down to a usually dry creek crossing, near the center of the campground, from which campers are more likely to start their hike.

53,54   From the South Yuba Campground entrance (23.2), drive northeast to a flat, wide, grassy ridge (2.4, 25.6), where you meet the Lake City Road. Branching east from the Foote Crossing Road only 0.3 mile north of Mile 19.8 in North Columbia, this road provides an alternate, 3.9-mile-long drive to the open-ridge junction. Fork right at this junction and drive down into Malakoff Diggins State Park, reaching **Trailhead 53 (0.8, 26.4),** on your left. Beyond this trailhead drive to a view (0.5, 26.9) of Malakoff Diggins, then arrive at **Trailhead 54 (0.2, 27.1),** on your right.

55,56   No sooner do you start up your car again than you reach in 300 yards **Trailhead 55,** on your left, from which the Diggins Trail climbs up a gully. Our road now takes us up a rustic hill capped by a cemetery—a chronicle of history—and well-preserved St. Columngille's Catholic Church, from which we descend to the Clampicnic Area, on our left, which serves as **Trailhead 56 (1.3, 28.4).**

57   In 50 yards reach a road signed *North Bloomfield Station,* on which you turn right and drive across Humbug Creek, then past a closed road on the right before you reach another road (0.8, 29.2) on your right. Turn sharply right and drive southwest on it to **Trailhead 57 (0.2, 29.4).** You may not be able to drive to the trailhead before Memorial Day, due to muddy road conditions; before then you may have to park back at the road junction.

58   Back at the junction near the Clampicnic Area (28.4), continue northeast on the main road, pass by the park headquarters and museum in 40 yards, then pull into the Blair parking area, which serves as **Trailhead 58 (0.2, 28.6).**

59   From the Blair parking area, drive north to the Shoot Hill Campground entrance (0.5, 29.1), turn left and follow its road to **Trailhead 59 (0.5, 29.6).** This trailhead serves the Blair Trail, on your left, and in 20 yards, the Rim Trail, a fire road on your right. The campground is open from about mid-April through the Labor Day weekend, and its popular campsites are subject to reservation.

Trailhead 60: Middle Yuba River, Lower Section

60   In North Columbia (19.8), continue your drive up the Foote Crossing Road (Road 19N14) and quickly pass the Lake City Road (0.3, 20.1), which branches right toward Malakoff Diggins State Historic Park. Next, encounter the Hill House Country Store near the Columbian Hill Station (1.0, 21.1) of the California Division of Forestry. Beyond it, drive your ridge road to merge (7.4, 28.5) with a road that climbs about four miles up from the Malakoff Diggins/North Bloomfield area. From this junction continue northeast along the ridge road to a cemetery on your right and a spur road (8.2, 36.7), signed *Bedbug Smith Trail,* on your left. This spur road is located just one-quarter mile west of Merk's place, in Graniteville, which has gas and a minimal supply of food available from late May through late October. Road 19N14 continues 6.4 miles east from Graniteville to a road junction above the west shore of Bowman Lake. See the Interstate 80 log for trailhead descriptions in that area.

We drive north on the Bedbug Smith spur road, quickly reach a fork and follow the descending branch 120 yards to a second fork (0.3, 37.0). Before Memorial Day you may want to leave your car here if the steep road on your left looks too damp to drive back up. On this road we descend, steeply at first, northwest down a gully, and then curve northward to road's end and two posts that mark **Trailhead 60 (0.4, 37.4).**

Trailheads 61–63: Ramshorn Area

61   From the Foote Crossing Road junction (11.5), drive north on Highway 49 through North San Juan (3.7, 15.2), then wind your way over the Middle Yuba River and finally down to a crossing (16.2, 31.4) of the North Yuba River. Immediately before reaching Fiddle Creek Campground, turn left on the Indian Valley Scales Road (1.0, 32.4), drive up it to a ranger station at Cal-Ida (4.5, 36.9), quickly fork right (0.2, 37.1) and then fork right (2.0, 39.1) on Road 20N25. Now on the

Eureka Mine Road, we follow it a short distance to our third right fork (1.9, 41.0), this one signed *Halls Ranch Forest Service Station.* Driving northeast on this short road, we see the ranch in 250 yards, pass its entrance, and above its north grounds reach roadside **Trailhead 61 (0.4, 41.4)**, signed *Halls Ranch Trail 9E03.*

62   On Highway 49 immediately beyond the Indian Valley Scales Road (32.4) we pass Fiddle Creek Campground, then Indian Valley Campground (0.7, 33.1), and arrive at Indian Rock Picnic Area, on our right. Park here for **Trailhead 62 (5.4, 38.5)**. To reach the start of Trail 9E03, walk 100 yards west on Highway 49 to the Ramshorn Summer Home Tract spur road, then 50 yards up it to the actual trail, on your left.

63   Just beyond Indian Rock Picnic Area (38.5) we cross Ramshorn Creek and turn left on the County Dump road (0.1, 38.6), up which we drive to a bend northwest— **Trailhead 63 (0.1, 38.7)**—situated between the upper and lower sections of Ramshorn Campground.

Trailheads 64–72: Upper North Yuba River

64   From the Ramshorn Campground/ County Dump road (38.6) drive east up Highway 49 to Downieville (5.7, 44.3), which has the Downieville Forest Service Station at the west end of town on the south side of the river. Continue east up to Sierra City, which is the most convenient settlement for gas, food and supplies if you are starting your hike from Trailheads 64 through 85. In town, turn north up County Dump Road (13.0, 57.3), which bends west in one block and climbs up to a large flat (1.2, 58.5) at the edge of the dump. Turn sharply right and follow a dirt road briefly east, then northwest up to **Trailhead 64 (1.4, 59.9)**, which is a junction with the steep, narrow Sierra Buttes jeep road. Don't attempt to drive up it—Trip 79—unless you have a 4WD vehicle.

65,66   Beyond Sierra City (57.3) we reach a bend from which a road forks right (0.5, 57.8), descends to a bridge across the North Yuba River and reaches a signed trailhead parking area (1.2, 59.0) on our right. A brief distance beyond this parking area, our road forks (0.2, 59.2). The left fork goes to **Trailhead 65 (0.2, 59.4)**, at the Wild Plum Station. Use the signed trailhead parking area 0.4 mile back if you are starting up from here. The

right fork immediately bridges Haypress Creek, enters Wild Plum Campground and loops to its east end, **Trailhead 66 (0.3, 59.7)**. If you're not setting up camp in this campground, then park back in the signed trailhead parking area.

67   From the Wild Plum turnoff (57.8) continue up Highway 49 to Bassetts Station— with gas, food and lodging—at the Gold Lake Road junction (4.6, 62.4). Highway 49 climbs past the riverside Carvin, Lodgepole and Pioneer camping areas, on our right, then comes to the Haskell Creek Summer Home Tract (2.5, 64.9). **Trailhead 67 (0.3, 65.2)** for the signed Haskell Peak Trail is near the end of the tract's north-climbing spur road. Park where you can without blocking the road.

68,69   Beyond the tract's spur road (64.9) Highway 49 reaches **Trailhead 68 (0.4, 65.3)**, on the left, which is only 25 yards before the Chapman Creek bridge. Just beyond the bridge is the entrance to Chapman Creek Campground (0.3, 65.6), at whose north end is **Trailhead 69 (0.1, 65.7)**.

70   Continuing from Chapman Creek Campground (65.6) we pass a road (1.4, 67.0) descending right to Lincoln Creek Campground, then meet a road (1.4, 68.4) climbing left up to the Lunch Creek Trail. We reach its start, **Trailhead 70 (0.2, 68.6)**, above the creek's west bank.

71   Beyond the Lunch Creek spur road junction (68.4) our highway tops Yuba Pass (1.1, 69.5), and at it we turn right and drive past the Yuba Pass Campground (0.1, 69.6) southeast to a saddle (0.9, 70.5). If you have a 4WD vehicle, you can descend southeast to Berry Creek, cross it and traverse southeast to the Berry Creek Trail. If you're driving a car, curve southwest from the saddle and drive to a fork (0.5, 71.0) almost on a broad saddle, branch left, and drive southeast up a gently ascending road to a junction (1.5, 72.5). From here, a dead-end spur road going left descends to a turnaround, **Trailhead 71 (0.9, 73.4)**, which is situated just above Berry Creek Trail's crossing of an alder-lined creeklet.

72   From the spur-road junction (72.5) wind southeast up to a gentle slope that has been selectively logged. A logging road (0.9, 73.4) descends east-southeast and crosses the obscure Berry Creek Trail in about ½ mile. Our road continues south to another logging spur (0.7, 74.1), which descends 0.9 mile to the same trail. Immediately beyond this spur and just before the Lincoln Creek saddle, our route forks southeast. We drive up its gentle ascent to a level roadend, **Trailhead 72 (1.2, 75.3)**, which is a few yards beyond a jeep road that descends steeply and briefly to the Berry Creek Trail.

Trailheads 73–76: Sardine Lakes Area

73 At Bassetts Station (62.4), drive up the new Gold Lake Road to the Sardine Lakes/ Packer Lake turnoff (1.4, 63.8). Drive west to a spur road leading south (0.3, 64.1) and follow it to limited parking just before it crosses Sardine Creek, whose crossing serves as **Trailhead 73 (0.2, 64.3)**.

74 Ten yards beyond the spur road, reach a fork at which the Sardine Lakes road branches left. Seventy yards on it takes us to an old jeep road—**Trailhead 74 (still 64.1)**—on our right. In two-thirds mile, the Sardine Lakes road ends at Sardine Lake Resort, which serves meals and rents boats. On your way to this resort, you'll pass Sardine Lakes Campground and Sand Pond Picnic Area.

75,76 Branching right at the junction (64.1), drive up toward Packer Lake, but first reach **Trailhead 75 (2.4, 66.5)**. Continue upward, driving past Packsaddle Camping Area in 100 yards and reaching a junction— **Trailhead 76 (0.4, 66.9)**. Drive about 80 yards southeast on the main road to the Packer Lake Picnic Area, where you can park.

Trailheads 77–79: Gold Lake Area

77 From the Sardine Lakes turnoff (63.8), continue up the new Gold Lake Road, quickly passing the Salmon Creek Campground entrance (0.2, 64.0) before climbing to a junction with the Salmon Lakes road (2.6, 66.6). Driving west on it, we pass a jeep road (0.6, 67.2), which descends south to Lower Salmon Lake, then we curve over to Upper Salmon Lake's east shore and **Trailhead 77 (0.5, 67.7)**, located about 150 yards before the lake's shoreline parking lot.

78 Gold Lake Road north from the Salmon Lakes road junction (66.6) takes us past Snag Lake Campground (1.4, 68.0) to an intersection with a road branching east toward Mills Peak Lookout and west down to Gold Lake Campground (1.4, 69.4). Beyond it we meet another intersection (0.3, 69.7), with a southwest branch to private property at Gold Lake's northeast end. We turn right, start northeast, and then drive northward to **Trailhead 78 (2.1, 71.8)**, which is the Frazier

Falls Picnic Area. Four miles beyond this trailhead our old Gold Lake Road joins the new one.

79 From the old road intersection (69.7) near Gold Lake, drive north and soon climb west up the new Gold Lake Road to an unsigned fork branching left just before our forest highway tops a broad divide. Go southwest 80 yards on this fork to a broadridge parking lot, **Trailhead 79 (1.0, 70.7)**, which is 100 yards east of Gold Lake Resort.

Trailheads 80–85: Lakes Basin Area

80 Beyond the Gold Lake Resort spur road (70.7), our forest highway descends to an intersection (0.9, 71.6), at which we turn sharply left toward Lakes Basin. Our road quickly ramifies into three branches (0.1, 71.7), the left one going south to private property, and the right one going west to Lake Center Lodge, which was permanently closed in autumn 1974. We take the middle branch and go south-southwest down to the center of Lakes Basin Campground (0.2, 71.9), where there are outhouses and a camp-fee sign. A few yards west of these fixtures, we spy campsite 10, and from it follow a camp road north 70 yards to campsite 7, at the camp's north end, which serves as **Trailhead 80 (0.1, 72.0)**.

81,82 From the camp's center (71.9), drive southwest past campsite 10 to Elwell Lodge's signed entrance, which has **Trailhead 81 (0.3, 72.2)** 20 yards west of it. Beyond the entrance our road winds west to a parking area, which serves as **Trailhead 82 (0.2, 72.4)**. The Bear Lake Trail climbs south from it, while Trail 12E30 traverses west and in 60 yards reaches an organization campground.

83,84,85 Driving north from the Lakes Basin turnoff (71.6), we curve smoothly down past a signed highway turnout, **Trailhead 83 (1.1, 72.7)**, above Lily Lake. Beyond it we descend to a bend and the Gray Eagle Lodge spur road (0.6, 73.3). Head west on it to Gray Eagle Creek, then immediately come to a spur road (0.4, 73.7), branching right, which you take to its end, **Trailhead 84 (0.1, 73.8)**. There is only room for a few cars at most. Gray Eagle Lodge is private property, but you can park outside its grounds and walk from the last junction (73.7) along the lodge's road to **Trailhead 85 (0.2, 73.9)**, from which a trail starts south near the north side of the lodge's northwesternmost cabin.

From the Gray Eagle Lodge spur road (73.3), the new Gold Lake Road descends to a junction with the old one atop a forested moraine's crest (3.6, 76.9), then continues down to its end at Highway 89 (1.7, 78.6). Drive northwest on 89 to Graeagle (1.4, 80.0) to obtain supplies at its general store.

Trailheads 86–87: Plumas-Eureka State Park

86   From Graeagle's general store (80.0), drive north on Highway 89 to a junction with County Road A14 (0.4, 80.4), onto which you turn left. Follow this road southwest up into the state park and arrive at the Jamison Mines spur road (4.8, 85.2), on your left, just before the county road curves west and descends to Jamison Creek. The spur road is locked off during the night, so park outside the steel cable if you intend to leave after dark. Otherwise, drive up the road to **Trailhead 86 (1.4,** 86.6), which is a large parking lot among the Jamison ruins.

87   Beyond the Jamison Mines spur road (85.2) County Road A14 descends to a bridge across Jamison Creek, then reaches a junction with the Johnsville-LaPorte Road (0.5, 85.7). Southwest up this road are Upper Jamison Creek Campground (1.2, 86.9) and Ross Camp Unimproved Area (3.2, 90.1). At the junction (85.7), near which is the obvious park headquarters and museum, we curve northward through Johnsville (no services) to a junction, where our paved road up to Eureka Ski Bowl turns sharply left (0.9, 86.6). A moderate ascent up it takes us southwest to the bowl's parking lot (0.5, 87.1), from whose south end a narrow dirt road, open Monday through Thursday only, climbs to the northwest shore of Eureka Lake, where **Trailhead 87 (1.3, 88.4)** gives rise to a path leading southwest across the lake's dam.

69   South Yuba Trail

Distance: 12.2 miles, round trip

Total gain/Net gain: 1440'/440'

Classification: Easy

Season: March through November

Parking: More than ample in trailhead parking lot

Trailhead/Map: 52/22

Features: While most of the Tahoe Sierra's high trails are still under snow, the South Yuba Trail offers the backpacker a wild-flowered landscape in full bloom. Its low elevation allows hikers to enjoy moderately warm outdoor camping in both spring and autumn. In addition to swimming and diving in the river's many swimming holes—best during midsummer—you can fish, pan for gold or raft down the river.

Description: The first 1.4 miles of trail, which take you to Overlook Point Picnic Site, also double as a nature trail that introduces you to the area's more prominent species. In 1974 a booklet published by the Bureau of Land Management was available for those who wanted to know what the 39 posts stood for. Since this very informative booklet may not be available when you hike the trail, the points it elaborates on are listed here in slightly modified form: 1,5, Douglas-fir; 2, ponderosa pine; 3, poison oak (learn to identify and avoid this one!); 4,27, sugar pine; 6,22, canyon live oak; 7, black oak; 8, California buckeye; 9, incense-cedar; 10, wood fern; 11, sword fern; 12, Kenebec Creek rock formations; 13, Pacific dogwood; 14, mock orange; 15, broad-leaf maple; 16, gooseberry; 17,34, manzanita; 18, barberry; 19, mountain misery; 20, mistletoe on black oak; 21, mule ears; 23, mountain mahogany; 24, red berry; 25, California laurel (bay tree); 26,37, knobcone pine; 28, bush monkey flower; 29, toyon; 30, birds-foot fern; 31, Blue Tent and Sailor Flat hydraulic diggings south-southeast across the river; 32, buckbrush; 33, digger pine; 35, South Yuba River canyon; 36, creeping sage; 38, deer brush; and 39, yerba santa. If you hike along this nature trail in spring, you're likely to see, in flower, bleeding heart, Sierra iris, larkspur, miner's lettuce, lupine, Indian paintbrush, wild parsley, Indian pink, soap plant, star flower, triteleia, yellow-star tulip and wall flower.

During most of the summer and part of the fall, the South Yuba Trail will be dry; be sure to bring enough water to last you to the river. From the large, day-use parking lot, our trail descends about 200 yards and joins a spur trail from the campground. Then our nature trail swings around a low, forested ridge and descends slightly to just below the base of a picturesque Kenebec Creek cascade, which flows down black slate blocks. These metamorphosed sediments underlie the entire nature trail, though in places they have been further metamorphosed to phyllite. We cross the creek and in 200 yards reach an old jeep road. Another 200 yards down it takes us to a signed junction, from which the South Yuba Trail branches left.

An interesting side trip is the 0.6-mile, moderately steep descent on the jeep road—signed the *Kenebec Creek Spur*—which takes you down to the Illinois Crossing Picnic and Camping Area. This area is situated atop a level, 40-foot-high bench of gravel, cobbles and boulders which are waste products from the Malakoff Mine and other hydraulic mines (see Trip 72). Under the shade of live oaks are tables for those who like luxurious camping or picnicking. Since this bench is such an easy walk from the South Yuba Campground, you might consider carrying down a gold pan, for on B.L.M. lands panning gold is legal. From the far end of the bench follow a narrow trail that extends almost to Kenebec Creek. Along this trail you'll spot shallow eddy pools in which you can try your luck.

Kenebec Creek cascade

see MAP 23

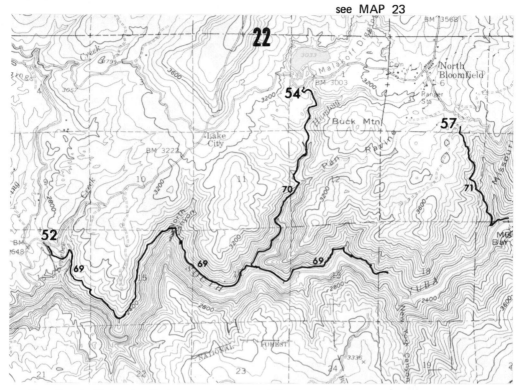

Our South Yuba Trail departs from the Kenebec Creek Spur and traverses southeast for one mile high above the unseen, faintly roaring river below and arrives at a spur trail that bears south 75 yards to the Overlook Point Picnic Site. This site provides a fair view down-river, but more than that, it provides tables shaded by live oak and Douglas fir—a welcome relief for those trudging up the South Yuba Trail on a hot summer afternoon.

Beyond this spur we traverse northward, start a descent and soon see the river below us. Along this descent, you'll notice the purple milkweed, which is a conspicuous, knee-high, purple-stemmed wildflower with dark-green, opposite leaves. As we approach a head-on view of a ridge that rapidly descends to a bend in the river, we encounter our third spur trail, this one particularly worth taking. Thirteen switchback legs carry you ⅓ mile down to the mouth of North Canyon's creek, which in springtime tumbles over a sunny bedrock bench into the South Yuba. On this broad bench are open campsites, but the best attractions are the river's pools—20 feet deep in places—and the high rock ledges from which you can dive into them. In late spring and early summer the current is too fast and

View up the South Yuba

cold (about 50°F) to safely enjoy, but by midsummer conditions improve. Since the water barely reaches 60°F, you'll appreciate the heat of a midsummer's day, which quickly warms you after an invigorating swim.

About 100 yards past the spur, we cross North Canyon, then climb up a southwest-facing slope, start a descent, curve northward and soon drop to a junction with the Humbug Trail (see Trip 70). Immediately west of this junction is a flat, wide bench—the Humbug Picnic Site—perched 60 feet above the river, and like the Illinois Crossing bench composed of gravel, cobbles and boulders wasted from the rubble created by hydraulic mining. Back in 1884, when Judge Sawyer issued an injunction against the dumping of mine debris into rivers, this bench *was* the South Yuba River's bottom! In the intervening time, the river has carried away most of the tailings so that it now runs clean, but a few debris segments—in the form of conglomerate-rock benches—still remain. Since this bench was built up to its present height in the late 1870s, the live oaks and ponderosa pines growing on it can be no older than that. With this in mind, you can see that at least one pine must have been growing at an average rate of about one foot per year. Before the pine can grow to full maturity, however, the bench will probably be eroded away. In the meantime, we can gaze down from its edge into the cold but tempting emerald-green pools of the river.

South Yuba Primitive Camp

Trail's end

Just beyond the bench, our path briefly descends to a boulder crossing of milky Humbug Creek, which still suffers from mine-debris pollution; then we follow the river 0.3 mile to the South Yuba Primitive Camp. Under shady walnut trees growing on a wide, grassy bench, you'll find tables and an outhouse in this not-so-primitive setting. A nice, sandy beach—great for sunbathing when the sun's upon it—awaits those who descend the 20-foot-high bench. Both upstream and downstream from this camp you'll find deep, beautiful pools. Diving into these for trout are common mergansers, which are large ducks with slender, "toothed" bills that are well developed for catching their slippery prey.

Continuing onward from this camp—the last flat ground we'll see—we immediately round a bend, then climb and parallel the river 1½ miles eastward on a course that takes us past some more-remote pools. At trail's end, 30 feet above the river, we encounter a beautiful, emerald-green pool bordered by water-rounded, massive exposures of bedrock that protrude part way into the river and make ideal diving platforms. If you're bold and energetic, you might carry in a two-man raft to this trail end, inflate it, and take an exciting, five-mile ride down the river to Illinois Bar, from which you have to hike only one mile back up to the trailhead. This alternative takes you through some pools seldom touched by other hikers.

70   Humbug Trail

Distance: 5.4 miles, round trip
Total gain/Net gain: 920'/800'
Classification: Strenuous
Season: Early April through mid-November
Parking: Park along roadside, but don't obstruct traffic
Trailhead/Map: 54/22

Features: Although steep and potentially dangerous in places, this trail is worth the effort because of the dramatic waterfalls, refreshing pools and scenic cliffs it presents to the hiker.

Description: Just beyond our signed trailhead, we reach a creeklet stained rusty orange by the oxidation of iron found in nearby rock deposits. Man, through hydraulic mining, has accelerated this process, and he has stained much of the state park landscape in more ways than one. A log bridge gets us across the creeklet, and then we curve east and follow its waters through a lovely Douglas-fir forest in whose shade grow pink bleeding hearts, purple larkspurs, scarlet Indian pinks and white, diminutive star flowers. Quickly we come to a bend and start southward down the creek from Malakoff Diggins before we encounter west-flowing Humbug Creek itself.

Humbug Creek and our route now both wind southward, and we pass a rusty pool followed immediately by an algae-choked, rusty spring. In May the dogwoods along this shady stretch of trail explode into blossom with large, white "petals," which botanically are bracts that surround tight clusters of small, greenish-yellow flowers. Beyond a log bridge over a creek, we pass a table on a flat just above us and then reach a bend and meet an old road that descends steeply to the point where our trail joins it. The road now descends gently 0.3 mile to its end at a fresh creek, encountered immediately beyond a small, round pond on our left. On small, grassy flats near this pond one could set up a fair campsite.

A short, steep ascent eastward up a trail takes us to a rocky ridge overgrown with moss and stonecrop. Then the trail drops us steeply to the oak- and poison-oak-lined creek, which has some tempting pools above the brink of its upper falls. We leave the creek's side, traverse a steep, rocky slope to a small, necessary bridge, and from it obtain a spectacular view back at the cascading creek, which jumps from one churning, milky-green pothole to the next via falls ranging up to 50 feet high.

Dogwood leaves

When you leave the bridge, water your step, for there are several bad spots where the steep trail almost disappears, and at them you could take a sudden, unintentional slide down the overly steep slope; don't let the captivating scenery distract you. Into this southbound stretch of creek below us, a 7874-foot-long tunnel from Malakoff Diggins once spewed its gushing, muddy water. You'll find evidence of sediments carried down our creek when you reach a tailings bench at the junction with the South Fork Trail, just above the river.

Our trail curves southeast and descends almost to Humbug Creek as it passes a massive outcrop that towers above the creek's opposite bank. Here, at the brink of the creek's lower falls, are two narrow swimming pools which have been cut into a bedrock bench. On a hot midsummer day, the two-mile hike down to these milky-green pools is more than worth the effort. In late spring and early summer, when the water flows faster, use your discretion, since a plunge over the falls could be fatal. Beyond these two oversized bathtubs, our path parallels the creek but stays well above it as it descends to meet the South Yuba Trail (see Trip 69). On it, you can hike east and enjoy the clear river's larger, colder pools.

Upper falls

71   Missouri Bar Trail

Distance: 3.4 miles, round trip

Total gain/Net gain: 1220'/1200'

Classification: Moderate

Season: Early April through mid-November

Parking: Very limited; park where you can without obstructing access

Trailhead/Map: 57/22

Features: Except for the long South Yuba Trail, most of the trails down to this river and to the Middle Yuba are steep. The Missouri Bar Trail is another exception; its short, moderate descent will take you comfortably down to the river in half an hour.

Description: Our trail starts out in a mixed forest of black oak, incense-cedar, ponderosa pine and Douglas-fir. Along shadier parts of the trail, such as those typified by Douglas-fir cover, you may find large banana slugs which oh-so-slowly scavenge the moist forest floor in search of decaying organic matter—orange peels included! Our route is an obvious one which steadily descends south-southeast across metamorphic bedrock to a campsite at the confluence of Missouri Canyon creek and the South Yuba River. Down here—at Missouri Bar—the river is about 40 yards wide, and even at peak runoff it is scarcely more than knee-deep, a feature that certainly pleased old-time miners on their way between the diggings and Nevada City.

Immediately upstream from the campsite, a portion of the river's flow curves clockwise back on itself, and this motion has scoured out a beautiful, deep, placid pool that remains safe—though cold—to swim in even when the river is flowing vigorously. The metamorphic bedrock near the pool is phyllite rather than slate, which is seen downstream, since the original rock both formed from has undergone greater change. A trail runs eastward from the pool about 200 yards to another wide, knee-deep crossing that will get you to campsites above the river's opposite bank. Just up from this crossing, the river narrows somewhat and deepens to 10 feet or more, and in late summer provides additional swimming opportunities.

South Yuba River at Missouri Bar

72   Malakoff Diggins Trails

Distance: See each of the three trails

Total gain/Net gain: All negligible

Classification: All easy

Season: Early April through mid-November

Parking: Small parking lot at Trailhead 58; all other trailheads have limited, though usually adequate, roadside parking

Trailheads/Map: 55,59/23

Features: In winter, Nevada County clears snow off the road into North Bloomfield, giving this rustic state park a 12-month season. History buffs will appreciate the "diggins," the old town and the museum. Botanists, entomologists and ornithologists will appreciate the flourish of life that abounds from April through June.

Introduction: The heart of the North Bloomfield mining district is the Malakoff Diggins, which became a state historic park in 1966. The first gold to be discovered in California was found in the late 1770s in the Potholes district of Imperial County. It was, of course, James Marshall's January 1848 gold discovery at Sutter's Mill in Coloma—situated between Auburn and Placerville—that triggered the 49er gold rush into the Sierra. Most of the mining claims were established in a belt that extended from Mariposa—gateway to Yosemite Valley—northward to the Quincy area (see Trip 91).

In Spring 1851 gold was discovered in the North Bloomfield area by an Irish prospector. He leaked his discovery to other miners in Nevada City, which was an 1849 boom town, and they secretly followed him back to his claim. When they got there, they tried their luck at mining, found nothing, and declared the project a "humbug." Because of this initial bad luck, the shanty community that grew there became known as Humbug, and the nearby creek became Humbug Creek. After several years gold was discovered, and Humbug grew to house a few hundred persons, including the expected saloon keepers, gamblers, dance-hall girls and merchants. At a mass meeting held in 1857, the populace decided Humbug was not a respectable name, and they changed it to Bloomfield. There was, however, already a California community bearing that name, so the residents changed their town's name again, to North Bloomfield.

With a change in the town name came a change in the miners' luck. At the American Hill mining district, which is about 10 miles northeast of their settlement, hydraulic mining was begun in 1852—the first in California. The following year, North Bloomfield's residents adopted this technique and by 1855 hydraulic mining had become a major industry. In order to spray vast amounts of high-pressure water against the gold-bearing gravels of the

Monitor in operation, circa 1880   *U.S.G.S.*

Malakoff mine, reservoirs were constructed, but since this area, like other mining districts nearby, was rather dry, over 50 miles of canals had to be built to divert water from the Bowman Lake area down to reservoirs near the gold fields. In Nevada County as a whole, some 700 miles of canals were built for this purpose. High-pressure water eroded the gravels down into sluice boxes, in which the gold—with a density 19.3 times that of water and about 10 times that of its associated sediments—settled to the bottom.

A problem developed over what to do with the remaining sediments, which at the Malakoff mine amounted to a total of about 50 million tons. As profits were pouring in, sediments were pouring out—down the Yuba River. Other Sierra rivers, particularly the Feather, Bear and American, suffered similar fates. Between 1866 and 1884, the Malakoff hydraulic mine yielded about 3.5 million dollars from its 30 million cubic yards of gold-bearing gravel. The large monitors, or water nozzles, had sprayed out a hole more than 7000 feet long, 3000 feet wide and up to 600 feet deep. The gravels from this mine, and from other nearby mines, brought a great change in the lower course of the Yuba River, particularly along a 16-mile stretch from Smartville down to Marysville. The added sediments built up the river bottom, so that it easily overflowed its banks in times of high water. Not only were farmers' crops ruined by flooding, but an immense amount of fine debris was deposited on the river's adjoining plains, covering an area of 25 square miles. These deposits of fine sand and gravel rendered much farm land unfit for cultivation and caused farmers to protect adjacent country by constructing costly levees.

The farmers who were affected took their claims to court in 1884, and in a landmark case, *Woodruff vs. North Bloomfield Gravel Mining Company,* Judge Lorenzo Sawyer issued an injunction against the dumping of mine debris into the Sacramento and San Joaquin rivers and their tributaries—one of the first environmentalist victories in this country. Other injunctions soon followed, and hydraulic mining all but disappeared. In its heyday, North Bloomfield could boast of a population of over 1200, but by the time it was considered for incorporation in the state historic park, its population had dwindled to nine.

Hydraulic-mining debris also changed the characteristics of rivers, thereby affecting river-barge transportation. Before the 2200 million tons of sediment choked up rivers, one could travel from Sacramento north 120 miles up the Sacramento River to Red Bluff and south 180 miles up the San Joaquin River to the Fresno area. Hydraulic-derived sediments, carried in flood waters, provided added thrust to scour away the rivers' banks, eroding good farm land in the process, but also leaving the rivers wider when the floods subsided, thereby making them shallower and less navigable.

Description:

Excursion A, The Diggins Trail: Mileage indeterminable—scramble where you wish; Trailhead 55

This trail takes you into the heart of the Malakoff Diggins. Start early if you're hiking it on a hot summer day, for there is little shade in this open pit. At the trailhead is a large sign that gives statistics of the 7874-foot-long drain tunnel engineered by Hamilton Smith, which was begun in April 1872 and completed 30 months later. At present, milky, yellow-brown water trickles from the Hiller Tunnel, which is a segment of the larger drain tunnel. During the mine's heyday, the drain tunnel must have transported a lot of muddy water and sediments down to Humbug Creek and along it into the South Yuba River (see Trip 69). To finance such a tunnel plus the reservoirs and many miles of canals needed to feed them required a lot of capital. The miners who worked these "diggins" weren't independent souls, but rather were company pawns. Except for the first few years, when individuals flocked to the hills in search of placer gold, the extraction of this ore belonged to big business—either in the surface hydraulic mines or in the subterranean bedrock mines.

Our trail starts north across weathered Paleozoic marine sediments which long ago were metamorphosed to slate, phyllite and schist. Then it tops a low saddle and presents the hiker with a sweeping panorama of the Malakoff Diggins, which are in a 600-foot-thick layer of Eocene sediments deposited by the ancestral Yuba River. The Diggins Trail, if one can call it that, now is an abandoned east-west road along the south side of a large, shallow, muddy pond. Just 40 yards east of your junction with this road, you'll find a

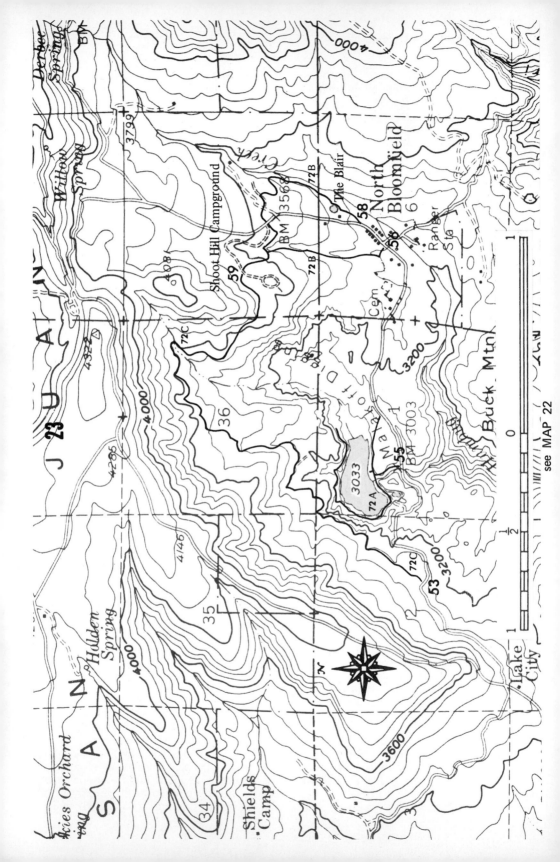

30-yard-long spur trail leading north to the end of the 556-foot-long Hiller Tunnel, which provides an alternate route to the Diggins (a flashlight is recommended if you take this route). At the pond's southwest end, a footpath begins northwest and gradually curves eastward around the iron-rich pond, dying out at its east end. From there, hike wherever you choose.

The pond is not lifeless. Cattails are invading it, and on them in spring perch male Brewer blackbirds, each singing a song that proclaims him the master of the adjacent territory he defends against landless males. Along the shore's white, quartz cobbles, the spotted sandpiper lays her eggs, which blend in perfectly with them. Invading the lower slopes above the lakeshore are alders, willows and ponderosa pines, each species dropping litter, which furthers soil development.

The Diggins resemble a miniature Bryce Canyon both in erosional patterns and in variety of colors. However, in Bryce Canyon, as in most canyons, the sediments get progressively younger toward the rim, but here, some older sediments lie on top of some younger ones. These older gravels were laid down by the ancestral Yuba River, which later cut down through them and then deposited the lower, younger layer of gravels in the cut. The upper layer of white gravels is called the bench gravel, since it was deposited on a wide bench cut by the ancestral river into the bedrock surface over which it flowed. That there was a wide river bench here tells us that the river had been eroding for millions of years in a low Sierran range—if the range had been higher, the river would instead have cut a gorge into the bedrock.

The Sierra was uplifted after the deposition of the bench gravel, and then the river cut a broad canyon several hundred feet deep. When the uplift ceased, the ancestral Yuba River stopped its canyon cutting and entered a phase of depositing gravels. At Malakoff these lower gravels are divided into two colors, the upper red and the lower pale blue. The gravels are essentially the same in composition, but the blue gravels once lay below the water-table surface, which protected them from being exposed to oxygen, while the red gravels got their color from oxidation of the iron in them. It was the blue gravels, the lowest 130 feet of sediments above the Paleozoic bedrock foundation, which contained the most gold. No wonder, then, that the first miners, who worked the uppermost sediments, declared this area "humbug."

Hydraulic-mined cliffs of Malakoff Diggins

Hiller Tunnel's outlet

Excursion B, The Blair Trail: 2.4 miles, semiloop trip; Trailhead 59

This trail is a pleasant stroll even on hot July days, for it is short and shady, and it takes you to an old swimming hole. Starting in Shoot Hill Campground, we descend southeast on an old road that has been narrowed to a wide path by encroaching shrubs. Black oak, ponderosa pine, incense-cedar and Douglas-fir—typical species for this elevation and slope—provide us with a convenient canopy. After 300 yards our trail levels, narrows to a true trail, and reaches the gully of a trickling, seasonal creek. Thirty yards beyond it, we reach the main creek, at which our trail splits. From here we'll make a loop trip, descending the steeper, creekside trail to the Clampicnic Area and returning via the shadier Blair Trail.

During spring our descent is accompanied by the refreshing song of a trickling creek, whose banks are adorned with Indian pink, soap plant, lilies and other water-loving plants. In the conifers, a woodpecker may search for bark insects while a gray squirrel may, after scrutinizing us, return to his forage for ponderosa-pine seeds and black-oak acorns.

After traversing across a drier slope covered with manzanita, we pass behind some buildings of partly reconstructed North Bloomfield, come to a bridge, cross it, and find ourselves in the Clampicnic Area, a beautiful, grassy picnic ground dominated by several immense incense-cedars. Across the road stands the silenced Hendy Giant—a 15-foot-

The Hendy Giant

Incense-cedars at Clampicnic Area

Aquatic garter snake

long, nine-inch-diameter monitor, which in its day shot down many tons of gravel cliffs with its jet of high-pressure water. After a few steps up the road, we reach Cummins Hall, which serves as the park's headquarters and contains a museum that is open daily from June 1st through the Labor Day weekend. A history buff could spend many hours in it and around the settlement's buildings, reconstructing in his mind how the town might have looked and what the townfolk were like back in the 1870s.

A brief walk northeast up the town's road gets us to Trailhead 58—the parking lot for the Blair. Up a short, closed road we walk to the Blair, which is today a somewhat murky but thoroughly refreshing swimming hole. This hole was the site of early hydraulic mining; then it later became a storage reservoir that provided water for one of the monitors at the Malakoff mine. In its deep, milky-green waters swim trout, other fish and kids. On less crowded days, you may find aquatic garter snakes near or in the reservoir's shallow, vegetated east end. On weekends you can expect all the picnic tables—sheltered under ponderosa pines, incense-cedars and Douglas-firs—to be occupied.

After taking a last drink from the water fountain, we start northeast along the narrow earth dam that separates the Blair from the deeply cut gully down which Humbug Creek courses boisterously in the springtime. Leaving the reservoir's shore on a splendid, shady path, we follow a ditch that once fed the reservoir, and pass an iron pipe and then a wooden flume, both used to transport the canal's water across small side gullies. We near the bank of delightful Humbug Creek, then climb up an old road that first curves west up a slope before it curves north and almost dies out as it joins a road climbing northeast. We start southwest on this road, cross through a missing section of fence, and descend its westward-curving path 170 yards to a prominent, south-southwest descending road. Don't follow it, but continue west on a trail for 120 yards to the park's main road, which you cross just 10 yards southeast of its junction with the campground's entrance road.

Found along this terrain are large but harmless alligator lizards, which slither down our path as we hike along it and parallel the entrance road above us to the creeklet down which the Clampicnic trail descends. We continue west a short way, then climb the stiff, narrow road back up to Trailhead 59.

Two mining flumes

Excursion C, The Rim Trail: 7.0 miles, round trip; Trailhead 59

This trail provides you with an entirely different perspective of the Malakoff Diggins than does the Diggins Trail. Our trail—really a closed fire road—starts west from Shoot Hill Campground, curves southwest, and emerges on a grassy flat that also supports plantain, lupine, western buttercup and other wildflowers together with a few walnut trees, perhaps planted by townfolk. Our road soon crosses the first of many creeklets we'll see along this route, but by midsummer all of them will be dry. Growing by most of them are water-loving broad-leaf maples. On drier ground above the first creeklet grow black oaks, incense-cedars and ponderosa pines, beneath which you'll spot kit-kit-dizze, called "mountain misery" by early pioneers who found walking through patches of this sticky, fernlike wildflower rather unpleasant. Miwok Indians used its leaves to make a tea, which they used to cure various illnesses.

Farther along our route we encounter the first of several headward-eroding gullies, each cutting into the road. Note the recently exposed roots of plants and the steep headwall of the gully. The headwall is subject to further collapse during a heavy spring rainfall, when there may already be ground water seeping from its base. The lower sections of most of these gullies have been somewhat stabilized by the growth of shrubs, which help trap

sediments. The upper, actively eroding sections, however, are usually devoid of vegetation.

Beyond a small pond we enter a sunny thicket of manzanita, which attracts an army of bumblebees during May when these plants are in flower. Through this thicket we descend south along our now-rocky road before coming to a level area with ponderosa pines. The rocks and boulders are derived from volcanic flows—similar to those at the Sierra crest—which were laid down during the Pliocene. In this state park, these flows cap much of the gold-bearing Eocene gravels of the ancient Yuba River. In all likelihood, less than half of this area's gold was removed by the hydraulic operations. Now the gold is protected by state park status as well as by the overlying burden of volcanic rock. Despite the dramatic rise in gold prices during the 1970s, nearby mines are unlikely to be reopened. Tough antipollution standards, used now to protect fish and game as well as downstream settlements, would prohibit most operations. Furthermore, the cost of machinery and labor makes such a project uneconomical. In these foothills, conservationists should be more concerned with a decrease in open space due to subdivisions than due to expansion of surface mining. California, in the meantime, will continue to get most of its gold the way it has since the early 1950s, when gold mining became unprofitable: the ore is extracted as a by-product in some other mining operation, such as North Columbia's gravel works.

The diverse environment of brush and conifers we now stroll southwest through provides many habitats for animals. The most conspicuous animals are birds, and here you'll see, among others, the robin, Oregon junco, California quail, green-backed goldfinch, mourning dove, black-throated gray warbler, Steller jay, mountain chickadee and several species of sparrows. Each species of bird has a specific dietary requirement that is at least somewhat different from that of every other species; in this way direct, head-on interspecific competition is avoided. Instead, competition is *intraspecific,* that is, among members of the same species. A principal mechanism for keeping a population in check is the establishment of territories during mating season—a practice found among other vertebrates besides birds. Only those dominant

Retreating rim of Malakoff Diggins

males that can establish and hold a territory will mate. Hence an overabundant surplus of young will not be produced.

Our aromatic route turns south and proceeds down a usually dry creeklet, crosses to a larger, longer-lasting one, leaves it, and then soon descends steeply back to it. We bid farewell to its cloistered grove of incense-cedar, madrone, black oak, Douglas-fir and ponderosa pine, and hike westward to an open bend, from which we get our first view of the gravel cliffs. Beyond it we wander through a 10-foot-high manzanita thicket, meet a closed road that descends southeast, and continue our brief westward, brushy traverse to a forest of ponderosa and sugar pines. Two gullies working headward into our road are passed before we encounter in a deep gully a small outcrop of cross-bedded sandstone, which is part of the gold-poor bench layer of Eocene gravels.

Our road traverses around the deep gully and emerges on the northwest rim above the large, shallow pond of Malakoff Diggins. Almost immediately a view opens up and we get a sweeping panorama of most of the open pit and its colorful cliffs. Old trees and shrubs grow right up to our rim's edge, indicating that the rim is retreating. Roots protruding from the tops of cliffs together with fallen trees on the slopes below confirm our suspicion. While following the Diggins Trail on the flat below us, one gets the impression that little erosion has occurred since the end of hydraulic mining. Up on the rim, however, we can see that a fair amount has occurred, and by at least three processes. First, heavy rains can send streams of water downslope, which erode the cliffs in bits and pieces. Second, when the upper portions of the steep cliffs get wet from surface water and/or from ground water, the cliffs are likely to suffer small rockfalls. Finally, if clay is present in sufficient amounts, it can adsorb enough water to weaken the cohesion of the gravels and cobbles it binds, and cause a good-sized slump. In several places our road has been eradicated by these slumps, and we can see the debris they deposited on the lower slopes 300 feet below us.

If these gravels had been of Jurassic age or older, they would be much better cemented and perhaps also metamorphosed by Cretaceous granitic plutons. If so, the gravels would have been too solid to be mined by hydraulic methods, and their gold concentration would

have been too low for any other method to be economical. Precious and rare minerals can be found in many sites, even in soils, but unless they are sufficiently concentrated, they don't merit exploitation.

Leaving the Diggins, you commence a traverse through a fairly open field, in which you're almost certain to encounter cattle and may also see, particularly in early morning, a jackrabbit or mule deer taking off through the deer brush and past the buckeye trees. Our closed road ends at three posts along the park's main road, and you can either retrace your 3.5 miles of route or you can start down the main road. The author suggests you descend this road to a signed viewpoint, descend a closed road from it down into the Malakoff Diggins, explore them to your heart's content, and then head east from the large pond's south shore until you once again reach the main road. Hike along it into North Bloomfield, then take the shady Blair Trail back to your trailhead.

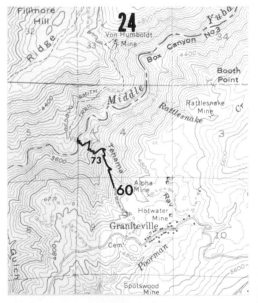

73   Bedbug Smith Trail

Distance: 2.0 miles, round trip

Total gain/Net gain: 1300'/1300'

Classification: Strenuous

Season: May through November

Parking: Room for one-half dozen cars at trailhead

Trailhead/Map: 60/24

Features: The only accessible, respectable trail that descends to the lower middle portion of the Middle Fork Yuba, this path takes you to shaded, river-bench campsites close to small, invigorating, emerald-green pools.

Description: We start our hike at two posts and descend a ridge trail that is mostly shaded by Douglas-firs, but also by sugar pines, white firs and occasional ponderosa pines. Lining the path in places are manzanita, chinquapin, huckleberry oak and (watch it!) poison oak. Short, steep switchbacks help ease the grade down this ridge route. Just beyond its halfway point, our path swings west, crosses the ridge, and continues to switchback down gradually easing slopes.

Just before arriving at a fair campsite on a gravel bench 50 feet above the Middle Fork, our trail leaves metamorphic rock behind and enters granitic bedrock. The forest cover still contains Douglas-fir, and beneath these shady false-firs—whose cones hang from, rather than perch on, the branches—grows a profusion of kit-kit-dizze. Usually going unnoticed are the inconspicuous Indian-hemp plants, but when touched with late October's frosty finger, they turn a brilliant yellow. Sugar pine and white fir have dropped out from the forest cover, replaced by incense-cedar, black oak and live oak.

A better campsite is found just upstream on a lower bench. To reach it, head upstream a few yards to a gully—named Tehama Ravine on the topo map—and follow a narrow path down it to the lower bench. In addition to typical hydrophytic plants, such as maple, alder and willow, which line the river, there also thrives the umbrella plant, or Indian rhubarb. Identified by its large, umbrellalike leaves that grow up to a foot in diameter, this annual grows waist-high out of shallow water. Indians peeled its leaf stalks and ate them fresh or stewed them. A peculiar feature of this plant is that it first grows flower stalks; then these die back and are replaced with new stalks that produce the large leaves. (In like manner, deceptive redbuds, which also grow in this canyon, produce a show of blazing maroon flowers on otherwise barren, woody twigs. These later become covered with clusters of round leaves and lose all traces of petals.) You'll find rather chilly the water in which umbrella plants grow. Climbing the thermometer to the mid-fifties at best, the river's icy pools on a hot midsummer afternoon are nevertheless worth the refreshment that a shocking plunge into them brings.

Middle Yuba River

74   Ramshorn Campground Area

Distance: See each of the three trails

Total gain/Net gain: 2100'/1540', 960'/960', 2230'/2230'

Classification: All strenuous

Season: Late March through mid-November

Parking: Ample

Trailheads/Map: 62,61,63/25

Features: While the higher, more scenic Highway 49 trails are still under snow, you can hike these trails to get in shape. Both ends of the Halls Ranch Trail direct you to verdant, creekside environments. The Ramshorn Trail transports you up to some interesting rock-and-mineral assemblages.

Description:

Excursion A, Halls Ranch Trail to Fiddle Creek: 6.0 miles, round trip; Trailhead 62

Our signed trail begins 50 yards up the Ramshorn Summer Home Tract spur road. We climb westward up to a gentle slope, on which people have camped above the muffled noise of passing traffic below. In early season this noise is almost drowned out by the roaring North Yuba River. On our slope and the steeper one above us, we are shaded by Douglas-fir, incense-cedar, canyon live oak, black oak and ponderosa pine. Switchbacks, together with shade, make the 700-foot ascent of the steeper slope tolerable, and from the last turn we curve southwest around a ridge onto sunny, rocky slopes. The river's roar is now noticeably quieter as we arc westward to our four final switchbacks, which lead us to the top of Fiddle Creek Ridge. Our trail now bears

southwest about 0.4 mile along the ridge, which is mantled with a manzanita thicket that harbors mountain quail. Dominating the skyline to the east-northeast are the unmistakable Sierra Buttes (8587').

If we had climbed up to this ridge some 20,000 years ago—at the height of the last major glaciation—we would have surveyed a different landscape. The difference would be subtle. We wouldn't see any glaciers, for they got no farther west than the Sierra City area. The North Yuba canyon may have been slightly shallower and its tributary gullies less pronounced. The main difference would have been in the vegetation.

During the last glaciation, the average annual temperature was about 9°F lower than it is today. Meteorologists have observed that temperature decreases about 3.5°F for every 1000 feet of elevation. Therefore a 9°F drop is achieved by a 2500-foot gain. Keeping this in mind, we can deduce that 20,000 years ago, our 4000-foot-high Fiddle Creek Ridge, if 9°F cooler, would have had the climate and vegetation of a present-day 6500-foot-high ridge. Then, rather than standing among scattered ponderosa pines, Douglas-firs and sugar pines, we would have been shaded mostly by white firs and Jeffrey pines, and perhaps also by an occasional lodgepole pine or red fir. The tree cover might have even been thick enough to block our present-day view of Sierra Buttes.

How can one tell the climate was colder back then? One approach to this problem is through the examination of varves, which are annual layers of sediments laid down in lakes

Umbrella plants at Fiddle Creek

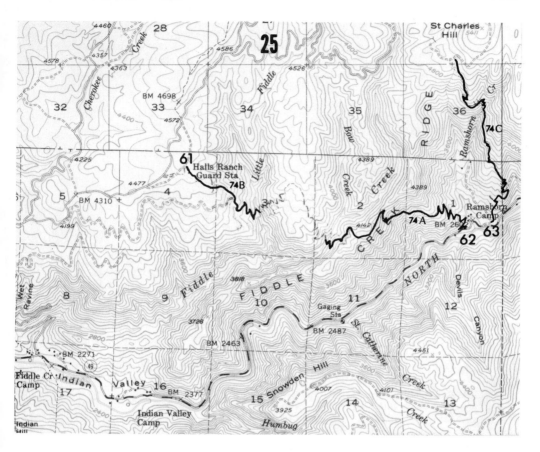

(see Trip 45). Trapped in each varve are pollen grains which came from nearby plants that existed while the varve was being deposited on a lake bottom. By identifying the various pollen grains in a long series of varves, you can detect changes in species and in their relative abundance as time progressed. Varves laid down when glaciers began to retreat about 12,000 years ago indicate that conifers which existed around lakes back then are the same species that exist several thousand feet above them today.

Returning to a warmer subject—the higher temperatures on our open ridge—we seek shade by following the trail southwest to a minor spur ridge, down which our trail swings northwest. Our path, brushy in places, then descends southwest and crosses two gullies before switchbacking quickly down to the verdant cover cloaking Fiddle Creek. Under the shade of alder, dogwood and broad-leaf maple, trout swim lazily in the creek's rocky, knee-deep pools. Within this filament of deciduous greenery, the temperature is pleas-

antly cooler, even on the hottest days. Ferns and umbrella plants add to the decor of this creek environment. A tricky crossing on rocks gets you to the wide creek's west bank, up which the trail continues about 35 yards to a small campsite. You probably won't want to hike any farther, since the route only switchbacks up to a maze of old logging roads before descending as a trail to Little Fiddle Creek. Those interested in the regeneration of a logged-over forest will find this 1.9-mile hike to Little Fiddle Creek informative. It also provides you with good route-finding practice. Use Map 25 and look for yellow blazes painted on trees.

Excursion B, Halls Ranch Trail down to Little Fiddle Creek: 2.8 miles, round trip; Trailhead 61

The trail from this end is not too obvious at first. Starting from the signed trailhead, walk 80 yards south-southeast, until you are east of a large building with a curved roof. Now look downslope for a blaze. Walk in its direction—

east-southeast—for 50 yards, by which distance the trail will become obvious. We now descend through the Forest Service's Experimental Forest, reach a dirt road, and at a trail sign *9E03* head east down a ridge from it. Curving from east to south, our blazed trail passes old logging scars and logging roads before its steep descent takes us to the end of a spur road that crosses a gully 70 yards west of us. From the road's end, our trail continues onward, now switchbacking down increasingly shadier and cooler slopes to the verdant banks of Little Fiddle Creek. If you cross it and walk 25 yards downstream, you'll come to a beautiful 20-yard-long swimming hole, which gets up to five feet deep. The trail beyond climbs to an old logging area mentioned at the end of the preceding trail description.

Growing from shallow, submerged bedrock in this stream are umbrella plants, some with leaves up to 16 inches in diameter. You can see this distinctive plant in isolated creek sections along northern Sierra river systems. One might wonder when these wildflowers became isolated. In the preceding trail description we noted that today's vegetation grew about 2500 feet lower during the peak of glacial periods. Umbrella plants back then would probably have thrived in creek environments between 1000 and 3000 feet in elevation. Since the confluence of the North and Middle Yuba rivers was about 1200 feet elevation during the last glaciation, it was above the lower limit of these plants, and the plants grew in both the river and its tributaries. It is possible that today's umbrella plants were isolated as recently as 12,000 years ago, when their distribution migrated upstream as glaciers retreated and temperatures warmed. In their 12,000 years of isolation, these separate clusters of umbrella plants have not diverged in characteristics from each other; evolution of plant life can be a very slow process.

Just how slow evolution works can be appreciated by tracing the history of arctic flora, which eventually migrated south into the Sierra Nevada. Conifer species similar to, but not identical with, today's Sierran conifers once existed near the Pacific in latitudes close to the Canadian border during the Paleocene epoch, about 70 million years ago. By 20 million years later, average temperatures had lowered sufficiently to allow the conifers to migrate into northern California. Finally, in the late Pliocene, as the Tahoe Sierra rose almost to its present height, conifers underwent zonal differentiation, as each species selected the climatic characteristics best suited for it. Today we see three main belts of evergreen vegetation, the lowest being ponderosa-pine forest, then lodgepole-fir forest, and finally subalpine forest. Major canyons in the northern Sierra were cut largely during the late Pliocene through the middle Pleistocene, a span of several million years, and during that time, perhaps about three million years ago, a continuous band of giant sequoias (see Trip 53) was sliced into separate groves. How much have these groves diverged from each other during the ensuing time? Very little.

Mammals, on the other hand, underwent some fantastic diversifications during the Pleistocene, many large forms becoming extinct during the last major glaciation—quite likely due to the arrival of that new Asian predator, man. Genus *Homo* perhaps underwent the greatest change of all in the last three million years, starting as a four-foot-tall, small brained, large-jawed, erect hominid and evolving into what he is today.

Excursion C, Ramshorn Trail: 5.2, round trip; Trailhead 63

Because this trail is so obvious and so close to Halls Ranch Trail, it is included along with it. Perhaps the best feature about this trail is that it will give you a good workout; views, pools and cascades are lacking. The forest cover, however, is pleasant and the geology is interesting.

From the signed trailhead, hike steeply up an old road to a gully, then go 80 yards gently up from it to a bend, at which we branch right and start northeast up a steep trail. Douglas-fir, incense-cedar, ponderosa pine and black oak provide shade which makes our effort pleasant enough. Beneath the trees grow kit-kit-dizze, mock orange, barberry and poison oak. We round the nose of a descending ridge, and climb up to a junction from which an old trail segment once descended eastward to the highway.

Our route switchbacks up the ridge, which is composed of a resistant band of volcanic rocks laid down in the Triassic and/or Jurassic periods and was subsequently metamorphosed by intrusive rocks. Immediately west of this band of metavolcanics is a slightly younger band of ultrabasic intrusive rocks, which has a geologic history similar to that of a granitic pluton, but this band is dark in color, for it lacks quartz and feldspar. Late Paleozoic marine sediments lie west of this dark band.

About ¼ mile before we encounter Ramshorn Creek, we see our first outcrop of white, blocky, vein quartz, in which early miners had hoped to find gold. When we reach the creek, shaded by mountain dogwood and broad-leaf maple, we see considerably more quartz. This outcrop was sufficiently luring to entice miners to excavate two short tunnels just about the creek. Narrow tracks for the mines' car still remain, but the abandoned mines are mostly filled in for your protection.

Near a gully with a trickling spring, our trail comes to an end at a road which is bordered with conifers that now include sugar pine. Rockhounds will want to hike east up the dirt road about 250 years or so, where, just past the gully, they'll find a varied assortment of rocks and minerals. This exposure is near a contact between the ultramafic and metavolcanic rocks. You'll find good quartz crystals, serpentine and other altered ultramafics, plus multihued metavolcanics. St. Charles Hill, immediately above the gully, is a remnant of Pliocene andesitic rock.

On the Ramshorn Trail

75 Trails of the Wild Plum Area

Distance: Various

Total gain/Net gain: 540'/490', 1640'/1400', 1990'/1790', 1700'/1680'

Classification: Easy to moderate

Season: May through mid-November

Parking: Ample in signed trailhead parking area

Trailheads/Map: 65,66/26

Features: The lake-dotted terrain extending from Sierra Buttes north to Plumas-Eureka State Park remains largely snowbound until mid-July. Before then, the hiker can get in shape by hiking on trails that originate from Wild Plum Campground. The first of these is snow-free by early April; the remaining three are snow-free by early June. Ski tourers will appreciate Excursion B.

Description:

Excursion A, Lower Haypress Creek: 2.6 miles, loop trip; Trailhead 65

From where the main road curves right to bridge Haypress Creek and enter Wild Plum Campground, we start a level hike east-northeast up a paved road, reaching the Wild Plum Guard Station in ¼ mile. Only 25 yards west of a metal gate is a sign, *Haypress Creek,* which is near an outhouse and a shack, and from the sign we hike on a trail that starts initially toward Haypress Creek, running immediately below the south edge of a flat. This flat is a *stream terrace*—that is, an almost level layer of sediments deposited by the stream perhaps several thousand years ago. Since then, the stream has cut down through more bedrock, leaving these sediments high and dry.

Our trail, becoming more obvious, curves east and follows the south edge of the flat, crosses an ephemeral creek, passes fire rings among black oaks and incense-cedars, and comes to the east end of the flat. Here, you can hear the muted roar of some impressive cataracts that can be seen by pacing 50 yards east to the flat's brink. The trail now runs north briefly, climbs east via short, fairly steep switchbacks, and arrives at step-across 1001-Mine creek, which flows over and between boulders that are twice as wide as it. About 100 yards beyond the creek, our trail starts to round a ridge, and, looking back, we

A Haypress Creek cascade

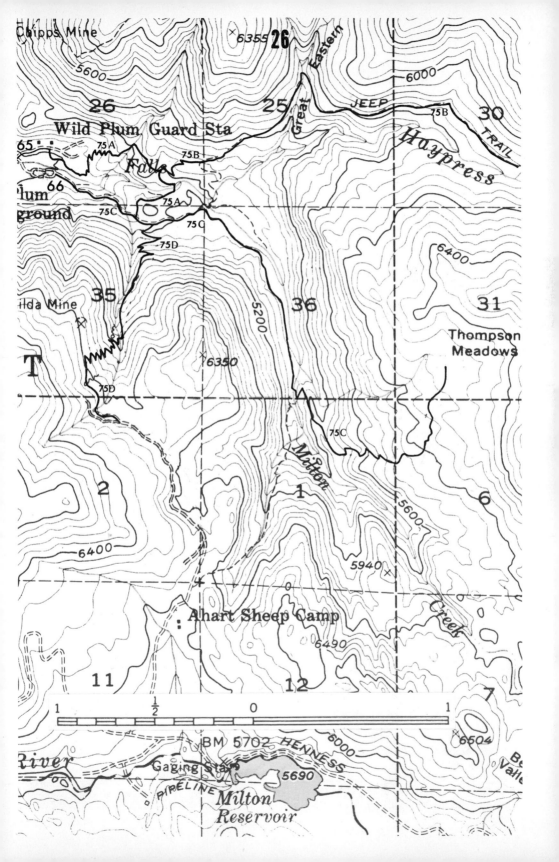

get a head-on view of the towering crest known as Sierra Buttes (see Trip 79 for its geologic history).

Most of the terrain from the Wild Plum area north well past Sierra Buttes is metamorphic, but the ridge on which we're standing is granitic. It differs from granitic rocks seen around the Lake Tahoe basin in two ways. First, it is richer in iron and magnesium, and hence darker. Second, it is coarser, containing conspicuous feldspar crystals up to an inch long. Large crystals such as these, when present in a matrix of smaller crystals, are called *phenocrysts* and the overall texture is said to be *porphyritic*. That some crystals are larger is due to the chemical composition of the molten granitic pluton in which they first solidified, together with the cooling rate of that pluton.

Leaving the ridge and entering a shady forest of incense-cedar, black oak, ponderosa pine and Douglas-fir, we reach in 200 yards a sign, *Wild Plum Guard Sta. 1,* which points back the way we came. Excursion B continues straight ahead, but we branch southwest and go 40 yards before turning abruptly left and descending eastward to the Haypress Creek bridge. Campsites can be found on flats above both sides of the creek, and on weekends fishermen are certain to be seen along its bank.

From the bridge our trail traverses west about 200 yards through an open forest of incense-cedar and black oak before entering a shadier Douglas-fir/white-fir forest. At this vegetation boundary, a faint fishermen's trail branches right and descends west-northwest, reaching in 100 yards a turbulent, roaring cascade. Photographers will certainly want to visit it. In addition to cascading water, you'll find umbrella plant, alum root and penstemon clinging to the damp, granitic rocks. Below this cascade are several hundred yards of cascades, pools and small falls—all accessible to the hardy hiker who doesn't mind mixing easy rock climbing with occasional bushwhacking.

The main trail west quickly leaves the forest's darkness, reaches a more open ridge with an oak-shaded view of the Sierra Buttes, then turns south and just as quickly reaches the Milton Creek Trail—an old jeep road closed to vehicles. Here our route turns west, following the first part of Excursion C in reverse down to Trailhead 66 at the east end of Wild Plum Campground, from which we walk west ⅓ mile to Trailhead 65.

Excursion B, Haypress Creek Trail: 8.2 miles, round trip; Trailhead 65

Just beyond the granitic ridge where Excursion A branches southwest, this route continues eastward. We start up along the northwest side of a gully, cross its usually dry wash, then quickly reach a bedrock flat above a gorge cut by Haypress Creek, from which a glance back provides a view of the domineering Sierra Buttes. Our trail now switchbacks northwest, curves eastward up past white blocks of quartz derived from large quartz veins, and soon joins an old jeep road where that road bends. If you were to hike southeast down the road, you would reach Haypress Creek in a few minutes. The road's bridge is washed out, but you can cross the creek— treacherous in springtime—on a large log located midway downstream between the washout and the Milton Creek union. Within 100 yards from Haypress Creek you can log-cross Milton Creek and climb a few feet up to the Milton Creek Trail.

From the road's bend we climb eastward, pass a shortcut ridge path descending steeply to Haypress Creek, and commence a shady, steady climb northeast. Old license plates, nailed high above us, mark this route for winter travelers. Our approach to the Great Eastern Ravine is heralded by an abrupt change from granitic rocks to metamorphic ones. In 100 yards we are beside its jump-across creek, which has cut and polished its bed of light-gray, banded marble.

After an initial moderate ascent from the creek, the grade eases and traverses a brushy slope covered by huckleberry oak, snowbush, manzanita and chinquapin. Among the thick grasses that line the trail, Oregon juncos in late

Junco eggs, ½ actual size

spring weave grass blades into small, cup-shaped nests, in which females lay four or five eggs. This brownish, sparrow-sized bird—perhaps the most numerous avian species in the Tahoe Sierra—is easily recognized by its black or dark-gray head and neck, its pale bill and its conspicuous white outer tail feathers.

From this open slope we can survey parts of the Great Eastern Ravine and Haypress Creek canyon. As we climb east, the gain in elevation brings us into a different forest cover, in which white firs and sugar pines are present. The already familiar species—incense-cedar and Douglas-fir—are still present for the moment, and you can't fail to be impressed by one magnificent ponderosa pine, a 200-foot giant growing near the trail's south side. Not far beyond it we pass a second ponderosa pine with wide-spreading limbs. Foresters call such a conifer a "wolf tree," for its spreading branches shade much ground, thereby preventing the growth of other lumber-producing conifers. Because of its many branches, its wood will be knotty and therefore generally undesirable. For maximum yield, conifers should be tall, straight and close-spaced, with only a few branches.

Views disappear altogether as we enter a solemn white-fir forest, and in it we soon come to a step-across creek, which cascades steeply down to our trail after emerging from a curtain of bushes that cloak its bedrock channel. Ferns grace its downstream channel, and with them crowd verdant alders, in which you may occasionally see western tanagers foraging for food. The scarlet-headed male bird of this species easily outshines his drab yellow-green mate.

We now traverse through the grand forest, with its 200-foot-tall firs, and after a while encounter three close-spaced creeks. Within 20 yards of the first one, and within sight of the trail, is a campsite complete with logs and a fire ring. Along the third, or main, creek—difficult to cross before late June—grow white-barked aspens, which contrast with the creekside vegetation we've seen thus far. Our trail gives way to an obvious jeep road in less than 100 yards, and down it, motoring enthusiasts from Haypress Valley roar during the summer. Hikers may wish to stop at this point, but ski tourers will want to follow the creekside road as it climbs three relatively easy miles up to wide, spacious Haypress Valley.

Excursion C, Thompson Meadows: 7.8 miles, round trip; Trailhead 66

Wild Plum Campground and its environs, shaded by ponderosa pines, incense-cedars, Douglas-firs and black oaks, provides a variety of habitats for birds we are likely to see along the first part of our trail. As in much of the Tahoe Sierra, you'll see the Oregon junco, Steller jay, robin and several species of sparrows. Living an almost unnoticed existence is the small, unobtrusive brown creeper, a sparrow-sized bird that blends in well with its surroundings. You'll see it on a tree trunk climbing a spiral path upward—never downward, like nuthatches—and sticking its fairly long, curved bill into cracks in the tree's bark to extract a juicy insect here and there. More conspicuous are the multicolored males of the Bullock's oriole, black-headed grosbeak and western tanager populations.

From the upper end of the campground, we start up a closed road, which is well signed with mileages to various points. Soon a short clearing opens and from it we obtain a view back which reveals the prominent mass of the Sierra Buttes. One-quarter mile from the trailhead, a trail branches left to a creek that originates from the slopes above Hilda Mine. Our old road ends at this creek in another ¼ mile, and a springtime crossing of it can be wet if a log isn't available. A trail starts from its

Sierra Buttes from near Milton Creek

east bank and we go but 50 yards on it before we come to a signed junction. Striking north is a ⅓-mile-long trail to a steel-and-wood bridge across Haypress Creek (see Excursion A).

Our route, now a road again, continues 200 yards east to another junction, from which the Hilda Trail (Excursion D) climbs up to Hilda Mine. The temporary route of the Pacific Crest Trail leaves our route here and follows that trail. We continue an easy climb eastward on the largely overgrown jeep road, cross a seasonal creek and get another view of the Sierra Buttes just before our road descends gently and turns abruptly right (south-southeast). Here you'll find a campsite just above Milton Creek. Straight ahead, a road forks 30 yards east to the creek's edge. If you're heading toward Haypress Creek, then cross Milton first on large, obvious logs, sometimes used by gray squirrels. A larger log across Haypress Creek gets you over to Excursion B.

Once across Milton Creek, you can also follow it upstream, staying a short distance from its bank. You may find a faint path that takes you through a fairly large, level meadow, and near its edge you can certainly find isolated campsites. Fishing for trout is

fair—up to 8 inches—but most fishermen prefer the locality where Haypress Creek joins the North Yuba. There, about one mile west of Wild Plum Campground, is where the trout are planted. About 0.2 mile south-southeast of the meadow, you can cross over to the Milton Creek Trail.

From the campsite junction our Milton Creek Trail starts south-southeast, quickly becomes a true trail, and soon climbs a brief

Creekside dogwood flower-bract

Umbrella plants at Milton Creek crossing

100 yards steeply up to a rocky prominence composed of Jurassic-Triassic volcanic rocks that were subsequently metamorphosed. The creek is almost unheard as we begin a gentle descent to a cool, shady forest that borders it. Along this descent you're likely to spot lupines, senecios, wallflowers, and in late spring, snow plants. Lining the creek are ferns, gooseberries, thimbleberries, alders, dogwoods and maples, and growing out of it are large-leaved umbrella plants (see Trips 73 and 74).

Our path now ascends gently up a creekside bench, taking us past an abandoned, roofless cabin which signals a crossing of Milton Creek in 400 yards. The Milton Creek Trail once climbed all the way up the west bank without crossing over. Today, however, we cross the creek on stones—take your pick—that are located 20–50 yards upstream from where the actual trail crosses the creek. These are immediately above a waist-deep pool. Hikers crossing after late July can cross anywhere.

Walking 100 yards up the creek's east bank, we reach a signed junction. In less than 20 yards the creekside trail recrosses Milton Creek, executes short switchbacks up a rock pile, then becomes a ducked, little-used route up to a ridge-crest swampy meadow above and northeast of Ahart Sheep Camp. Adventuresome hikers can follow this route—or go cross-country if they lose it—and then hike north up a spur road that leads to a logging road. Once on this, they have a 0.9-mile winding route northward to the Hilda Trail, which starts out as a jeep road (see Excursion D).

The trail that climbs to Thompson Meadows—our ultimate goal—starts steeply north-northeast, climbing indistinctly in places. Blazes on trees, however, identify the route. The route climbs moderately south-southeast up a ridge, then curves eastward and switchbacks steeply up a gully. About 1000 feet above the Milton Creek crossing, our trail thankfully levels off and commences a rolling traverse northward. Two low ridges are crossed, the second one providing us with our last view of the Sierra Buttes. Then we enter a forest and soon reach the linear, sloping meadow. Its water-saturated soils support a healthy growth of corn lilies, grasses, aspens and water-loving wildflowers. If you wish to camp in this area, you can find suitable dry sites on the forested flats above either side of this three-acre meadow.

Excursion D, Hilda Mine: 5.0 miles, round trip; Trailhead 66

Starting from Wild Plum Campground, the first part of this route follows the jeep road—the temporary Pacific Crest Trail described in Excursion C. Along this road, as along almost any dirt road or trail in the Tahoe Sierra, you may encounter deer, although they are usually unseen, leaving only their tracks. Suddenly startled, a doe will spring off into the bushes, perhaps with a fawn or two close on her tail. In such a chance meeting, the author encountered a doe and her fawn. The doe instantly disappeared into the brush, but the fawn, after a few steps, stumbled and froze where it fell, pretending it was fully camouflaged. Not so much as batting an eye, it lay there motionless for a minute while the author took several close-range photographs of it, and not until he walked away did it spring up and scamper off into the brush. The fawn had done the right thing, but at the wrong time and place. A coyote wouldn't be fooled. It may seem unfortunate that a doe never tries to defend her young or to distract the potential predator away from them, but since she takes flight, she can always breed again.

At the junction with the Hilda Trail, our route and the Pacific Crest temporary route both start up it. Unlike the steep climb to Thompson Meadows, this climb is only moderate, the steep slope made tolerable by plenty of switchbacks. After our first set of switchbacks, which approach the unseen but heard Hilda Creek, we catch a conifer-framed glimpse of Sierra Buttes as we start a ½-mile climb up the creek's canyon. The singing creek offers us a refreshing drink where we cross it, but as if its water were not good enough, someone has built a pipe spring about 100 yards up-trail from the crossing. Beyond it we touch upon a small, usually dry gully, beside which we climb steadily upward via 12 short switchback legs.

Our trail ends at some old, dilapidated mining shacks that served as workmen's quarters for several mines that were dug in this area. The miners sought to extract gold that was trapped under the volcanic rocks you see above the shacks. Beside the shacks the volcanic rock is in direct contact with the metamorphic rock on which our trail has climbed up, but small amounts of gold are found within Eocene sediments that are trapped between the two rock types. After Pliocene lava flows buried these sediments

Mule-deer fawn

about 10 million years ago, the course of the ancestral North Yuba River was diverted toward the Sierra Buttes, and since that time, the river has cut about 1500 feet down to where it flows today. Most of the cutting occurred within the last few million years while the northern Sierra renewed its uplift and glaciers actively scoured out the canyons.

From the mining shacks, an old jeep road replaces the trail, and up it we walk, passing an icy spring emanating from the base of a white fir located midway between the shacks and Hilda creek. Beyond the spring we climb gently up to Hilda Creek, our last water source. Our southbound jeep road now bends eastward, paralleling a larger forest road above it and meeting that road at a *Hilda Trail* sign, which marks the end of our excursion. Here in a large clearing that is being invaded with gooseberries, we once again get a view of the towering Sierra Buttes. Hikers in late summer or early fall will find the tasty but spiny berries in season.

76   Haskell Peak

Distance: 9.2 miles, semiloop trip
Total gain/Net gain: 2460'/2390'
Season: Early July through mid-October
Parking: Half dozen cars on south side of highway just above bridge
Trailhead/Map: 68/27

Features: Rivaling Sierra Buttes for views is Haskell Peak. The little-used trails that make up this trip contrast strongly with the Sierra Buttes jeep trail, which is heavily used—and driven—on summer weekends.

Description: The signed Chapman Creek Trail begins only 25 yards down the road from the Chapman Creek highway bridge. Wisely located within the forest's edge, our trail skirts above the creek's damp bank. Douglas-fir intermingles with white fir, lodgepole pine and Jeffrey pine, but it quickly disappears upstream, having reached its altitudinal limit. After crossing a shady gully with a trickling stream usually flowing down it, we round a bend, spy Chapman Creek Campground beyond the opposite bank, and in 100 yards cross the creek via logs and rocks. Don't continue up the old trail along the creek's west bank—it soon dies out.

Fifty yards beyond the ford, we join a path from Trailhead 69, in the campground. This blazed, initially wide path dwindles to trail width by the time its 200-yard-long route reaches ours. As we hike eastward, a quiet walker can observe the dipper, or water ouzel, which is a chunky, drab-gray bird that hunts for aquatic insects along the bottom of swift-flowing streams.

Just over ½ mile from the campground trail junction, we ford a permanent tributary, then parallel a logging operation—active in 1974—that sometimes reaches, but doesn't cross, our trail. Briefly leaving the logging scars behind, we soon log-cross a large creek from Beartrap Meadow, then curve left and climb around a low ridge before reaching Chapman Creek again, ⅓ mile beyond Beartrap Meadow's creek. Now only jump-across width, Chapman Creek is easily forded, and after 50 yards we meet the creek's abandoned west-bank trail. Beyond this junction our route swings north through a small bog, then east up to an old logging road, intersecting it only 40 yards from the creek. Another 120 yards east takes us up to a larger road, where, 70 yards from the creek, our trail ends. A short, moderate climb

northwest up this road through a selectively logged area brings us to a quick reunion with the first road we crossed. Then an easy 150-yard jaunt northeast gets us to a road junction immediately west of a low knoll.

With our route-finding problems now over, we can hike unconcerned northward up the wide road, quite likely passing cows in the man-made meadow below before we reach the headwaters of Chapman Creek. Here, at our last source of permanent water, we turn left onto Road 21N09, and walk southwest up it to an obvious, signed saddle. We have now left Mesozoic granitic rocks behind and tread on volcanic rocks of Miocene age or slightly older. Associated with these volcanic rocks are fragrant, large-leaved mule ears.

From the sign we start north-northeast on a faint trail through an open field of grass and mule ears, then veer west into a forest of white and red firs and silver and Jeffrey pines. Rock ducks and plastic streamers mark our route up the southwest side of a seasonal creek that soon becomes lined with alders that obscure our route. Just before reaching a steeper

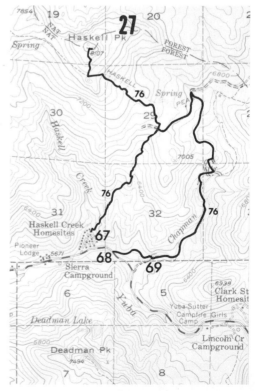

slope, we cross the creek and attempt to follow the cryptic trail upslope. Should you lose sight of it, continue straight up through the forest to where the trees diminish, and there find an obvious, manzanita-lined trail that transports you 400 yards west up to a saddle, giving you your first view of Sierra Valley to the east. From the saddle you also get a glimpse of the Sierra Buttes, to the southwest, but views of them will improve with elevation.

Leaving the saddle and the main trail, we strike north, following volcanic ducks across a slope mantled with creeping manzanita. Our ⅓-mile-long spur trail ascending to Haskell Peak becomes quite brushy midway up it, but cross-country climbing through the low brush isn't very difficult. When we are due east of a low prominence, our trail briefly climbs northwest, and then it climbs due north through a shallow bowl, shaded with silver pines and red firs, which lies between the peak's two blocky summits. From the saddle between them, a rocky footpath guides us easily to the higher, east summit, capped by a 10-foot-high cairn.

Although Haskell Peak lacks the Sierra Buttes' dramatic escarpment, it provides us with equally revealing panoramas. The buttes, seven miles southeast, are seen as a serrated crest of rusty and dark brown rock. North from them extends a long ridge—on which runs the Pacific Crest Trail—that links the buttes with the Lakes Basin Recreation Area. To the west-northwest and separated from this ridge stands pyramidal Mt. Elwell (7812'), whose metavolcanic mass divides Lakes Basin from Plumas-Eureka State Park. To the north and east of us lie fault-bound Mohawk and Sierra valleys, which broke off from surrounding mountain blocks as the blocks rose in the late Pliocene. Both offer relaxing atmospheres for the visitor who wants to escape the hectic congestion found around Tahoe's shores. You might also notice that our peak's north face has been oversteepened by repeated glacier action, which has been occurring on and off for perhaps the last one million years.

After you have explored the two summits and have taken in their views, return the way you came, descending to Road 21N09. A sign near the saddle indicates that our route—the Haskell Peak Trail—descends southwest down a prominent gully. Turning onto it, we leave mule ears behind as white firs and

Cairn atop Haskell Peak

granitic rocks soon prevail. Old blazes guide us down past creeklets to a gently sloped bowl, in which we find large Jeffrey pines. Leaving the bowl and its verdant creekside vegetation of alder, gooseberry, bracken fern and wildflowers, we traverse to a ridge, cross it, and steeply descend its west slope, which is clothed in white fir and chinquapin. After crossing a second gully, we begin a traverse to a second ridge and notice the logging operations downslope which have worked up to our trail. Quickly leaving these behind, we cross the ridge and make a final ½-mile descent, catching glimpses of the Sierra Buttes before our fir-bound path ends at signed Trailhead 67, which is located near the uppermost cabins of the Haskell Creek summer homes. We descend this tract's main road to Highway 49, then engage in a brief walk east up it to our trailhead.

77   Lunch Creek Trail

Distance: 3.4 miles, round trip

Total gain/Net gain: 740'/700'

Classification: Easy

Season: Late June through late October

Parking: Limited parking 50 yards up creek's east-bank road

Trailhead/Map: 70/28

Features: Except for the presence of a few cows, you can expect to have this short route entirely to yourself. Nearby logged-over slopes contrast strongly with our forest-and-meadow route. Bracken fern, pennyroyal, scarlet gilia and lupine seasonally adorn the trailside.

Description: We start north up the slopes that rise from the west bank of Lunch Creek. After a short stroll through a forest of white and red firs, we descend briefly, cross Lunch Creek, and almost touch the east-bank logging road where it turns abruptly east. After a couple minutes' walk up-trail, we recross the little-visited creek, hike up to a cattle drift fence, scramble under it or use its gate, and continue our journey.

We almost touch Lunch Creek, then cross a seasonal creek lined with alders, and climb moderately up a small ridge. Lodgepoles and gooseberries indicate the presence of ground water close to the surface, and we soon enter a grassy meadow that confirms this observation. Near a conspicuous granitic knob above us on the right, our trail bends eastward and grass gives way to water-saturated soils supporting a meadow densely populated with corn lilies. Blazes on lodgepoles adjoining the meadow guide us across it, and, about 300 yards beyond the knob we cross the head-waters of Lunch Creek. Keeping to the meadow's east edge, we follow a now-drier path 0.4 mile up to trail's end at an old road that marks the southern border of an extensive logging area.

Silver pine cone (left) and red fir cone (right), ¼ actual size

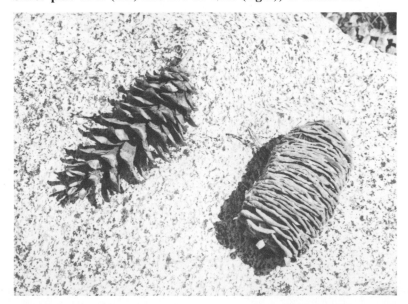

78   Berry Creek Trail

Distance: 6.6 miles, round trip.
Total gain/Net gain: 1960'/1800'
Classification: Strenuous
Season: Early July through mid-October
Parking: Ample at both trailheads
Trailheads/Map: 71,72/28

Features: The Berry Creek Trail is the last remaining walkable trail on which a hiker in the Tahoe Sierra could climb westward from a valley floor up to the Sierra crest. (However, it is described eastbound because of parking problems at the east end.) Delightful, cascading Berry Creek brings joy to the heart of the hiker who takes this little-used route.

Description: There are at least six places one could start his hike along the Berry Creek Trail. Only two trailheads are given, since the others all have one or more drawbacks. We're going to start our hike from Trailhead 71, which is located a little more than midway up the trail from the edge of Sierra Valley to Coburn Lake. The advantages of this trailhead are that it is readily accessible by auto, it lies away from lumber operations above but close to a permanent stream, and it has adequate level space to camp at.

The trail from the flat isn't obvious at first, but a sign points north-northeast toward a trail blaze on one of the giant red firs immediately downslope. We descend in that direction, steeply at first, veering away from the alder-lined stream as we progress along the canyon slopes. Soils derived from loose volcanic rocks that have gradually worked their way downslope from the Pliocene flows near Coburn Lake give way to a less dusty underfooting of decomposed granitic rock. Needles from silver pines and red firs cushion our descent, which after ⅓ mile has taken us to a creeklet in a deep gully that has been selectively logged. After crossing the creeklet, we reach, in 70 yards, an abandoned road, on which we descend northeast. In 0.4 mile our road curves left (northwest), and eventually it joins the major lumber road on a saddle about one mile southeast of Yuba Pass.

We start northward down another old road, veer left from it on a path after 35 yards, but soon cross the road again where it swings westward. With the old roads now behind us, we start northwest down a slope, temporarily bend north, and then curve east-southeast down to an open, cow-visited flat perched

upon a broad ridge just west of a low, forested granitic knoll. After diagonaling northeast across this flat, we angle southeast down to the knoll's lower north slope, then shoot north to jump across Berry Creek.

From here the trail is perfectly obvious all the way down Berry Creek canyon. All signs of logging and grazing are left behind as we pass an outcrop of large, granitic boulders on the slope north of us, then descend steeply beside the roaring creek choked with alders and large boulders. Farther downstream, the creek disappears beneath the boulders, and alders, lacking surface water, are not found. Where our trail eases its steep descent, the creek and the alders have both reappeared, and the forest cover of red fir and silver pine has now yielded to one of white fir and Jeffrey pine with an understory of huckleberry oak and chinquapin.

Where the larger, Coburn Lake tributary joins smaller Berry Creek, you'll spot Franklin Cabin, perched on a small flat immediately before their union. Jump across Berry Creek and investigate the cabin. Probably long used by ranch hands, this three-walled, roofless structure dates back to 1923—if you can believe the inscriptions carved into its logs. Beside its ruins you can camp; you're unlikely to find another flat campsite until you reach Sierra Valley. In addition to alder, this flat is bordered by other water-loving bushes such as willow, dogwood and mountain ash.

Beyond the cabin, we descend alongside beautiful Berry Creek, which cascades and bubbles around large granitic boulders that

Franklin Cabin

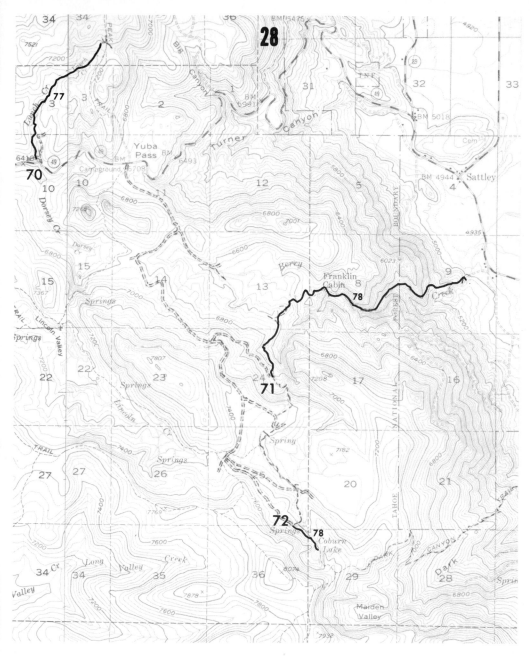

impede its progress. Our progress is not impeded, for our trail stays far enough away from the creek's bank to avoid all boulder problems. Numerous small pools and cascades are passed by unnoticed because of the brush and boulders that separate us from the creek.

Large-coned sugar pines and deliciously aromatic tobacco brush herald our approach

to a bend at the 6000-foot level, and brush cover becomes predominant as we now descend northeast. Incense-cedar and other conifers provide shade as we approach the creek's side, but then we curve eastward and erratically traverse up to a sloping ridge while Berry Creek drops 300 feet below us.

Crossing the narrow ridge, we are greeted with a picturesque view of broad, flat Sierra

Valley, whose fault-dropped origin is similar to that of the Lake Tahoe basin (see Trip 50). A steep, sandy descent on a trail of gruss (also see Trip 50) transports us quickly down to a low, logged-over, east-bearing ridge, on which manzanita and tobacco brush currently thrive, but they are gradually being succeeded by invading pines. To the north you're likely to see billows of smoke rising from Sattley's lumber plant, which processes the selectively logged timber being cut on Berry Creek's higher slopes.

Our route levels off at a broad trail—once a road—beside lower Berry Creek, and 20 yards downstream on it we cross the wide creek to a large campsite on its opposite bank. To keep your feet dry, you might try crossing just upstream, near the water-gauge station, by climbing from one alder limb to another. Our route ends at the large, shady campsite; there is no need to go an extra 0.3 mile northeast to Highway 49/89. Starting from the bend in this narrow highway is also not advisable, for there is no place near the ranch you must cross at which you could park your car. Return the way you came.

Back at Trailhead 71, adventuresome hikers may want to follow a 2.4-mile route—along trails and roads of all descriptions—up to Coburn Lake. This route is left undescribed for those hearty souls, but it has been mapped in detail (see map 28). About ½ mile up this route you'll traverse a gentle slope, whose red firs in 1974 were being selectively logged, cut

up and transported to the Sattley mill. Unhealthy or overly mature red firs, marked by Forest Service personnel, are cut and turned into fiberboard. Most of the mature firs are left standing, with the result that accelerated erosion does not become a problem. Bushes, together with young firs and pines invade the open spaces created by the tree removal. Man, then, is performing a beneficial role here similar to that of fire—clearing the forest understory to make room for new growth.

Unadventuresome hikers who nevertheless wish to reach Coburn Lake can start at Trailhead 72, a blocked road. Here you'll see a jeep road descending northeast to a meadow just below. Where it turns southeast, the Berry Creek Trail departs toward Trailhead 71. To reach Coburn Lake, however, start at the roadblock and traverse southeast along the closed road 0.2 mile to the aforementioned jeep road. A 0.2-mile moderate ascent up it gets you to placid Coburn Lake. You can enjoy this lake during the day, but its owner, the Fiberboard Corporation, prohibits camping and campfires, fearing that a careless match might start a forest fire. A trail continues along the lake's east shore, climbs southeast to a ridge and just beyond it meets an old logging road. Here, the hiker can follow an old road southwest ½ mile up to the Sierra crest or else northeast down a ridge west of Dark Canyon. This ridge trail, criss-crossed by logging roads, all but dies out before it reaches the lower slopes above Sierra Valley.

Peaceful Sierra Valley

79   Sierra Buttes Fire Lookout

Distance: 9.4 miles, round trip

Total gain/Net gain: 3440'/3440'

Classification: Strenuous

Season: Year round; snow is an advantage for this hike

Parking: Limited; park at turnouts near the junction with the *steep, narrow* road.

Trailhead/Map: 64/29

Features: The Sierra Buttes, at 8587 feet elevation, are the highest summit between Lassen Peak to the north and the Tahoe-Donner peaks to the south. Only Haskell Peak (Trip 76) comes close to the Sierra Buttes in providing excellent panoramas of Highway 49's high country. Unlike most peaks, however, the Sierra Buttes are best climbed when there is still snow on the slopes. When the snow is gone, usually from early July through late October, the summit's fire lookout is visited on weekends by dozens of people, almost half of them driving up in 4WD vehicles or on motorcycles. Hence, avoid the crowds and the noise by hiking on a summer weekday or by hiking when snow still blocks the motorists' access.

Description: Winter hikers may have to start their trek from the large parking area at Sierra City's dump, 1.4 miles down the road. All others should be able to drive up to the start of the road signed *steep* and *narrow.* We hike ½ mile eastward up this shadeless road to its tight bend west. Immediately east of this bend is a readily accessible, year-round creek, from which you should fill your water bottles. Climbing west, our steady, moderate ascent takes us past occasional incense-cedars and ponderosa pines, which provide us with convenient, shady resting spots. Along various road cuts you can't help but notice exposures of blue-green serpentine, which is the main alteration product of ultramafic rocks, such as the blue-black pyroxene you see associated with it. A once-active fault, trending northwest-southeast, approximately parallels the road we see below us. Along this fault these Mesozoic ultramafics probably welled up and intruded into the surrounding Paleozoic rocks. Once emplaced, these ultramafics were then invaded by superheated water under intense pressure, which forced water into their crystal structures, converting the rock to serpentine.

We think of water as being relatively harmless. We can drink it or bathe in it and it doesn't destroy us. When this same water, however, is *confined* within rocks and is subjected to temperatures that are several times greater than its boiling point, it builds up to tremendous pressures and becomes very corrosive. It then dissolves quartz, gold, silver, copper, lead, zinc and a host of other materials and carries them upward away from their plutonic, subterranean source. As it climbs farther from the pluton, its temperature—and hence its pressure—decreases, and the dissolved materials begin to precipitate out. If dissolved gold is present in the ascending fluid, it will precipitate out at the same temperature-pressure combination as the silica, which solidifies to form vein quartz. Hence miners look for quartz veins in the hope they'll find gold in them. About 60 million years ago, gold from quartz veins in the Sierra was eroded and transported downstream only to be redeposited where the gradient eased, the stream's velocity decreased, and the stream dropped its rich, heavy prize with other sediments. These Eocene sediments, such as those worked at the Hilda Mine (Trip 75), are the second major source of gold after veins.

The Sierra Buttes mining district is known for its large gold nuggets, and some are still occasionally found. In its heyday, this district produced at least $30 million in gold, but little has been mined since the 1930s. By far the most productive mine was the Sierra Buttes Mine—located ½ mile east of the right bend in our road—whose gold-rich veins yielded as much as $20 million.

Our 1½-mile, sunny, westward ascent ends at a saddle atop a southwest-descending spur ridge that separates deeply eroded slopes to the east from barely eroded ones to the north. The jeep trail up which we'll hike closely parallels this ridge.

No matter what month you hike in, you'll be able to follow the road up to this saddle. Beyond the saddle, snow is likely to be encountered except from midsummer through early autumn. After starting a walk east, we quickly encounter a road contouring north toward the Monarch Mine; then our road curves northeast and climbs ½ mile through a forest, rich in shady silver pines, to a signed junction with the Sierra Buttes jeep trail.

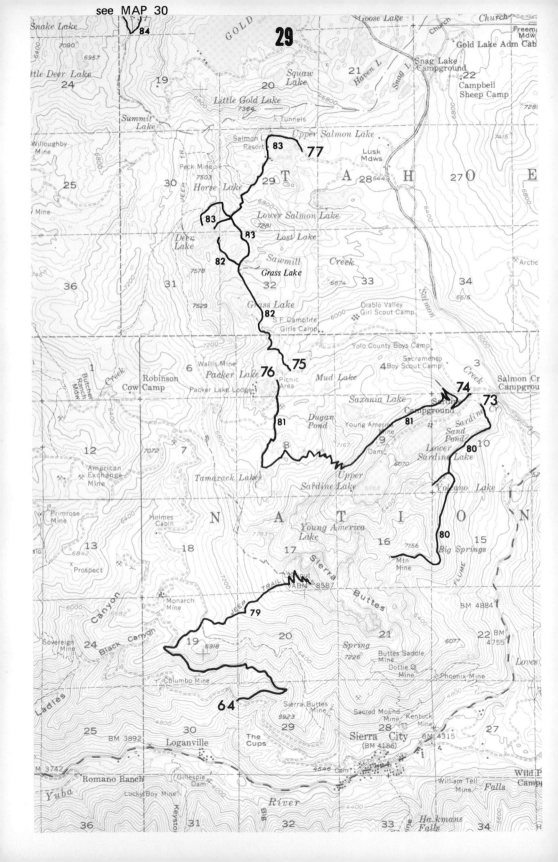

Winter and spring hikers will probably miss this sign, if not the entire road up to it, for both will be under fairly deep snow. The forest, however, is open enough for the snowbound hiker to pick any route he chooses. Perhaps the best route to follow under these conditions is to hike up to an obvious saddle immediately north of Summit 6918, then climb northeast straight up to the crest, staying near or within the forest's south edge.

From the signed junction the jeep trail climbs steeply eastward up to some exposed bedrock on the southwest-descending ridge. From there, it climbs almost 1000 feet as it winds up the forest's edge to the start of some fairly long switchback legs. We now leave most of the shady red firs and silver pines behind as we zigzag up toward the now-visible lookout tower. As we approach the crest and come to a point about 50 yards from the northernmost switchback turn, we spy a usually snow-covered trail starting west from our switchback leg. One can descend on this trail via short switchback legs to the ridge that curves northwest down from the Sierra Buttes. From a signed, level spot on that ridge, one can then descend north-northeast to Tamarack Lakes and beyond (see Trip 81) or one can continue north-northwest along the ridge to a ridge road that eventually descends eastward to Packer Lake. Both routes have been logged over in places and therefore are unesthetic—except when the snow is still deep.

Beyond the trail junction, our route doubles back and we start a southeast climb just below the buttes' crest. From here you can climb Class 2 or 3 up to the sharp crest and obtain a revealing view of the precipitous summit the lookout is built on. You will, of course, also get a sneak preview of the spectacularly glaciated Sardine Lakes canyon below you in the northeast. If you are hiking up to this crest through deep snow, you'll want to rope up from here to the lookout. A 25-yard rope should be sufficient for any climbing you'll have to do.

The jeep trail ends at a notch immediately below the summit pinnacle. Now we climb a series of steel ladders up a cliff to our goal, the lookout. Winter and early-spring hikers may find parts of this final ascent iced over, making a rope mandatory for safety's sake.

Regardless of the season in which you make this climb, you'll find the view well worth your hiking effort. The lookout is usually open and

maintained from early June through early September, but even when it isn't, you can still walk completely around its view deck, which protrudes in space over the buttes' 600-foot-high, near-vertical northeast cliff. On the distant northwest horizon stands snowy Lassen Peak (10,457'), North America's southernmost active stratovolcano. Seven miles northeast and slightly below us rises Haskell Peak (see Trip 76), whose gentle summit is composed of volcanic debris and flows that date back 20 million years or more. Numerous high peaks dot the Lake Tahoe environs to the southeast. With compass in hand you can identify Mt. Rose (10,776'), 174°; Mt. Lola (9143'), 126°; and the Crystal Range of Desolation Wilderness (9983' maximum), 155°. Many lower summits and ridges, both near and far, are seen in every direction.

What immediately captivates one's attention, however, is the deep, glaciated canyon immediately northeast and ½ mile below us. It lies in stark contrast to the unglaciated, little-eroded west slope up which we hiked. That slope has changed little in the last 10 million years. Back then, the Sierra Buttes weren't a jagged crest at all, but rather an elliptical dome, with minor irregularities, that was about six miles in diameter east-west, and about 5 miles in diameter north-south.

On the basis of the configuration of the west slope, one can determine that the original summit was located about ½ mile northeast of today's summit and stood perhaps 500 feet higher—possibly surpassing 9000 feet elevation *by today's standards*. Back then, however, the entire Sierra was considerably lower than it is today, and the Sierra Buttes dome, rather than reaching to 9000 feet, was more likely about 5000 feet above sea level. Today, the buttes stand about 4500 feet above the North Yuba where it flows past Sierra City. Back then, the broad dome climbed gracefully 3500 feet above the ancestral North Yuba, which was as much as a mile south and a mile east of its present, southwest-curving course. The ancestral river meandered through the broad, flat-floored valley much as it did 40–50 million years earlier, during the Eocene epoch, when the river was depositing gold-bearing sediments on the valley floor.

During the Miocene epoch, volcanic activity commenced on a grand scale, and lava flows buried most of the terrain that today lies northeast of the Plumas-Eureka/Sierra Buttes

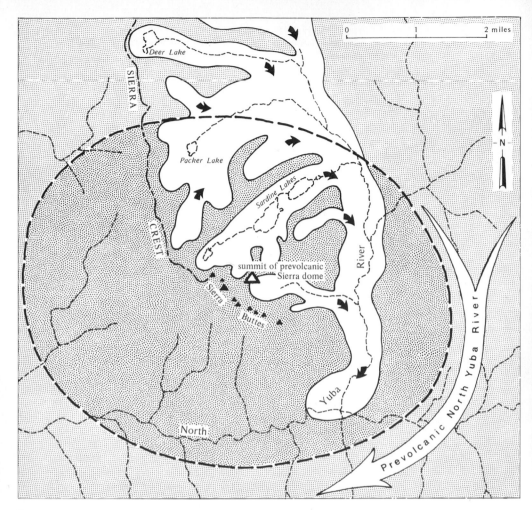

Evolution of the Sierra Buttes landscape. During the Eocene epoch, the buttes existed as a broad, elliptical dome (heavy dashed line). The ancestral prevolcanic North Yuba River flowed around its east and south flanks. Miocene and Pliocene lava flows from the east forced this drainage northwest to the present drainage (shown as light dashed lines). Pleistocene glaciers deepened the canyons along this drainage and cut deeply into the dome, thereby creating the steep northeast escarpment of the Sierra Buttes (maximum extent of glaciation, with arrows to indicate glacier movement, is shown as white).

area. The closest the flows got to the dome's slopes was the Salmon lakes area, about four miles northeast of us. It is possible that some flows actually lapped up and buried the lower north slope of the dome, but all material evidence has long since been eroded away.

Flows continued to erupt onto the surface during the Pliocene, and about 10 million years ago, these new ones buried the lower portions of the dome's east and south slopes, as well as virtually all the adjacent landscape up to 10-plus miles beyond them. The ancestral North Yuba River valley, with its Eocene-epoch placer gold, now lay under 1000 feet of lava. We know these flows piled up to this approximate thickness because today we can see parts of them, 1000 or more feet thick, making up all the ridges above Haypress and Milton creeks.

The slowly eroding dome now stood only ½ mile above the new volcanic floor, which lay close to today's 6500-foot contour line. Creeks descending gullies on its slopes went only as far as the volcanic floor's edge, then turned downstream and gradually cut a new channel, whose position was very similar to the North Yuba channel today.

Since all volcanic evidence has been stripped from today's deeply eroded east and south slopes, how can one be sure that the dome wasn't buried any deeper (the Haypress ridge flows, after all, exceed the 7800-foot contour)? The answer lies with the buttes' west slope, which, between the elevations of 6800 and 8000 feet, is little changed from that of the Pliocene dome. Had the flows drowned the valley by an additional 300 feet, they would have touched upon the west slope's lower portion and would have escaped erosion. No volcanic rocks, however, are found on this very old surface today.

With late-Pliocene uplift followed by cooler temperatures in the Pleistocene, glaciers began to grow in the uppermost portions of small canyons on the dome's north and east slopes. Evidence found along Trip 80 indicates that these canyons were repeatedly glaciated, and each major glaciation—lasting many thousands of years—deepened and widened the canyons. From the lookout we can see two large lateral moraines making up much of the sides of the Sardine Lakes canyon. That the west moraine stands at least 1000 feet above Upper Sardine Lake indicates that the last major glacier was at least this thick, and it probably was 200 feet thicker (see Trip 81). The glaciers in this canyon, like glaciers in canyons to the north, at times coalesced to form a larger, trunk glacier that advanced down Salmon Creek into the North Yuba canyon, and down it to the west end of Sierra City. Repeated advances by trunk glaciers helped scour away the 100 feet of flows that had originally buried the Pliocene dome's lower slopes, but they didn't stop there; they scoured away an additional 1500 feet of very resistant bedrock that underlay the flows.

Today, Sierra City lies in a canyon deepened and steepened by the action of the glaciers. In response to these changes, streams vigorously cut deeply into the south slope of the buttes, deeply eroding them and steepening them further. The first gold miners, who founded Sierra City in 1850, learned the dangers of over-steep slopes the hard way—a catastrophic avalanche swept down the south slope and destroyed their settlement in 1852. Not until the 1860s or later was much of the town rebuilt. Perhaps the hard life in that mining town led to the creation of the roisterous society called E. Clampus Vitus, which soon spread throughout the Mother Lode. The buttes had played a not-so-practical joke on Sierra City inhabitants, and they, in turn, formed this organization which played practical jokes upon naive newcomers. Today, the city is more of an easy-going retirement-and-vacation community rich in history, folklore and the magnificent scenery ruled over by the lordly, long-lived Sierra Buttes.

Sierra Buttes Fire Lookout in April

80   Volcano Lake and Mountain Mine

Distance: 6.2 miles, round trip
Total gain/Net gain: 1490'/1170'
Classification: Moderate
Season: Mid-June through October
Parking: Only a few cars near creek; plenty of parking in Sand Pond parking lot
Trailhead/Map: 73/29

Features: An introduction to glacial chronology unfolds to hikers on this trip. Regardless of whether they go to placid Volcano Lake or up to Mountain Mine, they will get awe-inspiring views of Sierra Buttes plus instructive panoramas of this glaciated landscape.

Description: Our jeep road, at first looking deceptively drivable, immediately crosses Sardine Creek. We cross this wide, azalea-lined creek on logs, if they're available, then commence an open ascent southeast up a rocky road. After ¼ mile, we round a low ridge, then cross a narrow gully and round a second low ridge before bending southwest. The ridges we have just passed are two stages of a lateral moraine. The gully separates the younger, inner one from the older, outer one. On the opposite side of Sardine Lakes canyon are two matching stages—mirror images of the ones we see here. To identify them on the map, look at two small contour lobes about ⅛ inch above the *m* in *Sardine Campground*. The two stages of each moraine coalesce into one ridge closer to the Sierra Buttes. The age difference between the younger and older stages is not great—several thousand years at most.

Now look northeast across Salmon Creek and above the new Gold Lake Road. The massive ridge you see descending southeast to Highway 49 is a huge lateral moraine that once bordered a glacier whose icy waves inched slowly down toward the North Yuba River. If you look closely, you should be able to identify at least three of the half-dozen stages within this moraine, the closest, innermost ridge being the product of the glacier's most recent advance, and each successive one being slightly older than the last.

Where is the matching lateral moraine that borders Salmon Creek's west bank? It's gone. Or at least, mostly so. To unravel what happened to it, we've got to walk a short distance southwest up the road from its bend around the older stage of the south Sardine Lakes moraine. About ⅓ mile up our route, the abandoned road has narrowed to a wide path that is being overgrown with manzanita, chinquapin, huckleberry oak and wild plum.

The long, sloping ridge in the foreground is a Salmon Creek lateral moraine

Sierra Buttes looming above Volcano Lake

Numerous rockfalls on the road attest to the instability of the morainal debris piled high by the Sardine Lakes glacier.

Slightly off to the left ahead of us lies the explanation of Salmon Creek's missing moraine. It was buried under the Sardine Lakes moraine, and only its mile-long end protrudes today. This overridden, partly buried moraine together with its counterpart northeast across Salmon Creek are considerably older than the Sardine Lakes moraine. The Sardine is almost certainly the product of glacial action lasting from 30,000 to 10,000 years ago, whereas the Salmon is perhaps derived from the 60,000 to 40,000 year period. Where our road crosses the Salmon moraine, stop and take a look at its soil and rocks, and compare them with those of the Sardine moraine. You should conclude that the Salmon's soils are better developed and its rocks are more weathered, both signs of greater age.

Beyond the Salmon moraine, a short, easy uphill walk takes us to a junction with the signed, steeply climbing Volcano Lake jeep road. Pioneers thought that the Sierra Buttes were the eroded hulk of an Ice Age volcano, and from it the lake received its name. Our direct route narrows to a brushy trail after 100 yards and then parallels the lake's outlet creek ¼ mile up to the terminal moraine above the lake's northeast shore. (A *terminal* moraine is just the debris left at the end of a glacier; terminal, lateral and ground moraines, taken together, are the deposits left by a glacier at its end, sides and bottom.) From this moraine we see the jagged Sierra Buttes rising above the "granitic" bedrock that borders the lake's southwest shore. The best campsites are among the pines along this shore, which is below a conspicuous saddle in the bedrock. From these sites, close inspection reveals that the bedrock is not granitic at all; rather, it is Jurassic-Triassic age metamorphic rocks that superficially resemble granite in color and gross morphology. A short 200-foot climb up to the saddle provides you with a face-to-face confrontation with the Sierra Buttes' towering northeast wall as well as with a view down at deep, azure-blue Upper Sardine Lake, almost 600 feet below.

Returning to the junction with the Volcano Lake jeep road, we veer southeast on the main trail, immediately cross the lake's refreshing outlet creek, then climb steadily south to a rocky ridge, through which our road has been blasted. We are immediately exposed to the massiveness of the often-snow-covered Sierra Buttes, which tower above us like a compressed version of the Swiss Alps.

Our ascent now is westward, past scraggly junipers, and in spots the road is overgrown with brush and is reduced to a footpath at best. Approaching a conspicuous saddle, we spy Mountain Mine, at the base of a five-foot-thick quartz vein that miners hoped would be rich in gold. It wasn't, but lying around its almost-closed entrance are flecks of malachite, a green copper ore, which make good souvenirs, but the ore is not present in sufficient quantities to warrant economic exploitation. One can squeeze into the abandoned mine, and with a flashlight explore its compact, rough-bottomed, T-shaped structure. Don't stay in its cool confines for long, since carbon dioxide can accumulate within its dark, damp space.

Outside the cave, you can explore the surrounding terrain, making an easy 80-foot gain to the saddle above the mine. This saddle approximately marks a division between Jurassic-Triassic metavolcanics to the east and the Paleozoic metavolcanics of the Sierra Buttes to the west. From it you can obtain the best view of Sardine canyon's huge west moraine, which has two conspicuous trails climbing up its brushy slopes (see Trip 81). Looking in the opposite direction—down-canyon toward Haypress Creek—we can identify two sets of relatively young moraines that may be about the same age as the Sardine Lake moraines. The inner moraine completely encircles a prominent, isolated stand of conifers located midway between the mine and Highway 49. The pair of older, larger lateral moraines, on the other hand, descends all the way to the highway.

Mountaineers and rock climbers, equipped with the necessary ropes and climbing equipment, may wish to tackle one of the many potential routes leading up to the crest of the buttes. Most hikers, however, will be content to enjoy the easy, all-downhill route back to the trailhead.

81 Sardine Lakes Moraine

Distance: 4.9 miles plus a 2.8-mile shuttle
Total gain/Net gain: 1380'/1280'
Classification: Moderate
Season: Late June through mid-October
Parking: Only a few cars along roadside; plenty of parking in Sand Pond parking lot.
Trailhead/Map: 74/29

Features: This short stretch of the Pacific Crest Trail carries you up and over one of the most prominent lateral moraines in the Highway 49 area. The open, uphill part of this trip provides you with a continually changing panorama of the Sardine Lakes and the Sierra Buttes.

Description: Our route at first is a jeep road that begins just beyond the Packer Lake Road cutoff from the Sardine Lakes Road. Our shadeless route climbs moderately southwest through dense manzanita up to a switchback. From this point we clearly see the sawtooth nature of the Sierra Buttes crest, and we can see that a traverse along it would be impossible without the aid of ropes and climbing equipment. Just in front of a massive wall of bedrock is deep-blue Lower Sardine Lake, which, like its twin hidden behind the wall, has been slightly raised by a low dam. In the foreground lies a favorite mid- and late-summer swimming hole, Sand Pond.

Sand Pond owes its origin to mining operations at the Young America Mine, whose large buildings once stood on a gentle slope above the lower lake's southwest shore. Higher up on our route, there will be several spots where you'll be able to take a few steps south from the trail and see the rocky, gravelly tailings left by the long-abandoned mine. The mine was a major operation as early as 1885, with a large mill in which ore blasted out of the Jurassic-Triassic metavolcanic bedrock was crushed to extract its gold, which, over about 50 years, amounted to $1½ million worth. The gangue, or waste material, was then flushed down via a closed conduit to the flat below Lower Sardine Lake, where it was deposited as tailings. In the early 1900s some tailings were removed and were treated by the cyanide process to recover more gold. The depression left by their removal became Sand Pond. If you go swimming in this shallow, clear pond, note that its bottom *is* sandy, due to the crushed gangue. If the pond had formed by being dammed behind a terminal moraine, its bottom would be quite rocky until enough sediments were deposited to bury the rocks.

From the switchback, our jeep road heads north to forested slopes and a trail junction. Here we turn left onto the trail and switchback up the end of a huge lateral moraine to its long, southeast side. Because most of the moraine is clothed only in manzanita, huckleberry oak, chinquapin and snowbush, our views up the steadily climbing trail are largely continuous and unobstructed. Occasional Jeffrey pines punctuate the moraine's brushy cloak and some provide us with shady, picturesque, trailside resting spots. Looking southward across Lower Sardine Lake, we see a large lateral moraine (see Trip 80) which is the same age as the one we're hiking along.

Midway along our trail's ascent we encounter a spur trail that descends steeply ¼ mile down to the rocky bench at the outlet of deep, azure-blue Upper Sardine Lake. Beyond the junction, the Mesozoic metavolcanic rocks making up our trail's bed gradually

yield to Paleozoic ones, which, like the former, come alive with blazing colors after a rainstorm.

Soon the trail switchbacks up to the open-forested crest of the moraine, from which the buttes are still visible through firs. The 1000-foot-high moraine we've just topped shows us the *minimum* depth of the Sardine Lakes canyon glacier, which filled the canyon until about 10,000 years ago. Since this lateral moraine is composed of debris dropped by the flowing glacier, the glacier had to be higher than the moraine, perhaps by 100 feet. The glacier, whose immense thickness generated a pressure of over 35 tons per square foot, scoured out a deep basin in which lies today's Upper Sardine Lake. At its maximum thickness, then, the glacier's icy surface stood about 1200 feet above the lake basin's floor. It must have been a very dramatic, alpine sight.

Leaving the moraine's crest, the trail switchbacks steeply down to gentler slopes and becomes a closed jeep road, which undulates and winds past seasonal ponds

Upper Sardine Lake and Sierra Buttes

before ending just below shallow lower Tamarack Lake. Here we encounter a second jeep road, on which vehicles are allowed, and on weekends you'll probably see campers and fishermen who have driven this far. The road continues southward, and at the lower lake's west shore it forks, the left branch climbing gently up to nearby upper Tamarack Lake while the right branch climbs steeply to a logged-over area. Campsites at both lakes are adequate if you don't mind the company of motorized vehicles. The lakes derive their name from the fringe of lodgepole pines that encircles each. Back in the 1800s, John Muir and his contemporaries called these two-needled conifers *tamarack* pines.

Our route down to Packer Lake is an obvious one. We follow a jeep road north down to a junction with the Butcher Ranch Meadows Road, and follow it ¼ mile gently down to Trailhead 76, which is its junction with the Packer Lake Road. An 80-yard walk southeast on it will take you to the Packer Lake Picnic Area, at which you can rest under conifers or on the lake's beach. Lacking any icy, inflowing streams during the summer, this sun-drenched shallow lake is the warmest swimming hole you'll find in the Highway 49 area. When you're ready to move onward, walk or drive 2.8 miles down the Packer Lake Road to your trailhead or retrace your steps.

The buttes and lower Tamarack Lake

82   Deer Lake Trail

Distance: 4.0 miles, round trip

Total gain/Net gain: 1100'/1000'

Classification: Moderate

Season: Early July through mid-October

Parking: More than ample at nearby Packsaddle Camping Area

Trailhead/Map: 75/29

Features: A short hike, this section of the Pacific Crest Trail takes you up to deep, sparkling Deer Lake, whose shores see many a backpacker and fisherman. In addition, two shallow, less visited lakes are easily reached from this trail. In a good day's walk you can hike to four Grass Lakes in the Highway 49 region. Two of them lie close to our route—the Deer Lake Trail—another is in Lakes Basin and the northernmost is in Plumas-Eureka State Park.

Description: Leaving the trailhead on Packer Lake Road, we quickly meet and cross by various means four unequal-size creeks that drain Packer Lake and the slopes north of it. Departing from the lush, streamside vegetation, we begin to climb upward, execute two well-graded switchback legs, and swing past a two-stage lateral moraine (see Trip 80). Our comfortable trail underfooting becomes rocky as we curve over to the first Grass Lake's outlet creek, and it remains so almost to the second Grass Lake turnoff.

The first Grass Lake turnoff is about ¼ mile up the trail from the outlet creek. Where you encounter a ridge jutting 10–15 feet above the trail's west side, you can climb up it, and from it an easy, 100-yard, cross-country descent to the east shore will become immediately apparent. Of the region's four Grass Lakes, this one is the smallest, diminished by invading grass to about half the size shown on the topographic map. It is a short-lived lake that is in its last stages. The 50-yard-long terminal moraine that dams it is quite likely the

The first (southernmost) of 4 Grass Lakes

Sierra Buttes and Deer Lake in mid-June

product of the Little Ice Age, which produced small Sierra glaciers at least three times in the last 4000 years. The latest surge of "glacierets" occurred while the Pilgrims were trying to survive bitter winters on the eastern seaboard. Two small flats provide adequate campsites. One is above the lake's east side, the other is just southwest of its outlet creek.

From the trailside ridge, we confront a steady, bush-lined ascent. In 0.6 mile our trail levels off at an open-forested flat, on which a sign, bearing 100°, reads *Grass Lake* ¼. The mileage is correct; the bearing is not. If you wish to hike to the lake, start at 50°, cross a seasonal creek in 30 yards, then follow a *faint,* ducked trail that crosses a gentle ridge and gradually descends its north slope to the willow-lined lake, which provides warm mid-summer swimming. Larger and deeper than the first Grass Lake, this chest-deep, grass-bottomed lake also differs in that its water is not crystal clear. Should you decide to camp at this hard-to-find lake, obtain fresh water from audible Sawmill Creek, which is 300 yards from the lake's north shore.

Only 60 yards north of the *Grass Lake* ¼ sign we come to a post and leave the Pacific Crest Trail as we bear 300° toward a conspicuous gully from which a seasonal creek flows. At its bottom, a rocky path, ducked and blazed, appears and guides us ½ mile up to a moraine immediately above Deer Lake's southeast shore. Small campsites can be found along the west, south and east shores, and diving and swimming are best on the east. If you've brought along a fishing rod, you can try to catch the fairly deep lake's rainbow and brook trout.

Brook trout

83 Salmon Lake Trail

Distance: 3.8 miles, round trip
Total gain/Net gain: 1050'/620'
Classification: Moderate
Season: Mid-July through mid-October
Parking: Ample at Upper Salmon Lake
Trailhead/Map: 77/29

Features: A slightly shorter, alternative approach to popular Deer Lake, this trail provides scenic vistas across the Salmon lakes basin.

Description: From the east end of the parking area, the Salmon Lake Trail begins a rocky, moderate ascent up a classic brush slope covered with huckleberry oak, western serviceberry, deer brush, snowbush, manzanita, wild plum and barberry. Scattered, big-leafed mule ears—plants usually associated with volcanic soils—add their own decoration and aroma to this slope, which is the south side of a large lateral moraine. Below us, several picturesque islands, easily reached by short swims from one to another, grow more distant. Upon reaching a flat, our trail

commences a moderate descent that takes us down to Salmon Lake's rocky northwest corner. As you approach outlying buildings of Salmon Lake Resort, stay high, contouring about 50 feet above the water, and reaching a bridge over Horse Lake creek 120 yards up from the resort's main building.

Beyond the creek, our trail climbs southward, passing a small pond before arriving at shallow Horse Lake, bordered by lodgepoles, silver pines, red firs and brush. Rounding the lake's southeast shore, the trail gets swampy in places, and an abundance of corn lilies reflects this water-saturated soil condition.

A few short switchbacks carry us up to a sloping bench just south of a creeklet that descends to Horse Lake, visible below us. Higher up, our steeply climbing, switchbacking trail provides us with better views of this lake plus views of Upper Salmon Lake and the massive moraine behind it. Note that the moraine isn't all that thick; rather, it covers the bedrock with just a mantle of earth and loose rock.

We soon reach the signed Pacific Crest

Morning calm over Upper Salmon Lake

A low moraine on Deer Lake's southeast shore dams the lake

Trail, atop a forested saddle. Here we have a choice of three routes to Deer Lake. (1) The first starts northwest as a faint trail—up a shallow gully—that leaves the Salmon Lake Trail only 15 yards north of the saddle. It then leaves the gully, climbs and descends a slab into a larger gully, ascends west to its head, and then bends southwest across a slope to a jeep road. The PCT heads north on this jeep road and others to Summit Lake and Oakland Pond. We head south steeply down it and quickly reach the north shore of Deer Lake. (2) The second route follows the PCT 0.6 mile southward, passing a small pond on Sawmill Creek midway along its journey to a post at the Deer Lake Trail junction (see Trip 82). (3) The third and shortest route is along a faint, unmaintained trail, bearing west-southwest, which ends near the lake's northeast shore. Cross-country hiking to this shore is easy enough that you need not follow the hard-to-see trail. At Deer Lake, ice melts late, entirely disappearing around late June. By late July, the lake's temperature is suitable for swimming, and the northeast shore has good rocks to bask on after an invigorating dip.

84   Lakes Basin Ridge Loop

Distance: 7.5 miles, loop trip
Total gain/Net gain: 1420'/980'
Classification: Moderate
Season: Mid-July through early October
Parking: Usually ample, but may be crowded
   on weekends
Trailhead/Map: 79/30

Features: Several trails of the Lakes Basin are
joined with the Pacific Crest Trail to produce a
loop trip that passes basin lakes as well as the
Sierra crest. The two contrasting perspectives
will give you a good feel for this glaciated
landscape.

Description: Just 50 yards east of Gold Lake
Resort and only 35 yards west of the crest
parking area is a signed, closed jeep road
which traverses southwest toward Round,
Bear, Silver and Long lakes. We start a gentle
ascent up this road, and, after a few minutes'
walk, meet a signed trail that departs for Bear,
Silver and Long lakes. Most hikers turn right
here. Over the next mile of road, our hike
through the white- and red-fir forest is
uneventful, although we do get a glimpse of
justifiably popular Big Bear Lake below.

Gold Lake

After a mile, our road curves left, passes
two seasonal ponds—one on each side—then
immediately reaches a trail junction. An old,
signed trail to Gold Lake starts up a
deep gully, but it doesn't get even as far as the
crest. Walking on, we wind westward for
⅓ mile—steeply at times—up to an abandoned tin shack on a ridgetop. Beyond the
shack our road descends about 60 yards to a
stone-and-mortar foundation—one of the few
remains of a gold-mining operation. Continuing 50 yards down the road, we reach a fork
and take the left branch, which climbs 50 yards
up and dead-ends at signed Trail 12E34.

We immediately start a steep ascent, which
remains steep up a ridge, through its low cleft,
and beyond. Looking back, we see Lakes
Basin spread out before us, with Round Lake
below us and mile-long Long Lake at the foot
of Mt. Elwell. As the ridge eases off, the trail
goes through a miniature pass, swings southeast toward a gully and briefly gives us a
glimpse of Gold Lake.

The largest natural lake in the Highway 49
region, Gold Lake lies dammed behind a
recessional moraine left by a glacier that once
extended seven miles down-canyon from its
source, which was an ice field at the Sierra

crest near Summit Lake. As the glacier's front
was making a prolonged, erratic retreat, it
would occasionally advance slightly and then
stagnate for a while. While it was stagnant,
rocks and other debris that the glacier had
carried or pushed along were deposited as an
arc-shaped moraine. The fingers of Gold
Lake's shore that jut out into the lake—
particularly along the south side—represent
other, partly drowned recessional moraines
that were deposited after the glacier's front
had retreated further. (Only the moraine
farthest down-canyon is called the *terminal*
moraine.)

Goose, Haven and Snag lakes, all smaller
bodies east of Gold Lake, were also formed
when drainage was trapped behind morainal
deposits. Within the last 10,000 years—after
the last major glaciation—Salmon Creek
eroded its headwaters northward until they
reached Snag Lake and Church Creek. Now
rather than drain north as they once did, Snag
Lake and Church Creek drain south down
Salmon Creek. This was a case of *stream
piracy,* that is, one stream capturing a
drainage area from another stream.

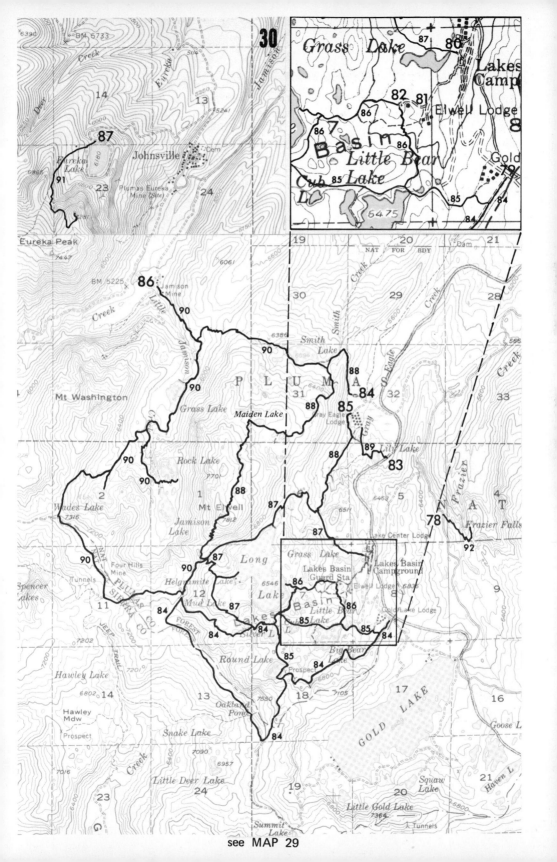

30

Beyond the gully with a view of Gold Lake, our faint trail turns south and climbs to a small saddle just west of a hidden, rock-rimmed pond. From the saddle we climb south, then southwest, and just before reaching a signed junction with the Pacific Crest Trail, we can look back and see the pond. (Northbound hikers take note: the route isn't too obvious, so make sure that you end up at the west side of the pond, not its east side. Furthermore, 300 yards below the pond, be sure you curve northwest to a five-foot-deep pass rather than descend a gully northeast toward the broad saddle above Gold Lake.)

To circumvent Peak 7550, the Pacific Crest Trail—a jeep road here—veers northwest and descends past a temporary pond before arriving at larger, deeper Oakland Pond. Just north of the pond's west shore, the jeep road bends west and descends very steeply to Snake Lake. From this bend the Pacific Crest Trail, which is now an adequately marked footpath, climbs northwest, moderately at times, up the west slopes below the crest, passing through acres of wildflowers before entering an open red-fir forest. After a mile of trail, we come to within 50 yards of a saddle on the crest. A brief walk up to it surprises us with a dramatic northeast escarpment. Bold granitelike cliffs on our right, which climbers may wish to investigate, block our view east, but the view northeast to Mt. Elwell and Long

Lake is unobstructed. The pseudogranite cliffs are composed of metarhyolite—erupted as rhyolite during the late Paleozoic era and later metamorphosed. This process produced large crystals of quartz in a matrix of much smaller crystals of quartz and mica, thus giving the rocks its granitic, crystalline appearance.

Our path continues northwest, guiding us into a lodgepole forest and to within a few yards of the crest itself. A few steps northeast from the path give us a better overview of the Lakes Basin than the one we just got from the crest saddle. Returning to our shady trail, we curve westward down to a shallow gully, then descend northeast in it to a small spring-fed creek and a view of the Lakes Basin in the east.

From the creek's north bank a road begins, and we follow it for only two minutes before we come to the first of two signed trail junctions. Our route turns right at the first trail, which descends quite directly to Silver Lake. (The second trail, starting 70 yards north down the road, follows a ridge northward about ½ mile before splitting in three directions—see Trip 90.)

As we descend moderately to steeply southeast down the first trail, red firs, mountain hemlocks and silver pines block our views across the Lakes Basin. However, as we turn

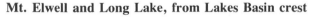

Mt. Elwell and Long Lake, from Lakes Basin crest

Helgramite and Long lakes

eastward and progress toward a rocky bench, views of Long and Mud lakes appear. Beyond the short bench we descend to a gully, then labor south up its steep slope before cresting a low-angle ridge. An easy southeast descent from it gets us down to the outlet creek from the highest of three small lakelets. Looking southwest up toward the high point on the Sierra crest, we can see immediately northwest of it the saddle we had previously gazed down from. Climbers who are impressed by the dramatic "granite" (actually metarhyolite) cliffs should start their approach to climbs up them from the lakelet just above us.

Crossing the outlet creek, our trail avoids the grassy shores of the middle lakelet by briefly climbing east before descending northeast past the lower, deepest lakelet and reaching a trail junction only 50 yards east of it. Here are good views of beautiful, blue Long, Silver and Big Bear lakes, but the views improve after we turn right on a trail and

descend a slope mantled with low, bushy huckleberry oak. Our trail enters red-fir and mountain-hemlock cover as it approaches the north arm of Silver Lake and then it arrives at a signed junction with a trail from Round Lake, described in Trip 85. The remainder of our route coincides with, and is described in, the second half of that trip.

Don't be in a hurry to leave Silver Lake. Most of its shoreline is readily accessible for exploration or relaxation, and by early August, when the mosquito population has largely abated, this shallow lake's relatively warm water is near its best for swimming. As at other lakes throughout the Lakes Basin, overnight camping is prohibited due to the heavy visitor use this very compact area receives. No lake in this area, however, is more than an hour's walk from the Lakes Basin Campground, so you can still get up early in the morning and do some sunrise lake fishing.

85   Round Lake Loop

Distance: 4.3 miles, loop trip

Total gain/Net gain: 590'/360'

Classification: Easy

Season: Early July through mid-October

Parking: Usually ample, but may be crowded on weekends

Trailhead/Map: 79/30

Features: This relaxing trip, an easy day hike, takes you to the five lakes in the southern half of Lakes Basin. Round, Silver and Big Bear lakes are fishermen's favorites, and are also appealing to photographers and swimmers.

Description: As in Trip 84, we follow the southwest-heading road 1¾ miles up to the abandoned tin shack atop a ridge. However, rather than forking left and up at a junction 110 yards beyond it, we curve right and descend toward Round Lake, our road diminishing to a trail before it touches the south shore. Mine tailings and mechanical debris, both derived from the now-abandoned mine located at an old foundation near the shack, now fill part of the deep lake's south side. Quartz blasted from the mine's veins is recognizable among the rock fragments in the tailings, and it was in this vein quartz that miners had hoped to find gold.

Fishing in Round Lake

Old engine in Round Lake

A fishermen's trail skirts the lake's southeast shore, and on it we reach the jump-across outlet creek. From here an evident, rocky trail makes an open climb northwest above the lake toward the crest of a moraine. Just south of the moraine's crest—and an easy walk west from us—lies a large, triangular pond that is sometimes shaded by stately Jeffrey pines growing near it. Atop the crest, we start north and immediately see our next goal, Silver Lake, before we descend to its east shore. Fringed with silver and lodgepole pines, mountain hemlocks and red firs, this lake has considerably more appeal than Round Lake, whose shoreline tends to be more brushy. Before August, however, shade-loving mosquitoes may make you prefer Round Lake. Most of the shoreline around Silver Lake is readily accessible, if not by main trail then by fishermen's trail. Like all lakes in the Lakes Basin, Silver Lake is heavily fished. The

Round Lake and checkered bark of silver pine

lake's shallow, warm August water invites an enjoyable swim, but by late August the temperature begins to drop and the lake's outlet creek has already dried up. Our trail crosses this east-flowing creek, near which we have a glimpse down-basin at Cub Lake and the Bear lakes, and then it curves over to a junction just above the lake's north arm. Starting southwest here is a trail that soon divides, one branch climbing to the Pacific Crest Trail (Trip 84), and another one rambling over to the Long Lake environs (Trip 87), from where another trail zigzags up to the top of Mt. Elwell (Trip 88).

Within 200 yards from this junction, our sometimes vague trail starts northeast, curves north, crosses a small flat, and then climbs northeast to a view of island-dotted Long Lake, which is also wide and deep. Although less than a mile long, it appears larger than it actually is, perhaps because of the stunted growth of the shoreline conifers. Leaving this ridge view, from which the east-dipping strata of Mt. Elwell are readily apparent, we descend east to a junction in a small flat that lies between the crests of two low moraines. The trail going northeast takes you to Long Lake's southeast shore (Trip 86) before descending to Elwell Lodge and Lakes Basin Campground.

We climb southeast over a low moraine, descend past a small pond on our right, and approach but don't reach circular, shallow Cub Lake. Paralleling this lake's drainage eastward, our trail soon crosses above the north shore of linear, pine-rimmed Little Bear Lake. From a trailside stump about 150 yards beyond this shallow lake, a fishermen's trail departs southeast toward it, then parallels its east shore, and ends at its 10-yard-long outlet creek, which drops four feet into Big Bear Lake. Along this larger lake's wavy, rocky shoreline, you'll find good spots to fish, and to dive and swim from.

Back at the trailside stump, from which both Bear lakes are seen, we briefly ascend and then descend to Big Bear's north shore, and cross east over a peninsula. Momentarily paralleling this lake's north shore, we reach its northeast corner and a trail junction. Here, Trip 86, which has coincided with our route since the last trail junction, departs northeast toward Lakes Basin Campground and Elwell Lodge. We turn south, in 45 yards cross Big Bear's outlet, and then leave this extremely popular, moderately large lake behind as we start down beside its outlet creek.

At first, the outlet creek is a flowing pond, but it soon constricts before enlarging into a second pond, which is seen as the trail curves right around a ridge above it. Our trail now traverses southeast to a shallow creek in a shaded gully. After jumping across the creek, we climb east moderately and then steeply up our blazed trail, cross a boggy flat, and parallel the edge of a cluster of willows as we climb northeast toward the outskirts of Gold Lake Lodge. Just before leaving the willows, we reach a steeper gradient and an easily missed trail junction. The route straight ahead climbs northeast moderately up to nearby Gold Lake Resort. Our route veers east, climbs moderately southeast, and curves eastward back up to the closed road we first started hiking on. On it we hike 300 yards northeast to the trailhead, to the Gold Lake Lodge entrance and to the parking area.

Silver Lake

Cub Lake (above), Big Bear Lake (below)

86   Bear Lakes Loop

Distance: 2.5 miles, loop trip
Total gain/Net gain: 480'/360'
Classification: Easy
Season: Early July through mid-October
Parking: Limited and usually crowded; walk to trailhead from your campsite
Trailhead/Map: 82/30

Features: The easiest lakes loop in the Lakes Basin, this trip takes you to four lakes, including one short excursion to giant Long Lake. For those who desire a quick taste of the Lakes Basin's beauty and charm, this short hike is perfect.

Description: Walking west on Trail 12E30, we immediately cross a creek where it flows through a conduit, then in 50 yards find ourselves in a flat, shady, spacious organization campground. Climbing moderately westward from the flat's far end, we exchange the shade of white firs and lodgepoles for fairly continuous sunlight on a more open, brushy slope. Yarrow milfoil, aster, cinquefoil, pennyroyal and Indian hemp are some of the wildflowers that adorn the trail's side, and a short distance up-trail we pass a low, granitelike cliff of metarhyolite, on which rock climbers can brush up their techniques.

Just beyond the low cliff we cross a short-lasting creek, bordered here and there

Silver Lake

by western serviceberry, which is recognized in early summer by its round, fine-toothed leaves and its half-dollar-sized, five-petaled flowers. Late-summer hikers will find its white flowers replaced with purple, pulpy but edible berries. From the creek we climb to a small flat, shaded by lodgepoles, and on it meet an old trail, not well maintained, which curves southeast and then progresses eastward, crossing the Bear Lake Trail before ending at the west grounds of Elwell Lodge.

A hike equally as short as the one we've just completed takes us up almost to a ridge, and we arrive at a trail junction. Being very close to Long Lake, we continue west in its direction up a short spur trail, cresting the ridge and almost immediately dropping to a small bay on the lake's northeast shore. At this bay, which is one of the huge lake's three readily accessible shores, summer visitors can rent small boats to fish from or cruise in.

After exploring the small bay or perhaps trying our luck at shoreline fishing, we backtrack over the low ridge and cruise down to the last junction. From the junction, the main trail climbs southwest and then descends a gully to a trail junction in a small flat. Trips 84 and 85, coming from the west, descend to this junction, while Trips 87 and 88 head west up from it. You might note that although we're very close to Long Lake's south shore, which is over 100 feet below us, we can't see the lake at all. A moraine blocks our view north down at it, as another moraine blocks our view southeast down toward the Bear lakes. The gully in which our trail descended to this flat separates these two linear products of glacial deposition.

Our route for the next 0.8 mile coincides with that of Trip 85. We climb briefly southeast over the low, bouldery moraine, descend to Cub Lake, and pass the north shores of Little Bear and Big Bear lakes. At Big Bear's northeast corner, our trail splits from Trip 85, and we descend northward, briefly touching a meander in the lake's outlet creek. Not far beyond this meander our trail forks. The Bear *Lakes* Trail descends right to Elwell Lodge. We take the Bear *Lake* Trail, which traverses around a small ridge before descending to our trailhead near the organization campground. Midway along this descent, we cross the old east-west Elwell Lodge-Long Lake Trail, which we previously encountered on a small, lodgepole-shaded flat.

Crest, from Big Bear Lake's outlet

87   Long Lake Loop

Distance: 6.7 miles, loop trip
Total gain/Net gain: 1420'/810'
Classification: Moderate
Season: Early July through mid-October
Parking: Limited and usually crowded; walk to trailhead from your campsite
Trailhead/Map: 82/30

Features: All three good access points to the shores of Long Lake are encountered along this route. One need not, of course, restrict himself to these three limited shorelines, but rather can investigate cross-country alternatives to virtually untouched shores.

Description: Trip 86 describes the first mile of trail up to a trail junction above the south shore of Long Lake. From this junction we follow part of Trip 84 in reverse as we first wind quickly up to lovely Silver Lake, which merits at least a brief delay, and then scramble westward up a brushy ridge packed with pleasing panoramas that extend across virtually all of the Lakes Basin. Momentarily leaving the ridge, our trail switchbacks and then climbs back on to it at a trail junction to which Trip 84 descends from the west.

We continue along our current direction, and traverse over to the north shore of a nearby lakelet which is signed *Helgramite Lake, 7040* feet—contrary to the topographic map. Since the sign is incorrect about the lakelet's true elevation, which is about 100 feet lower, perhaps then it is also incorrect about the name. Regardless of name or elevation, the grass-bottomed, fairly deep lakelet on a tranquil day pleasingly reflects the bold cliffs southwest of it that climb to the skyline. Attaining the high point of the climb before plunging down toward Long Lake, one may feel compelled—particularly on a hot day—to plunge his feet into the lakelet's calm, soothing water.

Continuing onward, we quickly reach and cross the lakelet's murmuring northbound creek, and then descend its rocky gully, pausing momentarily to glance north toward domineering Mt. Elwell, which is the only *real* mountain in the Lakes Basin vicinity. The subsequently metamorphosed volcanic rocks that make up this 250-million-year-old mass appear as distinct layers—which perhaps are individual flows—all dipping, or descending, northeast. Although the rocky mass is very

old, its form is not, having been largely sculptured in the last two million years.

Our sometimes steep descent northwest enters a red fir/mountain hemlock forest, lessens its gradient, and levels off near the crossing of a major but seasonal creek, which debouches from a striking V-shaped canyon and empties into chest-deep Mud Lake. Steering clear of the water-saturated west-shore meadow, which is being invaded and conquered by alders and willows, our trail keeps within the dry confines of red firs before curving north and climbing gently up to the base of a steeper slope, where we reach a signed junction. Only 25 yards beyond it, the main trail turns northwest and begins a moderate ascent. At that turn is a second junction. The trails departing east from the two junctions quickly unite into one, and on it

Long Lake

we hike briefly up, and then descend gradually toward Long Lake. This spur trail almost reaches the shore, and then becomes indistinct and overgrown, but a smaller path, branching left, traverses 60 yards northeast to the lake's edge. Just north of trail's end are rocks suitable for diving off or fishing from, and temptingly close lies the first of several rocky islands. Because the lake is the basin's largest, it is also the slowest to warm up, although it does get into the mid-60s by mid-August, making a swim at least to the first island feasible.

Returning to the main trail, we engage in a moderate ascent northwest up to the edge of some orange-brown metamorphic bedrock, then switchback up through a soggy, sloping meadow. Thick vegetation at times obscures the trail as it continues to switchback upslope. Eventually the trail diagonals north up to a trail junction on a small, almost level, tree-dotted bench. Our trail's sign, *11E14,* is seen 30 yards before this not-too-obvious junction. From here, a half-mile-long lateral trail departs southwest, soon following a narrow crest over to the Pacific Crest Trail (see Trip 90). Another trail initially goes north-northwest a few yards before turning left and diagonaling west-southwest over to the ridge, which is snow-free by early July. The ¾-mile climb to the top of Mt. Elwell (Trip 88) is well worth the effort.

Our trail northeast is an indistinct one at first. We hike in this direction through a clump of manzanita and willows, then arrive at a gully and start northeast down it. A rocky trail descending a huge talus slope in the near distance should quickly become apparent. (Route finding is a real problem only when you are going in the opposite direction—up the gully. If you're doing this, don't yield to temptation by heading over to a conspicuous saddle and low knoll just east of the gully; the junction you are trying to reach lies on a flat about 150 yards due west of and above the saddle.)

Once on the ducked, talus-slope trail, we can concentrate our attention on the spectacular island-studded lake below us. A steady descent down the unstable talus trail takes us almost to the lake's waters, which lie just beyond a few yards of dense willows and tobacco brush. Now we climb briefly, and then traverse across a brush-covered bench to two very different, cabin-sized boulders. The first is smooth, looks granitic, and bears no

resemblance to the cliffs above us or the bedrock we stand on. Where did this 100-ton boulder come from? If you've walked along the Pacific Crest Trail—a little over one mile southwest of here (Trip 84)—you'll recognize the mega-boulder as a huge chunk of Paleozoic metarhyolite, which was transported here by the Lakes Basin glacier. Glacier-transported boulders, which are usually smaller than this one, are called *erratics,* and most are easy to spot because they rest on a rock type that is quite different from their own composition.

The rough, second mega-boulder obviously broke loose from the cliffs above. It, too, is a metamorphosed Paleozoic volcanic rock, but its composition is a grade of andesite or basalt. The watermelon-sized blocks within its structure bear close resemblance to the blocky, autobrecciated, young lava flows seen near Round Lake on Trip 49, and this large boulder probably had a similar origin.

In 120 yards, just beyond a Jeffrey pine, we come to our third and final approach to the shores of Long Lake—a short spur trail to a small check dam at the lake's north end. The shoreline vegetation is open enough for you to scramble around on bedrock to a good fishing site, a swimming area or a sunbathing slab.

Once back on the main trail, we cross some springs just after our last lake view disappears. Decorating them and our trail's sides are yarrow milfoil, aster, pennyroyal, paintbrush, parsley and other wildflowers. Lending contrast to this ephemeral show of color are rugged, long-lived junipers, which seem to prefer dry bedrock to moist soil. These slow-growing trees send out roots that seek—and sometimes enlarge—every nearby crack in the bedrock. Like the wildflowers, a juniper needs soil nutrients and water.

Immediately east of us we see an unmistakable "footprint" of a former glacier—a smoothed-over bedrock knoll. Closer inspection will reveal that rocks and grit the glacier dragged along its bottom have striated the rock in the direction of glacier movement and have gouged out small, angular cavities. Seeking out all nearby cracks atop this glacier-polished knoll are the massive roots of a large Jeffrey pine.

Continuing northward, we begin a descent, immediately negotiate two switchbacks, and then descend across *joint-controlled* (see Trip 39), shallow gullies that have been polished by glaciers. Beyond them we skirt the north edge

Glacier-polished knoll; glacier moved from right to left

of a grassy meadow, which cradles a small lake that diminishes greatly by Labor Day. Beyond low bedrock outcrops above the meadow's east edge, we descend northeast down a brushy slope and soon find ourselves briefly alongside a seasonal creek before we abruptly turn southeast and head for Long Lake's outlet, Gray Eagle Creek. Midway down to it, we traverse a small, spongy meadow, and by a creek near its far end we note that the trail has eroded, exposing ground water that had previously flowed through the porous soil only inches below its surface. Much of the drainage of a basin, such as Lakes Basin, is accomplished through the ground. The lakes and creeks we see are just surface exposures of ground water.

Only 25 yards before Gray Eagle Creek we come to a junction, from which a trail—poorly defined for the first few hundred yards—descends to Gray Eagle Lodge and its environs (Trip 88 comes up this route). Wide, swift Gray Eagle Creek is a dangerous ford in early season. The crossing is only 20 yards before the lively creek turns east and cascades down a rocky cliff. Be extremely careful.

Beyond the ford we have an uphill hike rich in verdant growth. Alders and dogwoods rise above thimbleberries, currants, mountain ash and willows that might hide a lurking coyote. Except in autumn, when it is blazing yellow, Indian hemp goes unseen while swamp whiteheads, corn lily, Indian paintbush and at least four species of sunflowers add their colors to the greenery. We keep our feet dry by skirting around a boggy meadow rather than slogging through it, then climb up on a low moraine, which we'll tread upon almost every step of the way to trail's end.

After a climb up to a bend in the moraine, we encounter a short spur trail that descends to a shallow, reflective pond overly rich in pond lilies. Curving eastward, we now have a gently undulating path to follow, which takes us past the northern fringe of poorly defined Grass Lake—more of a meadow in late summer. Boulder-hopping its outlet creek, we can see, 20 yards downstream, a delightful pool—molded into a swimming hole by previous owners of Lake Center Lodge. Complete with steps and a poolside grass lawn, this crystal-clear pool provides the satisfying swim needed after a long day's hike. The lodge was permanently closed by the Forest Service in autumn 1974.

Fifty yards beyond the creek crossing we reach the trailhead, which is located just north of Campsite 7 in Lakes Basin Campground. Now we have a half-mile walk back to our original trailhead. We walk 70 yards south on the campground's road to its hub, from which the remaining route back to our vehicles is perfectly obvious.

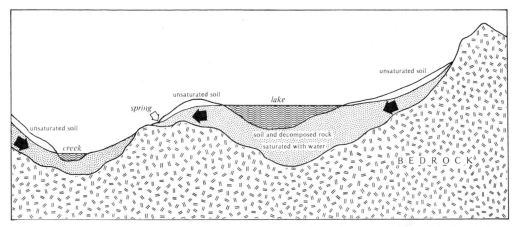

In the Lakes Basin area, most water flows through the ground rather than over it.

Lake Center Lodge swimming hole

88   Mt. Elwell Loop, from Lakes Basin Campground

Distance: 11.2 miles, round trip
Total gain/Net gain: 2790'/2020'
Classification: Moderate
Season: Mid-July through mid-October
Parking: A few cars at most; walk to trailhead from your campsite
Trailhead/Map: 80/30

Features: Unbeatable for Lakes Basin views is a climb to Mt. Elwell's summit. This loop trip traverses lake, stream, slope and crest terrains and exposes you to all the species of trees you'll find in the basin. Rock climbers will find numerous opportunities to practice their art, particularly on the south slope of Mt. Elwell.

Description: The first halves of Trips 86 and 87 describe our route up to a signed junction on a vegetated bench that is located on the south slope of Mt. Elwell. We go a few yards north-northwest before turning left and diagonaling west-southwest up an easy grade to the mountain's well-defined south ridge, which is usually snow-free by early July. Starting north up a trail, climbers will immediately notice that the massive metavolcanic cliffs ahead, which make up most of the south slope, offer dozens of Class 5 climbing routes.

At our first switchback, red firs add a photogenic touch to our view of Long Lake, and these trees offer shade along various parts of our steep ascent. Associated with this scattered cover are the trees' usual companions, spiny-seeded chinquapin and lowly mat manzanita. About 300 feet below the top, our trail veers west far enough to present us with views of Jamison and Rock lakes. A series of short, steep zigzags now confront us, and they are being ruined by thoughtless descending hikers who are shortcutting downslope from one switchback leg to the next.

Climbers will find some easily accessible routes just below the peak's southeast summit, and not far above them the trail skirts the base of the peak's northwest summit, which has enjoyable, blocky climbing routes—some of them overhanging.

Before we know it, we're at the cleft between the two low summits, and are surprised to find that aromatic species of ceanothus, tobacco brush, thriving up here above the red firs we passed along the trail and the mountain hemlocks we'll soon pass.

Both summits are Class 2 scrambles, although harder ways up each are very easy to find. The lower, southeast summit provides the more impressive views, for the entire, glaciated Lakes Basin, dominated by Long Lake, is spread out before you. Beyond Silver and Round lakes lies the deep canyon of unseen Gold Lake, and rising above all on the horizon are the unmistakable Sierra Buttes. The higher, northwest summit looks down on the definitely glaciated form of the Little Jamison Creek canyon, whose sides were smoothed and steepened by the ice.

From the top, the shortest way back is to return the way you came. Most people do. Our route, however, completes a loop trip, utilizing the less used trail from Smith Lake. Snow patches just below the summit cleft linger till September, and if you are hiking this route in July you'll have a route-finding situation waiting for you.

A brief, steep descent northeast leads us over blocks and into the outskirts of a predominantly mountain-hemlock forest—the kind of forest mosquitoes love. Red firs and silver pines soon increase their numbers along our winding, usually descending trail, and just before rounding a ridge and commencing a steeper descent, we pass through a small, sloping meadow. One-quarter mile from the ridge, we can't help but note a large, house-sized block off on our right, which certainly will appeal to climbers. It even comes with a Jeffrey pine on its summit, from which you can rappel or set up a top-rope belay. There are several Class 3 routes up to its summit that can be done unroped by cautious climbers, and the view from its almost-flat top is worth the brief effort. To the northeast and southeast below you lie Maiden and Hidden lakes, and between them, in the middle distance, stands Beckwourth Peak (7255'). Beyond it lies flat, fault-formed Sierra Valley and to its north rise the 8000-foot peaks of the Dixie and Diamond mountains.

Our trail now descends north, levels off and turns southeast, immediately encountering the shoreline of waist-deep, grass-lined Maiden Lake. A thoroughly integrated forest surrounds it, composed of mountain hemlock, red fir, silver pine and lodgepole pine. Beyond this small lake, an almost level, eastward-winding trail leads us past three lakelets.

Summit view of Long Lake, Lakes Basin and Sierra Buttes

Between the first and second, a trail sign points the way to not-so-hidden Hidden Lake (Lake 6847 on the topo map). A faint trail, blazed and ducked, departs south toward it but dies out before reaching it. We'll leave this hemmed-in, green gem, which is good for swimming but not for fishing, for those who want to try a little bit of route-finding on their own.

After arcing around the north shore of the second lakelet, we climb above and away from the third, and smallest, lakelet, which dries up before summer's end. We now meander northeastward down the broad crest of a lateral moraine, shaded by an open stand of red firs, silver pines, and—amazingly—sugar pines. Foot-long cones, drooping from the ends of long branches, identifies this good lumber tree. Farther down the moraine, our route becomes more brushy and open, and then we curve left, leave the crest and re-enter forest cover.

Soon we meet a short, east-curving spur trail, which ends at a viewpoint on the moraine's crest. From it we see what we just saw a few minutes earlier. Mills Peak Lookout rises above us in the southeast while flat-topped Beckwourth Peak stands in the northeast. Directly across the canyon, the large, linear, east-side lateral moraine of the Lakes Basin glaciers is readily apparent.

Back on the main trail, we descend a gully northward, and just before reaching Smith Creek come to a trail fork. The left branch, followed by those taking Trip 90, traverses over to campsites on the forested southeast side of nearby Smith Lake. Our route continues north, quickly reaches Smith Creek, and immediately beyond it comes to a signed trail junction. Smith Lake's outlet is attained by following the trail that goes upstream. We hike downstream, following the creek's damp bank, whose lush vegetation provides a good home and hunting ground for orange-striped garter snakes—harmless unless you're an amphibian, a small fish or an invertebrate. One way of differentiating the aquatic Sierra garter snake from the terrestrial mountain garter snake is that, when frightened, the former tends to escape into water while the latter tends to hide on land.

Not far downstream, we come to a junction, leave the Smith Creek Trail, and immediately cross three close-spaced channels of Smith Creek before we leave the shade of red and white firs behind and top our lateral moraine's low crest. An open, steady, usually hot trail south now guides us down the moraine's brushy, bouldery slope, and we can be thankful we're not engaged in a sweaty climb up it. At first, Beckwourth and Mills peaks are visible, but both disappear before we reach trail's end at Trailhead 84, which is a spur-road turnaround under patriarchal Jeffrey pines.

We follow the spur road southeast, come to its union with the Gray Eagle Lodge road, and walk southwest up it to the lodge's northwesternmost cabin (Trailhead 85). From near its north side, a faint trail climbs first southwest and then south up a gully to a low saddle, from which it descends at a lesser gradient to a level area and a trail intersection. If we were to continue east, we would reach Gray Eagle Creek in 65 yards. Its ford is always a wet one, except late in the season, and from its east bank the trail continues 95 yards southeast to the Lily Lake Trail (Trip 89).

From the intersection, we hike south-southwest on a trail from the south end of Gray Eagle Lodge, and relish its easy, almost level, up-canyon climb through a mid-Sierran forest belt of Douglas-fir, white fir, incense-cedar, sugar pine and Jeffrey pine. Midway to our reunion with Trip 87's route, we come to the Fern Falls spur trail. Certainly worth taking, this shady trail branching left arcs southeast over to nearby Gray Eagle Creek and briefly follows a chain of pools upstream to 20-foot-high Fern Falls—a cascade cutting through a narrow, fern-decked slot.

Beyond this divertissement, our main trail climbs more steeply up to a ducked ridge and crosses it, only to recross it in 200 yards. Before doing so, however, climbers will note tempting routes on the north face of Summit 6511, ¼ mile southeast. Our trail heads south, working closer toward this summit, then turns right (southwest) and climbs moderately, though briefly, across a meadowy, sometimes swampy slope. The exposed bedrock over which Gray Eagle Creek tumbles now lies ahead of us. A somewhat-ducked, hard-to-see trail up it takes us quickly to a trail junction and a reunion with Trip 87, which we follow back to the trailhead. Climbers attempting to reach the base of Summit 6511 should cross the creek before making the final bedrock climb to the junction.

Immature sugar-pine cones

89   Lily Lake Trail

Distance: 1.4 miles, round trip

Total gain/Net gain: 180'/140'

Classification: Easy

Season: Mid-June through late October

Parking: About 8 cars at trailhead turnout and same at next nearby turnout

Trailhead/Map: 83/30

Features: This short trail is a pleasant diversion best suited for an early-morning or late-afternoon stroll. It also is the start of an alternative route into the Lakes Basin.

Description: On this short, obvious trail, you can wind down to tranquil Lily Lake in a few minutes' time. White fir, Jeffrey pine and sugar pine rim this shallow lake, which is named after the large, floating, water-lily leaves so prominent in it. Growing out of shallow water, particularly at the south end, are grasslike, round-stemmed rushes.

Our trail skirts the lake's north and west shores, and then, near its southwest corner, climbs over a low ridge and in 60 yards arrives at a junction. Before the new Gold Lake Road was completed in 1973, a trail from Lakes Basin Campground descended north to here. We angle westward for a brief spurt, then, under a power line, reach a second junction, from where a trail once climbed to Long Lake. We follow the line north, climb over a low ridge, and end our walk at a small waterfall near the south end of Gray Eagle Lodge.

The Gray Eagle Creek Trail (Trip 88), which climbs from the lodge south up to Long Lake, can be reached by watching for a small spur-path that departs northwest about midway along our power-line traverse. This path starts in a 7-yard-wide grassy flat just before the low ridge. Look for a *Lily Lake* sign that marks this junction. Cool, wide Gray Eagle Creek, which must be waded before you reach the Gray Eagle Creek Trail, turns out to be a worthwhile goal in itself.

Pond lily

90   Mt. Elwell Loop, from Jamison Mine

Distance: 15.4 miles, semiloop trip

Total gain/Net gain: 4050'2550'

Classification: Strenuous

Season: Mid-July through mid-October

Parking: Two dozen cars, crowded on weekends

Trailhead/Map: 86/30

Features: In all of the Lakes Basin Recreation Area, there are only five lakes you can legally camp at: Grass, Jamison, Rock, Wades and Smith. This trip includes a stop at each of them. For those who enjoy swimming, fishing, diversified landscapes, geology and flora, this hike is a must. Climbers will find the recreation area's best climbs along this backpack trip.

Description: Our trail begins at a large parking lot among the ruins of buildings that were the site of a bustle of activity in the late 1800s. From quartz veins in the nearby Jamison mine complex, over $1½ million worth of gold was extracted. These veins rose from a gabbro pluton that intruded the late-Paleozoic volcanic rocks of this locality.

We start up-canyon on an old mining road, which becomes a trail just past the last building. Scattered Douglas-firs and abundant manzanita and huckleberry oak at first line our trail as we parallel Little Jamison Creek, about 100 feet below. Short switchbacks soon take us away from the creek view and away from the forest's shade. Our path, over the previously mentioned gabbro pluton, has dark rocks rich in pyroxene, olivine and calcium feldspar. Before leaving this rock, we come to a signed junction with the Smith Lake Trail. On this trail we'll be returning.

Beyond the junction, we again re-enter forest cover, receiving shade from incensecedar, Douglas-fir, white fir, lodgepole pine and Jeffrey pine. After bending south at a gully, we climb a short distance and then are alerted to a short spur trail by a sign, *Jamison Falls*. Like every other glaciated canyon in the Highway 49 lakes region, Little Jamison Creek canyon has its noteworthy fall—a 60-foot-high, silvery leap into freedom.

Making an easy climb up to Grass Lake, we cross a small canal—the same one we'll see along the Smith Lake Trail—which served operations down at the Jamison Mine. The campsites along the east shore near shallow Grass Lake's dam are unattractive. However,

late-summer ducks, migrating south on the Pacific flyway, find this lake—and other shallow ones like it—attractive. Flowing into the south end of the lake as well as into its inlet creek are numerous creeklets. Some are lined with thimbleberry, currant and gooseberry—three shrubs producing edible berries—as well as with Bolander's yampah, a large, edible parsley that closely resembles some of its poisonous relatives. Backpackers disgruntled with the accommodations of the Grass Lake campsites set up their camps at slightly better ones on a bench above the lake's south end.

As your southbound trail heads for an obvious headwall, which supports hidden Rock Lake above it, stay alert for a sudden bend west in the trail. An older pathway continues southward before dying out. Our trail west traverses an aspen-bordered meadow, veers northwest, and for 50 yards crosses one channel after another. Look for rocks, logs or whatever to make this wet ford of not-so-little Little Jamison Creek. Early-season hikers: resign yourself to a pair of wet boots. Dry ground is welcomed as we climb west, then south up to a nearby junction. Our main trail toward Wades Lake and the Sierra crest climbs moderately southwest, but first we'll take an excursion south up to Jamison and Rock lakes.

The forested path at first climbs gently, but just beyond a collapsed log cabin it veers southwest and executes several short, steep switchbacks up brushy rock benches. Those accomplished, we soon treat ourselves to a refreshing drink from Wades Lake's outlet creek, which crosses our path midway up this side trip to Jamison Lake. Before we reach Jamison, we have to surmount a low ridge of granitelike metarhyolite, and climbers will certainly spy short crack and face routes up it. On the west slopes above Jamison Lake, climbers will find additional appealing climbing routes, but the east slopes above Jamison, being composed of brown metabasalt or a close analog, are uninviting.

Descending the low ridge before Jamison Lake, we quickly arrive at the lake's outlet creek, frequented by water ouzels, and cross it 50 yards downstream from its broken-down dam. Just before this crossing, however, a trail splits south to the dam and the undesirable bedrock campsites not far beyond it. Of all the lakes one can camp at along this circuit, Jamison probably offers the greatest solitude,

Lodgepole pines at Rock Lake

for not many hikers go cross-country to the lake's southern shore. We, like others, cross its outlet creek and follow a brief, winding trail over and across low, glaciated ridges to campsites along Rock Lake's south shore.

Aptly named Rock Lake is perhaps the most appealing lake along our circuit, and it may well be the finest of the entire Highway 49 lakes region. Photographers will certainly appreciate its beauty, and from selected rocky ledges near its southeast corner swimmers can dive into seemingly bottomless, invigorating water. Contrasting with the depth of this lake is a steep-sided rock island that rises a full 20 feet above the lake's northwest waters. Everywhere you turn, you'll find evidence of past glaciers in the form of long scratches, or glacial striations, which were cut by the rock and grit that glaciers dragged along. What makes this lake so attractive is the way the glaciers sculptured its terrain, breaking off blocks of bedrock and thereby exposing dramatic bluffs. You'll certainly be tempted to linger awhile in this rockbound paradise.

Returning to the main trail, we begin a steep ascent that leads us up past an outcrop of white, vertical-foliated metarhyolite before reaching the signed Wades Lake spur trail. The foliations are parallel alignments of the minerals in this metamorphic rock, alignments due to applied forces, which in this case were compressing the rock in a horizontal direction.

Our hike up the Wades Lake spur trail is an easy ¼-mile walk. Just before reaching the lake's outlet, we pass a very good campsite—beneath red fir, lodgepole pine and silver pine—located on our left. Like Jamison, Wades has had its dam mostly removed, and the lake has returned to its natural level. Our lake, resting in a bowl of greenish-tinted, light-gray metarhyolite, has a shallow north end which slowly gets deeper, allowing the reluctant swimmer to gradually get used to this fairly deep lake's water.

Back again on the main trail, we start southwest, immediately pass a flat meadow on our right, and engage in a steep ascent up the crest of a lateral moraine, occasionally

Campsite near Smith Lake outlet

scented with tobacco brush, before traversing across slopes up to a saddle. A grove of red firs, ascending east to this saddle, obstructs our view west down into glaciated Florentine Canyon, but our sweeping view east toward Mt. Elwell reveals the four miles of crest we'll have to circle to reach the peak's two summits. The saddle also marks the boundary between the metamorphic rocks we've just climbed and volcanic ones to be ascended. These rocks—the only geologically young volcanics we'll walk upon in the Plumas-Eureka/Lakes Basin landscape—are auto-brecciated andesitic mud flows of Pliocene age, and are similar in origin to the flows described in Trip 49. We struggle south steeply up a ridge crest made of this loose material before attaining the Sierra crest.

On the crest we turn left and climb—steeply at first—up a dusty jeep road, which doubles as the temporary route of the Pacific Crest Trail. Our climb southeast quickly levels off, leaves a field of mule ears and the volcanic rocks behind, enters a red fir forest and soon descends. Where our winding route comes within 100 yards of the Sierra crest and bends south, we encounter the Four Hills Mine. Now abandoned, this mine in its day produced $2 million in gold from its quartz veins. A ¼-mile descent south gets us to a junction with the Spencer Lakes jeep road. Down this road, about ½ mile west of us, lie pockets of magnetite, which is a magnetic, iron-rich ore. The composition of iron in these pockets is pretty high, about 40%, but the quantity, under 5000 tons, is unprofitable to extract.

We follow the Pacific Crest Trail up a supposedly closed jeep road, which is at times transgressed by cyclists and jeepsters alike. On a broad, crest saddle, marked by a small, circular, semistagnant pond, we enter the Lakes Basin Recreation Area, and after a few minutes' walk cross a spring-fed creek, which provides the only pure, year-round water we'll find between Wades and Smith lakes (Maiden and Hidden lakes are usually tolerable). Beyond it, we hike a steady ⅓-mile ascent east to a sharp bend where the road turns south. Near it are two trail junctions only 70 yards

apart. Trip 84, which follows a segment of the Pacific Crest Trail past the Lakes Basin crest, descends northeast to the southern junction and then descends southeast on a trail into the basin.

Our trip goes northward from the northern, slightly lower junction, balances along a knife-edge crest or traverses immediately below it, and then briefly contours over to an amply signed junction on a tree-shaded bench ½ mile south of the top of Mt. Elwell. Our traverse across this ridge crest, which exhibits near-vertical foliation like that of the Wades Lake area, exposes us to our first good views of the Lakes Basin topography. From the signed junction we now follow the trail description in Trip 88 up to the two summits, over to Maiden Lake and finally down to a trail junction immediately before reaching Smith Creek.

Trip 88 crosses Smith Creek, but our route veers northwest and quickly arrives at a good, large, pine-shaded campsite near Smith Lake's outlet. Beyond it over a low ridge lies a second good campsite, which is nestled beside a lively creek lined with alder and dogwood. Our rollercoaster trail west climbs another low ridge, this time over blue-green-gray metavolcanic bedrock, then descends close to the lake's shallow south arm, which is being choked with grasses and rushes. A third and final ridge climb leads us over to the cascading creek that empties into this clear, green lake. Seeking the creek's life-giving water are alder, dogwood, mountain ash, vine maple, thimbleberry and many wildflowers.

West of Smith Lake our trail snakes ¼ mile up to a small notch on a broad, ill-defined saddle, then makes a gradual descent through a forest of red fir and silver pine that also contains sugar pine—an unusual bedfellow for them. Beyond a shallow pond, our trail west drops more steeply and crosses the north-heading, bouldery crest of a lateral moraine midway down to an old mining canal that originates at Grass Lake. A brief descent southwest now takes us to the end of our loop, and on the main trail we descend Little Jamison Creek's canyon trail back to our trailhead.

91   Eureka Peak Trail

Distance: 3.0 miles, round trip

Total gain/Net gain: 1180'/1100'

Classification: Moderate

Season: Early July through mid-October

Parking: Ample

Trailhead/Map: 87/30

Features: This summit climb is the shortest one in the Highway 49 region, and it provides views that are more than worth the effort. Peak 7281's north slopes contain steep, solid rock, which should attract any nearby rock climbers.

Description: First we cross over Eureka Lake's earth fill dam to the start of an old, overgrown road. Snags within the lake's shallow water indicate the position of its shoreline before the dam was built. Leaving this popular fishing lake, we immediately pass the branching west-shore road as we climb to a forested slope of a lateral moraine and pass a snow-survey shelter. Along our moderately climbing road, we find rocks of almost every color: from blue, green and gray to red, brown and white. The reason for this diversity in color is, simply enough, the diversity in rock types: various metasediments, metavolcanics and mafic intrusives (plutonic rocks rich in magnesium and iron).

Beyond a steep, open ascent past a red-brown cliff, our road reaches, and dies out upon, a forested, gentle slope. Replacing it is a trail, heading south, which stays close to the dropping edge of the main canyon. In this forest of red fir and silver pine you may encounter two furry predators, the long-tailed weasel and the pine marten. Both feed mainly on rodents, but the weasel also attacks small birds. Look for them in tree cavities or ground burrows among rocks or logs or under tree roots—particularly those of red fir.

Our trail up-canyon gives us glimpses of Eureka Lake just after we cross a small, splashing creek and start to parallel its east bank. As we approach a cluster of the creek's willows, we leave the creek, cross an often dry gully, and climb steeply to a minor ridge, on which, by taking a few steps northeast, we get a good view of the lake and the countryside beyond. Two distinct rock types now confront us as we climb southeast up the trail: granitelike metarhyolite on our left and near-vertical beds of metasediments on our right.

Stimulating our olfactory nerves are tantalizing aromas of a few plants of tobacco brush, which are encountered as we enter a classic forest assemblage of magnificent red fir, delicate mountain hemlock, checker-barked silver pine and lowly mat manzanita. Our southward, shady trail up the southwest slope of Peak 7281 soon turns northeast and climbs to a saddle south of the peak's rocky summit. Standing between us and the summit is a rocky crest, which drops off to a low saddle immediately below the summit. The safest, easiest way to this second saddle is to round the crest on its east side. First descend briefly, then parallel the base of the crest over to a gully, which you ascend to the saddle. The short, Class 2 scramble to the top is evident and not exposed.

The summit is cleaved in half, and through the cleft we get a framed view of Eureka Lake. Standing on either half of the summit, we get a more complete view, which includes not only Eureka Lake and its distinctive moraines, but also the huge lateral moraines of Jamison Creek canyon, whose floor lies almost ½ mile below our summit. The 500-foot-high moraines extend up to two miles beyond the old mining town of Johnsville. Placer gold was first discovered near this site in the first days of the 1849 gold rush, and gold in vein quartz was discovered two years later. The placer gold never amounted to much, but the bedrock gold, mostly mined from 1872 to 1890, brought in about $8 million to the Sierra Buttes Mining Company. Beneath our feet, into the bowels of Eureka Peak, were sunk 70 mine shafts, all now closed.

If you want to climb to the top of Eureka Peak, you can reach it by hiking ½ mile up the crest that curves southwest up from Peak 7281's first saddle. Eureka's summit, however, is less defined and doesn't offer as good views as those from Peak 7281. Beyond the nearby landscape, we see flat-topped Beckwourth Peak (7255') in the east, the pointed Sierra Buttes (8587') in the distant south-southeast, and closer Mt. Elwell (7812') just left of the buttes. Dominating the northwest horizon is snowy, royal Lassen Peak (10,457'), the southernmost active volcano of the Cascade Range.

Botanists will be pleased to find that plants grow on this rocky, inhospitable-seeming summit. Phlox, buckwheat, currant, and—surprisingly—rabbit brush manage to survive.

Rabbit brush is usually associated with a closely related high-desert sunflower, sagebrush.

Descending to the saddle above the gully, you'll see just west of it—if you haven't already noticed—a small, natural window, which was formed when a block of bedrock lodged between the summit's slope and a resistant pinnacle. Climbers will find many opportunities to either boulder or rope-climb near the summit or its dramatic north escarpment. The metarhyolite rock, superficially resembling granite in color and texture, also has similar rock-climbing characteristics.

Summit view of Eureka Lake

92   Frazier Falls

Distance: 1.2 miles, round trip
Total gain/Net gain: 200'/140'
Classification: Easy
Season: Late June through late October
Parking: Ample
Trailhead/Map: 78/30

Features: Easily the highest falls in the Highway 49 region, this sheet of water continues to impress visitors late into the summer, after twice-as-high Feather Falls has almost dried up. Standing at the viewpoint opposite the perennial falls, you can gaze out over the canyon that drops before you and imagine what it must have looked like when an enormous glacier filled it.

Description: From the roadside picnic area—complete with tables and toilets—we start to walk southeast, shaded by firs and pines. Brush becomes more prominent as we wind around and over low, glacier-polished ridges before coming to Frazier Creek, which is lined with aspen, dogwood and willow. The dark, blue-gray bedrocks over which we walk are lava flows that were derived from nearby sources back in the late Paleozoic era, about 250 million years ago. Since the time they solidified, they have been tilted so that now, rather than being almost horizontal, they dip almost vertically down. The texture of these flows, which are approximately basaltic in composition, has been altered by heat and pressure generated by the earth's shifting crust. Initially richer in dark minerals, these

Frazier Falls

metabasalts differ in color and texture from the granitelike metarhyolites seen along Trips 84 and 90.

After crossing the bridge over Frazier Creek, we wind among some more low ridges, whose bedrock has been split and intruded with white vein quartz, then turn north and descend to a fenced-off viewpoint directly opposite 248-foot-high Frazier Falls. Located 1.9 miles downstream from Gold Lake's outlet, this cascade marks the resistant midpoint in a canyon that once contained a seven-mile-long, 800-foot thick glacier. Originating at the crest above Gold Lake's southwest shore, the glacier had a tortuous path to follow. Gold Lake, of course, didn't exist back then, but ½ mile beyond the site of its outlet the glacier was forced to bend northward, and the bend undoubtedly caused crevasses, or deep cracks, to form at this stress point. Then, straightening its course, the icy mass traveled less than a mile before it tumbled—in very slow, frozen motion—down the bedrock that Frazier Falls cascades over today.

Just how fast did the glacier cascade over this brink? On the basis of large, present-day glaciers existing in more northern latitudes, we can estimate that the glacier ice might have "fallen" at the rate of about 30 feet per day, or about ¼ inch per minute. This rate of motion would have been barely noticeable if it were constant. It wasn't. If we had been present, we would have heard the glacier groan as crevasses slowly opened and closed, and ice broke off, fell and was buried under the slow onslaught of ice behind it. The rate of ice movement at less steep locations, such as the area where Gold Lake is today, was much less, probably being on the order of 1-3 feet per day.

Standing at the viewpoint, you can look down-canyon and see the high lateral moraine that makes up the canyon's west wall. About 20,000 years ago, a glacier filled this canyon to the moraine's height, if not higher. Try to imagine what a different landscape this area must have been back then! On your way back, note how glacial action, exerting a pressure of 20 tons per square foot, has abraded and smoothed the low ridges you wind along. Remember also that all the soil and vegetation you see before you have appeared in the last 10,000 years, that is, since the mammoth glacier finally retreated back up Frazier Creek canyon.

Trails of the Highway 70 Region

Introduction

Except for one trail in the Feather Falls Scenic Area (Trip 93), the trails of this region lie in or close to the Bucks Lake area (Trips 94–100). Between the two areas Highway 70 winds and climbs up a scenic section of the North Fork Feather River that is long on reservoirs and swimming holes but short on hiking trails. Virtually every trail that once climbed up to the Feather River canyon's rim has been abandoned or has been replaced by a jeep road. One inaccessible, compact, lake-dotted area in this region is a particular loss to the hiker. This is the Ben Lomond-Spring Valley area, which contains 12 small-to-medium named lakes on rocky benches above the south slopes of Chips Creek canyon. The steep, unrelenting Ben Lomond Trail once provided direct access to them from a Highway 70 trailhead, but the upper section of this trail has become greatly overgrown with brush. Logging roads to the west of this lakes area extend into it, unfortunately reaching some of them, but all these roads are closed to the public. Thus you and I are left with only the Feather Falls and Bucks Lake areas. The hearty souls who

struggle cross-country up to these lakes will find their efforts rewarded with excellent fishing at the larger lakes.

The well-maintained Feather Falls Trail can be hiked in almost any month of the year, although most hikers would prefer mid-to-late spring. Those who want to frolic in the swimming holes above the falls should hike in July or August, when the water has warmed up to the high 50s or low 60s and Fall River has diminished from a torrent to a gentle flow.

Bucks Lake—a boaters' paradise—has a wide assortment of trails in the landscapes above and beyond it. Glacier-formed lakes, forested ridge crests and impressive-walled canyons await the hiker who ventures into this area. Like Highway 50's Desolation Wilderness, Interstate 80's Granite Chief area and Highway 49's Sierra Buttes-Lakes Basin area, Highway 70's Bucks Lake area can be traversed via the Pacific Crest National Scenic Trail. The last trip in this guide is along this lengthy trail, and although the route description stops at the approximate northern border of the Sierra Nevada, you—the hiker—can continue on it north all the way to Canada.

Trailheads reached from Highway 70

The following trailhead descriptions begin from Oroville, which is about 72 miles north of Sacramento via Highways 99 and 70. Our mileage begins where Highway 162 crosses under Highway 70. In Oroville, you'll find the Oroville Ranger Station at 875 Mitchell Avenue, which is reached by heading east on 162, turning left on 5th Avenue and following it a brief distance to Mitchell.

Trailhead 88: Feather Falls
88   From Highway 70 (0.0) drive east on Oroville Dam Boulevard (Highway 162) to a right turn on Olive Highway (still 162) (1.7). We head east and climb to a junction with a road (3.8, 5.5) that climbs to Lake Oroville's strategically located Visitor Center. Another road from the center descends southward, and we descend and meet it (1.6, 7.1). At a bend

just beyond it, the Olive Highway forks right (0.2, 7.3) and winds 2.1 miles up to the Forbestown Road. You can take this route, but a simpler one is to curve left on the main highway to its junction with the Forbestown Road (1.2, 8.5). Climb east on this to a junction past a reunion with the Olive Highway (1.1, 9.6) to the narrower Lumpkin Road (5.2, 14.8), veering left. We drive northeast on this winding road to a junction with the Feather Falls Road (11.2, 26.0), starting north. One-half mile east on Lumpkin Road you'll find pleasant Feather Falls Village, with year-round facilities that include a general store, picnic tables, library, laundromat and the Feather Falls Post Office (95940). Our route, Feather Falls Road, quickly becomes dirt as it starts a descent to the Bryant Ravine creek, beside which you can camp. Then it climbs 250 yards north above the bank to obvious parking spaces for

---
Left: Feather Falls, from Cooper Point

Trailhead 88 (1.8, 27.8), from which the road curves eastward uphill.

Trailheads 89-90: North Fork Feather River

89   From Highway 162 in Oroville (0.0), drive north on Highway 70 past junctions with Highways 149 (7.2) and 191 (1.0, 8.2), then continue to a crossing of an arm of Lake Oroville. Beyond the crossing, our highway climbs northeast, descends to North Fork Feather River, passes its good swimming holes in the course of crossing the river four times, and comes to Chambers Creek Campground (35.7, 43.9). Our next significant landmark is Chips Creek (5.4, 49.3), from which we curve to **Trailhead 89 (0.5, 49.8).**

90   Immediately beyond the trailhead, our highway crosses Indian Creek (0.1, 49.9), passes the Belden Rest Area and Yellow Creek (0.7, 50.6), then comes to the Belden junction (0.1, 50.7). We turn right, bridge the Feather River, and arrive at the small riverside settlement of Belden (0.1, 50.8), which has a store, restaurant, gas pump and post office (95915). Driving westward, we encounter Belden Campground (0.3, 51.1), but continue on the narrow, paved road to Western Pacific's railroad tracks, on whose south side is **Trailhead 90 (0.3, 51.4),** immediately west of a small gully.

Trailheads 91-96: Bucks Lake Area

Leaving the Belden junction (50.7), we drive eastward up the scenic Feather River canyon to where Highway 89 (18.7, 69.4), from the northeast, joins our highway. We soon arc south and climb to broad, spacious American Valley, in which lies the old mining community of Quincy. At this town's west end we reach a **Y** (10.4, 79.8) and turn sharply right onto the Bucks Lake Road. Driving west, we soon parallel Spanish Creek upstream, then turn right on Deanes Valley road (4.0, 83.8), which ascends Slate Creek. Our road bridges this creek (0.7, 84.5), then Deer Creek (1.9, 86.4), and climbs to a ridge (0.6, 87.0) before starting a descent to a fork (0.2, 87.2). We keep right, continue descending to Rock Creek, and spy the Rock Creek Campground (0.6, 87.8) immediately beyond it. Just upstream (0.2, 88.0) a 4.8-mile-long road from Meadow Valley joins ours, and we drive onward to usually peaceful Deanes Valley Campground (0.8, 88.8).

91   Beyond the campground, our route gets complicated due to so many spur roads, but we follow *Middle Fork Trails* signs. Near the upper drainage of South Fork Rock Creek, we turn right (2.9, 91.7), climb past Bottle Springs and some mining cabins, then reach a flat crest and a junction (0.7, 92.4). We go straight ahead for 20 yards, swing left around the Bottle Springs Heliport, descend past the Grizzly Creek spur road (0.5, 92.9), and come to a fork (1.0, 93.9). Park your car here unless you have a 4WD vehicle or a sturdy pickup truck. Ignore all left forks and descend steeply downslope to **Trailhead 91 (0.2, 94.1),** signed *Rocky Point,* which is an almost level parking area.

92   From the Deanes Valley Road junction (83.8), drive westward to a lateral road (2.2, 86.0), signed *Middle Fork Trails,* which climbs 4.8 miles up to the Deanes Valley Road. On our right, we immediately pass Lowel Baden Memorial Park, then the Meadow Valley Post Office (95956) (1.3, 87.3), and we drive up to the valley's end, where our road curves right and we meet the Silver Lake Road (1.3, 88.6), on our right. Take this crest-hugging road up past the Jacks Meadow Trail (5.1, 93.7), which isn't worth hiking, then finish your moderate climb at a merger (0.8, 94.5) with a road on your right. Just ahead lies Silver Lake Campground, and you wind southward through it up to the shore of Silver Lake, **Trailhead 92 (0.5, 95.0).**

93   Beyond the Silver Lake Road junction (88.6), the Bucks Lake Road climbs steeply up to Bucks Summit, **Trailhead 93 (4.0, 92.6),** from which the Spanish Peak Road climbs northward. Don't attempt to drive up this deeply rutted, rocky, one-lane road.

94   Leaving Bucks Summit, we drive down an easy grade to Whitehorse Campground (1.6, 94.2), then shortly after it reach a dead-end road (0.4, 94.6) branching right only 50 yards before the Bucks Lake Road crosses Bucks Creek. We branch right and follow this rutted spur road to a fork, **Trailhead 94 (0.2, 94.8),** near which is a parking area 100 yards from the lake's shore. A section of the California Riding and Hiking Trail starts about 50 yards along the right fork.

95   Beyond the spur road and Bucks Creek (94.6), our road soon parallels the south shore of Bucks Lake and comes to Lakeshore Resort (1.1, 95.7), which has a store plus a dining room, among other features. Farther on, we reach Bucks Lake Lodge (0.7, 96.4), which, in addition to good meals, has a small service station. Down our road we come to PG&E's Haskins Valley Campground (0.3, 96.7), then in 35 yards Haskins Valley Resort, which has food and some supplies. Beyond them, our southbound road reaches a junction (0.2, 96.9) where it turns abruptly west. We turn left, drive east up Haskins Valley to a road fork (0.5, 97.4), at which we leave the Haskins Valley floor by veering right, southeast, gently up to a second fork (0.1, 97.5). Again, we veer right, and climb Highlands road steeply up to a slope-traversing road (0.6, 98.1), which we cross, then top the ridgecrest and descend gently to Lookout Rock road (0.2, 98.3). Turn left and descend this winding road southeast to a junction with the Willow Creek Road (3.4, 101.7). Turn left again and wind southwestward alongside Willow Creek, squeezing down through a one-lane roadcut just before crossing the creek (1.7, 103.4). Our winding road now climbs to a high traverse near the Middle Fork canyon's north rim before dropping into China Gulch (2.2, 105.6). A fairly level traverse from it then takes us past impressive columnar-basalt cliffs just before reaching a signed trailhead (1.5, 107.1). Rather than start your hike to Hartman Bar from here, drive 40 yards west to a gully, then continue south beyond it to a ridge and a spur road (0.3, 107.4). Turn left and follow the spur road east down the ridge, then northward to the gully, from which it turns south and descends to a parking area, **Trailhead 95 (0.6, 108.0).**

96   From the Haskins Valley junction (96.9) just south of the resort, drive west to Bucks Lake Dam road (1.1, 98.0), on which you veer right, climb to a saddle, steadily descend to the dam, and drive across it to a junction (2.8, 100.8) at its north end. We go right, pass a spur road (0.3, 101.1) descending to Bucks Lake Beach, then wind northeastward up to a saddle (0.7, 101.8), from which a spur road veers right and descends to campsites along the north finger of Bucks Lake. Our road climbs gently but steadily northward, steepening its gradient up to a spur ridge (1.7, 103.5), from which it traverses northwest before dropping in a brief distance to **Trailhead 96 (0.7, 104.2).** This signed trailhead is encountered 10 yards before our road crosses an eastward-descending tributary. The California Riding and Hiking Trail can be located above Mill Creek's east bank only 35 yards from our road. Our road forks in 100 yards, and the right fork goes 80 yards to a creekside campsite.

93   Feather Falls Trail

Distance: 10.6 miles, round trip
Total gain/Net gain: 2250'/940'
Classification: Moderate
Season: March through November
Parking: Ample
Trailhead/Map: 88/31

Features: This instructive, amply signed nature trail takes you to a view of the Tahoe Sierra's highest waterfall, which, unlike most other falls in the Sierra, was not formed through glacial action. Spring hikers will find flowers in full bloom and the fall at its peak. Midsummer hikers will find more than half a dozen tempting, trout-inhabited swimming holes upstream from the fall.

Description: Warm spring weather in April and May brings about the blossoming of many wildflowers and shrubs. In March, small, pink, bell-shaped flowers on manzanita bushes are among the first flowers to blossom along the Feather Falls Trail. Late April to early May is perhaps the best time for flower lovers to visit this area, for then, abundant deer brush is in bloom, and its panicles of creamy white flowers release a delicate aroma that permeates the warm air. Descending to Frey Creek, the springtime hiker is likely to see scarlet Indian pink and Indian paintbrush, yellow star tulip, pine violet and sunflowers, bluish-purple lupine and larkspur, and white Sierra iris and parsley.

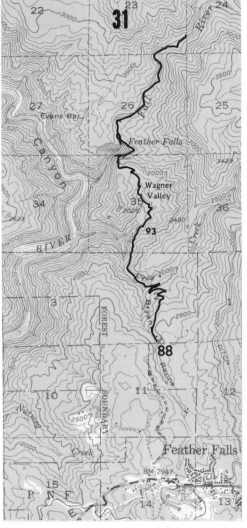

You may have noted in roadcuts along the road to the trailhead that the granitic bedrock has been deeply weathered to a red-brown, thick soil. This soil contrasts markedly with the soils of Lakes Basin and Desolation Valley, which are mostly 10,000 years old or younger. Feather Falls country, however, did not have its soils repeatedly swept away by glacial advances. On this red-brown soil our trail begins in an airy forest of ponderosa pine, incense-cedar, Douglas-fir, madrone, black oak and interior live oak. Very soon, a vignette of Bald Rock Dome, in the northwest above the Middle Fork canyon, catches our attention. Beyond it, broad-leaf maple and then California nutmeg make their debut, and a trailside sign identifies poison oak for those unfamiliar with this shiny, rash-producing plant.

On weekdays, the sound of distant lumber trucks may be heard until you reach the Frey Creek environs. Just before our trail's ½-mile

sign, we round a large granitic rock that contains a noteworthy interior live oak growing from a crack in it. Its massive, expanding roots help to enlarge the crack, which originally developed as a hairline crack that formed in response to the rock's new environment. Solidifying several miles beneath older bedrock over 100 million years ago, the crystals in this granitic rock developed in response to the high temperatures and extreme pressures characteristic of that environment. When the overlying bedrock was finally eroded away—a process that took about 70 million years—the granitic rock responded to its new, low-temperature-low-pressure environment by expanding and cracking apart.

As we switchback down to Frey Creek, Oregon juncos and robins sing and search about while gray squirrels busily collect acorns. In spring, the creek fairly roars, drowning out all man-made noise. In this creekside environment, shaded by Douglas-fir, maple, California laurel (bay tree), dogwood, tanbark oak and toyon, grow delicate ferns, yellow cinquefoil, scarlet Indian pink and orchid bleeding heart. Receiving about 60 inches of precipitation per year—most of it rain—this verdant landscape is home for a host of moisture-loving animals. Larger animals flee from us, but smaller ones can't. Careful observation may lead you to discover an eight-inch banana slug or a five-inch millipede. Under a log or in some dead leaves you may find the California newt, a slow-moving amphibian that feeds on even slower worms, insects and small mollusks. Feeding on it, as well as on almost every other small creature in reach, is the western garter snake.

Bleeding heart (above); millipede, actual size (below)

A wooden bridge carries us over Frey Creek to a small, inviting creekside campsite, then our trail parallels the cascading creek downstream a short distance before curving north. Rounding a bend, we emerge from thick forest cover and once again see Bald Rock Dome, whose 1000-foot-high cliffs have been largely untouched by climbers because of their relative inaccessibility. Alum root, stonecrop and sunflowers now replace the water-loving wildflowers, and buckbrush—a short-leaved ceanothus—together with California storax—recognized by its white flowers with united, yellow-orange stamens—complete the understory of a more open, drier forest.

Our trail levels off, crosses an ephemeral creeklet, then starts to climb and crosses two more. Along with bracken fern, you'll see woodwardia fern, which is the Sierra's largest fern, producing fronds ("leafy" stems) six feet long or longer. The native Maidu Indians used the fibers of frond stems to weave baskets and textiles.

Just beyond these creeklets, on the left, are ponderosa-pine snags—victims of bark beetles. These ¼-inch, chunky beetles successfully attack every kind of Sierra pine, but pines low in resin, such as ponderosas, are hard-hit. Resinous pines, such as lodgepoles, drown these burrowing invaders in sap, but these pines are subject to needle-miner attacks. Predators usually keep bark-beetle numbers in check, but the development of a homogeneous, over-mature, often-diseased stand of pines sets the stage for an epidemic. Likewise, tree farms, whose grounds are planted with acres of similar-age pines of one species, invite destruction. A forest that is well diversified in species and age is the most resistant to bark-beetle and other attack.

Beyond the ponderosa snags, our dry forest trail presents the midsummer hiker with a sweaty climb ahead. Before leaving the floor of Wagner Valley, however, we stumble across some mortar holes that were ground into the granitic bedrock by the Maidu Indians who foraged in this bowl-shaped valley. This site represents one of several that belonged to the local Maidu community, and in the mortar holes, acorns and seeds were ground. Acorns from black, golden and interior-live oaks together with sugar-pine nuts were highly prized for flour. One would imagine that the gray-squirrel population back in those days was smaller than it is today, for these animals competed with, and sometimes served as

dinner for, the Indians. The flour-grinding chore was relegated to the women and children, as was the procuring of ants, grasshoppers, crickets, other insects, worms, other invertebrates, and small game. Men were responsible for catching birds, trout, rabbits, deer, and—after the proper ceremony—black bears, grizzly bears (now extinct) and cougars. Coyotes, wolves, vultures, reptiles and amphibians were all avoided, for they were thought to be poisonous.

A Maidu village was located near a year-round stream, such as Fall River not far above Feather Falls. It may have had 10 families and a total population of 70. The total population of the Maidu people, who were divided into three dialect groups, probably never much exceeded 4000 individuals or 60 villages. Their north and south territorial boundaries were almost identical with the ones that limit the scope of this book. To the west their territory extended down to the higher foothills east of the Sacramento Valley. This valley was occupied by the Wintun, who had much in common with the Maidu, for both groups belonged to the same linguistic family, the Penutian. From the Wintun, the Maidu received beads (money), salt, digger-pine nuts, and, in some instances, salmon. In return, they gave the Wintun bows and arrows, deer skins and sugar-pine nuts.

To the east the Maidu territory extended up to, and sometimes beyond, the Sierra crest. Their relationship with the Washoe, who belonged to the Hokan linguistic family, was a hostile one.

The Washoe lived mostly in the fault-dropped valleys east of the crest, but to them the center of their world was Lake Tahoe. They were a scarce group—perhaps 3000 individuals at most—who moved with the seasons. A family or group of families would slowly work its way up toward the Lake Tahoe high country in late spring as snow retreated and certain food came into abundance. In early June, this food was trout plus large suckers, both of which spawned in the creeks that drained into Lake Tahoe. As fish spawning declined, the Indians ascended mountain canyons in search of game, vegetable food in meadows, and trout in streams and high lakes. On these excursions, they were most likely to encounter the Maidu, who had been working east toward the crest, following in the wake of retreating snowfields.

Maidu mortar holes

With the approach of autumn, the Washoe returned to the Carson Valley and other east-side valleys. This season was a time of plenty, with the harvest of berries, pinyon nuts and seeds, followed by rabbit, deer and antelope hunts. Doves, quail, sage grouse and rodents were also hunted, but like the Maidu, the Washoe avoided reptiles and amphibians. Their bountiful harvest had to last until spring, when they could harvest wild lettuce, wild spinach and wild potatoes. The Washoe understood their dynamic environment and lived totally within it.

The Maidu, on the other hand, modified their environment with almost annual fires, which had the distinct advantage of clearing brush that might hide a lurking enemy. (Fighting was a way of life *between* Maidu settlements as well as with the less numerous Washoe.) This practice also increased the distribution of *Ceanothus,* a genus of aromatic shrubs that sprout profusely after a fire. Since deer often browse on these plants, the size of the herd was increased.

The worlds of the Maidu and the Washoe were little changed by the coming of the Spaniards, who kept to the Coast Ranges and the Central Valley. With the discovery of gold in 1848 came lusty men who destroyed the environment to get rich quick. Maidu forests were logged for mine timbers and for boom-

town shanties. Goats and cattle were turned loose in Maidu meadows that had once yielded a rich grain harvest. Professional hunters overkilled animal populations in order to supply mining settlements with food. Gravels washed by high-power monitors choked up the rivers and their fish populations. A similar fate lay in store for the Washoe when silver was discovered in the Comstock Lode in 1859.

Returning our thoughts to the present world, we climb an increasingly shadeless trail up to a ridge that has a steep, west-facing escarpment. Don't be too surprised if, on this ascent, you see a striped racer slithering through the tops of bushes. This long, sleek snake is almost as adept in bushes and trees as it is over bedrock or through grassy meadows. Its varied diet includes amphibians, lizards, birds, rodents and other snakes, even rattle-snakes!

At the escarpment we get a view down into the Fall River box canyon, and a sign warns us not to get too good a view, for people have fallen off the brink to their death. A minute's walk later, we come to a fenced-in viewpoint, from where we can see the green, quiet Middle Fork of the Feather River. With the completion of Oroville Dam in 1967, after five years of construction, Lake Oroville gradually rose behind it to the 900-foot elevation contour. When the reservoir is at this height, boaters can cruise up the Middle Fork to lake's end, about ⅓ mile upstream from Fall River. Fortunately, the rugged scenery from Evans Bar north through Bald Rock Canyon is out of the boaters' reach and has been protected by Wild River status since 1968.

Through late spring, the roar of unseen Feather Falls is heard from this viewpoint onward. Just before we turn east, we encounter a rocky, barely noticeable trail that climbs eastward up to the Johnson Ranch Road via a chaparral ridge route. As our traversing trail curves east, we enter forest shade once again and quickly meet a short spur trail that descends west to a fenced observation deck. From the deck we confront Feather Falls face-to-face. Perched on Cooper Point, which juts out over Fall River's box canyon, this deck also allows us to get a birds-eye view down it to the river's entry into Oroville Reservoir.

During April and May, Feather Falls, like our trailside flowers, is in full glory. It then looks every bit as impressive as a 640-foot fall should look. Only two falls in the United

Brink of Feather Falls

States have a higher drop: Ribbon Fall (1612') and Upper Yosemite Fall (1430'), both in Yosemite Valley. But like Yosemite's falls, Feather Falls dwindles to a misty spray by late summer. If it weren't for the area's 75-inch annual precipitation, most of which builds up a considerable snowpack at its mile-high headwaters, this low-elevation waterfall would dry up in early summer.

A sign indicates that the fall's origin is linked with volcanic activity. This is not so. During the Pliocene epoch, andesite flows—and to a lesser extent basalt flows—buried the Feather River country, including the ancestral Fall River. The burial of river valleys, as we have seen on other trips, is quite a common occurrence, and it does not result in the formation of waterfalls. By the early Pleistocene, the new Fall River had cut deep into the volcanic mantle, and in the Feather Falls area it had eroded away much of this dark-gray rock and had begun to cut into the underlying granite. Back then, the Feather River may have been 900 feet above its current level where Fall River joined it. The huge Feather, with tremendous erosional powers, was able to cut down into the granite, and the Fall, like Frey Creek and other tributaries, attempted to

match its rate. Small tributaries, with virtually no eroding power, have made hardly a dent in the Feather canyon walls we see today. Fall River and Frey Creek, with greater drainage basins, were more successful, but why do they differ from each other?

Frey Creek cut down and back into rather uniform granite, but Fall River, near its union with the Feather, cut into moderately-to-highly fractured granite, then encountered massive, fracture-free granite. Look on the map and you can see where the granite was most fractured—immediately downstream from Feather Falls. Just above Section 26's border, you'll note an east-west expansion in the width of Fall River's canyon. Here, a master joint, or major fracture, runs east-west through the granite. Fall River was able to cut down easily along this fracture—thereby widening its canyon—but it failed to cut at an equivalent rate into the unjointed bedrock immediately upstream. The Feather and the lower half mile of the Fall continued their relentless downward cutting, but the upper Fall River was unable to overcome the massive granite. First a rapid formed, then it lengthened to a cascade, and then that grew into a full-fledged fall. Today, Feather Falls

A Fall River pool

no longer has a clean brink; the river has cut back slightly into the massive granite and it therefore cascades about 150 feet before it jumps into its airy abyss.

Returning to our main trail, we start a moderate ascent east and quickly meet a junction with a spur trail traversing southwest over to the ridge trail that climbs up to Johnson Ranch Road. Beyond the junction, we traverse northeast and soon reach a gully that has been eroded along the conspicuous east-west, vertical master joint. We now make a descending traverse northwest and reach a junction where our trail forks. The two forks head upstream, but before heading in that direction, take a short spur downstream to the brink of the falls, where, from railings, you can see that the vertical cliff Feather Falls tumbles over is slowly breaking along very conspicuous vertical joints.

Back at the trail fork, take either branch north, for they quickly rejoin, and in about 80 yards pass the first of several campsites, all nestled under trees in a grassy woodland. Pools exist nearby, as they do downstream to the brink of the falls, but larger, safer ones are found upstream. Our trail bends eastward, passes a large pool, and quickly reaches and passes through a shady, 30-yard-long campsite. Beyond it we turn northward and soon spy a 30-yard-long pool, which is perhaps the best swimming hole along Fall River. Those who come in springtime to admire the fall and the flowers at their peak will find this pool and others too cold and swollen with swift water to permit safe swimming. In the heat of the summer, the river warms up to about 60°F, which is still cold, but there are beautiful slabs for warming up on after you emerge from a brisk swim.

Beyond this pool, our forested trail—now a footpath lined with poison oak—continues just over a mile upstream, passing more pools and campsites before ending at the river's edge. Along the peaceful, little-travelled last half mile, our trail crosses metamorphic and mafic-intrusive rocks, and the river has eroded them, in places, into photogenic formations. Found within the metamorphic rocks is talc, whose soapy feeling readily identifies it. Near trail's end, we encounter some large sugar pines, whose pine-cone nuts were probably harvested by Maidu Indians over 100 years ago. From trail's end, you can log-cross Fall River and reach a campsite on a fairly large flat, shaded by Douglas-firs and incense-cedars, on which Indians may once have camped among the delicate spread of false Solomon's seals and star flowers.

94   No Ear Bar Trail

Distance: 2.6 miles, round trip
Total gain/Net gain: 1580'/1580'
Classification: Strenuous
Season: Late June through early October
Parking: Several cars at most
Trailhead/Map: 91/32

Features: The No Ear Bar Trail is the shortest foot trail down to the Upper Canyon Wild River zone of the Middle Fork of the Feather River. The trail ends at a cliffbound section of river, whose beauty, fishing and swimming more than compensate for the stiff, but short-lasting, climb you'll have to make back to the trailhead.

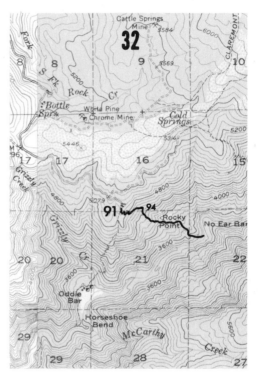

Description: Our entry into the Upper Canyon Wild River zone is marked with a sign that prohibits motor vehicles. A steep descent from it 100 yards down the ridge brings us to a second sign, from where the Oddie Bar Trail descends south and the No Ear Bar Trail descends east. The Oddie Bar Trail is not recommended because, as an unimproved mining trail, it is extremely steep, the stretch of river it descends to is not very scenic, and the short, overgrown spur trail from Grizzly Creek west to the Oddie Bar mines is ideal tick and rattlesnake country. Only the attraction of shady, refreshing Grizzly Creek, lined with umbrella plants, may justify taking this trail. We turn left and start down the slightly longer, but less steep, No Ear Bar Trail.

Starting among ponderosa pines, Douglas-firs and sugar pines, we find our switchbacking descent to a talus slope of dark blocks a steep one, but compared with the Oddie Bar's descent, it's not bad. The dark blocks are ultramafic rocks—composed of olivine, pyroxene and amphibole crystals—which were intruded into overlying bedrocks during the Jurassic period. Our entire trail runs along these iron-and-magnesium-rich dark rocks, which weather to form a rusty-brown soil.

From the talus slope, our trail almost levels out, and then it plunges down a forested secondary ridge to a gully, which it crosses before entering a second one. Now shaded mainly by live oak, but also by Douglas-fir, ponderosa pine and incense-cedar, our slightly abating descent arrives at a good campsite on a shady flat perched 25 feet above the river. Our trail ends on a bouldery bank just upstream from where the river curves west. At this bend the river has cut the slope opposite us into a rugged, vertical cliff, and below it lies a large, sandy pool which is deep enough for swimming. Another inviting pool lies not far downstream. Fishermen claim the fish here are smart and hard to catch; yet some fishermen do catch their legal limit.

Middle Fork Feather River canyon at No Ear Bar

95   Hartman Bar Trail

Distance: 9.2 miles, round trip
Total gain/Net gain: 2810'/2770'
Classification: Strenuous
Season: Early July through mid-October
Parking: Ample
Trailhead/Map: 95/33

Features: This trail takes you down to undeveloped Dan Beebe Campground, located on Hartman Bar beside the Middle Fork of the Feather River. Here, in the federally designated Upper Canyon Wild River zone, you'll find one of the best swimming holes in California.

Description: Shaded under the cover of white firs and sugar pines, our trail starts eastward from an almost level slope that is northeast of small but impressive Peak 5495. This peak, a knob of Pliocene olivine basalt, is fractured into many near-vertical columns. Climbers will certainly want to try some of the dozens of steep cracks between the columns, which are as high as 200 feet. This volcanic knob is part of the same flow that stands ½ mile north of it, which we drove past on the way to the trailhead. Together, they offer some of the finest *volcanic* rock climbs to be found in the Sierra Nevada. During the Pliocene, this olivine basalt flowed down valley bottoms, but today it stands on high ridges—a clear case of *topographic inversion* (see Trip 54). If you break open a piece of this volcanic rock, you can see crystals of olivine, which appear as yellow-brown-to-green specks in a finer groundmass.

Our shady trail switchbacks down a ridge of old metamorphic rocks, which are infused with veins of quartz, passes a pipe spring, and soon reaches a saddle. From it we can look

A pool at Hartman Bar

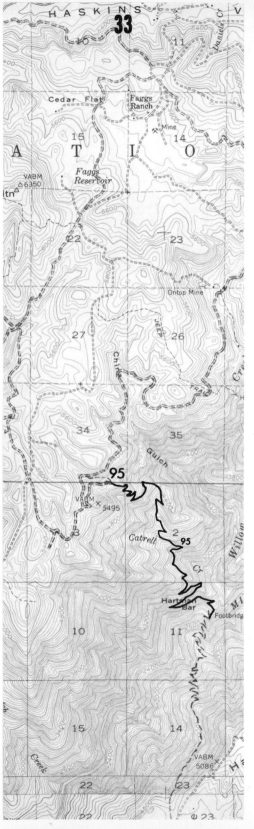

north down into China Gulch or south toward Catrell Creek. Our route switchbacks down toward this creek under a forest cover that now includes incense-cedar, ponderosa pine, black oak and Douglas-fir. One third of the way down to Hartman Bar, we arrive at an old "homestead," if it can be called that. Here, within a tiny plot bounded by an old, piecemeal fence, is a weather-beaten shack standing within a pea garden gone wild. You can obtain fresh water from a nearby creek that runs through the west side of this plot, but don't plan to camp here, since it is a good habitat for rattlesnakes.

Beyond the abandoned shack, our shady, switchbacking trail descends across an assortment of old, metamorphosed volcanic rocks to our route's midpoint—splashing, invigorating Catrell Creek. On your grinding way back up this trail, you'll certainly want to stop here and cool off before the steep climb ahead. Our descent beyond Catrell Creek is only moderate, and we pass by several creeklets and around one low, descending ridge before we curve southwest to drier, warmer slopes. We switchback northeast to the descending ridge, just barely cross it, then immediately recross it and head southwest down a long switchback leg. Along this leg we can see Hartman Bar's suspension bridge and a flat immediately west of it, which is the Dan Beebe Campground. Our descent, now on granitic rock, is shaded by live and black oaks plus occasional Douglas-firs and California nutmegs. The nutmeg is easy to recognize because its spiny-tipped, firlike needles are sharp enough to draw blood. Characteristic of this plant community is poison oak, which lines our rocky path, and being at rather low elevations, we encounter flies rather than

Bee-like fly

mosquitoes, which are associated with higher, wetter environments.

In almost no time we are down to the wide, 40-foot-high suspension bridge. The river is deep here, and one can high-dive into the clear, invigorating water, which at its maximum climbs up into the cool, low 60s. Sunny, granite slabs, however, provide a quick warmup after a chilly dip. Just upstream from the bridge is a 300-yard-long, granite-lined pool, beautifully fed by two cascading creeks and the river's rapids. It is certainly one of the best pools in the whole Tahoe Sierra, and the only detraction from it is that in the past, motorcyclists descended to it, gutting trails and bringing trash and noise into this section of Upper Canyon Wild River. It is hoped that future cyclists, perhaps backed by Forest Service enforcement, will observe the *Motor Vehicles Prohibited* signs, thereby leaving the wild river in a clean state for those who like to peacefully fish, dive and swim in its life-nourishing waters.

The kit-kit dizze is a common plant near canyon bottoms

96   Gold Lake Trail

Distance: 3.4 miles, round trip

Total gain/Net gain: 710'/290'

Classification: Moderate

Season: June through October

Parking: Cramped at trailhead; park in Silver Lake Campground

Trailhead/Map: 92/34

Features: Gold Lake is the only good cirque lake in the Bucks Lake area that you can easily hike to. The hour-long hike up to it reveals the most dramatic evidence of former glaciation to be found in this entire area.

Description: Starting from the south end of Silver Lake Campground, we hike southeast along a signed, curving trail, which skirts along a retention wall, one of two dams on Silver Lake. Since the lake is the domestic water supply for Meadow Valley residents, no swimming is allowed. Very soon, our trail forks left from the shoreline trail and climbs up a steep gully that separates two stages of a lateral moraine (see Trip 80). Jeffrey pines and white firs offer occasional shade, but most of our short, gruelling ascent is through shade-

less manzanita and huckleberry oak. Interspersed among the brush are giant granitic boulders, whose 20-foot heights are testimony to the strength of the river of ice that dropped them here. Topping the moraine's crest, we get our last view of sometimes sparkling Silver Lake, which after Labor Day diminishes to a shallow, unattractive, rock-studded puddle.

From the crest, we briefly descend, then start up a well-graded trail segment that carries us high above swampy Jacks Meadow, in the canyon below us. From high on our 400-foot-high moraine, which once bordered an equally high glacier, we can look southeast across the canyon at the east moraine of former glaciers, and if we stare hard enough, we can identify the faint, distant, pointed summit of the Sierra Buttes (8587'). Tobacco brush adds an aroma of sweetness to our journey just about the time we spy Gold Lake, nestled on a bench below flat-topped Spanish Peak. Soon, we are greeted with shade provided by a large, solitary sugar pine, beyond whose widespread limbs with drooping cones our route descends almost to a saddle on the crest of the moraine. Passing a

Large lateral moraine descending from Spanish Peak

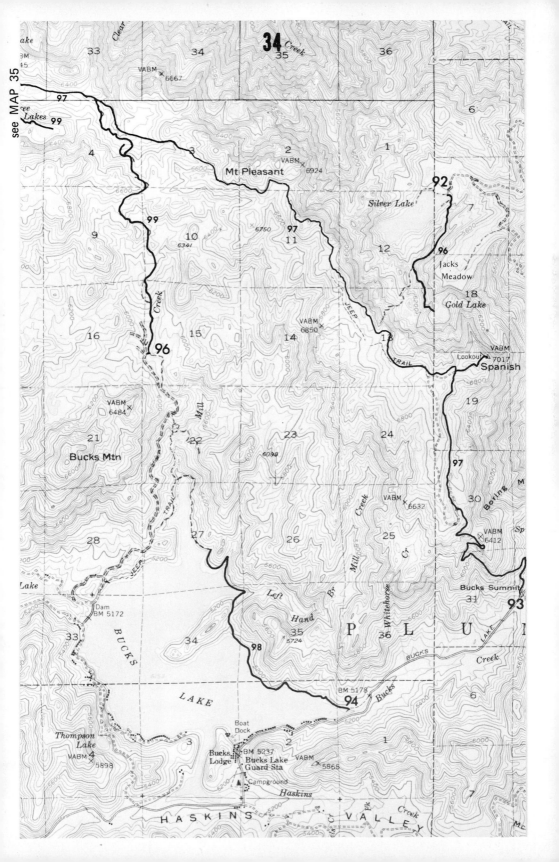

few feet below this brushy saddle, our trail comes just shy of providing us with a view of Silver Lake, below its other side.

Leaving this saddle, our trail begins to climb once again, and in 100 yards passes between two Jeffrey pines. Only a few yards before this point, a faint, old, ducked trail climbs 1⅓ miles up to the rim and the Pacific Crest Trail (see Trip 97).

Our Gold Lake Trail passes between the two Jeffrey pines, and then rambles for ½ mile over brushy, undulating, glacier-polished terrain toward a prominent cleaver. In this knife-edge ridge, you'll see a conspicuous notch. Our sometimes indistinct trail climbs through this notch, then very steeply descends to the west shore of hemmed-in Gold Lake. By early August this cirque lake warms up to present excellent swimming, and from rocks along its northeast shore you'll find good diving. Campsites above this shore are the only ones around, and they are spartan at best. Above them rises a second, more dramatic cleaver, which ascends southeast up to the very summit of Spanish Peak. Climbers may wish to try their skill on routes up this pyroxene-rich diorite ridge.

Senecio growing among granitic rocks

97   Bucks Summit to Belden, via the Pacific Crest Trail

Distance: 19.6 miles + a 43.3-mile shuttle

Total gain/Net gain: 2430'/4710'

Classification: Easy

Season: Mid-July through early October

Parking: More than ample at large, scenic Bucks Summit viewpoint, 0.1 mile north of the Spanish Peak Lookout Road junction

Trailhead/Maps: 93/34,35

Features: This 19-mile section of the Pacific Crest Trail takes you past glaciated landscapes, through several vegetation zones, and even across gold-bearing gravels. Midway along the crest traverse, you'll find some of the most isolated campsites to be found in the Tahoe Sierra. A short excursion to Three Lakes reaches less isolated lakeside campsites. Climbers will find challenging cliffs at Three Lakes and at Spanish Peak.

Description: The first 2.8 miles of route follow a narrow, closed road that switchbacks up slopes covered with shallow, granitic soils. Once forested, these slopes were logged over before 1950, and they now support a thick, mature mantle of chaparral. Because our moderate ascent is open, it can be hot, but the early-morning hiker experiences almost ideal temperatures. The openness allows us to measure our progress as we wind ever higher, and about two thirds of the way up, just south

of and below Summit 6412, we get a view northeast down into peaceful Meadow Valley.

You'll know you're getting close to an actual trail when your road begins to climb up through dark, volcanic rocks, which are andesitic mudflows that were derived during the Pliocene epoch in a manner similar to those described in Trip 49. Also, you are certain to see roadside mule ears—those leafy sunflowers which are almost synonymous with andesitic mudflows in the northern Sierra and the southern Cascades. We enter the forest's fringe and soon arrive at the trail's start, signed with a Pacific Crest Trail emblem, which is located on a shady flat where the road turns sharply counterclockwise from northwest to south.

The Pacific Crest Trail skirts along the base of the north-trending volcanic ridge, staying just high enough above meadows to keep our feet dry. Snow doesn't finally melt in this vicinity until mid-July, and until at least then, you'll encounter two large, shallow ponds that give rise to thousands of croaking tree frogs. Even before snow melts from the ponds' edges, corn lilies sprout and begin to grow skyward through the freezing water. Late-summer hikers will find the ponds replaced by chest-high corn lilies growing in dense clusters within damp meadows.

Our gradual climb north soon leaves the

Meadow Valley and distant American Valley

meadows behind, passes through a dense forest, and emerges high on fairly open slopes that are garnished with clusters of magnificent red firs. Our route traverses above a conspicuous granitic bench, whose low, brushy cover permits us to look east and 3000 feet down on serene Meadow Valley. Its flat floor once supported a shallow lake, but today only lake-bed sediments remain, which cover a belt of dark ultramafic rock that cuts across the valley and the terrain northwest and southeast of it.

Beyond the bench, our trail gradually becomes a faint, old road, which passes a cluster of water-loving shrubs and trees that tap a near-surface water table. Our road comes to an open gully, and beside it we see a deteriorating log shelter, which, during a rainstorm, would provide only minimal protection. Above it, we enter a pure stand of mature red firs, whose tall, straight trunks are embellished with a chartreuse cloak of staghorn lichen. Note that the lower 10–15 feet of each tree is devoid of lichens, for this part of the trunk is annually buried by snow.

A brief stroll up our road along the shady, forested, gentle slope brings us to a shallow saddle, on which we meet the Spanish Peak Lookout Road. Since the lookout is only ½ mile east of us, it is well worth the effort to hike up the easy road to it. The saddle approximately marks the boundary between ridge-crest volcanic mudflows and much older, intrusive, crystalline diorite on which the flows were deposited. The volcanic rocks are only a few feet thick on the saddle, and by walking east 100 yards, we leave them behind. Pay close attention to the next 150 yards, however, since a small pocket of Eocene sediments was trapped when descending mudflows buried a low, rolling-hills landscape. The Eocene sediments are gold-bearing gravels similar in age, composition and origin to those found in Malakoff Diggins State Historical Park (see Trip 72). From isolated pockets like this one, gold has been carried downstream and deposited along with other sediments on the floor of Meadow Valley. The gold, however, is not concentrated enough for commercial exploitation.

Past the gold-bearing pocket, the lookout road winds northeast up almost to the crest itself, then bends east toward the nearby fire lookout. From this bend a spur trail descends northwest a short distance along a sharp diorite crest, where you can get an impressive

Spanish Peak Fire Lookout in 1974

view of the steeply descending northeast escarpment of Spanish Peak. Rock climbers will have their hike up to here justified by finding virtually unclimbed routes. From near the site of Spanish Peak's lookout cabin, you can see, in the north-northwest, magnificent Lassen Peak (10,457'), whose snowbound slopes contrast with the fiery furnace burning deep within it. Jutting out below us in that same direction are the huge, smooth lateral moraines left by equally large glaciers that periodically filled Jacks canyon, between them. On the distant southeast horizon stand the pointed Sierra Buttes (8587'). Along the crest north of the buttes runs the Pacific Crest Trail, and if you've hiked this trail before, you can trace the trail's approximate route from the buttes northward to Lassen Peak.

Returning down the lookout road to the Pacific Crest Trail, we start north along it, then make a relaxing traverse along the crest above usually unseen Gold Lake. As we curve northwest along the rim of a cirque wall, we can see large, shallow Silver Lake in the distance below. Partly obscuring it is a smooth, rounded, brushy moraine that the conspicuous Gold Lake Trail traverses. This lateral moraine buries a bedrock ridge that separated the Silver Lake glacier from the Gold Lake glacier. Abundant red firs, together with some silver pines and a few Jeffrey pines, filter this view. Notice in the nearby firs growing just below our trail that the large, upright female cones grow on the uppermost branches. The small, hard-to-see male cones hang from lower branches. This positioning of female and male cones makes self-pollination rather difficult, since pollen can't fall up to the female cones. Cross-pollination, however, is favored, for winds can blow the pollen from one fir to the next. This is an advantage. Self-pollination, or inbreeding, greatly increases the chances that recessive traits—usually detrimental or even lethal—will be expressed. Cross-pollination, on the other hand, usually assures that a recessive gene—say, from a pollen grain—will be linked with a dominant gene from a seed, and this latter gene will prevent the recessive trait from developing.

Beyond the brief views of Silver Lake, the Pacific Crest Trail enters forest cover, curves west, and descends to the head of a gully. Down it a faint trail descends to the Gold Lake Trail (see Trip 96). Our scenic rim route continues northwest through open forest, ascending and descending increasingly larger ridge knolls. The first is barely noticeable; the second we breathe a little heavily to top, then, on the third, begin to wonder why our trail doesn't contour around them. On the third we cross a jeep road, which climbs up to its bouldery summit. This road has more-or-less paralleled our path ever since we began it. This area's snow pack lasts well into July, and before then you may want to follow the road, although much of it too is then snow covered. The fourth and last knoll is climbed almost to its very top, only to start us on a 250-foot-descent to a forested saddle. Now below the east end of Mt. Pleasant—the high point of our ridge—we traverse west across its slopes, cross its low west spur ridge, then descend northwest to cross the headwaters of Clear Creek.

The miles of granitic slopes we have crossed have changed very little since the beginning of the Ice Age, about two million years ago. These slopes are part of a *relict* erosion surface, which is one that has survived with little change for a long time, and therefore indicates what the adjacent topography must have looked like back then. Since this gentle surface has existed for quite some time, it has developed fairly deep soils, composed mostly

Silver Lake, Gold Lake Trail and red fir with cones

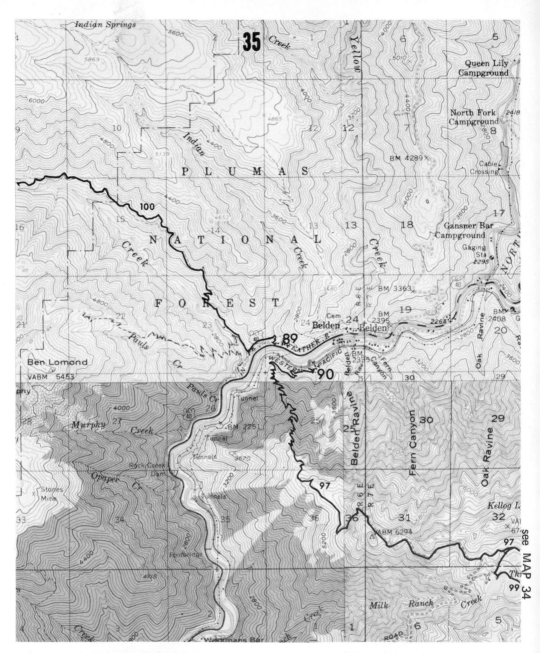

of *gruss* (see Trip 50). Our granular road bed traverses through several meadows, almost all of them dominated by mildly fragrant lupines, then ends where a trail starts.

From here we follow a Pacific Crest Trail segment that descends west into a small, deep valley, skirts the west side of a moist meadow, and rounds slopes as it traverses northeast to a creek. A short climb beyond the stream takes

us up to a broad saddle on a ridge that runs south from the unseen summit of forested Mt. Pleasant. Our trail, now largely shaded by red firs and signed with PCT diamonds, blazes and other trail markers, leaves the saddle, traverses over to the west ridge of Mt. Pleasant, and then descends to cross the headwaters of Clear Creek.

Our route west—faint at times—descends usually within sight or hearing of refreshing, cold Clear Creek, then it soon almost levels off, and crosses an unsigned north-south trail. Not far beyond this intersection, our trail crosses Clear Creek where it turns north to flow down through a deep gap. Before leaving this creek you might consider establishing camp on the nearly level ground east of it. Campsites in this area are about as isolated as one can expect to find in California.

At one time, our trailside creek flowed west, eventually emptying into Milk Ranch Creek, which drains the Three Lakes, located about one mile west of us. However, as the Feather River continued to deepen its canyon throughout the late Pliocene and early Pleistocene, its tributaries cut back into the canyon's walls. One of these tributaries, Clear Creek, actually managed to cut through the crest and beyond it, thereby capturing the drainage of our trailside creek. This stream capture—sometimes called *stream piracy*—probably occurred around one million years ago.

We head west across Clear Creek, then follow the Pacific Crest Trail northwest up to its junction with the old California Riding and Hiking Trail. Trip 99, which descends north on the CRHT to this junction, coincides with our route for the next mile. Just west of this junction we pass a shallow pond choked with grasses and pond lilies. Our gently undulating trail then skirts the base of a granitic ridge and along our traverse we pass a second, larger but shallow pond. Late-summer hikers will see only a wet meadow. Beyond it our fern-lined trail passes a more distant pond, but white and red firs hamper our efforts to see it. Then we come to a trail junction, from which a new segment of the PCT climbs right but the old CRHT descends left. If you want to descend to Three Lakes, head down the CRHT, following Trip 99's route description.

After a brief climb, we come to another junction, from which a lateral trail descends to the CRHT. This spur is for the convenience of southbound PCT-trekkers who want to camp in the Three Lakes area. From the junction we have an easy, generally downhill, ⅓-mile traverse to a bend on an old fire road. If you descended to Three Lakes, you can rejoin our route at this bend by following the Pipe Line Road ¼ mile down-canyon from the lowest lake, then veering west up a brush-lined jeep road, which quickly switchbacks northeast up to the bend.

From the shady bend, we climb west out onto sunny slopes, which are clothed with manzanita and chinquapin, and lesser amounts of wild cherry and aromatic tobacco brush. Looking south across the canyon, we see Pipe Line Road winding a tortuous route toward Bucks Lake. When the Belden Trail that we'll soon hike on was being rebuilt in 1974, some of the trail crew said that when they wanted to "go to town," they preferred to hike down the Belden Trail rather than drive down the rutted Pipe Line Road. The Forest Service plans to close this winding road at the west end of Lower Bucks Lake, thereby closing the Three Lakes area to all but backpackers and horsemen.

Our sunny, curving road descends northwest toward a crest saddle, and, approaching it, we see snowy Lassen Peak (10,457′) on the horizon ahead of us. Leaving the saddle, we pass some low, granitic blocks and pinnacles that cover the broad crest and tempt rock climbers to boulder a while. A second northwest descent takes us to another saddle and another view of Lassen. Seen in the north-northeast is a fire lookout atop well-named Red Hill (6330′), whose rusty color is derived from an iron-rich belt of ultramafic rocks—the same fault-bounded belt that underlies Meadow Valley. Our road continues beyond the saddle, descends the north slopes of Peak 6294, then crosses its west ridge just before a secondary summit and dead-ends in 200 yards. From the road's left side, the Belden Trail segment of the Pacific Crest Trail begins.

A long switchback leg starts south on a moderate-to-steep descent, then quickly bends southwest and maintains its gradient across brushy slopes. We pass a trickling spring before reaching a ridge and switchbacking north past a few scattered pines. The descent ahead of us is perfectly clear, and we soon pass a second trickling spring before our trail curves northwest and descends toward Chips Creek canyon, which is a prominent cleft in the opposite wall of the Feather River canyon. Both the Pacific Crest Trail and Trip 100 follow the Chips Creek Trail up that canyon.

Our rapidly descending section of the PCT reaches a prominent ridgetop, briefly curves northeast across it, and then quickly rejoins it. The ridgetop descent is only momentary, for we soon leave brush behind and switchback under verdant forest cover northward down toward the Feather River. Note the succes-

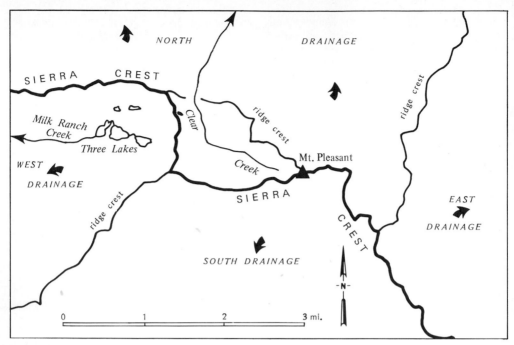

Present drainage of the Clear Creek area

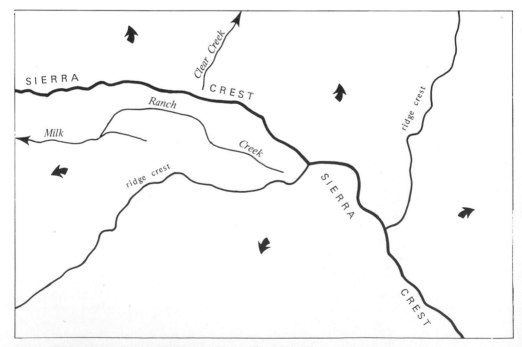

Early Pleistocene drainage of the Clear Creek area

sion of vegetation zones as we descend on the PCT. Mt. Pleasant's slopes of red fir and silver pine gave way to the Three Lakes area's cover of white fir and sugar pine. Brushy, deforested slopes along the Belden jeep road interrupted the sequence, but now, as we descend some 36 switchbacks, we enter the realm of Douglas-fir, ponderosa pine, black oak and incense-cedar. Growing along moist gullies traversed by our winding trail are dogwood, broad-leaf maple, thimbleberry and bracken fern. Found in this zone are the usual hazards of poison oak, ticks and rattlesnakes. These aren't problems if you watch your step and what you brush against. Unrelated to this change in vegetation is a change from diorite to phyllite and metachert—metamorphosed sediments of the Calaveras formation (see Trip 100).

As our trail approaches the river, California laurel and live oak put in their appearances. Nearing the end of our route, we traverse eastward past some four-petaled mock orange and cross an ephemeral creeklet. Not far beyond, our trail zig zags across a bushy gully, then it descends northwest a brief distance to a signed trailhead beside Western Pacific's two railroad tracks.

Sugar pine along Belden Trail; Chips Creek canyon in distance

98   Bucks Lake Shore Traverse

Distance: 6.6 miles, round trip
Total gain/Net gain: 640'/100'
Classification: Easy
Season: May through October
Parking: Several cars—but the road in is impassable when muddy, which is often.
Trailhead/Map: 94/34

Features: This walk along a piece of the old California Riding and Hiking Trail is a good one for swimmers and fishermen who want easy access to a lot of shoreline. There are also adequate campsites for those who want to stay longer than just one day.

Description: Old orange-and-blue signs nailed to trees mark our route along the California Riding and Hiking Trail, which was one precursor of the Pacific Crest Trail. As the PCT now does, it once carried horsemen and hikers along many miles of mountain ranges in California. Horsemen are rarely seen today, having been replaced by backpackers with efficient, lightweight equipment which frees them from the necessity of camping where there's pasture.

Our trail west is usually shaded by white fir and lodgepole pine, but not enough to completely block out views over Bucks Lake. Bracken fern, corn lily and yarrow milfoil grow in damp soils we must traverse before we climb to a low point of exposed grantic bedrock, atop which are several small campsites. A larger campsite lies at its east base. Leaving this point, we descend northwest and pass some good sunbathing beaches before entering a small lakeside grove of aspen. Beyond the grove, our trail leaves the lake's shore and climbs north through a shady, bracken-floored forest up to a low saddle at the base of a peninsula. Mixing with the white firs are some red firs, Jeffrey pines and incense-cedars. If you stay close to the ridge of the peninsula, you'll find that a cross-country route out to its rocky tip is not very difficult.

The granitic rocks we see on both sides of our saddle are well weathered, but if you were to chip off a fresh piece from each side of the saddle, you might notice a difference between them. Both rocks are diorites, but the dark minerals in the peninsula's rock are mostly chunky pyroxene, while the dark minerals in the other rock are mostly columnar hornblende and flaky biotite mica. Neither rock looks older than the other, but the

Aster

peninsular diorite, which solidified about 150 million years ago, is about 20 million years older than its counterpart.

As we descend from the low saddle we encounter some log-constructed towers (the handiwork of Boy Scouts?), then quickly reach a large, well-equipped lakeshore campsite. During the summer months, large lakeshore camps such as this one are likely to be used more by water skiers than by hikers. Beyond it we cross the wide Left Hand Branch of Mill Creek, whose waters cascade down a bouldery bed. Continuing onward, we make a short, curving traverse that stays just above beaches found along the forest's fringe, then climbs to a jump-across creek that empties into a narrow cove.

After crossing the creek, we climb briefly upstream to a switchback, then arc clockwise around a ridge to our last bay, which has a small, sandy beach when the water isn't at its highest level. Draining past alders into this cove is a trickling creek that adds its harmonious sounds to those of the lapping waves. Like all the lake's beaches, this one was formed by wave action after this reservoir was formed. You'll find good rocks to dive from along the shoreline south of us, near the point. Our trail description ends at this bay, since the California Riding and Hiking Trail rapidly deteriorates into an almost impenetrable tangle one has to crawl through to reach campsites at the tip of Buck Lake's north arm.

Aspens on east shore of Bucks Lake

99   Mill Creek to Three Lakes

Distance: 11.4 miles, round trip

Total gain/Net gain: 1730'/660'

Classification: Moderate

Season: Early July through mid-October

Parking: Several cars, but always room due to little use

Trailhead/Maps: 96/34,35

Features: This once-popular section of the California Riding and Hiking Trail sees little use now that the nearby Pacific Crest Trail has attained national fame. When the tortuous Pipe Line Road to Three Lakes is closed, these lakes will be accessible only by trail, and the CRHT is by far the easiest approach to them. Its route, however, is obscure in places and is therefore not recommended for novice backpackers.

Desciption: Next to wide Mill Creek, we see a sign, *California Riding and Hiking Trail 100 yards.* The CRHT, in actuality, is only 100 feet beyond a boulder-hop of Mill Creek. The three-mile stretch of CRHT heading south from us to the end of Trip 98 is—in places—discontinuous, overgrown or just hard to follow. Our trail north is marked by old CRHT signs, which have a blue image on an orange background. We progress along this little-used trail, strolling through a lodgepole-pine flat that borders the creek. The creek soon forks, and near this fork we jump across the east branch, which drains the south slope of forested Mt. Pleasant.

Beyond the ford we quickly reach a meadow with a highly visible snow gauge planted in it. Grazing cows are likely to be seen in this meadow or in other meadows we'll pass along the way to Three Lakes. We skirt the west edge of the meadow, then start up through a red-fir forest, whose floor is bedecked with lupine and pennyroyal. Soon our trail forks, and we keep right, rejoining the old, abandoned left branch farther upslope. Beyond this reunion near the top of a gully, our trail eases off, traverses a flat, damp meadow, climbs up and around a low, forested knoll on the right, and reaches an alder-lined gully. Our soles are dampened as we traverse along its east edge, but beyond its corn lilies we are again on dry soil, which is characterized by pennyroyal and lupine growing among granitic boulders. Before curving northwest around a second knoll,

our trail bifurcates but the segments quickly reunite.

Our traverse along the north slope of the knoll stays high enough to keep us out of the damp soils of the wildflowered gully below and to the right. Upon, reaching a saddle, our trail climbs northwest up a low ridge, arcs northward up to a second low ridge, and then traverses northeast through deep gruss (see Trip 50) to just above the west edge of a flat, wide saddle. Just beyond the saddle, the trail splits for the third time, the left branch climbing a few feet before diagonaling down through a meadow of silvery-green lupine, while the right branch continues down to a fallen red fir—used as a salt trough for cattle—before turning northwest and rejoining its mate.

From the reunion a 100-yard traverse above a corn-lily meadow takes us to a junction with a faint, ascending trail, which we ignore as we veer north and start downward. In ¼ mile we come to another junction, this time with a short, dead-end trail on our right that starts southeast almost back the way we came. We go northeast down to a low divide, cross it, and are once again faced with a choice. As you start west down from the divide you *might* notice a faint trail (the *old* CRHT) climbing upslope to meet you. If you do see this trail, follow it north down to gentler slopes on which it curves west past old trail signs to a level meadow. If you don't see it, your trail west will soon turn north and very steeply descend a slope before curving northeast and dying out. Never fear. Continue northeast a few yards into a meadow and descend it 150 yards to the old CRHT. Where you join it, you are only 100 yards south of Clear Creek, which is about 100 yards south of the Pacific Crest Trail. Near the meadows of this fairly level area, you can find isolated, unused campsites.

We bear west-northwest as we leave the level meadow, then curve west, and after 120 yards of walking, arrive in a small meadow abundantly covered with corn lilies. In it we turn northwest and in 70 yards cross a trickling creek. Then, rather than continuing northwest 120 yards to a salt trough made from a red fir, we angle west-southwest, staying close to the east side of a row of alders. Our trail then climbs 100 yards northwest up a dry wash to a ridge, heads 35 yards north on it, and descends 110 yards to a small, sloping meadow—

wedged between two ephemeral creeklets— which is mostly barren except for a cluster of corn lilies. On a bearing of 350° we cross this meadow over to the base of a low slope, on which we rediscover our trail. (Southbound hikers should follow old CRHT signs, not a trail that leads southeast.) With our route-finding problems over, we now hike down an obvious, 300-yard, gentle descent northwest to a junction with the Pacific Crest Trail (Trip 97).

The CRHT coincides with the PCT for the next mile. Just west of this junction we pass a shallow pond choked with grasses and pond lilies. Our gently undulating trail then skirts the base of a granitic ridge and along our traverse we pass a second, larger but shallow pond. Late-summer hikers will see only a wet meadow. Beyond it, our fern-lined trail passes a more distant pond, but white and red firs hamper our efforts to see it. About this time, we come to a trail junction, from which a new

segment of the PCT (Trip 97) climbs right, but the old CRHT descends left.

Our winding descent to the PCT was mostly through a forest of red fir, silver pine and lodgepole pine, but now, after our westward traverse, white fir becomes quite abundant. Our route starts a southwest descent, quickly encounters a short lateral trail that climbs northwest back up to the PCT, then makes a fairly steep, fern-lined descent past large boulders before dead-ending at a curve in a road.

To get to nearby Three Lakes from the end of the CRHT segment, turn left and follow the road southeast to the north arm of the lower lake. This lower lake, when full, extends all the way up to the middle lake, but in late season its level falls at least 15 feet, turning it into an unattractive mudhole. From the north arm, a muddy, rutted road curves eastward over to the northwest shore of the more scenic middle lake, which has trout—ranging up to at

Middle lake

least 16 inches—jumping from its warm
waters. Like the lower lake, this one is
dammed, and its level drops considerably, but
not drastically, in late season. Our road
traverses to the lake's east end, from where a
trail starts up the north side of the refreshing
outlet creek from the upper lake.

Starting on a terrace at a point about 12
yards north of this creek, our trail climbs up a
brushy slope of huckleberry oak, tobacco
brush, manzanita and chinquapin. Nearing the
upper lake, we pass scattered specimens of
sugar pine and white fir, then encounter more
luxuriant growth in the form of mountain ash,
dogwood and bracken fern. The upper lake is a
pleasant surprise in that it is natural and its
level stays high. In late summer, however, its
fairly warm water becomes slightly cloudy,
and halazone tablets may be advisable. Rock
climbers will find prominent crack climbs on a
band of diorite cliffs above the lake's south
shore. Finding a good campsite is another
matter. Because this lake is so hemmed in,
there is very little level ground. Nevertheless,
small sites can be found just above the lake's
north, east and southwest shores.

Upper lake

100   Chips Creek Trail

Distance: 10.0 miles, round trip

Total gain/Net gain: 1900'/1530'

Classification: Moderate

Season: April through November

Parking: Very limited at trailhead, but room at other nearby turnouts.

Trailhead/Map: 89/35

Features: This segment of the Pacific Crest Trail bears the distinction of crossing the nebulous boundary between the northern Sierra Nevada and the southern Cascade Range. The trail up to a small cabin and close-by, cascading Chips Creek can be hiked throughout most of the year.

Description: Our signed trail, which doubles as a part of the Pacific Crest Trail, switchbacks up dry slopes into the cool confines of lower Indian Creek canyon, where we're shaded by broad-leaf maple, Douglas-fir, black oak, live oak and California laurel. Here a trail goes north ⅓ mile to the creek. Our brief shade ends as we exit from the canyon and traverse a shadeless trail for almost half a mile above Highway 70 and its inviting, long, roadside reservoir. Along this rocky traverse, we cross

nearly vertical beds of the Calaveras formation, which is an extensive, mile-thick wedge of sediments deposited in a shallow Paleozoic sea. Most of the sediments our trail traverses are phyllite, with lesser amounts of metachert interspersed. The phyllite was derived from clay, which, after deposition, was compacted to shale and later metamorphosed— due to burial by the accumulation of additional sediments—to slate. Later metamorphism— perhaps due to the intrusion of a nearby granitic pluton—converted this slate to phyllite, and if further metamorphism were to occur, the phyllite could be transformed into a schist. The metachert, of course, underwent the same metamorphism, and it is derived from chert, which is a form of microscopic silicon-dioxide crystals that can be derived from both organic and inorganic sources.

Beneath the buzzing of giant powerlines, we cross a low ridge crest, quickly spot Chips Creek below us, and once again enter a shady forest, which includes the previously mentioned trees plus incense-cedar and ponderosa pine. After a pleasant, level traverse through the forest, we reach a signed junction from

Chips Creek at Ben Lomond Trail crossing

which the Ben Lomond Trail forks down and left. This trail descends northwest to an old road, then follows it southeast until it diminishes to a trail and ends 20 yards past a soda spring. From there one can descend a few feet, cross a rusty creek and follow the wandering trail across a bouldery stream bed to a bridge across Chips Creek. The excursion to this spot is a worthy goal in itself, for just beneath the bridge is a small, bedrock swimming hole. Beyond the bridge, the steep Ben Lomond Trail climbs unrelentingly up a ridge to a dead-end just above the 5000-foot contour.

On the Chips Creek Trail

From the Ben Lomond trail junction, the Chips Creek Trail continues its shady traverse, begins to climb, and then executes four switchbacks to get us high above the creek. Beyond the last switchback, our ascent northwest is a moderate one, across metamorphic rocks that were metamorphosed in part when a granitic pluton—partly seen across the canyon—intruded them. In several places along our trail, we cross small, bedrock exposures of this granitic pluton, and these mark the northern boundary of the granitic Sierra Nevada. From the headwaters of Chips Creek, volcanic rocks extend northward in a continuous mantle to central Washington, where granitic rocks once again appear.

If you've already descended the Belden Trail (Trip 97), you will notice a reverse sequence in vegetation as we ascend Chips Creek canyon. We started among Douglas-fir, ponderosa pine and other associated species, and our path climbs into a zone of white fir and sugar pine. If you were to climb to the saddle above the headwaters of Chips Creek, you would find stately red fir and checker-barked silver pine. Particular species of trees, shrubs and wildflowers seek out particular environmental conditions, and the result is this variable vegetational pattern we see upon the land. Likewise, animals too are unequally distributed, each species seeking a rather specific habitat.

After a protracted, moderate ascent, our trail levels off, then even descends as it crosses several welcome seasonal creeks. Beyond them, our contouring trail slowly curves west and resumes its climb. As we start a traverse west, we can stare down lower Chips Creek canyon and see, above the unseen North Fork of the Feather River, the ridge down which the Belden Trail descends. Several more creeklets of varying size and duration are crossed, and then we arrive at a small cabin on a white-fir-shaded flat. This level area, only 100 yards north of bounding, noisy Chips Creek, makes a lovely campsite and is at the end of our trail description. The trail continues five miles up to a forested ridge, but the route doesn't stop there, since it has been extended—via the Pacific Crest Trail—another 1400 miles to the Canadian border. If you intend to continue along this National Scenic Trail, then consult *The Pacific Crest Trail*, published by Wilderness Press. Many hikers prefer to hike no farther than the cabin, near which they can splash around in bouldery Chips Creek's cascading, invigorating water.

Index